Asia-Pacific Crossroads

Regime Creation and the Future of APEC

Edited by Vinod K. Aggarwal
and Charles E. Morrison

St. Martin's Press
New York

ISBN 0-312-21110-4 (cloth)
ISBN 0-312-21148-1 (paper)

Library of Congress Cataloging-in-Publication Data
Vinod K. Aggarwal and Charles E. Morrison
Asia-Pacific crossroads : regime creation and the future
  of APEC / edited by Vinod K. Aggarwal and Charles E. Morrison.
p. cm.
    Includes bibliographical references and index.
    ISBN 0-312-21110-4 — ISBN 0-312-21148-1 (pbk.)
    1. Asia Pacific Economic Cooperation (Organization) 2. Asia-
-Economic integration. 3. Pacific Area—Economic integration.
    I. Aggarwal, Vinod K., 1953 II. Morrison, Charles Edward, 1944-   .
HC412.I5212   1998
337.1'5—dc21   97-50523
                                                            CIP

Design by Acme Art, Inc.
First published: May, 1998
10 9 8 7 6 5 4 3 2 1

CONTENTS

ACRONYMS

ABAC	APEC Business Advisory Council
AEM	ASEAN Regional Forum
AFTA	ASEAN Free Trade Agreement
AID	Asian Industrial Development
ANZCERTA	Australian-New Zealand Closer Economic Relations Trade Agreement
APEC	Asia Pacific Economic Cooperation
ARF	ASEAN Regional Forum
ASEAN	Association of South East Asian Nations
ASEM	Asia Europe Meeting
BIAC	Business and Industry Advisory Committee
BIS	Bank for International Settlement
CAP	Common Agricultural Policy
CEPT	Common External Preferential Tariff
CER	Closer Economic Relations
CG18	Consultative Group of 18
CMEA	Council of Mutual Economic Assistance
CPR	common pool resource
CTI	Committee on Trade and Investment
CUSTA	Canada-United States Trade Agreement
DFI	direct foreign investment
DSM	Dispute Settlement Mechanism
EAEC	East Asian Economic Caucus
EAEG	East Asian Economic Group
EC	European Community
ECB	European Central Bank
ECSC	European Coal and Steel Community
EEA	European Economic Area
EEC	European Economic Community
EFTA	European Free Trade Area
EMU	European Monetary Union
EPA	Economic Planning Agency

EPC	European Political Cooperation
EPG	Eminent Persons Group
EPO	European Patent Office
EPU	European Payments Union
ESCAP	Economic and Social Commission for Asia and the Pacific
EU	European Union
FDI	Foreign Direct Investment
FTA	Free Trade Area
FTAA	Free Trade Area of the Americas
GATS	General Agreement on Trade in Services
GATT	General Agreement on Tariffs and Trade
GDP	Gross Domestic Product
GNP	Gross National Product
IAPs	individual action plans
IMF	International Monetary Fund
INGOs	international nongovernmental organizations
IPR	intellectual property rights
ITA	International Technology Agreement
ITO	International Trade Organization
ITU	International Telecommunications Union
IVANS	International Value-Added Network Services
LDC	Less Developed Countries
MAI	Multilateral Agreement on Investment
MAPA	Manila Action Plan Agenda
MFA	Multi-Fiber Arrangement
MFN	Most Favored Nation
MITI	Ministry of International Trade and Industry
MRAs	mutual recognition arrangements
NAFTA	North American Free Trade Agreement
NBIP	Non-Binding Investment Principles
NGOs	nongovernmental organizations
NTBs	nontariff barriers
NTMs	nontariff measures
OAS	Organization of American States
ODA	Overseas Development Association
OECD	Organization for Economic Cooperation and Development
OEEC	Organization for European Economic Cooperation
OPTAD	Organization for Pacific Trade and Development

PAFTAD	Pacific Trade and Development Conference
PATAD	Pacific Trade and Development
PBEC	Pacific Basin Economic Council
PCT	Patent Cooperation Treaty
PECC	Pacific Economic Cooperation Council
PLO	Palestine Liberation Organization
PRC	People's Republic of China
RTAA	Reciprocal Trade Agreements Act
SPARTECA	South Pacific Regional Trade and Economic Cooperation Agreement
SRTAs	subregional trading agreements
TRIMs	trade-related investment measures
TRIPS	Trade-Related Aspects of Intellectual Property Rights
TUAC	Trade Union Advisory Committee
UNCTAD	United Nations Conference on Trade and Development
USPBEC	United States Committee on the Pacific Basin Economic Council
WIPO	World Intellectual Property Organization
WTO	World Trade Organization

PREFACE

In 1993, U.S. government interest in Asia-Pacific economic cooperation suddenly escalated. Winston Lord, the new Assistant Secretary of State, made the "Pacific community" the theme of his activity. President Bill Clinton invited the heads of the Asia-Pacific Economic Cooperation (APEC) governments to join him in an economic leaders meeting immediately following APEC's annual ministerial meeting. This escalated what otherwise would have been a somewhat obscure international meeting into a major media event, and it has been followed by annual leader meetings in Bogor (1994), Osaka (1995), Subic Bay (1996), and Vancouver (1997). In Bogor, APEC adopted a vision statement calling for free trade and investment in the region by 2010 for developed countries and 2020 for all countries.

As Americans became interested in and committed to building an Asia-Pacific community, we were gratified. As scholars of international regionalism, however, we were also concerned about increased expectations of what regionalism could accomplish and how soon. We believe it is essential to have a realistic, multilateral perspective on the state of Asia-Pacific regionalism and its likely future. This book was born out of this concern.

There were many professional reasons to examine the institutionalization of regional cooperation in Asia and the Pacific. The APEC forum dates only from 1989 and has sometimes been called the first post–Cold War international organization. Despite its relative newness, it had already begun to raise some important questions about the region's political economy. APEC explicitly advocated the notion of "open regionalism," calling for close ties with the existing GATT and its successor organization, the World

Trade Organization. At the same time, its members expressed concern about not undermining existing subregional organizations in the region. As a consequence, the formation of APEC raises both theoretical and policy issues about the prospects for reconciling or "nesting" this new institution within the broader trading system, while at the same time attempting to have subregional groupings nested within its purview. How such reconciliation might be accomplished provided a natural starting point for our project and is one of the central themes addressed in the book.

The Center for Global Partnership (CGP) of the Japan Foundation agreed to support this inquiry through a grant made to the East-West Center. We are very grateful to the CGP's former director in New York, Jun Wada, and its current director, Juichi Chano, for the interest they have shown in the project as well as CGP staff members Kim Ashizawa, Norio Fukushima, and Nicholas Szechnyi. Shu Urata brought the valuable collaboration of the Waseda Institute for Social Sciences as well as his own talents and expertise as a specialist on regional foreign investment trends to the project.

The editors also wish to express their appreciation for those who read or commented on parts of the manuscript. These include James Caporaso, Merit Janow, William James, Bunn Negara, Sadao Nagaoka, Hugh Patrick, and Steven Weber. We are also grateful to Donald Hellmann and the University of Washington APEC Study Center for its assistance in hosting a project meeting in Seattle.

We are especially indebted to the staff of the East-West Center APEC Study Center and the Berkeley APEC Study Center (BASC). At the East-West Center, Marilu Khudari and June Kuramoto played a key role in organizing our meetings and facilitating communications with the contributors. At BASC, Trevor Nakagawa assumed yeoman duties in preparing the manuscript for publication, for which we are extremely grateful. In his efforts, he was assisted by Vipur Andleigh, Vandana Bhatia, Paul Dosh, Stefan Kang, Keith Nitta, and Catherine Oliver.

Finally, we would like to thank our editor, Karen Wolny, at St. Martin's Press, for her expeditious management of the review and publication process. Without her stimulus and encouragement, this book might still have been languishing in e-mail attachments and on floppy disks.

CONTRIBUTORS

VINOD K. AGGARWAL is Professor in the Department of Political Science, Affiliated Professor in the Haas School of Business, and Director of the Berkeley APEC Study Center (BASC) at the University of California, Berkeley.

CHARLES E. MORRISON is Director of the APEC Study Center at the East-West Center, Honolulu.

RICHARD W. BAKER is a Senior Fellow at the East-West Center, Honolulu.

MAXWELL A. CAMERON is Associate Professor at the Norman Paterson School of International Affairs, Carleton University, Ottawa.

CÉDRIC DUPONT is Assistant Professor at the Graduate Institute of International Studies, Geneva.

JOSEPH M. GRIECO is Professor in the Department of Political Science at Duke University.

PAOLO GUERRIERI is Professor in the Department of Economics at the University of Rome.

TSUTOMO KIKUCHI is Professor of International Politics at Nanzan University, Nagoya.

SUMNER J. LA CROIX is Professor in the Department of Economics at the University of Hawaii, Manoa.

SYLVIA OSTRY is Distinguished Research Fellow at the Centre for International Studies at the University of Toronto.

MICHAEL G. PLUMMER is Associate Professor in the Department of Economics at Brandeis University.

JOHN RAVENHILL is Senior Fellow in the Department of International Relations at Australian National University, Canberra.

SHUJIRO URATA is Professor of Economics at Waseda University, Tokyo.

YOSHINOBU YAMAMOTO is Professor of International Relations at the University of Tokyo.

ZHANG YUNGLING is Director of the APEC Policy Research Center and Institute of Asia-Pacific Studies, Chinese Academy of Social Sciences.

CHAPTER I

APEC: THE EVOLUTION OF AN INSTITUTION

Charles E. Morrison

I. INTRODUCTION

Two striking features of East and Southeast Asia over the past three to four decades have been the unprecedented rates of economic growth among many of the economies of this region and the weakness of a regional institutional framework for facilitating growth and easing adjustment problems that arise because of it.[1] It was only in 1989, after almost 25 years of proposals for an Asia-Pacific cooperation organization, that the Asia-Pacific Economic Cooperation (APEC) forum was established as the first broad regional institution for intergovernmental dialogue on economic policy issues.[2] The name itself, "four adjectives in search of a noun" in the words of former Australian Foreign Minister Gareth Evans, is a legacy to the reluctance of the ASEAN (Association of Southeast Asian Nations) group of developing countries to "institutionalize" a regional cooperation organization that they feared might compete with their own subregional organization and result in large power domination.

At first blush, therefore, it would appear to be an academic conceit to analyze APEC as an institution for regime-building, that is, for developing governing arrangements or principles, norms, rules, and procedures for handling issues in international economic relations.[3] It might also seem wildly premature to worry whether APEC can be comfortably "nested" at an intermediate level in a hierarchy of international organizations and institutions proceeding from the subregional to global level.[4] Formally, APEC is not a rules-making organization. Its 18 (soon to be 21) members are referred to as "economies" since two (Hong Kong and Taiwan) are not recognized by the others as sovereign countries. They span all or parts of four continents and include societies as technologically sophisticated as Japan and the United States and as underdeveloped as Papua New Guinea. In population they range from China with 1.2 billion to Brunei with less than 300,000 persons, and in area from the United States, Canada, China, and Australia, all with about 3 million square miles, to Singapore, with less than 250 square miles.

This group seemingly has little geographical, economic, or political coherence, raising the question of what its members might be able to do together that could not as easily be done at the global level or more efficiently in subregional institutions. Yet in Bogor in November 1994, the APEC leaders adopted a vision—"free trade and investment in the region" by 2010 for developed countries and by 2020 for developing countries. They seek to operationalize this vision through the adoption of individual and collective actions. During any given year, dozens of APEC meetings, several at the ministerial level and one at the "leader" level, take place, covering cooperation or potential cooperation across a broad sweep of economic topics. In Osaka in 1995 the APEC leaders approved a framework for trade and investment liberalization in 15 areas and a program of economic and cooperation in 13 areas that could lay the basis for coordination and harmonization in regulatory regimes.[5] The November 1996 Manila Action Plan for APEC

(MAPA) included a set of individual and collective action plans as well as joint activities for economic and technical cooperation that began the "action phase" of APEC. APEC is thus an evolving process that is moving in ways not envisioned by all its original creators and that may serve to facilitate the establishment, strengthening, or extension of regimes.

This book asks and seeks answers to a series of questions regarding APEC's likely evolution and its impact on the broader international process of regime creation. This chapter is descriptive, painting a picture of the institution's creation and development in the broadest brushstrokes. The next chapter sets out a general conceptual framework for analyzing APEC based on the literature of institutional formation, particularly the work focusing on "international regimes." This framework is used in the body of the book to explore four interrelated sets of issues.

In Part One, we look at the environment for regional regime creation in the areas of trade, investment, and intellectual property protection. What are the basic economic trends that underlie a growing perception of Asia-Pacific as a region? Is there a bias toward greater intraregional trade and investment? Are there prospects for developing regimes in these areas at the regional level that are compatible with and supportive of global regimes?

Since APEC is the creation of sovereign states, each with its own set of interests determined through domestic decision-making processes, Part Two examines the domestic political processes and national attitudes and interests that affect policies toward APEC cooperation in several leading countries: Australia, China, Japan, and the United States. Do these processes suggest a convergence of interest around greater regime creation through APEC, or will they inhibit regime creation?

Part Three examines the international institutional context that influences APEC's evolution and particularly the issue of how well APEC "nests" with global and subregional institutional arrangements. Those concerned with developing global institutions have always been suspicious of regionalism, fearing that despite pretensions to openness, regional arrangements are inherently discriminatory and may undermine global regimes or divert political resources toward the suboptimal regional arrangements. At the same time, more intense subregional arrangements such as the North American Free Trade Agreement (NAFTA) and the ASEAN Free Trade Agreement are creating regimes that affect APEC and global regimes. Thus Part Three examines the relationships among these various layers of organizational and institutional arrangements. Are they compatible? If not, where will the likely points of friction lie and how will they affect APEC's evolution?

Finally, Part Four recognizes that APEC is an unfinished work whose future may be influenced by other models of international cooperation. APEC advocates claim that APEC is a new model of international cooperation. How valid is this? How does APEC differ from the OECD and the European Union, and what lessons might cooperation in these institutions hold for the APEC process?

II. THE CREATION OF APEC

Economic and Political Forces

Asia-Pacific regional organization had a false start in 1980. Toward the end of the 1970s, considerable interest had developed in the notion, although in rather confined academic and political circles.[6] The Australian and Japanese political leaders sponsored a semiofficial conference in Canberra for further exploration, but ASEAN opposition to a formal intergovernmental organization delayed the concept from going forward. The notion's supporters organized a fall-back, the Pacific Economic Cooperation Conferences (PECC)[7] involving government officials in their private capacities, business persons, and academics. The PECC maintained and lobbied for intergovernmental cooperation and deserves much of the credit for seeing it through to fruition.

During the 1980s, there was growing governmental interest in and commitment to regional organization.[8] Of the numerous proposals, the one that finally launched APEC successfully was that of Australian Prime Minister Robert Hawke in January 1989. It is pointless to argue over whether this success owes more to economic or political drivers. A number of economic and political factors in the 1970s and 1980s converged to set the stage for the establishment of a broad-based regional economic cooperation organization. Of these, three stand out: the region's economic growth, the related growth of Asia-Pacific economic interdependence and fear of protectionism, and the shift of political and diplomatic forces associated with the end of the Cold War.

The story of Asia's economic miracle hardly needs retelling here. Not all Asian economies are miracle economies, but the region as a whole has experienced average rates of economic growth that are the envy of the world.[9] This was accompanied by growing economic interdependence. U.S. investment and the relatively open U.S. market played a vital role in the region's economic success, but the rapid increase of Asian manufacturing exports to the United States was accompanied by growing trans-Pacific trade and economic frictions, first with Japan and then with others. In more recent years, as noted by Paolo Guerrieri in chapter 3, the most rapidly increasing economic interactions in the Asia-Pacific economy have been within Asia rather than across the Pacific. Thus a less vertical and more horizontal picture of multilateral economic interaction was emerging, both strengthening the prospects for cooperation in Asia and broadening the loci of economic frictions.

These developments buttressed arguments for creating regional economic institutions.[10] Such institutions, their advocates argued, were needed to analyze emerging problems and facilitate adjustments, exerting pressure on the more closed economies to open up and on the more open economies to remain open. Some

Asian countries hoped that regional organizations might alleviate pressures from the United States for enhanced market openness. Moreover, in the late 1980s, the trade-oriented Asian countries were concerned about what was perceived as a tendency toward closed regionalism elsewhere as the completion of the Common Market moved forward in Europe and negotiations started in North America toward extending the U.S.-Canadian Free Trade Agreement into the three-cornered NAFTA with Mexico.

The Americans and Canadians who advocated Asia-Pacific economic institutions in the 1980s also focused on economic goals: opening up Japan and other Asian markets through more multilateral than bilateral external pressures,[11] boosting the North American economies through their increased association with the dynamic East Asian economies or providing an international economic alternative to what some perceived as a less and less open Europe.

If the arguments for Asia-Pacific institutions were often cast in economic terms, political drivers certainly played a strong role. Asia-Pacific cooperation was pushed forward by leaders who saw political or diplomatic benefit in the idea: Australians Malcolm Fraser and Robert Hawke, Japanese Takeo Miki and Masayoshi Ohira, Korea's Roh Tae Woo, Thailand's Thanat Khoman, and a variety of American members of Congress.[12] The end of the Cold War played a critical role in the ultimate success of the Hawke initiative in that it removed a major political barrier to cooperation and provided a stimulus for trans-Pacific institutional ties. During the Cold War era, any proposed regional arrangement involving the United States but not the Soviet Union, even if exclusively confined to economic cooperation, was bound to be seen as a form of alignment and was heavily criticized domestically in many Asian countries. The end of the Cold War removed this obstacle. It also provided an incentive. Among some Asian and American foreign policy elites, an Asia-Pacific organization was seen as a means of maintaining beneficial special ties between the United States and

East Asia at a time when binding security ties had become less important. Asian commentators have noted that APEC served a variety of political and security purposes.[13]

Models of Cooperation

Months of hard effort by the Australian Ministry of Foreign Affairs and Trade brought ministers to Canberra in November 1989, but even then there was no real consensus on exactly what forms or objectives the institution should have. Within the strands of intellectual thinking in governments and the academic community that lay behind Asia-Pacific cooperation, one can discern three basic models, parts or all of which have been molded into the contemporary APEC.

The first, a minimalist model, draws from the early history of ASEAN. It basically focuses on APEC as a community-building process rather than as an organizational structure, and sees the APEC meetings as a means of "getting to know you better."[14] The ASEAN governments opposed rapid institutionalization of APEC, and they thought that the meetings should have concrete benefits for ASEAN.[15] However, in recent years, they have accepted and at times contributed to the creeping institutionalization of APEC, with Malaysia the most reluctant to do so. In the minds of the minimalists, community-building or mutual understanding is an end in itself. While it may lead to further activities, a premature push toward institutionalization may overstretch what is still a very delicate fabric.

A second model can be called an "OECD model." As John Ravenhill notes in chapter 6, the OECD model particularly attracted the Australian planners of APEC in 1989, and it was foreshadowed in earlier academic research calling for an intergovernmental "Organization for Pacific Trade and Development (OPTAD)."[16] According to this notion, the new organization, like the OECD, should provide a venue for identifying and discussing international economic issues, although the actual negotiations might be transferred to another venue. It would also have a substantial research and analytical capacity. The OECD is not a rules-based institution, and, as Sylvia Ostry points out in chapter 13, its informality and flexibility combined with access to rules-makers through its networks have been used to considerable effect. Why not then just extend the OECD to Asia? Although the advanced countries of the Asia-Pacific region were already in the OECD, the OECD was conceived in Asia as a basically trans-Atlantic institution, not suitable to deal effectively with the special issues of the mixed economies of the Asia-Pacific region. Moreover, many of the most important Asian economies—China, Korea, and Taiwan, for example, were not OECD members, although Korea has subsequently joined the organization.

The third "trade agreement" model makes trade liberalization the overriding purpose to be achieved through a formalized process similar to that in other regional trade schemes such as the North American Free Trade Agreement. The concept of an Asia-Pacific trade arrangement dates back to 1965, but more recent advocates have shied away from the term "trade bloc." In their view, the Asia-Pacific economies should promote "open regionalism," as distinct from the "closed regionalism" being pursued in Europe. The practical implications of open regionalism (often regarded as an oxymoron) has never been well defined, with the major split between those who believe that APEC liberalization measures should be offered on a global basis and those who argue that concessions should be confined within the group to prevent free-riding. But both positions converge on the point that APEC should be part and parcel of a broader effort through the GATT/WTO to promote global freer trade and capital flows.

Elements of all three models have been incorporated in the present APEC, but there is a continuing tension between the minimalist model and the regional free trade institution model. The last, which has become increasingly prominent, drives forward both the institutionalization of APEC and a new function for the body as negotiating forum. The first notion opposes these directions.

III. APEC's EVOLUTION

During the first years of APEC's existence, four major developments shaped its evolution. These were the broadening of its membership, the addition of leaders' meetings, the creation of new international institutional arrangements involving some but not all of its members, and the adoption of an "action agenda" focused on trade.

Prior to 1994, APEC did far more broadening than deepening. Twelve countries came to the Canberra meeting, the then-six ASEAN nations (Brunei, Indonesia, Malaysia, Philippines, Singapore, and Thailand), the five developed nations (Australia, Canada, Japan, New Zealand, and the United States), and South Korea. It was agreed from the beginning that it would be desirable for the People's Republic of China, Chinese Taipei, and Hong Kong to join. This was accomplished in 1991. Mexico and Papua New Guinea were added in 1993, and Chile in 1994. These later additions expanded APEC beyond its original core of western and northern Pacific developed or rapidly developing economies, adding substantial diversity. By this time concern arose that further expansion would result in APEC's loss of focus and cohesiveness, although some members, notably Malaysia, favored continued expansion. It was agreed that the issue could be postponed, and a three-year moratorium on new members was declared.

The second development, the "heightening" of APEC through the addition of annual leaders' meetings, was the result of a United States initiative during its turn to be the host member economy in 1993.[17] Prime Minister Mahathir refused President Clinton's invitation to come to this first summit,[18] but for the other leaders the invitation was a welcome sign that the newly elected American president was interested in Asia. The delicate question of representation for "noncountries" Taiwan and Hong Kong was finessed by having them represented at a lower level. Although the meeting initially was presented as an ad hoc event, Indonesian President Suharto followed with a second invitation to leaders in 1994 during Indonesia's host year. Since then the summits have been held annually and constitute the top decision-making structure in APEC.

These meetings coincide neatly with the "getting to know you" notion of APEC. For the host leader, they provide a measure of domestic and international prestige, and for the other leaders, the APEC summit provides an efficient means of seeing counterparts of the other main Asia-Pacific countries and conducting other business on the side. The bilateral "side meetings" became an increasingly important aspect of APEC leaders meetings.

The leaders meetings have also driven forward the institution-alization of APEC. The involvement of the leaders helped resolve an institutional tension within APEC among the foreign and economic ministers who previously shared equal top billing at the ministerial level. It also strengthened and accelerated APEC's substantive agenda. The leaders required greater achievements to give APEC (and their meetings) credibility. Each successive host government wanted to associate the meetings with some distinctive accomplishment.

A third development has been the evolution of the subregional arrangements within APEC membership as well as regional or plurilateral arrangements involving APEC members with non-APEC members. The ASEAN Free Trade Agreement (AFTA) and the North America Free Trade Agreement (NAFTA) both came into being since APEC was created, and a Malaysian proposal for an East Asia Economic Caucus (EAEC) was mooted. Of these, only the AFTA was noncontroversial. The NAFTA created concern in Asia about trade and investment diversion from Asia to Mexico and the future direction of American trade policy. As for the EAEC, some U.S. foreign policymakers, especially former Secretary of State James Baker, were concerned that, if launched, the Asian-only arrangement might become an inward-looking bloc, undercutting Asian participation in APEC.

These arrangements, with one exception, involved entirely APEC members.[19] Other new regional institutions in 1994-1996 connected APEC members with nonmembers. The American APEC members became engaged in a parallel dialogue in late 1994 with the other countries of their hemisphere that envisioned a Free Trade Area of the Americas (FTAA) accord by 2005. In March 1996, an Asian initiative led to the first Asia Europe Meeting (ASEM) involving the countries of the European Union and those Asian countries that would have been members of the EAEC.

In general, the development of these other institutional arrangements has benefited APEC, just as APEC has stimulated some of them. The NAFTA probably strengthened Asian interest in upgrading its ties with the Americas through APEC. The EAEC proposal encouraged the Americas to take a more active interest in APEC. As APEC became more institutionalized, particularly after the leaders meeting was added, its members grew more confident in the institution, and this made less threatening subregional or extraregional relationships involving some but not all of the members. Appropriately nested, APEC could be one element in a hierarchy of global, regional, and subregional institutions involving Asia-Pacific countries, one parallel to overlapping megaregional arrangements such as ASEM and the FTAA.

The final development, enabled by the leaders meetings, was the adoption of the trade and investment liberalization and facilitation vision at the Bogor leaders meeting as a principal objective. From the beginning, trade had been the focus, but the early ministerial meetings resulted in little more than rhetorical statements supporting the completion of the GATT's Uruguay Round. The driving force for developing an APEC free trade and investment vision came from the organization's Eminent Persons Group (EPG), above all its dynamic chair, C. Fred Bergsten. The EPG had been established at the 1992 ministerial meeting out of the concern that APEC lacked impetus and direction. The group's first report coincided with the first leaders meeting and obviously appealed to the leaders who wanted a stronger image attached to their activity. Host President Suharto's embrace before the second summit of the EPG's vision of free trade and investment in the region by 2020 (2010 for developed countries) ensured the adoption of the vision.[20]

At Bogor, the leaders saw APEC as a three-legged stool with trade and investment liberalization, trade and investment facilitation, and economic and technical cooperation ("eco-tech") as the legs.[21] In subsequent years liberalization and facilitation were combined, and the dates of 2010 and 2020 gave this combined liberalization-facilitation agenda a goal-oriented appearance that made it the standard-bearer of APEC.

IV. IMPLEMENTING THE VISION: OSAKA AND SUBIC BAY

As noted above, the annual leaders meetings put a premium on politically visible accomplishments. As the first, the 1993 leaders meeting in Blake Island, Washington, was a breakthrough in itself, while the Bogor meeting resulted in the vision. As APEC moved toward implementation, the senior officials in charge of APEC coordination have come under increasing strain to come up with what some cynically refer to as impressive "announceables." Both the Osaka ministerial and leaders meeting in November 1995 and the Manila/Subic meetings in November 1996 were hailed as important turning points in APEC cooperation. While they cannot yet be evaluated from a longer-term historical perspective, they began to move APEC from vision toward implementation. Many of the details remained to be filled in.

The 1995 Osaka Action Agenda provided a "template" for the realization of the Bogor economic goals. Although individual members also made "down payments," that is, pledges of actions in one area or another, these were uncoordinated and largely symbolic. In Part One of the Osaka Action Agenda, the APEC economies agreed on objectives and general guidelines to govern individual action plans, and some collective actions for 15 specific areas of liberalization and facilitation.[22]

Following Bogor there had been controversy about how the trade and investment liberalization and facilitation should proceed. The Osaka Action Plan embodied numerous compromises that were reflected in nine "general principles." The American officials, with an eye to their need for Congressional "fast-track" trade negotiating authority, reportedly would have preferred a more GATT-style trade liberalization process involving explicit reciprocity. Ultimately, however, the consensus-dependent APEC took the only avenue open to it—that of voluntary concerted liberalization. Member economies would prepare individual action plans specifying near- and medium-term actions and an outline of the basic direction toward full liberalization in 2010 or 2020. They would then exchange these plans and ensure "comparability" of effort through a consultative process, taking into account the extent to which each economy was already open. The Americans could claim that the principle of "comparability" meant substantially the same thing as reciprocity.[23]

Another compromise involved agriculture. Prior to Osaka, the Northeast Asian economies, led by Japan, sought to exclude politically sensitive rice from the free trade vision. The agriculture exporters in APEC, led by Australia, argued that the inclusion of agriculture was essential. This was resolved by adopting the principles of "comprehensiveness," thus including agriculture, and "flexibility," meaning that the more politically difficult decisions could be postponed to the end of the process.

The question of whether liberalization plans should be extended on a global basis (inviting free-riders) or limited to other

APEC members was not resolved. Osaka also left hanging the question of whether there is sufficient incentive and political will on the part of the major APEC actors to achieve the 2010/2020 objectives through concerted liberalization. In chapter 10, Joseph Grieco suggests that this process is unlikely to move significantly ahead of global processes and may even generate economic conflict.[24] Zhang Yunling in chapter 7 on China, Tsutomu Kikuchi and Yoshinobu Yamamoto in chapter 8 on Japan, and Richard Baker in chapter 9 on the United States all suggest difficult political constraints on trade and investment liberalization in the three economies that most matter.

Manila provided the first test of unilateral concerted liberalization. While some of the individual action plans (IAPs) did go beyond existing multilateral commitments—those of China and Indonesia, for example—the IAPs of Japan and the United States were regarded as disappointing.[25] To dampen expectations, APEC officials stressed that the plans were cumulative and "rolling," and serious review for comparability and strengthening would begin in the following year. Having little trade authority, Washington had to plug for an APEC commitment to zero tariffs in the information technology sector, in which it did have negotiating authority. This got a qualified boost from the Subic summit, propelling it into the WTO ministerial meeting in Singapore the following month and toward an early global agreement in 1997. The press and leaders turned away from the tedious detail of the individual and collective action plans and focused on the International Technology Agreement proposal and the political dimensions of the leaders' side meetings.

Fearing domestic criticism for overspending on hosting APEC, one of Philippine President Fidel Ramos's priorities for the Philippine year of APEC was to develop the third technical and economic cooperation leg of the APEC stool, which he could point to as of direct benefit to developing countries. The Osaka Action Agenda had adopted common policy concepts and agreed upon joint activities and/or dialogues in the 13 areas listed in Part Two.[26] But Part Two received much less attention than liberalization and facilitation. The United States tended to look upon it as a diversion from the more important Part One liberalization and facilitation agenda, while those more intrinsically interested in Part Two failed to provide the basis for a stronger thrust in the area.[27]

The result of the Philippine efforts was a declaration on an APEC "Framework for Strengthening Economic Cooperation and Development." The language was largely hortatory, but it established six priority areas: human capital, capital markets, economic infrastructure, future technologies, environment, and small and medium enterprises. Since virtually all existing APEC projects could be fit under one or another of these broad topic areas, it is unclear that the declaration will have any practical meeting for the APEC working groups that largely develop their own agendas, often quite independently of the broader APEC processes.

V. APEC AND REGIMES

This chapter so far has examined the developments largely associated with the leaders' meetings. Much of the substance within APEC occurs at more specific working group meetings, meetings of specialized "networks" or technical experts, and ministerial level meetings in areas of technical and economic cooperation such as those of education, labor, transportation, and environmental ministers. To provide some sense of APEC's progress through such activities, it is useful to review APEC's ambitions and progress in some specific areas related to regime and institution building. These areas are chosen because of their relationship with the topics addressed elsewhere in this volume or of interest to policy and business communities.

Foreign Investment

Shu Urata in chapter 4 discusses investment trends in Asia-Pacific and their implications for APEC. Current APEC work consists primarily of collecting information on member-economy investment regimes and encouraging the governments through their APEC action plans to improve dialogue with the business community, advance transparency, and liberalize their regimes, and implement Uruguay Round commitments. There has been a collective APEC effort to formulate what might be called a protoregime, the 1994 Non-Binding Investment Principles. Considering the strong emphasis among the developing countries in the region on attracting foreign investment, this initial APEC collective action was disappointingly weak.[28] In its assessment of the twelve principles toward which members should "aspire," the EPG found that five were at or above other international standards but that five others fell short of these standards.[29] Recognizing the difficulties of strengthening the code on an across-the-board basis, the APEC Business Advisory Committee (ABAC) recommended that demonstration APEC Voluntary Investment Projects be established where stronger principles would be maintained.[30] The 1996 IAPs included various measures to improving investment access, but these are not linked with each other, nor can they be said to be a part of a coordinated regional regime.

Intellectual Property Rights Protection (IPR)

IPR has become an increasingly contentious area in Asia-Pacific trade relations as Asian countries have developed the capacity to manufacture and market goods embodying foreign intellectual property and Western manufacturers, particularly in the United States, became much more aggressive in seeking to protect intellectual property from unlicensed use. In this area, rules-building is occurring at the global level and through bilateral agreements, and

APEC commitments largely reaffirm promises already made to participate in the global regimes. The Manila Action Plan for APEC, for example, listed its first IPR objective as to "align domestic legislation with the WTO Agreement on Trade-Related Aspects of Intellectual Property Rights according to WTO timetables." Sumner La Croix elaborates on this subject in chapter 5.

Standards and Conformance

This was identified in November 1993 as a priority item for trade and investment work, and a framework for future work was adopted the following year.[31] It was agreed that APEC would address three areas: alignment of the members' standards with international standards, links with relevant regional and international bodies, and progress toward mutual recognition of conformity assessment arrangements. The Subcommittee on Standards and Conformance meets regularly and hopes to develop a network of mutual recognition arrangements (MRAs) by the year 2000 for developed and 2005 for developing countries. It is also conducting a survey on information access and transparency and developing a database and network systems on standards and conformance systems, accredited laboratories, the status of MRAs, and the alignment of APEC economy standards with international standards.[32]

Human Resource Development

APEC's Human Resource Development working group meets twice a year and comprises four networks for education, business management, national economic development management, and industrial technologies. These networks have sponsored a multitude of small projects, many of them reflecting an initiative of one of more of the governments or educational institutions. One major activity, for example, provides information and training in export credit procedures in APEC member-economies and others focus on small and medium-sized industries and comparisons of APEC labor markets.

VI. CONCLUSION

As APEC moves into its implementation phase, it is clear that a number of key questions remain hanging. Perhaps the most prominent is whether concerted liberalization will work successfully to move APEC effectively toward achievement of the 2010/ 2020 targets. For some this is a key issue of APEC credibility. For others the target dates themselves are less important than sustaining the direction.

A related question is how any faltering of the trade liberalization and facilitation agenda and schedule would affect the APEC project as a whole. Is there enough other "there" to justify continued leaders meetings and the devotion of considerable resources to the APEC process?

The membership issue was unresolved until late 1997. Coming to the end of the self-imposed moratorium on new members in 1996, APEC found at least eleven countries knocking at the door, including Vietnam, Peru, Russia, and India.[33] There were no agreed-upon criteria to make choices, and if all were admitted the leaders meetings would be nearly impossible. Finally at its 1997 Vancouver Leaders Meeting APEC agreed to admit Peru, Russia, and Vietnam, but no other countries for ten years. The issue of optimal size may appear subsidiary but could be extremely important for whether APEC continues to function effectively at the higher levels and can build consensus around specific programs of action.

As the following studies make clear, the development of international institutions and regimes among national entities jealous and protective of their own sovereignty is a politically difficult process. Whether broad, heterogeneous regional institutions such as APEC can be a vehicle for this process remains to be seen. The following chapter by Vinod Aggarwal establishes the framework for inquiry that will be pursued throughout the volume in addressing this question.[34]

NOTES

1. Barry Buzan has commented that "what is remarkable about Asia is its combination of several quite highly industrialized societies, with a regional international society so impoverished in its development that it compares poorly with even Africa and the Middle East." See "The Post–Cold War Asia-Pacific Security Order: Conflict or Cooperation?" in Mack and Ravenhill (1995, p. 150).

2. Two other intergovernmental economic organizations that preceded APEC were the Economic and Social Commission for Asia Pacific (ESCAP), established in 1947 as the United Nations Economic Commission for Far East (ECAFE) and mainly noted for statistical compilations, and the Asian Development Bank, created in 1967 to facilitate development capital investment.

3. Krasner (1983, p. 2) defines regimes as "sets of implicit or explicit principles, norms, rules, and decision-making procedures around which actors' expectations converge in a given area of international relations."

4. Aggarwal (1985).

5. These are human resource development, industrial science and technology, small and medium enterprises, economic infrastructure, energy, transportation, telecommunications and information, tourism, trade and investment data, trade promotion, marine resource conservation, fisheries, and agricultural technology. APEC Secretariat (APEC #95-SE-05.3, December 1995, pp. 26-38).

6. For an extensive historical treatment of the intellectual and institutional history of Pacific economic cooperation, see Woods (1993).

7. The final "C" in PECC was later changed to "Council."

8. Soesastro (1994, p. 13).

9. The eight highest performing East Asian economies since 1960 have grown twice as fast as the rest of East Asia, three times as fast as Latin America and South Asia, and five times faster than Sub-Saharan Africa. See World Bank (1993, p. 2).

10. For an insightful anecdotal account of APEC's development based on extensive interviews, see Funabashi (1995).

11. Several of the more prominent Americans associated with such organizations at PAFTAD, the Pan-Pacific Community Association, and the succes-

sor U.S. Committee for Pacific Economic Cooperation had a deep interest in Japan and saw positive benefits to the United States–Japan relationship in establishing a broader Asia-Pacific context. Such individuals included Hugh Patrick and Richard Sneider. At the political level, the ambassador to Japan, former Senator Michael Mansfield, advocated regional cooperation on this basis.

12. The Americans included Senators John Glenn and William V. Roth, Jr. and Congressman Lester Wolff as early as the late 1970s and Senators Alan Cranston and Bill Bradley in the late 1980, both of whom made proposals for intergovernmental Asia-Pacific cooperation in the year prior to the Hawke initiative.

13. Jusuf Wanandi in February 1990 noted seven of these: (1) help the United States maintain its presence, (2) stabilize United States–Japan relations, (3) provide a regional structure to accommodate China's participation, (4) provide a basis for the Russian role in the region, (5) counter inward-looking European tendencies, (6) maintain the region's attractiveness in the face of a larger European community, and (7) provide a framework for constructive North-South relations. See Soesastro (1994, pp. 31-32, see also Funabashi, pp. 112-117).

14. Mohamad Mahathir had argued this position as early as 1980 in his position at the time as Malaysia's deputy prime minister. See Crawford and Seow (1981, pp. 41-45).

15. ASEAN officials took the position that "APEC should essentially be a forum for consultations and constructive discussions on economic issues" and that it "should proceed gradually and pragmatically, especially as regards its eventual institutional structure. . . ." See Ali Alatas in Soesastro (1994, pp. 27-28).

16. Drysdale and Patrick in Crawford and Seow (1981, pp. 63-82). The OECD-based OPTAD proposal first appeared in 1968 at the first Pacific Free Trade and Development Conference. See Woods (1993, p. 43).

17. From the beginning the main ministerial meeting and chairing responsibility has rotated, alternating each year between an ASEAN economy and a non-ASEAN economy. Although there were an equal number of ASEAN and non-ASEAN economies until 1991, the later additions of non-ASEAN economies have meant a slower rotation among the latter.

18. The term "summit" has been studiously avoided by APEC officials because of the differential status of participation from Taiwan and Hong Kong, but it has been freely adopted by the press.

19. Vietnam, a member of ASEAN but not yet of APEC, is the exception.

20. This was somewhat surprising because Indonesia was the least open of the ASEAN economies, and strong elements within the Indonesian bureaucracy and body politic opposed the notion of free trade. Two years after Bogor, Indonesia adopted a controversial national car scheme widely seen as contrary to WTO principles and to the thrust of the Bogor vision. For the

EGP's recommendations, see APEC Secretariat (APEC #94-EP-01, August 1994, pp. 3-4).

21. At the time of Bogor, "development cooperation" was the usual terminology, but eventually "eco-tech" became the preferred term, primarily because developed countries, especially the United States, did not want to confuse APEC cooperation with traditional overseas development assistance or foreign aid.

22. APEC Secretariat (APEC #95-SE-05.3, December 1995, pp. 5-25). Part One combined liberalization and facilitation, hitherto two separate APEC emphases, along with "development cooperation."

23. Bergsten, *Economist*, 6-12 January 1996: 62-63.

24. The author's similar skeptical view is set out in Morrison (1997, pp. 39-48). Another view is that reiterated positive benefits from small, less politically difficult liberalization steps will cause actors to gain confidence in the process and be willing to take larger steps. Trade liberalization in ASEAN gathered momentum in this way, but there was a relatively low level of intra-ASEAN trade and thus relatively limited vested interests to oppose it.

25. Johnstone (1996).

26. APEC Secretariat (APEC #95-SE-05.3, December 1995, pp. 26-38).

27. Morrison (1997).

28. An American businessman, Joel Messing, damned the code with faint praise as a "constructive first step" that could do no harm. "As a nonbinding ministerial statement of mere aspirations, unsigned, unratified, and unenforceable, it presumably will not undermine existing bilateral and regional treaties, impede American efforts toward a multilateral investment agreement, mislead capital-importing countries regarding either the intentions or the requirements of American investments or establish a precedent that cannot easily be overridden" (Messing [1995, p. 59]). Mari Panestu, however, argues that negotiations over the nonbinding codes forced participants to think about their policies in a more regional context and may result in unilateral measures that "will bring us to the agreed upon principles faster than any binding code would." See Panestu in Soesastro (1994, p. 88).

29. APEC Secretariat (APEC #95-EP-01, pp. 66-70). For example, the EPG found the wording on transparency "excellent" and requiring "only" implementation to put APEC into international leadership on this issue, but on performance requirements the APEC language was inconsistent with the WTO ban on local contact and trade balancing requirements under the new Agreement on Trade Related Investment Measures.

30. The ABAC also suggested clarifying the investment principles, assessing progress toward implementation, and other measures. APEC Secretariat (APEC #94-EP-01, August 1994, pp. 15-17).

31. This area was given considerable emphasis by the EPG.

32. APEC Secretariat (APEC #96-SE-05.3, March 1996, pp. 19-20).

33. At the end of 1995, APEC had agreed that working groups could include nonmembers if the existing members agreed that the nonmember was relevant to the work program and as long as the nonmember understood that working group participation implied no commitment toward eventual APEC membership.
34. Aggarwal and Morrison (1998), in chapter 15, this volume.

CHAPTER 2

ANALYZING INSTITUTIONAL TRANSFORMATION IN THE ASIA-PACIFIC

Vinod K. Aggarwal

I. INTRODUCTION[1]

The development of the Asia-Pacific Economic Cooperation forum (APEC) in 1989 has been greeted with a combination of hope and skepticism. Unlike many regions of the world, regional institutions in Asia, and particularly the Asia-Pacific, have been scarce. With East Asian economic success, the end of the Cold War, and shifts in power among Asian states, many see APEC as a much-needed institution that will facilitate economic cooperation in the region. For some analysts, this institution will provide a mechanism to increase economic liberalization in the region and bolster the efforts of the World Trade Organization (WTO) to reduce impediments to trade. A few have suggested that this forum could provide a means to go beyond economic issues and foster security cooperation in the region as well.

A more skeptical group of analysts views APEC as unnecessary or even as positively harmful. Some emphasize that the Asia-Pacific region has been the most dynamic region in the world economy—in the *absence* of a formalized institution. For them, APEC will do little to facilitate economic growth in the region. More pessimistically, others argue that by encouraging further regionalization of the world economy, APEC will undermine global economic institutions, leading to regional-based competition and conflict.

The introductory chapter by Charles Morrison in this volume provides an overview of APEC and an update on its current status. The task of this chapter is to provide an analytical framework to analyze exemplars for APEC as well to consider APEC's future prospects. Although APEC has continued to widen and deepen as an institution, many obstacles remain in achieving the organization's stated goal of "free trade and investment in the region" by the year 2020. The framework presented in this chapter, together with the empirical chapters in the book, provide a basis for conceptually and analytically examining APEC's likely evolution.

One of the key original concerns of APEC members was to *reconcile* this group's formation with the broader world trade organization of the General Agreement on Tariffs and Trade (GATT). Member states have continued to maintain this as a key objective with the conclusion of the Uruguay Round and creation of the World Trade Organization (WTO) to replace GATT. This specific reconciliation effort, or what I term "nesting," could be accomplished in several ways. One option would be for member states simply to nest APEC in the WTO based on Article 24 of the GATT, which permits the formation of free trade areas and customs unions, but members have chosen a different route and proclaimed an interest in nesting APEC by pursuing "open regionalism." Still, the interpretation of "open regionalism" continues to be contested, although the idea behind this concept was to reduce barriers to goods and services in a GATT-consistent manner. This avenue thus raises the possibility of pursuing nesting in three additional ways: first, APEC could simply pursue unilateral liberalization measures that would be open to all GATT signatories—whether or not they are members of APEC.[2] Second, APEC members might simply liberalize in areas that are not currently covered by the WTO, thus "conforming" to the strictures of the WTO. Third, some type of conditional liberalization could be pursued, as suggested by the Eminent Persons Group. It remains unclear if this latter strategy would actually be consistent with efforts to pursue "open regionalism" because of the real possibility of discrimination against nonmembers. In this context, the further nesting of subregional groupings such as AFTA or NAFTA within APEC has also generated considerable controversy.[3]

A second key issue concerns APEC's appropriate mandate. The debate over how APEC might be *restructured* to formalize it further and increase its strength in regulating national behaviors has been hotly contested, with some preferring a looser, more informal organization. Another dimension with respect to institutional restructuring relates to APEC's appropriate issue scope: should it deal only with trade and investment issues, or should it address environmental issues, labor concerns, and even security problems as well?

In short, these and other debates on APEC's future pose interesting research and policy questions. In particular, as noted by Morrison, this volume begins with a focus on the changes that have stimulated the formation of APEC. We then go on to consider the role of national actors in the evolution of APEC and the impact of both broader and narrower institutions on its evolution. Finally, we are interested in possible exemplars for APEC, with the European Union (EU) and the OECD serving as two extremes on the continuum of institutional formalization.

The literature on institutional formation, particularly the body of work focusing on "international regimes," has been applied to examine institutional development in specific issue-areas such as trade, the monetary system, the environment, and security. Regime theory has also recently been used to understand the formation of regional institutions as well, both in the Asia-Pacific and in other areas of the world.[4] Because it goes beyond the analysis of formal organizations to examine the development of internationally negotiated principles, norms, rules, and procedures, international regime theory is particularly suited to examine the evolution of less developed institutions such as APEC.

To preview the analytical approach pursued here, my focus in this chapter is to understand the problem of institutional reconciliation and institutional restructuring. These topics have been relatively ignored in the existing international regime literature, but they are central to understanding APEC's evolution. To analyze these questions, I develop the notion of an "institutional bargaining game" based on three elements: (1) the types of goods or externalities that are involved in the issue area of concern; (2) the "individual situation" of actors—defined by their international power position, domestic coalitions, and politicians' beliefs, all of which combine to influence actors' national positions;[5] and (3) the presence or absence of institutions within which bargaining takes place. Together, these elements help us to understand how actors will respond to stimuli that set bargaining games in motion.

Institutional bargaining games generally lead to differing payoffs for actors. If actors are displeased with their payoffs, they may attempt to *modify* the bargaining game by using various resources to manipulate the three elements of goods, individual situations, and institutions that define the game. In this book, our primary focus is on understanding actors' efforts to use *institutional* approaches to game change rather than on changes in goods or individual situations.

If actors choose to create new institutions, they must decide on their specific characteristics, which include the strength, nature (in the sense of what objectives are being promoted), and institutional scope of the arrangements. They must also decide on an appropriate bargaining route to develop the institutions. Moreover, and critical to the questions posed in this study, how will APEC be linked to other existing arrangements? Specifically, will linkages be nested or parallel, and will they be substantive or tactical in nature? To preview these concepts, "nested" linkages point to a hierarchical, goal ordered arrangement; by contrast, "parallel" linkages among institutions refer to a division of labor among them. Issues are "substantively" linked when both the linker and target actor of the linkage agree on the causal connection between issues; by contrast, "tactical" linkages are based on power or exchange without a causal affinity. Based on these categories, this chapter presents a typology of outcomes that focuses specifically on linkages and concludes with hypotheses about institutional modification.

Section II begins with an overview of the literature on institutional formation and discusses the basic analytical framework that relates governance structures to economic interactions. In Section III, I focus on the concept and factors that define an institutional bargaining game as well as the changes in interactions that set the game "in play." Section IV discusses the notion of how "institutional bargaining games" might be modified and examines the possible outcomes that might result from such institutional change efforts. Finally, Section V turns to the causal factors that might explain actors' choices in their decision to promote game change through institutional manipulation strategies.

II. ANALYZING INTERNATIONAL INSTITUTIONS

Research on Institutional Change

Research on institutions has proceeded in a number of areas, with recent concerted attention being paid to the examination of "international regimes." These arrangements have been defined by a group of scholars as principles, norms, rules, and procedures around which actors' expectations converge.[6] Rather than focusing on international organizations, as was common in the literature of the 1950s and 1960s, this literature on institutions has concentrated on less formal arrangements that may or may not be further institutionalized through the formation of formal organizations.[7]

In examining the evolution of regimes, five different approaches in international relations have been brought to bear on this problem: neorealism, neorealist institutionalism,[8] neoliberal institutionalism, cognitivists, and radical constructivists.[9] Neorealist scholars from this tradition find regimes to be of little interest. For them, regimes and international institutions have no significant role in international relations because power considerations are predominant in an anarchic world.[10]

Within a power-based tradition, some scholars have examined changes in international institutions—a tradition that I label neorealist institutionalism. The central concern in this literature is on how regimes affect the distribution of costs and benefits of state interaction. For analysts in this school, institutions have distributional consequences (benefits may be unequal).[11] In previous work, I suggested that regimes can be seen as a device by which central decision makers control actors' behavior, that of other countries and/or domestic pressure groups.[12] From a domestic perspective, state elites can argue that their hands are tied and thus attempt to diminish pressure for particular actions from domestic actors. Examples of this include the Mexican government signing on to NAFTA or the American use of the Multi-Fiber Arrangement (MFA) to prevent textile and apparel interests from pressing for excessive protection. With respect to the creation of regimes, a central theme in this literature has been the role of hegemonic powers in fostering the development of institutions through both positive and negative incentives.[13] Benevolent hegemons, for example, may provide "public goods" because their large size makes it worthwhile for them to take action on their own to overcome collective action problems. But while suggesting that regimes may form when powerful states desire them, this approach does not tell us much about the nature of regimes, and it does not adequately account for new issue packagings because of the focus on tactical, power-based linkages. Moreover, scholars in this school overemphasize relative gains at the expense of understanding cooperative efforts that might lead to joint gains for all parties. And finally, this approach has little to say about actors' desire to pursue multilateral versus bilateral solutions to accomplish their ends.

Building on this critique, neoliberal institutionalists have examined the specific incentives for states to create regimes—as opposed to simply engaging in ad hoc bargaining. This body of work, building on seminal research by Oliver Williamson, examines the role of regimes in lowering transaction costs and has garnered a considerable following.[14] The inertial implications of regimes in constraining future regime change or construction has also been a theme in this work.[15] One aspect of this constraint is the possibility that existing institutions in broader areas will affect the negotiation of more specific institutions, or the "nesting" of regimes.[16] Thus, while the notion of transaction costs and sunk costs are central elements in this thinking, the role of regimes in providing states with information and reducing organizational costs can be distinguished from the role of existing institutions in constraining future actions.

A fourth approach to examining institutional innovation and change has been an emphasis on the role of expert consensus and the interplay of experts and politicians.[17] New knowledge and cognitive understandings may lead decision makers to calculate their interests differently. For example, work by Ernst Haas has focused on the efforts of politicians to use linkages to create new issue packages in international negotiations to form international regimes.[18] His specific focus on the use of substantive versus tactical linkages in the formation of regimes is a theme that I pursue in this chapter in developing my notion of institutional bargaining games.

Lastly, radical constructivists, while focusing on the role of ideas, argue that reality is in fact constructed in the minds of decision makers. These scholars, while drawing from Ernst Haas's work, go much further than he does in suggesting that "power and interest do not have effects apart from the shared knowledge that constitutes them as such."[19] Analysts in this school see norms and values as being dominant and ascribe considerable power to institutions not only in constraining actors but in fundamentally altering their basic interests. In summarizing their view, Peter Haas notes that this school contends "there is no 'objective' basis for identifying material reality and all claims for objectivity are therefore suspect."[20]

Because of the strong empirical record that institutions can and do constrain state behavior and my skepticism about the claim that reality is completely constructed, I emphasize variables only from the schools of neorealist institutionalism, neoliberal institutionalism, and the cognitive approach. Thus, I do not develop either a pure realist or a radical constructivist account in examining institutional transformation.

It is worth noting that economists have also focused on the evolution of international institutions, in particular the relationship between regional and international trade arrangements. One prominent example of this approach is an essay by Robert Lawrence on regional trading arrangements entitled "Building Blocks or Stumbling Blocks?"[21] Yet this literature has primarily examined trade diversion and creation and has slighted the political aspects of institutional formation both in the trading system and in other issue areas.

As this brief sketch illustrates, the literature on the evolution of international institutions is very rich. Yet on the whole, these theories are underspecified and unable to adequately account for two significant types of institutional adaptation that are crucial to understand the evolution of APEC: the *reconciliation* of old and new institutions and the *restructuring* of existing institutions.[22] To examine these institutional changes—which APEC has faced and is likely to face in the future—I develop an approach that goes beyond the existing literature, but which still draws on the variables identified by these approaches.

Figure 2.1: Pre-APEC Trade Bargaining

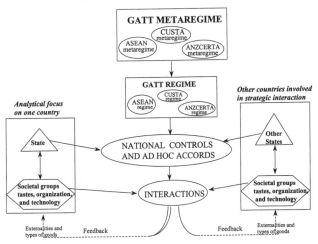

A Framework to Examine Institutional Bargaining

We begin with an overview of the institutional bargaining process. For discussion purposes, Figure 1 depicts the strategic bargaining problem—*prior* to APEC's creation.

Starting with the center of the chart, we can distinguish between two aspects of institutions: *metaregimes* and *international regimes*.[23] Whereas metaregimes represent the principles and norms underlying international arrangements, international regimes refer specifically to rules and procedures. Regimes can be examined in terms of their strength, nature, and scope: *strength* refers to the stringency of the multilateral rules that regulate national behavior, while *nature* (in an economic context) refers to the degree of openness promoted by the accord. Scope can be divided into two parts: *issue scope* refers to the number of issues incorporated in the regime; *institutional scope* points to the number of actors involved.

Prior to APEC's formation, the GATT was the major institution that regulated trade activities. Its underlying metaregime has been an encouragement of trade liberalization. The GATT regime has included rules on tariffication, antidumping, the use of quotas, and also includes a set of procedures for handling both trade negotiations and trade disputes. By and large, the GATT regime has been quite strong and specific in its rules and procedures, although countries have often breached these directives. With respect to nature, GATT and its successor organization have generally continued to encourage liberalization. Finally, with respect to scope, the GATT and its successor organization, the WTO, have expanded in terms of the issues that they cover.

Other institutions, such as the Association of South East Asian Nations (ASEAN) and the Australia–New Zealand Closer Economic Relations Trade Agreement (ANZCERTA) have also existed among a subset of members in the Asia-Pacific region. Each organization has its own metaregime and regime, with varying characteristics. In creating APEC, the member states had to concern themselves with two types of institutional reconciliation: (1) reconciling APEC with the broader institution of GATT; and (2) reconciling APEC with narrower institutions such as ASEAN and ANZCERTA. To date, the avenue to achieving institutional reconciliation has been through nested rather than parallel connections. More recently, the development of the North American Free Trade Agreement (NAFTA) as another subregional institution within APEC and the movement toward a free trade agreement among ASEAN members (AFTA) have further complicated this nesting problem.

International regimes, whether multilateral or bilateral, are developed to regulate the actions of states. *National actions* can include unilateral actions or ad hoc bilateral or multilateral accords. Examples of these include the use of Super 301 by the United States or bilateral discussions on specific issues between Japan and the United States.

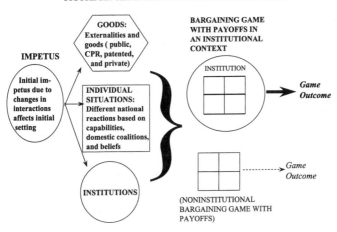

FIGURE 2.2: THE INSTITUTIONAL BARGAINING GAME

These measures in turn affect the types and levels of *interactions* that we observe in particular issue areas, such as trade, investment, or short-term capital flows.[24] In an apolitical world, we could imagine a closed loop with societal actors engaging in interactions without any governance structures—be they national controls, ad hoc agreements, or institutions—to influence these activities. But in the Asia-Pacific context, national regulatory efforts will influence the flow of interactions. National policies that affect trade and financial flows include policies that specify rules of origin, intellectual property, and competition policy.

III. THE INSTITUTIONAL BARGAINING GAME

The process depicted in Figure 2.1 of Pre-APEC Trade Bargaining helps to set the stage for understanding the institutional environment prior to APEC's formation. We now consider some theoretical elements that might help us to account for APEC's development.

We begin by describing the elements of goods, individual situations, and institutions that constitute an institutional bargaining game and show how they fit together to yield game payoffs. Figure 2.2 depicts the elements of the initial bargaining game, starting with an initial impetus that sets the game in motion.

The Initial Impetus

In general, an initial impetus significantly alters the preexisting bargaining context. Examples include the oil shock of 1973, the breakdown of the Bretton Woods system in 1971, and the end of the Cold War following the collapse of the Soviet Union. An impetus to change can also come from both endogenous and exogenous changes that are less dramatic, such as actions by currency speculators, or electoral victories that shift actors' individual situations. These changes will generally create differing incentives for actors.

Goods and Externalities

Initial shocks may create either a positive or negative externality on actors who are not immediate participants in the precipitating event. Alternatively, economic or political changes may stimulate or impede the provision of some type of "good," namely public goods, common pool resource (CPR) goods, inclusive club goods ("patented goods"), or private goods.[25] Differences among goods can be characterized along two dimensions: jointness, which refers to the extent to which goods are affected by consumption; and by the possibility of exclusion, which refers to whether noncontributors to the provision of the good can be kept from consuming it.[26]

In the case of public goods, actors face a collective action dilemma because all can benefit from the joint nature of the good (e.g., national defense). However, because exclusion is not possible, beneficiaries need not contribute to its creation or maintenance. In such cases, analysts have focused on the incentives for differently situated states to provide public goods. The classic representation of the provision problems for public good is the n-person prisoners' dilemma (PD): in such cases, cooperation can potentially help all players, but actors have a dominant strategy to defect and the good may not be provided.[27]

CPR goods include global commons concerns such as fishery resources or goods for which exclusion of noncontributors from consumption of the good is not feasible.[28] In such cases, providers of goods risk being exploited since they will not only end up paying for the cost of the good, but they will also suffer from free-riding that will diminish the goods due to the lack of jointness. Thus, at least in principle, the game that reflects the problem of provision of such goods will be a more severe form of a PD.

Inclusive club goods, or "patented goods," refer to goods that exhibit jointness (i.e., they are not diminished by use), but for which exclusion is possible (e.g., satellite transmission of television with scrambling technology to prevent noncontributors from accessing the goods). Because of the benefits of having additional consumers of the goods that one produces, we might expect that in the case of international institutions, actors will compete to have their institutional approach adopted as the standard by all participants to maximize their revenue possibilities.

Finally, private goods, which reflect the possibility of exclusion but not jointness, include the consumption of goods diminished by use. Individual actors will have an incentive to produce these goods and to charge according to their marginal cost of extension of these goods.

To better understand the implications of this basic characterization of the "type of goods" involved in an issue area, we need also to consider the effects of actors' individual situations and institutional context within which interaction takes place. Goods give us only a first cut into understanding the types of problems that actors face and their incentives: knowledge of the types of goods involved in the bargaining does not allow us adequately to determine specific payoffs of games because the position of national actors or the institutional setting may alter the bargaining problem. We now turn to these two elements.

Individual Bargaining Situations

States or other actors are likely to have varying interests in the issue area within which bargaining takes place. The most significant factors that will influence their payoffs include: (1) an actor's international capabilities; (2) its domestic coalitional stability; and (3) elite beliefs and ideologies. The first of these elements refers to the actor's position in the overall international system as well as its relative capabilities in the specific issue-area under discussion. These factors will influence a state's objectives as well as its ability to secure its desired outcomes. The second element, a state's domestic coalitional stability, focuses on the incumbency expectations of government decision makers. This variable taps into decision makers' discount rates. For example, in debt rescheduling negotiations, domestically unstable governments will be reluctant to undertake sharp economic adjustment measures for fear that they will be ousted. Finally, elite beliefs and ideologies about the causal connections among issues and the need to handle problems on a multilateral basis will also influence the payoffs and actors' responses.

The Institutional Context

As states attempt to secure their optimal outcomes, they will interact strategically, possibly in the context of one or more institutions. Institutions should influence how actors interact, and they may provide focal point solutions for coordination games or may help states to overcome collective action problems.[29] For example, neoliberal institutionalists argue that regimes help to provide information and lower organizational costs, thus helping to allow actors to come to bargains and solve collective action problems. Institutions are also likely to have important distributive consequences, and they may influence actors' bargaining behavior by tying the hands of other international and domestic actors.[30] And analysts from the cognitive school argue that international institutions may lead to fundamental changes in actors' basic interests and possibly facilitate greater cooperation.

The Institutional Bargaining Game and APEC

We can now attempt to consider the combined effect of the initial impetus with the three elements of goods, individual situations, and institutions to gain insight into different types of institutional bargaining games. Understanding these games gives us insight into the strategies that actors might subsequently pursue in an attempt to change the games in which they find themselves. It is worth noting that an exact a priori specification of the effect of the three elements on game payoffs—absent a specific empirical issue—is a difficult if not impossible task: instead, the discussion below focuses on some general considerations of the effect of different elements.

The neorealist institutionalist school hypothesizes that hegemonic powers will be willing to provide public goods and will allow free-riding because of purely economic calculations (as when the owner of a large number of ships pays for a lighthouse). Put differently, we should expect actors' payoffs to vary as a result of their differing positions, possibly changing the nature of the game as initially suggested by the goods involved. Lisa Martin presents an example of this and shows how a prisoner's dilemma game turns into what she terms a "suasion" game when a hegemon is present.[31] Because of this transformation, resulting from differing individual situations in my terminology, the outcome of the game will be unilateral provision of public goods by the hegemon. Alternatively, rather than a benevolent hegemon that provides public goods, we might also see aggressive powers that form institutions to monitor potentially shirking actors or simply use power directly by threatening free-riders. Public good provision might also be possible with small numbers of actors rather than only in cases of hegemony.[32] What might the public good provision game look like with two players? While one might argue that the game still remains a PD, given the jointness of the good, it seems more reasonable to consider the game as one of Chicken: each would like the other to pay for the good, but the joint nature of the good means that free-riders will not impair one's own consumption of the good. The exact form of the game in this case will depend on the size of each of the two players as compared to the overall cost of providing the public good.[33]

In the case of common pool resources, the problem of provision and maintenance is more severe than for public goods because of the lack of jointness. Following the logic of the relationship between individual situations and public goods, we would expect the resulting games for hegemonic and bipolar provision in the CPR case to mimic the games involved with provision of public goods. However, in view of the lack of jointness, both the suasion and Chicken games will have worse payoffs both for cooperation and defection, thus potentially making it more difficult for actors to come to agreement on the development of such goods. Yet this pessimism on the likelihood of provision may not be fully warranted.[34] While the lack of jointness inherent in CPRs makes it less likely that a hegemon would be willing to provide the good, this very "crowding" may actually *stimulate* the provision of CPRs as compared with public goods. Hegemons in CPR cases will be more likely to encourage joint provision of goods through coercive means. Thus, possible free-riders may be brought into the fold since their nonparticipation in provision has direct consequences for the supply of the good. If they are then forced to pay for the good in question, the hegemon's initial investment and maintenance costs will be lower. Drawing on neoliberal factors, I would also argue that CPRs should clearly stimulate group activity in monitoring and possible sanctioning in an institutionally thick context because of the negative implications involved in free-riding. Thus there is likely to be *more* active participation by all members, and the good may therefore be less likely to be eroded over time.

With respect to private vs. patented goods, I would hypothesize that the strong benefits that accrue to actors from the provision of patented goods will stimulate competition to provide the good. Thus, if benefits can be gained by "selling" the good to possible new adherents to an institution, we should see competition among groups of states to encourage nonparticipants to join their arrangement. The game in this case would look much like a coordination game, with each party vying to have its own institutional form adopted. In the technology standards area in a private setting, attempting to set up one's own standard as the national or global standard to subsequently reap benefits from this choice parallels this institutional hypothesis.

In sum, bargaining among actors—based on the games defined by goods, individual situations, and institutions—yields payoffs that are likely to differ for the actors involved in the initial negotiating game. We can briefly illustrate these points in the case of APEC's formation. The problems in the Uruguay Round and changes in the European Community provided a key impetus. With the Europeans moving forward to a unified market and the impasse in GATT negotiations, Australia and other like-minded countries were concerned about the externalities resulting from European integration and GATT's potential demise as a public good. For many state and nonstate actors in the region, the discussions about trade liberalization under GATT auspices (see Figure 2.1), resulted in unsatisfying payoffs for many actors. This provided the stimulus for the APEC's formation. Thus, faced with the payoffs that result from their initial strategic interaction, as we

Figure 2.3: Creating and Reconciling APEC with Existing Institutions

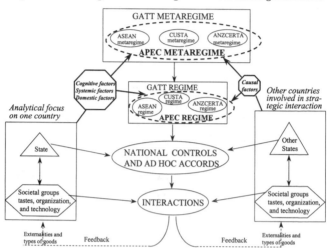

have seen, states did not simply accept the outcome of their bargaining. Thus the game did not simply "end" at this point: indeed, actors often make efforts to alter the bargaining game in which they find themselves to improve their payoffs in a new game structure.[35] It is to this latter possibility that we now turn.

IV. GAME CHANGE EFFORTS AND OUTCOMES

When will actors make efforts to promote game change? Logically, they consider their existing payoffs in the current bargaining game and compare these with their projected payoffs from instituting some form of game change. To make this calculation, states evaluate their ability to secure more favorable outcomes by assessing their own power resources in light of their own individual situation and that of their opponent or opponents.

In APEC's case, potential members were motivated to change the existing bargaining game. Figure 2.3 provides a schematic overview of APEC's creation and the strategic institutional bargaining game.

FIGURE 2.4: INSTITUTIONAL GAME CHANGE EFFORTS

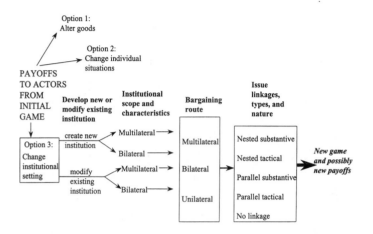

As noted before, a key consideration for the participants in APEC was the desire to be consistent with the GATT while also encompassing existing subregional agreements (ASEAN, the Canada–United States Trade Agreement (CUSTA), and ANZCERTA). Although the outcome in this instance was the formation of a new nested regional institution, this choice was only one of a number of possible outcomes.

To understand this particular choice, we must address the following points: (1) What institutional or noninstitutional options are available to actors? (2) Where do the different paths lead in terms of institutional and noninstitutional outcomes? and (3) What factors explain the choice of different bargaining paths? Together, the answers to these questions will help us anticipate future developments in APEC and its relationship to other institutions. Figure 2.4 provides a flowchart of decisions that actors must make. After discussing the nature of each of these choices, I will examine the logic underlying their selection in more detail.

The Choices Available to Actors

As this figure illustrates, actors have three options. First, they can attempt to manipulate the types of goods involved in negotiations directly, say by an exclusive alliance. Second, they can alter either their own or their opponents' individual situations. These could include such efforts as overthrowing governments, building up one's own capabilities in specific issue areas, or attempting to influence foreign decision makers. Third—and the primary focus of this book—they can change the *institutional context* within which actors are operating. Note that such institutional change strategies may indirectly influence the goods involved in the negotiations and may well change actors' individual situations.

In line with our emphasis on institutional strategies to alter games and influence bargaining outcomes, actors following such strategies must make several additional decisions. Specifically, they must (1) decide if they would be better off by creating a new institution or modifying the existing one(s); (2) choose the type of institution they prefer if they create a new one; (3) select the bargaining route they want to follow; and (4) decide whether to engage in issue linkages and, if so, determine the type and nature of these connections.

Creating New or Modifying Existing Institution(s)

When faced with unsatisfactory payoffs, and depending on their individual situations, states may develop new institutions. For example, since several states in the Asia-Pacific questioned the efficacy of the Uruguay Round but believed in GATT principles and norms, they decided to pursue the formation of APEC within the existing institution of GATT.

Institutional Characteristics

If a state decides to pursue the formation of a new institution, it must decide if such an accord should be bilateral (such as the

CUSTA) or multilateral (such as APEC) and also decide on its strength, nature, and scope. But if a state opposes a new institution, it could still work to modify it, possibly by changing its institutional scope (as with the expansion of the CUSTA to include Mexico). The next stage in the process is to decide on an appropriate bargaining route.

In the APEC case, the actual membership of this multilateral arrangement has been open to considerable debate. For example, there was some initial debate over inclusion of the United States. Prime Minister Mahathir of Malaysia has attempted to press for an organization such as the East Asia Economic Group (now Caucus) as an alternative to APEC. The question of regime strength has been of particular significance. Whereas the United States has pushed for binding rules and procedures, most Asian countries have shown considerable reluctance to move in this direction. The issue of regime nature has been an issue of much less contention, with all countries supporting (at least formally) an open liberal arrangement. Issue scope has been open to more debate, with some fear of U.S. agenda setting.

Bargaining Route

As indicated in Figure 2.4, states may choose to bargain multilaterally or bilaterally, or to take unilateral actions to achieve their ends.[36] Turning first to the bargaining route within an existing institution, although multilateral negotiations in a multilateral institution are common, states can also pursue bilateral and unilateral strategies. For example, even though the United States was involved in the Uruguay Round trade negotiations, it discussed specific issues with Japan on a bilateral basis (under GATT auspices) and took unilateral action with respect to other states using specific GATT provisions.

What about the use of different bargaining routes for the creation of a new institution? In the case of multilateral arrangements, multilateral strategies can include coalition building efforts. States can also use bilateral and unilateral strategies by "imposing" agreements on other states through either bipolar cooperation or hegemonic imposition. If the institution in question is a bilateral one, the case of a multilateral bargaining route to secure such an outcome is less obvious than the use of bilateral or unilateral strategies. An example of this could be actors engaging in multilateral negotiations and then deciding on an appropriate bilateral regime for a subset of the states involved. The emerging regime guiding relations between the PLO and Israel, resulting from negotiations in a multilateral forum, would seem to fit this notion.

In APEC's case, we have seen a multilateral approach to the creation of this institution. In contrast to the most common path of hegemonic leadership by the United States in the post–World War II era, in this case Australia, supported by Japan and encouraged by the United States, worked to develop APEC. Since then, although the major powers have had more say in the evolution of APEC, middle-level powers continue to play a key role. The development of APEC can thus be best characterized as a multicountry joint effort

Issue Linkages and Institutional Reconciliation

The final decision node in Figure 2.4 concerns an actor's decision to link issues or institutions in negotiations. In addition to choosing whether or not to make linkages, actors must also make two other choices when they link issues: the type of linkage (parallel or nested) and the nature of the linkage (tactical or substantive).[37]

Turning first to types of linkages, we can think of two types in the context of reconciling institutions: (1) nested arrangements, which draw on elements from the framework of broader institutions to make them compatible while providing an element of hierarchical goal ordering; and (2) parallel arrangements, which are compatible with other arrangements because of an institutional division of labor. Nested arrangements are well illustrated by

FIGURE 2.5: THE DYNAMICS OF ISSUE LINKAGE

LINKAGE TYPE	OBJECTIVE REALITY	TARGET DECISION MAKERS' PERCEPTIONS	BASIS FOR ISSUE CONNECTIONS	OUTCOME
Substantive link	Connected	Connected	Knowledge	(1) Stable issue-area
Failed substantive link (perceived as tactical)	Connected	Unconnected	Power	(2) Temporary solution to externalities
Tactical link	Unconnected	Unconnected	Power	(3) Unstable issue-area
Failed tactical link (perceived as substantive)	Unconnected	Connected	Misunderstanding	(4) "Contingent" (to unstable issue-area with knowledge change)

APEC's efforts to be consistent with the GATT. "Parallel" institutions deal with separate but related activities. In the case of the development of the European Economic Coal and Steel Community and the Western European Union, we had parallel organizations. The first was oriented toward strengthening European cooperation in economic matters while the WEU sought to develop a coordinated European defense effort.

The second consideration, the nature of the linkage, refers to the intellectual basis for the issue connection. If two issues are seen to be unrelated but are tied together in negotiations, this can be considered a power-based connection or tactical link. By contrast, if the issues exhibit some intellectual coherence, then the linkage can be labeled substantive. Figure 2.5 presents the alternatives under different conditions.

In the first case in this chart, we have a case of substantive linkage, which is likely to result in the creation of a stable issue-area. This outcome arises from bargaining in which one actor convinces the other (the "target") of the impact of externalities surrounding a particular set of negotiations, and the coherent packaging of the issues (e.g., APEC discussions of financial and trade policies). As we shall see in the case of the formation of institutions, substantive linkages should lead to more stable agreements and institutions because actors are more likely to accept this type of issue packaging.

More complicated is the second type of manipulated linkage— failed substantive linkage. Here, even though experts agree that two issues are interconnected (such as access to markets for trade and the ability to service debt), policymakers in the target country do not recognize the issues as substantively linked but perceive the issues as only tactically related. Without changes, even though the target actor treats the issues as connected, this will prove to be only a temporary solution to the externalities problem. Such a situation may provide hope for the actor trying to establish the link (the "linker"). When the policymaker's initial reaction is a rejection of substantive connections among issues, experts in both countries may play a prominent role in swaying decision makers' opinions.

The third type of link, tactical linkage, may foster even greater conflict. This method of connecting issues is a pure power play. If used as a carrot, it can diminish conflict. But if used as a stick, tactical linkage will create sharp conflict in negotiations and most likely lead to unstable agreements or institutions.[38] Many Asian countries see American efforts to discuss democratization or human rights as being a linkage of this sort.

Finally, in the last case, misperceived tactical linkages, policymakers in the target country see the issues as substantively linked—even though they are linked only tactically. Although the target decision makers' own experts will attempt to dissuade their policymakers from accepting the linkage, target decision makers may agree to some type of joint agreement and consider the issues in question as a package. Clever manipulation by the linker could produce a much more favorable outcome than might otherwise be the case. But because it is based on a misunderstanding, this is an unstable situation and will lead to unstable institutional formation.

FIGURE 2.6: LINKAGE BARGAINING AND INSTITUTIONAL ADAPTATION

	Linkage Type				
	Nested Linkage		Parallel Linkage		No Linkage
	Substantive	Tactical	Substantive	Tactical	
Use or Modify Existing Institution or Institutions	1. Stable hierarchical link between issues within existing institution or between institutions *Role of dollar, gold, and exchanges rates in IMF*	3. Contingent, hierarchical link between issues within existing institution(s) (to independent or conflict with power change) *Security Council vs. General Assembly role in the UN*	1. Stable, intra- or cross institutional link between related issues *IMF and World Bank*	3. Contingent, intra- or cross institutional link between issues (to independent with power change) *Voting power and economic standing criteria in IMF*	Institutionally-based negotiations on single issue *GATT dispute settlement body*
	2. Temporary hierarchy between issues within existing institution(s) (target perceives link as tactical link) *Southern Europe view of EMU convergence criteria*	4. Unstable, hierarchical link between issues within existing institution(s) (if target perceives link as substantive link) *Commodity fund aid within Lomé convention*	2. Temporary, intra- or cross institutional solution to externalities (target perceives link as tactical link) *Services & manufactures in Uruguay Round (LDC view)*	4. Unstable, intra- or cross institutional link between issues (target perceives link as substantive link) *Special and differential treatment for developing countries in the GATT (LDC view)*	
Create and Reconcile New Institution with Old Institution or Institutions?	1. Stable, hierarchically compatible institutions for related issues *WTO-APEC*	3. Contingent, hierarchically compatible institutions for issues (to independent or conflict with power change) *APEC-EAEC connection*	1. Stable, compatible inter-institutional link for related issues *IMF and BIS connection*	3. Contingent, inter-institutional compatibility for issues (to independent with power change) *GATT vs. UNCTAD role in global trade negotiations*	Independent institutions (no concern for compatibility) *World Health Organization and ITU*
	2. Temporary, hierarchically compatible institutions for issues (if target perceives link as tactical link) *MFA within the GATT (LDC view)*	4. Unstable, hierarchically compatible institutions for issues (if target perceives link as substantive link) *Global Environmental Fund and World Bank (LDC view)*	2. Temporary, inter-institutional compatibility between issues (target perceives link as tactical link) *GATT-UNCTAD Trade Development Center (LDC view)*	4. Unstable, inter-institutional compatibility for issues (target perceives link as substantive link) *Financial Support Fund and the International Energy Agency (French view)*	

Indeed, if and when the target comes to realize that the connection was tactical in nature, the bargaining connection will shift to a potentially unstable tactical one that relies on its superior power.

Institutional Outcomes

We can now look at the possible outcomes resulting from efforts either to modify or to create and reconcile institutions on the one hand and the types and nature of linkages on the other.[39] In each of the two rows of Figure 2.6, the top and bottom entries (separated by dotted lines) reflect a convergence and divergence of perceptions on linkages respectively.

Modifying Existing Institution(s)

In addition to the possibility of no linkages, there are two possible types of linkages that we must consider. The first example (1) reflects a case of nested substantive linkages. The relationship of issues in the IMF under the Bretton Woods system was clearly ordered. Fixed exchange rates were central and gold provided the basis for backing the dollar. The dollar played several key roles including the numeraire, the intervention currency, and the like, and there was widespread agreement on this structuring. By contrast, in the second case, the EMU convergence targets for debt, government spending, interest rates, and inflation have proved controversial. The Germans and some others see this as a natural economic connection between the higher level objective of monetary union and the subordinate goals necessary to achieve smooth progress toward fixed exchange rates in the Union. But some Southern European members of the EU have exhibited considerable skepticism about this claim (2), viewing the connection as a tactical effort by the Germans and other Northern Europeans to control their economic policies.

The next case (3) provides an example of a tactical linkage. Almost all states recognized that the decision-making structure with the dominance of the Security Council over the General Assembly in the United Nations was a tactical consideration based on the power of the major players in the system. The fourth case of nested linkages (4) contains an example of aid to Lomé convention members for commodity price stabilization. From the perspective of the poorer members of this agreement, this is a substantive connection to stabilize markets. But from the perspective of many EC members, this was simply a tactical exchange tied to political and economic interests in maintaining the Lomé agreements.

Moving across the chart to the case of parallel linkages, the relationship between the IMF and World Bank (1) provides a good example of parallel substantive connections with respect to financial assistance. In the Bretton Woods system, the IMF was to engage in short-term lending to help countries facing balance-of-payments difficulties to adjust. Meanwhile, the World Bank would provide long-term loans to help improve the functioning of countries' economies. The connection between services and manufactures in the Uruguay Round (2) provides an example of differing views involving negotiations within an existing institution. Whereas the United States saw this connection as a substantive one, many developing countries argued that this was merely a tactical ploy and that services had no place in GATT negotiations. In the end, the negotiation proceeded on two separate tracks but with an implicit connection between the two.

Moving to tactical parallel linkages, the notion of weighted voting is clearly seen as a power-based decision (3). In the IMF, countries are allocated voting shares based on economic criteria. While the indicators of economic wealth have come under increasing challenge, there is little question that this linkage is tactical in nature. Finally, calls for special and differential treatment for developing countries have been seen as a tactical concession to facilitate trade liberalization (4). Thus, developed countries have repeatedly made special provisions in negotiating rounds—dating back to the Kennedy Round and now in the Uruguay Round—that allow for delays in the implementation of WTO provisions. By contrast, this effort has been viewed by many developing countries as a substantive logical connection deriving from their relatively uncompetitive position.

In this row, the last example reflects a case of no linkage. The GATT dispute settlement body provides a forum for the resolution of issues without linkages to other concerns. In an ideal setting, these institutional mechanisms are to deal with the specific issue brought up for resolution by member states without connections to other issues.

Reconciling New and Old Institutions

We next turn to the second half of Figure 2.6. I have already discussed the WTO and APEC connection (1) as one that explicitly argued for a new arrangement in the Asia-Pacific that would be consistent with actors' higher-level concerns about continuing trade liberalization through the GATT. The claim by developed countries of the nesting of the MFA within the GATT (2) was seen by developing countries to be a tactical ploy to restrict their imports, and GATT consistency was seen as a sham.

Moving to the next column, we have a case of tactical linkages. In this example, the connection between APEC and the East Asian Economic Caucus (EAEC) (3), all parties recognize that this linkage exists because of pressure by Malaysia to create a separate grouping that would exclude North Americans and Oceania. Although some lip service is paid to the notion that this grouping is substantively connected, no one views this as credible.

Finally, as an example of a tactical link being perceived as substantive, we can consider the case of the Global Environmental Fund and its connection to the World Bank following the Rio environmental summit (3). From the developing countries' point of view, the promise of aid was a natural and logical connection to broader financial aid organizations such as the World Bank. But developed countries have a more jaundiced view of this linkage and generally see it as a tactical payoff to get developing countries to reduce harmful emissions.

Now we turn to parallel substantive linkages. When the IMF was created in 1944, there was initially seen to be conflict with the Bank for International Settlements (BIS) (1). But within a few years, the relationship between the two stabilized in a division of labor that actors have accepted as logical. In the next case, GATT's interest in trade liberalization was compatible with UNCTAD's focus on promoting exports—at least in the minds of decision makers in developed countries (3). These two institutions have been partially reconciled through the formation of a Trade Development Center,[40] although developing countries remain more skeptical about this connection and perceive it more as a tactical linkage. The decision to create UNCTAD and its relationship to the GATT (3) in the various trade rounds has been seen by all countries as a tactical development resulting from developing countries' pressure to create a forum for their interests. While GATT negotiations continue, UNCTAD often serves as a forum in which developing countries can get advice on how to improve their bargaining skills and obtain information. Finally, when the United States proposed the Financial Support Fund as a tactical linkage to encourage development of the International Energy Agency, the French saw this as a substantive link connected to helping countries facing balance-of-payments difficulties (4).

Finally, the last column presents an example in which no effort is made to reconcile institutions. This is a case of the persistence of independent institutions with no effort to make them compatible. An example would be the World Health Organization and the International Telecommunication Union, which traditionally have dealt with quite disparate issues.

IV. HYPOTHESES ON GAME CHANGE EFFORTS AND INSTITUTIONAL RECONCILIATION

What factors will determine decision makers' choices on whether to pursue institutional change strategies to influence bargaining games? And how will they decide if institutions should be reconciled? Because of the considerable overlap between the arguments about modifying versus creating new institutions, I discuss the hypotheses by group with respect to institutional innovation, institutional scope, bargaining strategies, and reconciliation through different forms of linkages.

Modifying Existing versus Creating New Institutions

One of the key issues in choosing whether to alter existing or create new institutions relates to the goods that are involved in the negotiations. For example, to prevent free-riding that might take place with public and CPR goods, neorealist institutionalists point to the possible role of institutional strategies in altering the nature of the good (e.g., the decision by major powers to prevent developing countries from free riding due to the Most Favored Nation norm of the GATT). Thus, in the Tokyo Round, only those countries who signed onto specific codes (e.g., subsidies) were given the benefits of liberalization entailed by these codes.[41]

Focusing on transaction costs, if an existing institution is providing valued goods, it might be possible for actors to link the provision of goods in one arena with the provision of goods in another. Thus, given the organizational and informational benefits of an existing institution, actors may be reluctant to free-ride in another area for fear of undermining the existing institution. With respect to new institutional creation and reconciliation, particularly in a nested context in which goals in the new institution are subordinate to higher-level concerns in a broader institution, a similar incentive for actors to work together to provide public goods or CPRs may exist. That is, in view of their higher-level objectives, actors may be willing to risk cooperation in light of possible defection because of their concerns for meeting these goals.

Cognitive perspectives do not directly address the problem of overcoming collective action problems to secure provision of public goods or CPRs. Instead, cognitivists point to the possibility that as a result of learning, it may be possible to achieve some convergence of interests. Of course, such convergence is hardly guaranteed; states might simply better understand that their interests are in conflict! But we might extend cognitive thinking on how institutions might be used to deal with the provision of goods. How might growing cognitive convergence overcome the problem of free-riding that is inherent in the provision of public goods—even when actors have common interests? I would argue that we can think of this problem in the context of thick interactions among states. In such a case, the convergence of interest would likely facilitate cooperation among states along standard neoliberal lines. A second cognitive effect on the provision of goods is the possibility that changes in knowledge may lead to changed understanding of the goods involved: this might mean that states could better understand how to exclude free-riders, or that the type of good involved in the negotiations was not really what they initially thought. Such changes do not point a priori to a greater likelihood of cooperation in the provision of goods. As noted above, actors may simply realize that the supply problem was more difficult than they had initially estimated, and they may therefore be less likely to cooperate.

Excluding the creation of an institution de novo and noninstitutional bargaining, actors can either use or modify existing institutions or develop new ones and reconcile them to existing arrangements. From a simple inertia perspective, we would expect that actors' first instinct is to utilize or modify an existing institution to their advantage rather than to pursue development of a new institution—both from a neorealist and neoliberal institutionalist perspective.[42] New institutions are expensive to create. Thus, if actors can achieve their objectives by simply modifying an institution, this will likely be the preferred course. Of course, if the institution has repeatedly failed to "deliver the goods," even with modifications, then institutional innovation will be the logical option.

Beyond these standard arguments, we can hypothesize that an important constraint on the innovation of new institutions will be the degree to which existing institutions in which an issue might be resolved are deeply embedded among other institutions. Thus, if actors see existing arrangements in which negotiations might take place as substantively connected to other arrangements, either in nested or parallel fashion, this will influence prospects for new institutional creation.

Institutional Characteristics: Institutional Scope

Institutional characteristics will be affected by several factors.[43] With specific respect to our interest in examining the issue of multilateralism vs. bilateralism, we would expect different predictions from neoliberals vs. neorealists. Neoliberals would expect that multilateralism would be the preferred avenue to reduce transaction costs and provide the widest dissemination of information. By contrast, from a neorealist perspective, unless an actor is exceptionally strong, it might prefer bilateral over multilateral arrangements to maximize its leverage.[44]

Second, the choice of a multilateral versus a bilateral institution will be affected by preexisting institutions. For example, I have argued that the norm of multilateralism in the GATT strongly constrained the formation of the Short and Long Term Cotton Textile Agreements in 1961-1962. This outcome can be explained as the result of actor concerns about institutional nesting and the fear that bilateral and unilateral actions would undermine this GATT norm—*independent* of the benefits of reducing transaction costs through a multilateral arrangement.[45] By contrast, without strong substantive linkages among issues, the decision between a multilateral or bilateral institution will be more influenced by transaction and control considerations.

Third, the question of the choice between a multilateral or bilateral approach to institutional formation can be considered from a more cognitive perspective. In a volume edited by John Ruggie,[46] a number of scholars argue that this choice derives from the preferences of states who fundamentally believe in the value of organizing the world system on a multilateral basis. Thus they are not concerned with the number of states involved in an activity but rather with examining state commitments to norms of collective action. In doing so, these analysts go beyond the neoliberal institutionalist view of multilateralism as simply a means for reducing transaction costs.

Bargaining Route

To achieve their ends, actors can pursue either a unilateral, bilateral, or multilateral route. The classic argument in this regard is a neorealist institutionalist one, with the view that hegemonic states will be tempted to develop regimes. Other work in this genre has shown that like-minded states may be able to cooperate on a bilateral or multilateral basis to secure regimes, and need not always fall victim to collective action dilemmas.[47]

Less has been written directly about reconciling international institutions. Although we would expect power considerations still to be important, material power usage in this case will be constrained by existing institutional power resources. Appeals to norms and rules could play a significant role in this instance, particularly when actors agree upon the substantive nesting of issues. In addition, I would suggest that the presence of a highly institutionalized regime will also constrain actors' efforts to develop a new institution for bureaucratic reasons. The bureaucracy and secretariat of extant organizations will be likely to oppose the formation of a new institution. In addition to direct resistance from the bureaucracy, it is likely that states will have vested interest groups that are also likely to resist institutional innovation.

Linkages and Institutional Reconciliation

With respect to linkages, specifically parallel versus nested connections, I propose several hypotheses. Within an existing institution, from a cognitive perspective, decision makers' choices will depend on their understanding of the relationships among issues. For example, if they perceive inherent spillovers and connections among issues and believe that there is a hierarchical relationship among issues, they will seek to make nested connections. Otherwise, it would be easier to cope with spillovers through a division of labor—through parallel connections.

In reconciling new and old institutions or in significantly modifying old ones, the choice of whether to support parallel or nested institutions will depend on the existing institutional environment. If institutions already exist, actors contemplating institutional innovation must decide how important it is to reconcile institutions. If one is developing narrow issue-area or regional-based accords, and the issue's salience is low relative to broader issue-area or regional arrangements, actors will make strong efforts to nest the new institution within the broader one—even if there is no clear substantive connection among issues. Thus we should also expect to see consistent goal ordering, and hence nested institutions, when threat is high. By contrast, if issue area or regional institutions are crucial to actors, they may be willing to risk conflict with other institutions by developing parallel arrangements.

Turning to substantive versus tactical linkage issues, when actors do not share a cognitive consensus on the relationships among issues, tactical linkages will be related to power-based efforts to assert the superiority of some issues or to deny the hierarchical ordering of connections proposed by other actors. On the specific question of differences between modifying existing institutions versus wholly new institutional reconciliation, we should expect it to be more difficult to achieve a clear cognitive consensus in the latter case. Whereas the question of cognitive consensus will apply to connections between individual issues in the case of minor institutional modification, in the case of new or significantly modified institutions, actors must actually agree on the relationship between different large packages of linked issues in an institutionalized form. This is likely to be a more difficult problem because of the number of issues involved and would suggest that the nesting of wholly new and old institutions will be more difficult than simply modifying old arrangements.[48]

Summary

This section has presented several hypotheses on the evolution of institutional bargaining games. In drawing on existing approaches to understanding institutions, as well as elaborating on undeveloped strands of thinking, my objective has been to allow us to explore choices about creating new institutions, institutional scope, and bargaining routes. Ultimately, our focus is on trying to understand the motivations and calculations of actors in the APEC process. Taken together with the ideas on construction of institutional bargaining games presented earlier in this chapter, the remainder of this volume explores facets of APEC's development and evolution.

VI. CONCLUSION

The creation and evolution of APEC will have important implications for the Asia-Pacific. This chapter has presented an approach to analyzing the evolution of APEC by focusing on the notion of an institutional bargaining game. I have suggested that this concept is helpful in understanding the reconciliation of new and old institutions as well as the modification or restructuring of existing ones.

The central effort in this chapter has been to draw upon research on institutional formation—particularly the literature on the formation and evolution of international regimes—to gain insight about APEC. I suggested that regime theory can be usefully applied to the analysis of regional arrangements. Because there is no single approach to understand the evolution of international regimes, however, Section II discussed five competing schools— neorealism, neorealist institutionalism, neoliberal institutionalism, cognitivists, and radical constructivists. In reviewing these literatures, I emphasized how each generates distinct expectations about the formation and implications of international institutions.

Building on portions of this work, the core of the chapter developed what I termed "institutional bargaining games" in the third and fourth sections. Based on some change in the external environment that may generate externalities or affect the provision of various types of goods, actors respond to this change through negotiations in an "initial" bargaining game. Their interests and choices will be affected both by what I have termed their "individual situations" as well as by the presence or absence of institutions. Subsequently, depending on the payoffs to actors generated by their interaction, actors may respond to possibly poor payoffs in the initial bargaining game through institutional innovation and the use of linkages.

Section V of this chapter focused on the causal factors that influence actors' choices in the institutional bargaining process. The central objective of this effort has been to consider factors that have led to the "nested substantive" reconciliation of APEC with the GATT and WTO. A second objective has been to provide a basis for understanding the institutional innovation process more generally with an eye to considering the development of other institutions that APEC might follow as exemplars.

The unified theoretical framework presented here provides a basis for the empirical analyses that follow in this volume. In particular, the first empirical section of this work considers several issue-areas that have influenced the formation of APEC and will continue to do so: trade, investment, and intellectual property. The second section then turns to national policies toward APEC, focusing in particular on the policies of Australia, the United States, Japan, and China. Section III then considers the question of nested institutions through an examination of the relationship between the WTO and APEC. It also focuses on "subregional" arrangements within APEC with a specific focus on NAFTA, ASEAN, and the EAEC. Finally, the concluding section examines two possible exemplars for APEC, the OECD and the EU with an eye to gleaning lessons on institutional development for APEC.

The concluding chapter by the co-editors of this volume examines the findings and implications of the analysis in this work and the utility of the analytical framework in helping us to improve our grasp of the likely evolution of APEC. By drawing on a unified set of analytical concepts, I hope that this volume will help us to gauge better the future of institutional developments in the Asia-Pacific.

NOTES

1. For comments on earlier drafts of this chapter, I am indebted to Charles Morrison and Cédric Dupont.
2. These options are discussed in Aggarwal (1994).
3. It is worth noting that nesting is not the only form of institutional reconciliation that might be possible. For example, APEC could develop as a "parallel" institution to the WTO and simply deal with non-GATT issues. This idea is developed below. Empirically, some have suggested that such an institutional division of labor might be a means of pursuing institutionalization in the Asia-Pacific without challenging the authority of the WTO in the trade area.
4. See Aggarwal (1994) for a comparison of APEC and NAFTA based on international regime theory.
5. See Aggarwal (1989) and (1996) on both the concepts of individual situations as well as parallel and nested linkages (discussed below).
6. See Krasner (1983).
7. For a recent discussion of formal organizations, see Abbott and Snidal (1995).
8. I have not seen this term used before, and will discuss my reason for using this label below. Moravcsik (1992) does note the difference between realist and liberal conceptions of institutions but does not use this specific term to refer to the school as I describe it below.
9. Peter Haas (1992, p. 21) uses the term "Radical constructivists."
10. See, for example, Waltz (1979). This view is most sharply represented by the work of John Mearsheimer (1990). Ironically, the most useful purpose of regimes for such analysts would be simply to reduce transaction costs along the lines of the neoliberal institutionalist model discussed below.
11. See Krasner (1983), Aggarwal (1985), Krasner (1991), and Knight (1992) for examples of this line of reasoning.
12. See Aggarwal (1985) for this discussion of "control."
13. Kindleberger (1973), Gilpin (1975), and Krasner (1976). Keohane (1984) provides a valuable critique and discussion of hegemonic stability theory.
14. Keohane (1984). This work draws on Coase (1960) and Williamson (1975). Grieco (1990) uses this term to describe the adherents to this school.
15. See Keohane and Nye (1977) and Keohane (1984).
16. This theme is developed at length in Aggarwal (1985).
17. See E. Haas (1980) and P. Haas (1989), among others.
18. E. Haas (1980).
19. Wendt (1995, p. 74).
20. P. Haas (1992, p. 21).
21. See also Krugman (1991). For recent references to this literature, see Frankel, Stein, and Wei (1995).

22. For analytical completeness, it is worth noting that one can also examine the creation of an institution in an issue-area where none existed before, or a decision to pursue bargaining without the use of institutions. While the approach developed here can be used to consider such questions, the focus of this volume is on bargaining within the context of existing institutions.

23. See Aggarwal (1985); Zacher (1987) and Zacher (1996) uses the distinction developed in this work in his analysis of regimes.

24. In security matters, we could examine weapons flows, the movement of fissionable materials, and so on.

25. For a discussion of these four types of goods and actors' motivations to provide them, see Aggarwal (1996). On common pool resources in particular, see Ostrom (1990). For an earlier insightful discussion of types of goods, see Snidal (1979). The best summary of the literature on goods is by Cornes and Sandler (1986).

26. The best discussion on these issues is by Snidal (1979).

27. Hardin (1982).

28. For a good discussion of CPRs and international institutions, see Keohane and Ostrom (1994).

29. See Stein (1983), Snidal (1985a), Axelrod and Keohane (1985), and Martin (1992), among others.

30. See Aggarwal (1985) and below on the use of institutions to control other actors. For additional discussions, see Krasner (1991) and Knight (1992).

31. Martin (1992).

32. See, for example, Snidal (1985b).

33. See Aggarwal and Dupont (forthcoming) on a more formal treatment of the relationship between goods, individual situations, and institutions.

34. I myself have contributed to this pessimistic view in Aggarwal (1996).

35. See Aggarwal (1996) for a discussion of game change efforts in debt rescheduling. While from a game theory standpoint, the choices that actors make in subsequent bargaining rounds are simply choice points in an elaborate extensive form bargaining game, the notion of "game change" efforts provides a useful metaphor. This idea allows us to distinguish between the repeated play of the game within existing constraints, and efforts to improve one's payoffs by modifying the constraints themselves.

36. On the use of unilateral, bilateral, and multilateral approaches, see Diebold (1952, p. 36).

37. For a discussion of tactical and substantive linkages, see Oye (1979), Stein (1980), and Haas (1980), among others. The distinction between nested and parallel linkages can be found in Aggarwal (1996). I also elaborate on the nature of linkages in this work (chapter 4), from which a portion of the following discussion is drawn.

38. See Haas (1980) for a discussion of this type of outcome.

39. For ease of presentation, I have left out the type of institution and the bargaining strategy that actors might pursue to accomplish their ends.

40. Another example, mentioned earlier in this chapter, is the parallel substantive link between the IMF and World Bank.
41. See Krasner (1979) and Grieco (1990) on this issue.
42. On this issue, see Keohane (1984) and Haggard, Levy, Moravcsik, and Nicolaïdis (1993), p. 181.
43. For a discussion of the factors that influence the strength and nature of regimes, see Aggarwal (1985).
44. For a discussion of these ideas, see among others Diebold (1952), Keohane (1984), and Gilpin (1987).
45. Aggarwal (1985).
46. See Ruggie (1992).
47. See Snidal (1985b).
48. One could argue that institutions may contribute to tight and accepted packaging of issues. If this is the case, then the problem should be no more difficult than in new institution creation.

PART ONE

ECONOMIC TRENDS

CHAPTER 3

TRADE PATTERNS AND REGIMES IN ASIA AND THE PACIFIC

Paolo Guerrieri

I. INTRODUCTION

Economic regionalization has progressed rapidly in the Asia-Pacific, and a variety of regional cooperation arrangements have come into existence. East Asian economies[1] have become increasingly important to each other due to the recent high growth of intra-Asian trade and investment. At the same time, strong economic linkages have been maintained between East Asia and North America, especially the United States.

In the past two decades, the exceptionally high economic growth of East Asian economies has been sustained by "export led" growth strategies that were mostly targeted at the North American and European markets. Since the first half of the 1970s, East Asian export growth rates have been significantly higher than that of world exports, helping to facilitate rapid regional integration into the global trading system. These include the four Asian NICs (South Korea, Hong Kong, Singapore, Taiwan), then most ASEAN economies (Malaysia, Thailand, Indonesia, and the Philippines), and finally China. Evidence of this trend can be seen from the

TABLE 3.1

SHARES OF SELECTED COUNTRIES AND AREAS IN WORLD EXPORTS*

(PERCENTAGE SHARES IN VALUES)

	1970	1975	1980	1985	1988	1991	1994
ASIA	11.17	12.43	14.76	20.55	21.91	23.18	26.76
JAPAN	6.73	6.99	7.00	9.82	10.07	9.09	9.38
ASIAN NICS	2.36	2.86	4.36	6.69	7.40	9.10	10.78
KOREA	0.29	0.64	0.95	1.69	2.31	2.08	2.28
SINGAPORE	0.54	0.67	1.05	1.28	1.49	1.70	2.29
HONG KONG	0.88	0.76	1.07	1.68	1.06	2.85	3.59
ASEAN	1.57	1.93	2.55	2.57	2.41	2.91	3.73
THAILAND	0.25	0.28	0.35	0.40	0.60	0.82	1.07
MALAYSIA	0.59	0.48	0.70	0.87	0.80	0.99	1.39
INDONESIA	0.37	0.89	1.18	1.04	0.73	0.84	0.99
PHILIPPINES	0.37	0.28	0.31	0.26	0.27	0.26	0.32
CHINA	0.51	0.64	0.85	1.48	2.04	2.08	2.87

*Ratio of country's or area's exports to world exports (percentage)

Source: Elaborations on U.N. and OECD trade data from SIE World Trade Data Base

spectacular growth of the share of East Asian economies in world exports, which increased from about 11 percent in the early 1970s to more than 26 percent in the first half of the 1990s (see Table 3.1). The first half the 1980s was marked by a sharp rise in intra-Asian trade and capital flows, especially direct investment, contributing to regionalization of the East Asian economies.

In terms of trade, capital, and (to a certain extent) labor flows, these intense regional interactions have been largely driven in the Asia-Pacific by private actors. Formal intergovernmental arrangements and regionally based regimes played only minor roles, and the institutional framework behind East Asian regional dynamics was always very weak. In this context, the recent relaunching of the Asia-Pacific Economic Cooperation forum (APEC), the major regional initiative in the Pacific, has been of great importance.

APEC has grown in scope and assumed ambitious goals in terms of trade and investment liberalization. In particular, the implementation of free trade by 2010 and 2020 has become a primary objective of APEC. Despite these positive recent developments, however, the success of the new course in the trade integration processes of the Pacific region is far from being taken for granted.

To examine the prospects for institutionally based APEC cooperation in trade relations, this chapter deals with economic interactions in the Pacific region—especially in terms of trade flows—in relation to the effects of national controls and ad hoc accords (to use Aggarwal's terminology).[2] There are two main reasons to focus our attention on this pattern. First, economic interactions in the Asia-Pacific (and especially how they are perceived) have been the driving force behind the formation of the main regional economic agreements and cooperation, as in the case of APEC. Second, there is still an open debate among scholars over the nature and the effects of trade and economic interdependence in the Pacific region. In particular, the question of whether the East Asia region could become an increasingly closed economic bloc continues to be heatedly debated.[3]

These issues are examined here in a historical and analytical context by using the collation of new trade data[4] and providing a stylized pattern of the great transformations that have characterized trade and economic interdependence in the Asia-Pacific region during the past two decades. Accordingly, the first three sections analyze patterns of trade flows and interdependence in the Pacific area as "stylized facts," grouped into three main phases covering the period from the late 1970s to the mid-1990s. The logic behind this analytic step is to disaggregate the complex changing linkages between the United States and the East Asian countries on the one hand and the development within the East Asian region on the other. These patterns, as the chapter tries to show, have exerted a significant influence on trading regimes in the overall Pacific area and on the APEC institutional framework. In the last section, by

TABLE 3.2

SHARES OF VARIOUS REGIONS IN TOTAL EXPORTS OF ASIA

(PERCENTAGE)

	1970	1980	1985	1989	1992	1994
WORLD	100	100	100	100	100	100
NAFTA	30.7	24.6	35.9	32.4	26.4	26.6
NORTH AMERICA	30.3	24.1	35.5	31.9	25.7	25.8
UNITED STATES	27.9	22.6	33.3	29.8	24.0	24.5
ASIA	32.4	36.8	35.0	38.9	43.6	46.9
ASIA (WITHOUT JAPAN)	25.1	25.1	25.7	29.5	35.9	38.9
JAPAN	7.3	11.7	9.3	9.3	7.7	8.0
ASIAN NICs	14.4	14.0	13.7	17.5	19.7	21.6
CHINA	1.9	2.6	5.8	4.5	6.7	8.5
ASEAN	7.2	7.1	5.1	6.0	7.2	8.8
APEC	66.4	64.3	73.7	73.9	72.0	75.6
UE (15)	15.2	16.0	12.5	17.1	15.2	14.5
REST OF THE WORLD	18.4	19.8	13.8	9.0	12.8	10.0

ASIA comprises: Japan, Asian NICs (Hong Kong, South Korea, Taiwan, Singapore), ASEAN (Malaysia, Thailand, Indonesia, Philippines), and China

Source: Elaborations on U.N. and OECD trade data from SIE World Trade Data Bank

using the evidence mentioned above, different scenarios of the institutionally based APEC cooperation in the trade arena are sketched out.

II. INDUSTRIAL GROWTH AND OUTWARD-ORIENTED STRATEGIES IN EAST ASIA

The first period of trade interdependence in the Asia and Pacific area, which runs until the first half of the 1980s, is characterized by accelerating growth and very rapid industrialization of the East Asian economies, driven primarily by an exceptional expansion of exports (Table 3.1). The share of developing East Asian economies

TABLE 3.3

SHARES OF VARIOUS REGIONS IN TOTAL IMPORTS OF ASIA

(PERCENTAGE)

	1970	1980	1985	1989	1992	1994
WORLD	100	100	100	100	100	100
NAFTA	27.4	20.7	20.7	21.9	19.1	18.4
NORTH AMERICA	27.0	20.3	19.9	21.5	18.8	18.2
UNITED STATES	23.5	17.9	17.5	19.1	17.0	16.6
ASIA	30.4	36.1	42.5	46.2	50.1	51.5
ASIA (WITHOUT JAPAN)	16.6	23.3	27.4	31.2	34.4	34.8
JAPAN	13.8	12.8	15.1	15.0	15.7	16.7
ASIAN NICS	4.1	6.5	9.8	13.6	12.8	15.9
CHINA	2.7	3.7	5.7	7.1	9.4	10.3
ASEAN	8.1	10.2	9.3	7.6	8.0	8.5
APEC	64.7	61.4	67.9	72.2	73.0	73.3
UE (15)	13.6	9.5	11.2	13.8	11.2	13.9
REST OF THE WORLD	21.7	29.1	20.9	13.9	15.8	12.8

ASIA comprises: Japan, Asian NICs (Hong Kong, South Korea, Taiwan, Singapore), ASEAN (Malaysia, Thailand, Indonesia, Philippines), and China

Source: Elaborations on U.N. and OECD trade data from SIE World Trade Data Bank

in world exports increased from about 5.4 percent by the second half of the 1970s to 10.8 percent in 1985. If Japan is included in this calculation, the East Asian share increases from 12.4 to 20.5 percent of world exports.

The United States, and more generally North America, played a crucial role as the major market for the products and exports of most East Asian countries as shown by the growing U.S. share in East Asian exports (see Table 3.2). The penetration of the U.S. market by East Asian products was favored by the high real value of the U.S. dollar during the first part of the 1980s.

The export-led growth of the area was thus strongly oriented outside the Asian region. The outcome was rapidly growing trade

TABLE 3.4

TRADE BALANCE OF ASIA TOWARD DIFFERENT REGIONS AND COUNTRIES

(THOUSANDS OF CURRENT U.S. DOLLARS)

	TOTAL TRADE					
	1970	1980	1985	1989	1992	1994
WORLD	-2,472,190	-6,854,662	63,317,430	106,769,083	106,895,621	113,297,611
NAFTA	354,458	9,278,443	68,891,334	93,250,948	81,233,019	112,927,550
U.S.A.	836,525	11,677,764	69,113,081	91,641,964	80,444,173	107,599,044
JAPAN	-1,914,751	-1,925,910	-9,209,665	-17,773,370	-41,819,826	-61,222,090
ASIAN NICs	2,718,341	14,514,491	14,510,548	29,888,131	52,931,124	50,802,887
CHINA	-297,489	-3,412,340	3,928,203	-9,846,719	-13,867,037	-9,489,345
ASEAN	-483,236	-9,246,179	-9,398,029	-2,590,046	1,028,795	13,581,075
EU (15)	332,549	17,338,891	12,136,620	36,942,678	48,530,026	22,507,376

ASIA comprises: Japan, Asian NICs (Hong Kong, South Korea, Taiwan, Singapore), ASEAN (Malaysia, Thailand, Indonesia, Philippines), and China

Source: Elaborations on U.N. and OECD trade data from SIE World Trade Data Bank

deficits with Japan and then with the other Asian NICs toward the United States as well (Tables 3.5 and 3.6). Asia's trade surplus increased from $11 billion in 1980 to $69 billion in 1985 (Table 3.4). Furthermore, East Asia's rising trade dependence on the American market brought about great tensions in trade relations at the global level. The United States undertook various bilateral initiatives against Japan and the Asian NICs, especially Korea and Taiwan, demanding greater openness of their markets in terms of relaxing border restrictions on trade and investment, and the granting of national treatment for products and firms.[5] However, bilateralism actually enjoyed little success. In this phase, the Asian NICs, with the notable exception of Hong Kong, pursued industrial strategies characterized by government intervention and orthodox protectionist measures, such as export subsidies, import controls, restrictions on investment and other sectoral measures.[6] Only minor changes in terms of greater openness of the domestic markets characterized their behavior in this phase.

TABLE 3.5

TRADE BALANCE OF JAPAN TOWARD DIFFERENT REGIONS AND COUNTRIES

(THOUSANDS OF CURRENT U.S. DOLLARS)

	TOTAL TRADE					
	1970	1980	1985	1989	1992	1994
WORLD	436,534	-10,349,253	48,082,340	67,683,520	108,515,223	120,857,783
NAFTA	28,147	5,204,669	39,050,694	43,893,427	45,994,074	55,271,198
U.S.A.	450,715	7,201,094	40,113,550	45,244,546	43,981,802	55,417,991
ASIA	1,914,751	1,925,910	9,209,665	17,773,370	41,819,826	61,222,090
ASIAN NICS	1,983,819	11,768,031	12,631,390	25,522,013	46,349,550	61,448,430
CHINA	315,062	754,943	5,994,052	-2,630,183	-5,004,064	-8,789,610
ASEAN	-384,130	-10,597,064	-9,415,777	-5,118,460	474,340	8,563,270
EU (15)	934,806	11,076,955	13,635,808	22,933,862	34,435,380	22,544,318

Source: Elaborations on U.N. and OECD trade data from SIE World Trade Data Bank

On the other hand, economic linkages within the East Asian region remained relatively less important: trends in intra-Asia trade and investment were relatively undynamic (Tables 3.2 and 3.3). Furthermore, no significant regional initiative in terms of major intergovernmental arrangements or economic cooperation took place in this period. The fact that trade patterns in East Asian countries were competitive rather than complementary and shared a common orientation toward outside markets is one reason for this very poor regional collaboration. The development of regional institutions was also complicated by the preferences of most countries in the area for informal and negotiated policy approaches rather than formal agreements.[7]

III. TRADE INTERDEPENDENCE AND ASYMMETRIES IN THE PACIFIC RIM

From the second half of the 1980s to the very early 1990s a second phase occurred in relations among countries within the Pacific

TABLE 3.6

TRADE BALANCE OF ASIAN NICS TOWARD DIFFERENT REGIONS AND COUNTRIES
(THOUSANDS OF CURRENT U.S. DOLLARS)

	TOTAL TRADE					
	1970	1980	1985	1989	1992	1994
WORLD	-2,543,247	-3,982,350	15,121,311	18,788,087	266,200	-1,755,853
NAFTA	494,310	5,267,573	27,206,470	37,770,875	35,927,158	40,734,543
U.S.A.	408,321	4,788,732	25,510,297	34,603,684	31,331,727	35,799,220
ASIA	-2,718,341	-14,514,491	-14,510,548	-29,888,131	-52,931,124	-50,802,887
JAPAN	-1,983,819	-11,768,031	-12,631,390	-25,522,013	-46,349,550	-61,448,430
CHINA	-559,755	-3,463,866	-1,640,760	-6,922,951	-8,385,100	-596,561
ASEAN	-174,767	717,406	-238,398	2,556,833	1,803,526	6,398,695
EU (15)	-144,272	5,379,295	1,756,188	11,027,129	11,926,375	5,443,722

Source: Elaborations on U.N. and OECD trade data from SIE World Trade Data Bank

Rim. In most East Asian economies, high growth and rapid industrialization continued to be based on the strong expansion of exports directed outside the region. North America remained the major market for most Asian exports, but Europe also significantly increased its absorption of East Asian products (Tables 3.2 and 3.3). Thus Europe also started to register increasing trade deficits towards East Asia as a whole (from $12 billion in 1985 to $48 billion in 1992), while the U.S. trade deficit with East Asian economies remained very high ($80 billion in 1992) (see Table 3.4). As a consequence, the United States maintained and increased the external pressures on Japan and the NICs to open and liberalize their domestic markets. In this period, U.S. demand also included behind-the-border trade-related issues like foreign investment questions, services, and intellectual property.[8] Under these pressures and rising domestic interests of what by then had become a huge export-oriented sector, East Asian NICs implemented gradual import liberalization programs, seeking to lower import tariffs and restrictions in a multilateral direction.

The new pattern in this phase was that East Asian intraregional economic ties increased remarkably, both in terms of growing intraregional trade and capital flows, especially foreign direct investments.[9] Both absolute figures (Tables 3.2 and 3.3) and relative measures of trading intensities provide evidence of this increased integration within the Asian region.[10]

One should also note that no formal policy initiatives and/or official economic agreements were taken across Asian governments in this phase.[11] ASEAN (comprising Brunei, Indonesia, Malaysia, the Philippines, Thailand, Singapore, and Vietnam), for example— the most firmly institutionalized of the subregional groupings— initially focused on political issues and experienced many unsuccessful attempts to promote intra-ASEAN trade.[12] In short, firms and private mechanisms were the main players in the process of Asian integration in this phase, leading to a de facto trade integration. Other factors played a role in increasing East Asian integration. These include the faster growth of East Asian economies that tended to increase trade regionalization, liberalization of trade and investment regimes undertaken by many East Asian economies, and exchange rate realignments.

The strong revaluation of the yen, together with other structural factors, led Japanese firms to invest intensively in the developing East Asia area.[13] In a very short period of time, Japan became the major investor in the area, replacing the United States. Japanese aid to the region encouraged this process.[14] Japanese investments were the outcome of strategies aimed at establishing networks of production at the regional level.[15] Automobiles and electronics, in particular, have been the preferred sectors. The two main goals of these investments are worth mentioning: (1) serving the domestic market of East Asian countries; and (2) even more important, building up regional production platforms with a strong export orientation, especially toward the rich markets of the West. First Singapore, then Thailand and Malaysia became important locations for Japanese investment in manufacturing, increasing the exports of East Asia toward the U.S. market and, to a lesser extent, the European market as well. As a consequence, the NICs and other East Asian countries held and even increased their already significant trade surpluses toward the United States, fully compensating for the slight decrease of Japan's trade surplus toward the American market in the period from the late 1980s to the early 1990s (see Tables 3.4-3.6).

During the same years, East Asian imports from Japan grew significantly, especially in terms of investment goods and high tech components that were intensively employed in their industrialization processes (Tables 3.7-3.10). This surge of imports has been only partially compensated by the modest increase of exports from the same East Asian countries towards Japan, despite the large appreciation of the yen in those years.[16] The trade deficit of the NICs and the whole East Asia area toward Japan therefore soared in a short period of time (Tables 3.4-3.5).

Looking at this evidence, one could point out that it is erroneous to argue, as scholars have done, that an Asian trading bloc has been emerging during this period. East Asian countries continued to depend heavily on extraregional export markets, especially on the United States. But it is also erroneous to believe that increasing intra-Asian trade was only the outcome of the fast growth rate of the East Asian economies. Increasing Asian trade integration has been taking place through corporate strategies and market forces following a strategic pattern of industrial restructuring and production reorganization.[17]

The development of regional production networks with strong intraregional interdependence—in terms of inputs, sales, and long-term corporate strategies of involvement in the area—shows that integration has been taking place increasingly in both factor and product markets. These supply-side linkages, driven mostly by the large increases in East Asian intraregional foreign investment and the related trade effects, gave rise to an asymmetrical "triangular" feature of economic interdependence in the Asia-Pacific in the

TABLE 3.7

TRADE BALANCE OF ASIA TOWARD DIFFERENT REGIONS AND COUNTRIES

(THOUSANDS OF U.S. DOLLARS)

	MACHINERY AND OTHER INVESTMENT GOODS					
	1970	1980	1985	1989	1992	1994
WORLD	-735,002	3,164,972	8,229,308	11,458,051	3,727,577	4,584,538
NAFTA	-434,989	204,246	5,094,535	8,966,296	4,778,980	7,383,443
U.S.A.	-482,275	-307,654	4,333,538	7,511,425	3,347,716	5,618,016
JAPAN	-715,794	-6,095,942	-7,263,335	-15,665,452	-22,903,301	-31,078,101
ASIAN NICs	383,977	3,287,400	3,065,911	8,777,873	12,852,021	11,819,485
CHINA	57,367	1,089,233	2,878,583	2,943,307	7,147,694	11,417,067
ASEAN	289,536	2,444,587	2,001,581	6,300,120	9,147,552	13,915,549
EU (15)	-764,548	-2,384,710	-2,692,531	-3,732,764	-3,008,156	-14,510,306

Source: Elaborations on U.N. and OECD trade data from SIE World Trade Data Bank

second half of the 1980s.[18] East Asia as a whole has maintained its main exports outlet outside the region and its huge trade surplus towards North America and Europe in particular.

These trade surpluses are certainly related to macroeconomic factors such as the asymmetrical disparities of saving and investment between the United States and Japan. But they also reflect structural features such as the institutional differences between the two sides of the Pacific that represent very significant "invisible barriers," such as regulations that close the Japanese market to outsiders.

The asymmetrical distribution of trade balances in the Pacific Rim has continued to be a source of increasingly frequent trade tensions between the East Asian nations and the United States.[19] U.S. bilateral pressures to liberalize East Asian markets further increased during this period. In response to the latter, significant programs of import liberalization were implemented by the Asian NICs in this phase. The liberalization efforts, however, also

TABLE 3.8

TRADE BALANCE OF ASIA TOWARD DIFFERENT REGIONS AND COUNTRIES

(THOUSANDS OF CURRENT U.S. DOLLARS)

	HIGH R&D INTENSITY GOODS					
	1970	1980	1985	1989	1992	1994
WORLD	-263,283	5,929,109	19,027,891	52,209,995	60,444,864	79,943,270
NAFTA	-488,658	-1,432,189	9,173,696	25,310,677	25,476,446	38,986,656
U.S.A.	-566,580	-2,012,554	8,052,508	22,868,667	21,918,645	33,591,918
JAPAN	-526,029	-4,851,256	-8,041,067	-17,761,454	-26,018,646	-55,441,111
ASIAN NICS	347,298	3,803,523	3,991,102	12,103,725	20,070,974	26,365,931
CHINA	22,177	485,077	3,111,954	3,627,899	6,048,456	9,195,879
ASEAN	192,862	1,538,314	1,503,676	4,224,999	5,945,859	10,632,236
EU (15)	-211,401	1,918,179	4,518,748	19,766,618	25,569,965	25,172,159

Source: Elaborations on U.N. and OECD trade data from SIE World Trade Data Bank

reflected the unilateral initiatives of individual East Asian economies as well as the more pragmatic bilateral policy of Japan, which aims at primarily achieving economic advantages for Japanese firms.[20]

In addition, the persistent U.S. market orientation of East Asian exports in this second phase tells us much about the lack of appeal of regional agreements that would leave out the United States. Accordingly, the Malaysian proposal for the creation of an East Asian economic bloc excluding Australia, New Zealand, Canada, and, in particular, the United States, provoked a negative reaction from most East Asian countries. The proposal was thus transformed into a looser consultative body called the East Asian Economic Caucus. By contrast, trade agreements involving small geographical areas formed by two or more countries have multiplied in East Asia, based on informal and pragmatic policy approaches pursued by most East Asian countries.

TABLE 3.9

TRADE BALANCE OF JAPAN TOWARD DIFFERENT REGIONS AND COUNTRIES

(THOUSANDS OF U.S. DOLLARS)

	MACHINERY AND OTHER INVESTMENT GOODS					
	1970	1980	1985	1989	1992	1994
WORLD	1,018,503	15,038,738	21,261,439	37,399,630	45,127,182	56,370,503
NAFTA	-25,358	2,305,556	6,244,265	11,270,535	9,790,413	13,105,584
U.S.A.	-76,215	1,788,745	5,488,513	10,007,717	8,246,416	11,515,314
ASIA	715,794	6,095,942	7,263,335	15,665,452	22,903,301	31,078,101
ASIAN NICS	390,396	3,292,530	3,901,107	10,155,881	14,178,687	18,065,074
CHINA	70,941	1,167,543	2,064,091	1,532,349	2,495,890	4,050,502
ASEAN	254,457	1,635,869	1,298,137	3,977,222	6,228,724	8,962,525
EU (15)	-178,569	1,161,918	1,857,420	4,635,890	5,990,448	5,903,742

Source: Elaborations on U.N. and OECD trade data from SIE World Trade Data Bank

IV. THE REGIONALIZATION OF EAST ASIA AND PACIFIC TRADE PATTERNS

The third and most recent period has been characterized by a strong acceleration of intra-Asian economic transactions, through a sharp rise of intraregional trade and investment shares as a proportion of the region's total trade and investment. Intra-Asian trade accounted for almost 47 percent of total East Asian exports and 51 percent of total imports by 1994, compared with 35 percent and 42 percent by 1985 respectively (Tables 3.2-3.3). A large and rising movement of labor across borders, originating especially from South Asian countries, has been also contributing to the growing intra-Asian transactions.

Several significant factors explain the rapid increase of regional integration of the East Asian economies. First, the yen's appreciation is partially correlated with the rise of Japanese investments into the region. During this phase, China and the other new industrializing economies in Southeast Asia have been the focal

TABLE 3.10

TRADE BALANCE OF JAPAN TOWARD DIFFERENT REGIONS AND COUNTRIES

(THOUSANDS OF CURRENT U.S. DOLLARS)

HIGH R&D INTENSITY GOODS

	1970	1980	1985	1989	1992	1994
WORLD	858,092	13,877,841	27,869,224	60,319,312	75,178,438	91,598,220
NAFTA	-273,760	1,298,590	8,502,687	20,281,880	22,366,080	28,979,288
U.S.A.	-356,458	743,026	7,469,753	18,449,499	19,743,756	25,750,788
ASIA	526,029	4,851,256	8,041,067	17,761,454	26,018,646	36,692,748
ASIAN NICS	328,180	3,221,233	5,172,062	13,184,772	18,826,920	25,654,629
CHINA	28,796	489,897	1,578,510	1,303,791	1,357,077	1,912,367
ASEAN	169,053	1,140,126	1,290,495	3,272,891	5,834,649	9,125,752
EU (15)	151,578	3,121,072	6,003,778	16,278,937	20,161,749	18,748,363

Source: Elaborations on U.N. and OECD trade data from SIE World Trade Data Bank

points of investment. Second, with the strengthening of the industrial development of the four Asian NICs, they have become an important source of investment and technological transfer towards the other countries in the region. Finally, the spectacular growth and the opening up of the Chinese economy has created a market outlet of primary importance in the East Asian region.

This increasing regional integration has contributed significantly to the increase of East Asian absorption during the first half of the 1990s. The Asian domestic market has become increasingly crucial to sustain the growth of the Asian region as a whole. Moreover, this new endogenous growth capability has in turn provided new incentives for investing in the Asian region.

Many industrial sectors exemplify this new trend. Consider the case of consumer electronics. In the past two decades, East Asian producers dramatically succeeded in capturing international market share and these countries accumulated huge trade surpluses. In this industry, intra-Asian exports have been significantly increasing in overall East Asian production and exports during the most recent period.[21] However, despite this increasing East Asian trade integration, the role of markets outside the region has remained very important for most East Asian economies. The Pacific trade network therefore has maintained a fundamental role. APEC accounted for more than 73 percent of total Asian exports by the mid-1990s. On the other hand, U.S. trade has been concentrated increasingly in Asia during this phase (Table 3.2).

Together with a number of economic and political factors,[22] the deeper Pan-Pacific trade integration pattern seems to have contributed significantly to the new wave of cooperation and institutional development that occurred in the region over the early 1990s.[23] Trade liberalization has rapidly become a key issue of these new institutional initiatives. At its fourth summit in Singapore in 1992, ASEAN announced its intention to implement a free trade area (AFTA) by 2007, and in January 1993, the common effective preferential tariff agreement was signed. Its goal was to reduce ASEAN tariff rates to 20 percent in five to eight years and subsequently to 0 percent in the following seven years. The timetable was subsequently accelerated.

The Asia-Pacific Economic Cooperation forum went even further toward constructing a program for regionwide trade liberalization, calling for a liberalization schedule of free and open trade and investment for the most advanced APEC members by 2010 and for developing member countries by 2020. Besides trade liberalization, APEC has considered launching several other initiatives well beyond the removal of barriers to trade at the border. It incorporated a review of competition policies, a common definition of product standards, and the establishment of a dispute mediation mechanism. The open nature of APEC regional agreements, favored by many Asian participants as nondiscriminatory regionalism, seems also to conform to the trade patterns and economic interactions in the area previously analyzed. The goal of reducing transaction costs in intraregional trade, therefore, seems to have played an important role for APEC.[24] But an important motivation for APEC was also the need for an insurance policy on the possible failure of the Uruguay Round and the consolidation of competing regional blocs at the level of the world economy.

Despite these positive recent developments in trans-Pacific trade integration, the progress and the direction of this new institutional regional arrangement in the Asia-Pacific is far from obvious. APEC's evolution could follow different paths in the foreseeable future.

V. PACIFIC TRADE INTEGRATION AND ALTERNATIVE SCENARIOS FOR APEC

Trade liberalization is undoubtedly a key and very controversial issue on APEC's agenda. All APEC members have accepted a key commitment to achieve free trade over the next two decades, but the content of this commitment is ambiguous. Since there are many variables that will affect the future Pacific trade regime—which is in an evolutionary stage itself—it is difficult to speculate on the likely future course of Asia-Pacific trade integration and its institutional dimension.

In what follows, two different scenarios will be tentatively drawn in light of the recent trends and economic interactions analyzed in the previous sections. The idea of a self-sufficient Asian trade bloc should be excluded from both scenarios. First, East Asian trade and output growth is still heavily dependent on extraregional markets. In particular, economic ties with North America remain very important. By the second half of the 1990s, more than 50 percent of the region's exports for many significant industrial sectors were still based on North American markets.[25] The second reason is the uneven distribution of political power in Asia and the history of fierce competition within the area. Smaller Asian economies would hardly welcome an East Asian regional arrangement dominated by Japan or China.

The role of trans-Pacific trade linkages, therefore, and the political problems associated with the distribution of power in Asia show that there are weak incentives for concluding formal free trade agreements in East Asia alone and make it unlikely that an exclusive East Asian bloc could emerge in the short-to-medium term.

With regard to the first likely scenario, East Asian growth would continue to be increasingly driven by domestic demand and the intraregional market. Trade patterns would contribute to support a larger and deeper trade network in the Asia-Pacific region. This would enable the East Asian region to absorb more exports from outside, easing the balance of payment problems of North America and sustaining most East Asian countries' outward-oriented growth. Recall that East Asia constitutes today almost 28 percent of the world purchasing power, and this share is bound to significantly increase to 34 percent by the year 2000. In this favorable context, one could assume that the institutionalization of APEC could be pushed ahead by trying to convert it into a robust organization, which would implement a long-term agenda of comprehensive trade liberalization throughout the Pacific.

In this scenario, APEC's evolution would be closer to the U.S. view of a formal active negotiating forum with strong rules and binding procedures. The United States is interested in using APEC to promote rules-building in the Asia-Pacific and harmonize domestic policies and regulations. Accordingly, the problem of APEC openness could be solved through the application of mild discrimination in terms of a conditional most-favored-nation basis to avoid free riding from outside the group. But that could lead APEC to transform itself into a discriminatory regional trade regime, representing a threat to the WTO.

With reference to recent developments and the evidence previously discussed in this paper, a much more likely alternative scenario can be presented. From this viewpoint, trade patterns in the Pacific will evolve much less smoothly and further institution building in APEC will be slow. Unless one assumes that radical events will take place, such as deep reforms of both trade and industrial policy in most ASEAN economies, together with structural reforms in Japan, the export dynamism of East Asian countries is likely to continue. This is likely to pose a serious challenge to those countries outside the region, especially the United States and Europe. If anything, the competitive pressures from East Asia may even increase with the accelerated industrial growth of China. Thus, due to structural reasons as well as macroeconomic differences of saving and investment rates, strong trade asymmetries in East Asian trade will persist. Many East Asian countries will continue to run huge trade deficits with Japan and large trade surpluses with the United States, as in the case of China. It follows that a marked asymmetry will persist in the distribution of trade balances within the region, especially between East Asia and the United States.

These trends will make it difficult to attain institutionalized cooperation in the Pacific setting in the medium-to-long term, with unresolved trade asymmetries within the region leading to tense relations across the Pacific Rim. This problem is likely to be exacerbated by the fact that East Asian trade investment liberalization still has a long way to go. Although tariffs have been declining, average effective protection rates are still high in most East Asian countries. Restrictions on trade and investments, in terms of standards, procurement practices, and administrative controls are also quite significant. Furthermore, there still exists wide variation among the current economic and business regimes and practices in the region. In other words, the diversity of APEC's members remains very high.

In this alternative scenario, therefore, due to trade asymmetries, institutional differences, and economic disparities among its members, APEC will not be able to play an autonomous role in the region's trade liberalization. The diversity of policy approaches makes highly institutional cooperative profiles and more ambitious goals difficult and unlikely. APEC's evolution would then follow the less ambitious Asian view of APEC—no formal institutions and very few legally binding obligations. APEC would thus be characterized by voluntary, individual action plans directed toward liberalization and deregulation, and harmonization would occur according to existing international agreements.

With regards to openness, a nondiscriminatory approach is likely to prevail in terms of an extension of APEC benefits on an unconditional MFN basis to nonmembers. In this view, the chances that APEC will move beyond the WTO, putting pressure on European and other partners to engage in global liberalization, are very slim indeed. By contrast, in many areas, APEC's goals are likely to be supportive of global processes rather than seeking the creation of a separate regionally based regime. One should not forget that despite their diversity, Asian nations share the common interest of supporting the multilateral trading system under the GATT/WTO regime. Much of the trade region's business therefore will be conducted through a mix of bilateral and regional initiatives that will be compatible with or nested into the multilateral order of the WTO.[26]

VI. CONCLUSION

In recent years, APEC has grown in scope and assumed ambitious goals in terms of trade and investment liberalization. Despite these positive recent developments, however, the success of the new course in the trade integration process of Pacific region is far from being taken for granted.

To assess the prospects for institutionally based APEC cooperation in trade relations, this chapter has dealt with economic interactions in the Pacific region in the period from the late 1970s to the mid-1990s, especially in terms of trade flows, and national strategies that significantly affected these patterns. Patterns of trade flows and interdependence in the Asia-Pacific have exerted a significant influence on the trade regime in the overall Pacific area and on the APEC institutional framework. Together with a number of economic and political factors, deeper Pan-Pacific trade integration patterns seem to have contributed significantly to the new wave of cooperation and institutional development that occurred over the early 1990s in the region.

Trade liberalization has rapidly become a key issue in these new institutional initiatives. All APEC members have accepted a key commitment to achieve free trade in the region over the next two decades, but the content of this commitment is far from clear. In this chaper, two different scenarios on alternative developments of the institutionally based APEC cooperation in the trade arena have been sketched out. The idea of a self-sufficient Asian trade bloc was excluded from both scenarios because of the prevalence of the high dependence of East Asian trade on extraregional markets and the political problems associated with the distribution of power in Asia.

In the first scenario, APEC's evolution would be closer to the U.S. view of a formal active negotiating forum with strong rules and binding procedures. From this perspective, the institutionalization of APEC could be pushed ahead by trying to convert it into a robust organization, which would implement a long-term agenda of comprehensive trade liberalization throughout the Pacific. This could even lead APEC to transform itself into a discriminatory regional trade regime, thus posing a threat to the WTO global negotiation process.

With reference to recent developments and evidence discussed in this paper, a second scenario is much more likely to occur. Trade asymmetries and tensions in the Pacific are bound to persist due to the export dynamism of East Asian countries and their different trade regimes. One could foresee, therefore, that these trends will make it difficult to attain institutionalized cooperation in the Pacific setting in the medium to long term. In this alternative scenario, due to trade asymmetries, institutional differences, and economic disparities among its members, APEC's evolution is likely to be slow and to follow what is the less ambitious Asian view of APEC, with no formal institutions and very few legally binding obligations. As to openness, a nondiscriminatory approach is likely to prevail, and in many areas APEC's goals are likely to be supportive of the WTO global processes rather than seeking the creation of a separate regionally based regime.

By contrast, in most of the behind-the-border issues, such as harmonization of domestic practices that restrict access to national markets, APEC is unlikely to move fast and realize substantial benefits. APEC's diversity will not permit effective agreement on rules, and unilateral initiatives, bilateral treaties, and other multilateral contexts would offer more negotiation opportunities. In such a context, it is very likely that bilateral pressures, especially by the United States, will remain an important political force leading to confrontation in the Asia-Pacific region.

NOTES

1. The regions referred to in this paper will be East Asia (Japan, Hong Kong, Singapore, South Korea, Taiwan, Malaysia, Thailand, the Philippines, and Indonesia), North America (Canada and the United States), and the Pacific Rim (North America, East Asia, Australia, and New Zealand).
2. See Aggarwal (1993) and chapter 2 (Aggarwal, 1998a) in this volume.
3. For example, see Dornbusch (1990); Lawrence (1991); Petri (1993); Saxonhouse (1993); and Frankel (1991).
4. The world trade database (Banca Dati SIE-World Trade) contains U.N. as well as OECD statistics. Unlike previous studies, which were based on sources providing information only on trade within the OECD area, the database used here makes it possible to consider the entire matrix of world trade patterns, including new important international actors such as the newly industrialized countries (NICs) in Southeast Asia. For further details on the trade database, see Guerrieri (1993; 1996).
5. Report of the United States Trade Representative (1994).
6. See Wade (1990) and Amsden (1989).
7. Kahler (1995).
8. Haggard (1995).

9. Urata (1993).
10. Petri (1993).
11. Petri (1993).
12. Imada and Naya (1992).
13. Ernst (1995).
14. Lincoln (1992).
15. Ernst (1995).
16. Hirata (1995).
17. Cohen and Guerrieri (1995).
18. Park and Park (1991); Petri (1993); Cohen and Guerrieri (1995); Ravenhill (1995).
19. Cohen and Guerrieri (1995).
20. Haggard (1995).
21. Guerrieri (1995).
22. See chapter 1 (Morrison, 1998) in this volume.
23. Yamazawa (1992).
24. Yamazawa (1992).
25. Guerrieri (1995).
26. Aggarwal (1994).

CHAPTER 4

FOREIGN DIRECT INVESTMENT AND APEC

Shujiro Urata

I. INTRODUCTION[1]

Foreign Direct Investment (FDI) has been increasing rapidly, both within the dynamic APEC region and globally. Of all APEC subregions, the growth rate of FDI has been remarkably high in East Asia.[2] In fact, the rapid expansion of FDI inflow has been one of the most important factors leading to rapid economic growth in East Asian economies.

In spite of the favorable impact on host countries from the transfer of investable funds and technologies associated with FDI, most host governments impose restrictions on its inflow. FDI is not permitted in "sensitive sectors" such as transportation and communications, and "performance requirements" such as minimum export regulations are imposed on foreign firms. Restrictions on FDI in the sensitive sectors are meant to protect and promote these industries for various reasons such as national security, and performance requirements are imposed in order to extract maximum benefits from FDI. However, these restrictions reduce the attractiveness of countries using these measures. To compensate for the unfavorable effect of restrictions, most governments offer incentives like special tax treatment. Government intervention, both to attract as well as to regulate FDI, takes many forms, thus making the investment regimes of countries complex and nontransparent.

Having recognized the important role that the private sector plays in promoting economic growth, and concerned about the possible harmful impact of restricting FDI flows, governments with complex FDI intervention schemes became interested in creating an environment conducive to the free flow of FDI. This interest led to discussions about FDI at the Uruguay Round on multilateral trade negotiations under the General Agreement on Tariffs and Trade (GATT, now succeeded by the World Trade Organization, or WTO). The round reached an agreement prohibiting Trade Related Investment Measures (TRIMs). Recognition of the need for open investment also motivated APEC members to improve their FDI environment. They established the Non-Binding Investment Principles (NBIP) in 1994. In addition to multilateral action by the WTO and regional action by APEC, there are other arrangements on investment already in existence and in the process of negotiation.

The purpose of this chapter is to examine FDI and APEC from various vantage points. Questions to be asked include: How did FDI affect the formation of investment rules in APEC? To what extent will trends in FDI be affected by the establishment of such rules? In addition, to emphasize special characteristics of APEC's investment rules, other multilateral arrangements regarding FDI will also be examined.

This chapter is structured as follows. Section II summarizes developments in FDI, with a specific focus on the APEC region. It also discusses the impact of growing FDI on the economic growth of the region. Section III examines measures applied to FDI by the governments of APEC members. Section IV discusses and compares multilateral arrangements concerning FDI being developed separately by the WTO, OECD, and APEC. Section V analyzes the possible impact of multilateral investment rules on FDI. Section VI concludes the chapter by presenting views on FDI and the FDI regime in APEC.

II. RAPID EXPANSION OF FDI IN APEC

An Overview of Worldwide FDI in Recent Years[3]

Worldwide FDI grew rapidly in the latter half of the 1980s, increasing from $58.3 billion in 1985 to $235 billion in 1990 (see Table 4.1).[4] Considering that world trade during this period increased approximately 1.8 times, a rate significantly lower then the increase in world FDI, the importance of FDI in international economic activities increased. After 1990, world FDI declined. In 1992 it amounted to only 80 percent of its peak level recorded in 1990. World FDI increased again in 1993, but this growth halted in 1994.

Although the amount of world FDI fluctuates widely year by year, it has exhibited a general upward trend. Several identifiable factors have led to this trend. First, an increasing number of countries have liberalized FDI regimes in an attempt to attract FDI inflow, as they increasingly realized that FDI contributes greatly to the economic growth of recipient countries. Indeed, a number of countries have provided a variety of incentives, including preferential fiscal and financial measures, in order to attract FDI. Second, structural changes, which were precipitated by the sizable currency realignment in the mid-1980s, have promoted FDI. Those countries whose currency appreciated found it difficult to compete in the international market, leading to a focus on overseas production. Countries whose currency depreciated attracted FDI from those whose currency appreciated, because a depreciated currency provides an environment for low-cost production. Third, technological advances in communications have encouraged firms to undertake FDI because there are considerably less expensive and faster ways to transfer investable funds and technologies. Fourth,

TABLE 4.1

FDI IN THE WORLD AND IN THE APEC REGION

OUTFLOW										
VALUE (US$MILLION)	1985	1986	1987	1988	1989	1990	1991	1992	1993	1994
WORLD	58292	91597	136974	168478	222214	235022	194283	189329	207265	201983
INDUSTRIAL COUNTRIES	57013	89735	133886	161649	211026	224204	187180	178366	193629	189290
U.S.	13170	17110	27180	16180	36832	29951	31378	42660	72600	49372
CANADA	3072	3863	8540	3854	4587	4725	5655	3635	5825	4781
AUSTRALIA	1879	3327	5114	4984	3319	186	3126	113	1087	5908
NEW ZEALAND	105	394	245	-2	1300	1039	574	-942	-1675	-486
JAPAN	6450	14480	19520	34210	44160	48050	30740	17240	13740	17970
DEVELOPING COUNTRIES	1279	1861	3089	6829	11188	10819	7103	10963	13636	12693
ASIA	956	778	1932	5805	9230	9190	5242	8139	9594	8138
CHINA	628	450	645	850	780	830	913	4000	4400	2000
KOREA	34	110	183	643	613	1056	1500	1208	1361	2524
SINGAPORE	238	181	206	118	882	2034	1024	1317	1784	2177
ASIA (NOT SPECIFIED)	82	66	704	4120	6851	5123	1634	1609	2151	2080
WESTERN HEMISPHERE	119	654	203	306	747	1043	1317	697	2020	2939
CHILE	—	—	—	16	10	8	123	378	431	925
MEXICO	—	—	—	—	—	—	—	—	—	—
APEC TOTAL	25658	39981	62337	64973	99334	93002	76667	71218	101704	87251
THE SHARE IN WORLD FDI(%)										
INDUSTRIAL COUNTRIES	97.8	98.0	97.7	95.9	95.0	95.4	96.3	94.2	93.4	93.7
DEVELOPING COUNTRIES	2.2	2.0	2.3	4.1	5.0	4.6	3.7	5.8	6.6	6.3
APEC	44.0	43.6	45.5	38.6	44.7	39.6	39.5	37.6	49.1	43.2
ASIAN DEVELOPING ECONOMIES IN APEC	1.7	0.9	1.3	3.4	4.1	3.8	2.6	4.3	4.7	4.3

INFLOW										
VALUE (US$MIL-LION)	1985	1986	1987	1988	1989	1990	1991	1992	1993	1994
WORLD	50975	78826	126882	156809	194518	201485	153643	162130	200652	212508
INDUSTRIAL COUNTRIES	38500	66382	113225	132056	166100	169687	112695	113221	127620	128267
U.S.	19030	35630	58220	57270	67730	47918	22020	17580	41128	49437
CANADA	-1773	1217	8040	6425	5029	7855	2740	4517	4997	6043
AUSTRALIA	2063	3484	3920	8056	7936	7077	4903	4912	3381	3789
NEW ZEALAND	424	283	293	308	1483	1924	1141	1610	1413	334
JAPAN	640	230	1170	-520	-1060	1760	1370	2720	100	890
DEVELOPING COUNTRIES	12476	12444	13657	24753	28418	31798	40948	48909	73031	84241
ASIA	4863	5725	8258	12593	14168	18302	20691	25607	44832	50178
CHINA	1659	1875	2314	3194	3393	3487	4366	11156	27515	33787
INDONESIA	310	258	385	576	682	1093	1482	1777	2004	2109
KOREA	234	435	601	1014	1118	788	1180	727	588	809
MALAYSIA	695	489	423	719	1668	2332	3998	5183	5006	4348
PHILIPPINES	12	127	307	936	563	530	544	228	763	—
SINGAPORE	1047	1710	2836	3655	2887	5575	4879	2351	5016	5588
THAILAND	163	263	352	1105	1775	2444	2014	2116	1726	640
ASIA (NOT SPECIFIED)	476	326	715	959	1604	1330	1271	879	917	1375
WESTERN HEMISPHERE	4068	3292	3744	8792	9249	8058	12831	14484	15821	21442
CHILE	114	116	230	968	1289	590	523	699	841	1795
MEXICO	491	1160	1184	2879	3174	2634	4762	4393	4389	7978
APEC TOTAL	25585	47603	80990	87544	99271	87337	57193	60848	99784	118922
THE SHARE IN WORLD FDI(%)										
INDUSTRIAL COUNTRIES	75.5	84.2	89.2	84.2	85.4	84.2	73.3	69.8	63.6	60.4
DEVELOPING COUNTRIES	24.5	15.8	10.8	15.8	14.6	15.8	26.7	30.2	36.4	39.6
APEC	50.2	60.4	63.8	55.8	51.0	43.3	37.2	37.5	49.7	56.0
ASIAN DEVELOPING ECONOMIES IN APEC	9.0	7.0	6.3	7.8	7.0	8.7	12.8	15.1	21.7	22.9

Note: Asia not specified is included in APEC, as a large part of Asia not specified appears to include Taiwan and Hong Kong.

Source: IMF, Balance of Payments Yearbook, various issues

increased competition on a worldwide scale, or "megacompetition," brought about mainly by active flow of FDI, has forced multinational firms to expand their overseas operations. Firms attempted to cope with megacompetition by locating operations in production and R&D in countries where they could be performed most efficiently.

FDI-Led Economic Growth in East Asia

FDI outflow and inflow in the APEC region increased at the same rate more or less as world FDI. As a result, APEC's share of world FDI remained constant between 1985 and 1994 with minor fluctuations. This share consisted of approximately 45 percent of world outflow and 55 percent of world inflow. FDI inflow to developing Asian members of APEC increased sharply from 9.0 percent in 1985 to 22.9 percent in 1994, a remarkable gain. FDI outflow from these countries also increased during the same period, albeit at a much slower rate—from 1.7 percent in 1985 to 4.3 percent in 1994. I will discuss later how the substantial increase in FDI inflow played a key role in promoting economic growth in East Asia after the mid-1980s.

Before analyzing the factors leading to rapid FDI inflow to East Asia and the impact of this inflow on economic growth in East Asia, it is useful to examine intra-APEC patterns of FDI. These patterns help us to analyze the impact of increased FDI on the formation of FDI rules by APEC.

Table 4.2 reveals that the share of FDI outflow by APEC members destined for other APEC members increased from 41.4 percent in 1980 to 51.4 percent in 1992, indicating the increasing importance of the APEC region as an FDI host of APEC capital. An examination of the table reveals that the importance of APEC members as host countries increased for most subregions in APEC over time. In particular, Northeast Asia, especially China, became a very attractive host—not only for other APEC members but also for the rest of the world. The increasing importance of the APEC region as a host to FDI from other APEC members does not necessarily indicate that the FDI relationship among the APEC members has intensified. Indeed, the FDI-intensity index, which indicates the degree of intraregional FDI relationships in APEC, increased only slightly from 0.52 in 1980 to 0.57 in 1992.[5] This finding indicates that the increase in the share of FDI by the APEC members going to other APEC members is largely due to the increase in overall inflow of FDI in the APEC region and does not reflect the increased intensity of its intraregional relationship.

Unlike the increasing importance of APEC as a host to FDI from other APEC members, the importance of APEC as a source of FDI to APEC members did not increase. The portion of total inflow into the APEC region originating from APEC members remained around 50 percent in both 1980 and in 1992. This finding shows that APEC should open itself to the rest of the world in order for the region to continue to attract the FDI necessary for further economic growth. I will return to this point below.

It should be noted here that the average figure for APEC as a whole masks an important trend observed among the subregions. A most notable development is the increased importance of Northeast Asia as an investor in the region. This is due to the significant increase in the amount of FDI that Northeast Asia receives, which is higher than the increase for other subregions.

I mentioned above that East Asian APEC members attracted a large amount of FDI in the 1980s. Several factors played an important role in attracting this inflow. First, a number of East Asian countries liberalized their FDI policies in the 1980s. Faced with serious foreign debts, these countries adopted liberalization policies in hopes that this would increase the inflow of foreign funds. Foreign firms responded to FDI liberalization by actively investing in East Asia. Second, compared with other developing economies, East Asian economies could provide well-educated, well-disciplined, low-wage labor, making them additionally

TABLE 4.2

INTRA-APEC FDI

DESTINATIONS OF FDI FROM APEC MEMBERS (%):1980

INVESTORS	RECIPIENT COUNTRIES											FDI STOCK
	N.AMERICA	L.AMERICA	AMERICA	N.E. ASIA	S.E. ASIA	OCEANIA	E.HEMIS.	APEC	EU	OTHERS	WORLD	(US$ MILLION)
N.AMERICA	24.4	2.5	26.9	3.9	2.2	3.7	9.8	36.7	34.7	28.7	100.0	242750
L.AMERICA	83.7		83.7			1.5	1.5	85.2	14.8		100.0	163
AMERICA	24.4	2.5	26.9	3.9	2.2	3.7	9.8	36.7	34.7	28.7	100.0	242913
N.E.ASIA	24.7	2.0	26.7	9.6	23.2	6.1	38.8	65.5	9.7	24.8	100.0	40982
S.E.ASIA	6.8		6.8	20.8	59.2	4.1	84.1	90.9	1.6	7.6	100.0	1616
OCEANIA	17.4		17.4	0.8	23.4	31.4	55.6	73.0	25.8	1.2	100.0	2607
E.HEMIS.	23.6	1.8	25.4	9.5	24.5	7.4	41.4	66.8	10.4	22.8	100.0	45205
APEC	24.3	2.4	26.7	4.8	5.7	4.3	14.8	41.4	30.8	27.7	100.0	288119
EU	32.6	0.4	33.0	1.9	3.5	5.0	10.5	43.4	31.8	24.8	100.0	164759
WORLD	49.4	0.0	49.4	8.3	0.3	0.5	9.2	58.6	33.5	7.9	100.0	491689

DESTINATIONS OF FDI FROM APEC MEMBERS (%):1992

INVESTORS	RECIPIENT COUNTRIES											FDI STOCK
	N.AMERICA	L.AMERICA	AMERICA	N.E. ASIA	S.E. ASIA	OCEANIA	E.HEMIS.	APEC	EU	OTHERS	WORLD	(US$ MILLION)
N.AMERICA	20.1	2.4	22.5	7.6	3.4	3.8	14.9	37.4	38.3	24.3	100.0	582803
L.AMERICA	95.2		95.2					95.2	4.8		100.0	1349
AMERICA	20.3	2.4	22.7	7.6	3.4	3.8	14.8	37.5	38.3	24.2	100.0	584152
N.E.ASIA	40.2	0.5	40.7	11.6	11.0	5.3	27.9	68.6	16.5	14.9	100.0	441227
S.E.ASIA	9.3	0.1	9.4	20.6	33.3	9.2	63.0	72.4	12.0	15.6	100.0	16852
OCEANIA	23.5	0.0	23.5	-1.1	6.8	26.9	32.6	56.0	41.0	3.0	100.0	33757
E.HEMIS.	38.0	0.5	38.5	11.0	11.5	6.9	29.4	67.9	18.0	14.1	100.0	491837
APEC	28.4	1.5	29.9	9.2	7.1	5.2	21.5	51.4	29.0	19.6	100.0	1075989
EU	27.1	0.4	27.6	2.1	1.6	2.4	6.1	33.6	47.7	18.7	100.0	799301
WORLD	28.2	0.1	28.3	21.3	0.8	1.6	23.8	52.0	38.7	9.3	100.0	2067944

TABLE 4.2 (CONTINUED)

SOURCES OF FDI IN APEC MEMBERS (%):1980

INVESTORS	RECIPIENT COUNTRIES											FDI STOCK
	N.AMERICA	L.AMERICA	AMERICA	N.E. ASIA	S.E. ASIA	OCEANIA	E.HEMIS.	APEC	EU	OTHERS	WORLD	(US$ MILLION)
N.AMERICA	39.6	0.1	39.7	3.9	0.1	0.4	4.4	44.1	41.0	14.9	100.0	137208
L.AMERICA	70.5		70.5	5.9			5.9	76.4	14.6	9.0	100.0	8459
AMERICA	41.4	0.1	41.5	4.0	0.1	0.3	4.5	46.0	39.5	14.6	100.0	145667
N.E.ASIA	39.5		39.5	31.8	4.3	0.2	36.2	75.7	18.4	5.8	100.0	13842
S.E.ASIA	14.0		14.0	35.4	10.2	2.7	48.3	62.2	19.7	18.1	100.0	23145
OCEANIA	39.3	0.0	39.3	6.5	0.5	5.0	12.0	51.3	39.2	9.4	100.0	15536
E.HEMIS.	28.2	0.0	28.2	25.9	5.8	2.7	34.4	62.6	25.1	12.3	100.0	52523
APEC	37.9	0.1	38.0	9.8	1.6	1.0	12.4	50.4	35.7	14.0	100.0	198191
EU	40.1		40.1	2.2		0.4	2.6	42.7	36.2	21.1	100.0	158948
WORLD	30.8	0.2	32.7	3.1	5.2	3.5	11.8	44.5	35.7	19.8	100.0	445174

SOURCES OF FDI IN APEC MEMBERS (%):1992

INVESTORS	RECIPIENT COUNTRIES											FDI STOCK
	N.AMERICA	L.AMERICA	AMERICA	N.E. ASIA	S.E. ASIA	OCEANIA	E.HEMIS.	APEC	EU	OTHERS	WORLD	(US$ MILLION)
N.AMERICA	20.3	0.2	20.3	20.2	0.3	1.6	22.1	42.4	45.9	11.7	100.0	534930
L.AMERICA	63.2		63.2	4.3	0.1	0.0	4.4	67.6	21.7	10.7	100.0	37474
AMERICA	22.9	0.2	23.1	19.2	0.3	1.5	20.9	44.1	44.3	11.6	100.0	572404
N.E.ASIA	27.3		27.3	47.1	3.7	-0.3	50.5	77.8	13.3	8.9	100.0	118518
S.E.ASIA	12.0		12.0	39.7	6.3	3.1	49.1	61.0	15.0	24.0	100.0	136492
OCEANIA	30.1		30.1	17.2	2.2	7.9	27.3	57.4	30.8	11.9	100.0	81344
E.HEMIS.	21.8		21.8	36.9	4.4	3.1	44.3	66.1	18.2	15.7	100.0	336354
APEC	22.5	0.1	22.6	25.7	1.8	2.1	29.6	52.2	34.7	13.1	100.0	908758
EU	25.0	0.0	25.0	4.4	0.0	2.0	6.4	31.4	48.6	20.0	100.0	724082
WORLD	27.8	2.0	29.8	6.2	7.1	4.2	17.5	47.2	37.6	15.1	100.0	1923881

Source: Adopted from the estimates made by Industry Canada

attractive to foreign firms interested in export production. Third, infrastructure such as transportation and communication services is relatively modern in East Asian countries, compared with other developing countries. This enabled foreign firms to operate efficiently at low cost. It should be noted, however, that these favorable characteristics have eroded somewhat due to the rapid economic growth of these countries. As rapid economic growth resulted in a shortage of labor and infrastructure, their supply could not meet the increasing demand created by rapid economic growth.

FDI has contributed to rapid economic growth in the Asia-Pacific through various channels. First, FDI has enabled foreign firms to allocate productive resources, such as capital and technologies, internationally so that they can be used productively. Both the investor and the host economy benefit from FDI, but the effect on economic growth in the recipient country FDI is particularly strong. Transfer of investable funds and technologies to the host economy leads to the expansion of that economy's productive capacity. The funds may be used as fixed investment to build factories and to install new equipment as well as to improve the technological capabilities of the host economy. Table 4.3 shows that foreign firms played a significant role in promoting economic growth throughout East Asia by enabling capital formation.

Second, FDI contributes to the recipient economies by linking them to the rest of the world. Specifically, FDI promotes the exports of recipient economies by providing marketing channels in foreign countries. Indeed, one important characteristic of FDI in the Asia-Pacific is its strong emphasis on exports. Taking advantage of abundant labor in the host economy, foreign firms carry out the production of labor-intensive products or labor-intensive processes for export. Foreign exchange earnings acquired from exports may in turn be used to purchase capital equipment, technology, and other items necessary for economic development, leading to further economic growth.

TABLE 4.3

THE RATIO OF FDI TO FIXED INVESTMENT IN EAST ASIAN COUNTRIES

	1988	1989	1990	1991	1992	1993	1994
CHINA	3.54	4.51	5.54	6.17	11.09	17.73	—
INDONESIA	2.17	2.05	2.85	3.58	3.87	3.93	3.55
KOREA	1.88	1.58	0.84	1.04	0.65	0.49	0.59
MALAYSIA	8.59	15.03	16.83	23.81	26.04	22.47	16.13
PHILIPPINES	13.89	6.35	5.17	5.98	2.06	5.77	—
SINGAPORE	42.41	27.66	43.16	30.59	12.40	22.48	—
THAILAND	5.84	7.10	7.09	4.97	4.83	3.46	—

Sources: IMF, *Balance of Payments Statistics Yearbook*, 1995, part 2 IMF, *International Financial Statistics Yearbook*, 1995 ADB, *Key Indicators of Developing Asian and Pacific Countries*, 1995

Successful economic growth attracts more FDI since favorable economic performance is regarded as evidence for the capability of efficient production. This marks the creation of a virtuous cycle consisting of FDI, fixed investment, and exports that resulted in rapid economic growth in the Asia-Pacific region. Furthermore, buoyant domestic demand, which was created by rapid economic growth, has attracted foreign firms oriented toward local-market sales, contributing to the economic growth of the region. It should be noted that not only foreign firms but also local firms contribute to economic growth. What appears to be happening in the Asia Pacific region is the emergence of self-propelled economic growth.

III. POLICY MEASURES AFFECTING FDI IN THE APEC ECONOMIES

Foreign direct investment promotes economic growth in host countries. However, a number of countries have imposed restrictive measures for two main reasons. First, FDI has been seen as a means to exploit host markets by powerful foreign firms. Second, a number of host governments impose restrictions in order to extract economic benefits from foreign firms. One such example is the requirement imposed on foreign firms to transfer technology. Recognizing the importance of obtaining advanced and efficient technologies from foreign sources, several host governments demand technology transfer before granting a firm permission to engage in FDI.

It is useful to examine government measures from four different perspectives: market access, national treatment, administrative impediments, and incentives.[6] The restriction of market access, national treatment, and the existence of administrative impediments discourage FDI, while the incentives attract it. Although the impact of these two types of measures are completely different, they share the common characteristic of distorting resource allocation or the flow of FDI.

The restriction of market access or the right of establishment by foreign firms takes various forms. Prohibiting foreign direct investment inflow in particular sectors is a typical form of restriction on market access. Channeling FDI to underdeveloped areas in a host country's economy for the purpose of reducing regional disparity is another common form. Restrictions may also impose limits on foreign equity.

An examination of current government policies toward FDI in the APEC region indicates that all APEC members place some restrictions on market access, although the degree of restrictiveness varies among the members nations (see Table 4.4). A number of members restrict or prohibit FDI in "sensitive" sectors. These sectors typically include defense, telecommunications, transportation, finance, and securities among others. Behind these restrictions lies the perception that these sectors are important for maintaining national security. Restriction of FDI inflow is also applied to promote or protect an industry. A case in point is the common restriction of FDI in the automobile sector mainly by restricting the level of equity participation by foreign firms. Unless restrictions are imposed, the local markets would be dominated by

TABLE 4.4

POLICY MEASURES TOWARD FDI IN THE APEC MEMBERS

	AUSTRALIA	BRUNEI	CANADA	CHILE	CHINA	HONG KONG	INDONE-SIA	JAPAN	KOREA	MALAYSIA	MEXICO	NEW ZEALAND	PHILIPPINES	PAPUA NEW GUINEA	SINGAPORE	TAIWAN	THAILAND	US
MARKET ACCESS																		
SCREENING/ NOTIFICATIONS	X	X	X	X	X	O	X	X	X	X	X	X	X	X	O	X	X	O
RESTRICTED/ CLOSED SECTORS	X	X	X	X	X	X	X	X	X	X	X	X	X	X	X	X	X	X
NATIONAL TREATMENT																		
PERFORMANCE REQUIREMENTS	O	O	O	X	X	O	X	O	X	X	O	O	X	X	O	X	X	O
INCENTIVES																		
FISCAL INCENTIVES	O	O	O	O	X	O	X	X	X	X	X	O	O	X	X	X	X	O
TAXATION INCENTIVES	O	O	O	X	X	O	X	X	X	X	O	O	X	X	X	X	X	O

Notes: "X" indicates the presence of impediments, while "O" represents the absence of impediments.
Source: PECC (1995)

competitive foreign firms, making it difficult for local automobile producers to become competitive themselves.

National treatment of foreign firms ensures that investment laws, regulations, and rules create a climate no less favorable than the one granted to domestic investors. Strictly speaking, national treatment should give foreign firms the same access and protection they offer to domestic firms in areas including taxation, labor, and government assistance. National treatment is similar to market access or the right of establishment because for foreign firms it means the assurance of market access and the right of establishment. However the terms national treatment and market access are used in different contexts. The issue of market access arises when foreign firms first enter a host market, whereas the term national treatment is applied to the time after foreign firms are established in the market.

Violation of national treatment usually takes the form of attempts to direct the activities of foreign firms or establish performance requirements. Performance requirements include local-content requirements, minimum-export requirements, and technology-transfer requirements. The local-content requirement forces foreign firms to purchase a minimum percentage of total procurement from the local market, while minimum-export requirements demand that foreign firms export a certain percentage of their total sales.[7] Table 4.4 shows that performance requirements are generally applied by developing countries with the objective of extracting the most benefits from foreign firms. In recent years, however, many countries have reduced the use of performance requirements because they discourage FDI.

Administrative impediments discourage FDI inflow because foreign firms are uncertain about the continuity of their application. As can be seen from Table 4.4, administrative impediments mainly in the form of screening exist in a number of countries, especially developing ones. Specifically, the lack of transparency includes the discretion and inconsistency exercised by government officials in processing FDI applications and in the variable application of performance requirements.

In recent years, recognizing the importance of FDI for promoting economic growth and the detrimental impact of FDI restrictions on inflow of capital, a number of countries have liberalized their FDI regimes. Moreover, many countries have extended existing incentives solely to attract FDI (see Table 4.4). These incentives, including preferential tax treatment and low-interest loans, are provided by both central and local governments. Rather than employing a protectionist viewpoint, Asian countries now engage in severe competition to attract FDI.

Restrictions on FDI prevent economies from achieving efficient resource allocation, and thus cannot be justified from the point of view of allocative efficiency. The provision of incentives may seem justified, as it may promote FDI and thus result in greater economic growth. However, incentives also lead to the misallocation of resources by discouraging investment by local firms. In other words, unless there is evidence that foreign firms contribute more to the local economy through nonmarket channels than local firms, or the presence of external economies, the provision of FDI incentives cannot be justified. It has been argued that foreign firms should be treated preferentially since they introduce advanced technology into the host economy and actively undertake R&D. Because technology gives rise to external economies, this argument may be valid. However, such a policy is not optimal. The optimal policy in this situation is to subsidize technological or R&D activities undertaken by any firm, regardless of national origin.

Moreover, incentives tend to result in a beggar-thy-neighbor atmosphere, which harms all countries involved. Incentives do attract FDI, but they incur costs to the countries offering them. For example, if incentives are given in the form of tax exemptions, the government in question loses revenue. Recognizing incentives as an effective means to attract FDI, countries continue to use them despite the harm done to each other.

IV. MULTILATERAL INVESTMENT RULES

Recognizing the importance of FDI inflow in promoting economic growth and responding to requests or pressure from multinational enterprises (MNEs) for a freer FDI environment, countries have established various institutional frameworks regarding FDI, including bilateral, regional, and multilateral approaches.[8] There are more than 900 bilateral investment treaties.[9] These treaties certainly have contributed to the expansion of FDI. However, bilateral treaties cannot be fully effective or efficient means for providing an environment conducive to FDI, since it would take thousands of treaties to negotiate each set of investment relationships the world over, thus sharply increasing transaction costs. Moreover, bilateral treaties result in imbalanced benefits between the two parties with the investing economies benefiting more than host economies. These observations indicate the advantage of having regional and multilateral frameworks for negotiating policies regarding FDI. It has also been suggested that trade and FDI regimes can be liberalized with less difficulty when liberalization is carried out regionally or multilaterally, because the negative effect of trade and FDI liberalization on some groups in the economy is likely to be offset by favorable effects in other areas.

Various regional agreements regarding investment have been established because the benefits of such agreements are shared more equally among economies having mutual interests. In addition, it is easier to reach an agreement when working with a small number of member economies.

This section discusses three major regional and multilateral frameworks concerning FDI, which involve some or all of the APEC member nations: the agreement on Trade Related Investment Measures (TRIMs) under the GATT/WTO, the Multilateral Accord on Investment (MAI) under the OECD, and the Non-Binding Investment Principles (NBIP) Act under APEC.[10]

GATT/WTO Trade Related Investment Measures (TRIMs)

The Uruguay Round of the GATT reached an agreement on investment rules, which was the first time in the history of GATT multilateral negotiations that members took up the issue of foreign direct investment. In particular, the dispute between the United States and Canadian governments over U.S. FDI in Canada in the early 1980s led to these negotiations. Canada restricted the establishment and behavior of foreign firms in Canada for the stated intention of protecting the interest of Canadians. Specifically, Canada imposed restrictions on equity participation, local procurements, exports and other areas. The United States appealed to the

GATT on the grounds that Canada's restrictions were illegal under the GATT rules governing national treatment in the areas on internal taxation and regulation. A GATT panel ruled in 1984 that local procurement requirements imposed by the Canadian government were a violation of Article III (4) of the GATT, and the Canadian government revised its rules on FDI to comply with the GATT decision.

Before agreeing to Uruguay Round negotiations, developed countries requested that the issue of FDI be taken up in the Round because they argued that restrictions on FDI imposed by recipient countries distorted the flow of trade. The United States was keenly interested in removing not only restrictions related to foreign trade but also restrictions on FDI in general. On the other hand, developing countries were opposed to broadening the GATT system to include services trade and foreign direct investment. After a series of intense talks, developed countries and developing countries agreed to address only the FDI issues related to foreign trade, or TRIMs in the Uruguay Round.

In the Uruguay Round negotiations, the United States argued that all TRIMs should be prohibited, while Japan and the EC argued that only some of them should be prohibited. Developing countries argued that TRIMs should not be prohibited since these measures are necessary to promote economic development in their nations. After a series of negotiations, an agreement was reached to prohibit TRIMs that violate the GATT rules. The agreement was a compromise between developed and developing countries, as neither side was entirely happy with the outcome. The United States argued strongly to prohibit export requirements, fearing that they might lead to the expansion of exports bound for the U.S. market. However, this provision was not included in the agreement. Developing countries argued for a clause to restrict the monopolistic behavior of MNEs, but that was not included either.

In the end, it was agreed to prohibit TRIMs that violate the two following GATT rules: national treatment applied to imported products (Article III) and general elimination of quantitative restrictions on imports (Article XI). The specific TRIMs that violate the national treatment rule include the local-content requirement and trade balancing requirements. Trade balancing requires that imports of foreign firms do not exceed their exports. TRIMs that violate the general elimination of quantitative restrictions are trade balancing requirements, restrictions on foreign exchange transactions, and local sales requirements. Local sales requirements force foreign firms to market a certain portion of their sales in the local market or to limit their exports.

Only TRIMs practiced by governments violate WTO rules, and thus TRIMs practiced voluntarily by the private sector do not violate these rules. Trade-restricting measures that are sanctioned under the GATT for security reasons, among others, are also recognized in the agreement on TRIMs. Furthermore, special provisions accorded to developing countries under Article XVIII also apply to the agreement on TRIMs. Specifically, Article XVIII, section B, permits developing countries to restrict their imports in order to deal with balance of payments difficulties. Article XVIII, section C, permits developing countries to apply the same restrictions to promote a particular industry.

The contracting parties of the WTO must abolish TRIMs that are reported to the Council for Trade in Goods within the agreed period—within two years for developed countries, within five years for developing countries, and within seven years for the least developed countries. To increase the transparency of TRIMs, WTO member countries are required to report all TRIMs that they apply. They are also required to furnish information on TRIMs to any member country that requests it.

Although the rules regarding foreign direct investment that were established in the Uruguay Round are limited to issues of foreign trade and TRIMs, it is worth noting that the Uruguay Round was the first trade negotiation under which measures related to FDI were taken up. However, no agreements were reached on other restrictive measures related to FDI, such as restrictions on the extent of equity participation, technology transfer, and exports. Because of this, there are still many government interventions to be removed before a true free FDI environment will be established. Despite these interventions, an agreement was reached that ensures services trade the right of establishment, a significant step toward assuring the right of establishment for firms involved in FDI.

At the first ministerial meeting of the WTO, held in Singapore in December 1996, it was agreed that a working group should be established to examine the relationship between trade and FDI. This was a compromise between developed countries, which were interested in setting up stronger regulation of FDI, and developing countries like Malaysia, India, and Tanzania, which are against such rules.[11]

OECD's Multilateral Agreement on Investment (MAI)

The most successful multilateral agreements on FDI have perhaps been those formulated under the auspices of the Organization for Economic Cooperation and Development (OECD).[12] The OECD has pursued investment policy harmonization in a variety of ways, providing a forum on international investment policy. In 1961, the OECD adopted the Code of Liberalization of Capital Movements. In 1976, OECD adopted the Declaration on International Investment and Multinational Enterprises.

Liberalization of capital movements in the pre-establishment stage and national treatment in the postestablishment stage are addressed in the 1961 code. However, the OECD has neither the enforcement authority nor comprehensive rules to protect investments or settle disputes. Thus, the OECD, like the WTO, falls far short of providing an environment to ensure free investment.

To improve this situation, the OECD opened negotiations on the Multilateral Agreement on Investment (MAI) in September

1995. The MAI is expected to contain a high standard for liberalization and investment protection such as market access, MFN status, national treatment, and an effective dispute settlement mechanism. The agreement is scheduled to be concluded in time for the next OECD Ministerial Meeting in the spring of 1998. The MAI is expected to become an international treaty, which will be accessible to OECD members and non-OECD members alike.

The APEC Non-Binding Investment Principles (NBIP)

Achieving free trade and investment in the APEC region has been one of APEC's central objectives. The APEC members have liberalized their trade and FDI policies unilaterally in recent years, but many areas remain to be liberalized in a number of APEC member economies. Recognition of these issues led to the agreement on Non-Binding Investment Principles (NBIP) in November 1994. It should be noted that an increasing number of developing APEC members that have been recipients of FDI are now becoming active investors, contributing to the establishment of the NBIP.

The expansion of FDI has been recognized as an important element for the promotion of economic growth in the Asia-Pacific region by APEC members since the inception of APEC in 1989. Since 1989, the framework for the liberalization of FDI has been shaped gradually. At the Canberra meeting in 1989, participating ministers selected investment and technology transfer as an area of focus for an APEC work program at APEC. At the Singapore meeting in 1990, this became one of seven work projects carried out by APEC. Specifically, members sought the establishment of information networks concerning FDI and technology and the creation of technology parks where technology-intensive foreign firms could operate.

In the 1991 Seoul Declaration, one key objective of APEC members was the promotion of FDI. APEC stated that obstacles to the promotion of FDI among member countries would be reduced in accordance with GATT principles. At the Bangkok meeting in 1992, ministers proposed that senior officials prepare a guidebook containing a detailed description of the APEC members' rules and procedures regarding FDI, which led to the APEC Guidebook on Investment Regimes.

At the Seattle meeting in 1993, reaffirming the importance of trade and FDI liberalization for economic growth in the APEC region, the ministers set up the Committee on Trade and Investment (CTI). CTI reports to the ministers through meetings of senior officials. CTI's objectives are twofold: to formulate opinions on trade and FDI issues in APEC, and to devise ways to reduce or remove obstacles to the free flow of trade and FDI. The newly formed CTI was given the task of developing a set of nonbinding investment principles.

In Indonesia in 1994, APEC leaders issued the Bogor Declaration, declaring their intention to achieve free and open trade and investment in the APEC region. The declaration established a target date for reaching that goal: no later than 2010 for the industrialized members and no later than 2020 for the developing members. Prior to the Bogor Declaration at the APEC meeting in Jakarta, the ministers endorsed the Non-Binding Investment Principles (NBIP). These were prepared by CTI in response to a request presented at an unofficial APEC leaders' meeting in Seattle. The PECC (Pacific Economic Cooperation Council) contributed to the preparation of the NBIP by developing a model voluntary code on direct investment in its Trade Policy Forum.[13]

The NBIP supports the need to liberalize FDI policies in order to promote economic growth in the region. It consists of four sections: principles that govern international relations, codes of conduct for governments, codes of conduct for investors, and a system for dispute settlement.[14] The three general principles of international relations are transparency, national treatment, and nondiscrimination. The codes of conduct for government stipulate the use of specific policies related to FDI: investment incentives, performance requirements, expropriation and compensation, transfer of funds, settlement of investment disputes, entry and stay of expatriates, tax measures, and capital movements. These codes of conduct are meant to discourage the use of investment-distorting policies, but the diversity of APEC members has made it difficult to implement these codes uniformly.

The Eminent Persons Group assessed ten specific principles of the NBIP and decided that five are equal to (or even above) other international standards. These five are transparency, nondiscrimination, expropriation, settlement of investment disputes, and tax measures. However the other five fall short of those standards: the transfer of funds, capital movements, national treatment, performance requirements, and investment incentives.[15]

The NBIP on performance requirement, for example, falls short of WTO obligations. The NBIP states that member economies will minimize the use of performance requirements that distort or limit the expansion of trade or investment, whereas the WTO bans TRIMs such as local content and trade balancing requirements.[16] The Eminent Persons Group recommends strengthening the principles and then converting the arrangement into a voluntary code that will ultimately lead to an agreement that is binding for all members.

Despite the presence of divergent views, codes of conduct for investors were included in the NBIP as they were considered to balance the set of principles.[17] These codes of conduct state that foreign investors should abide by the host country's laws, regulations, administrative guidelines, and policies, just as domestic investors do. A dispute settlement provision is included in the NBIP but lacks a detailed mechanism or procedure. It suggests only that disputes will be settled promptly through consultations and negotiations between parties through arbitration procedures acceptable to all. Finally, it is stated that the NBIP must not violate existing bilateral or multilateral treaties, including the agreement on TRIMs under the WTO.

At the Osaka meeting in 1995, the APEC economic leaders adopted the Osaka Action Agenda, carrying through the commitment they made at Bogor. At Osaka, economic ministers reaffirmed that liberalization in trade and investment, facilitation of trade and investment, and economic and technical cooperation are three pillars that APEC needs to achieve sustained economic growth. APEC members agreed on certain fundamental principles designed to lead to liberalization and facilitation, comprehensiveness, WTO consistency, comparability, nondiscrimination, transparency, standstill, simultaneous start, continuous process, differentiated time tables, flexibility, and cooperation.[18] These principles reflect the diverse levels of economic development among APEC member economies. Substantive action plans were agreed on at the 1996 Ministerial Meeting in the Philippines. Overall implementation of action plans began in January 1997 and are to be reviewed annually.

Regarding FDI, the Osaka Action Agenda put forth the objective of achieving free and open investment in the Asia-Pacific region by liberalizing restrictive investment regimes in the overall investment environment. Specific plans include providing for proper MFN and national treatment, ensuring transparency, and facilitating investment activities through technical assistance and cooperation.[19] To achieve these objectives, the Osaka Action Agenda emphasized guidelines that progressively reduce or eliminate exceptions and restrictions: it draws on the WTO agreement, the APEC Non-Binding Investment Principles, other relevant international agreements, and commonly agreed-upon guidelines developed by APEC.

At the Manila APEC ministerial meeting in November 1996, ministers from member economies reaffirmed their commitment to full and effective implementation of the Osaka Action Agenda by 2010 and 2020.[20] Yet even though ministers reaffirmed the importance of moving forward with progressive action plans, little progress was made regarding investment liberalization. The individual action plans (IAPs) submitted by member economies contained virtually no new commitments to promote FDI liberalization substantially.[21]

One significant achievement at the Manila meeting was recognition of the importance of continuing consultation and annual review of progress made concerning investment and trade liberalization. Review is meant to sustain the process of voluntary improvements as listed in the IAPs.

Another notable development that took place at the Manila meeting was greater participation by the business sector. This was due to recognition by APEC members, especially by President Fidel V. Ramos of the Philippines, that the business sector plays an increasingly important role in economic growth and trade and FDI liberalization. In response to the greater participation by the business sector, ABAC (APEC Business Advisory Council) submitted to the APEC ministerial meeting a set of recommendations for achieving prosperity in the APEC community.[22] Specifically, recommendations include measures for trade and FDI liberalization, building infrastructure, support for small and medium enterprises, investment in human resource development, and pursuing economic and technical cooperation. Recognizing the need to reduce and eventually eliminate border restrictions that prevent APEC's firms from remaining globally competitive, ABAC's recommendations on FDI include those calling for the reinforcement of the NBIP through further clarification, and for a commitment to the immediate implementation or a timetable for implementation of the NBIP. None of these recommendations was adopted in the APEC economic leader's declaration in Manila because of opposition from developing countries headed by Malaysia.

V. THE IMPACT OF INVESTMENT RULES ON FDI

The previous section examined recent developments concerning the establishment of international investment rules by the WTO, OECD, and APEC. Needless to say, the purpose of establishing these rules is to promote FDI, which in turn would promote economic growth.

One would therefore be interested in the impact of investment rules on the promotion of FDI. Ideally, statistical analyses should be carried out to examine the impact of investment rules on FDI decisions made by foreign firms. However, a lack of sufficient information precludes us from undertaking such analyses at this time. Instead, the analysis here examines the results of two questionnaires, one conducted with U.S. firms, the other with Japanese firms. These surveys asked the firms to rate the importance of investment rules in making decisions on FDI. The result of these two surveys indicate that investment rules play an important role in the decision-making process of surveyed firms. This finding implies that the further establishment of international rules would promote FDI.

The United States Committee of the Pacific Basin Economic Council (USPBEC) conducted a survey of corporate attitudes toward foreign investment in APEC economies.[23] The survey was conducted on 48 U.S. firms. Some of the results are reproduced in Tables 4.5 and 4.6. Table 4.5 reports the responses to questions regarding factors related to the investment environment, grouped into commercial factors, political factors, and investment policies. The respondents were asked to evaluate the importance of each item on a scale from 1 to 5; the higher the number, the higher the item's importance. An examination of the results reveals that investment policies are as important as commercial or political factors for firms deciding on FDI. The average scores for commercial factors, political stability, and investment policies are similar—3.2, 3.8, and 3.4 respectively. Among investment policies, currency transferability, currency convertibility, and national treatment were considered to be particularly important.

Regarding the impact of investment agreements in decision making on investment, 38 out of 46 firms responded that they are important (see Table 4.6). Of all the various provisions of investment agreements, significant importance is given to the following: the ability to repatriate profits freely (4.4 points out of possible 5.0) and transparency (4.0). These two provisions are followed in rank by

TABLE 4.5

IMPORTANCE OF HOST COUNTRY FACTORS TO FOREIGN INVESTORS: A CASE OF U.S. INVESTORS

(RATING: 1 TO 5)

1. COMMERCIAL FACTORS RELATING TO MARKET SIZE AND PRODUCT COSTS	
A) LARGE DOMESTIC MARKET	3.7
B) AVAILABILITY OF PARTNERS	3.5
C) OVERALL PROFITABILITY OF MARKET	2.7
D) QUALITY OF WORKFORCE	3.5
E) ACCESS TO KEY SUPPLIERS	3.0
F) PROXIMITY TO BUYERS	3.4
G) QUALITY OF INFRASTRUCTURE	3.4
H) LABOR RELATIONS	3.1
I) ACCESS TO FINANCIAL MARKETS	2.7
AVERAGE	3.2
2. POLITICAL STABILITY	
A) STABLE MACRO ENVIRONMENT	3.7
B) POLITICAL STABILITY	4.0
C) LOW FOREIGN EXCHANGE RISK	3.6
AVERAGE	3.8
3. INVESTMENT POLICIES	
A) ABSENCE OF PERFORMANCE REQUIREMENTS	3.0
B) REGULATORY TRANSPARENCY	3.2
C) INTELLECTUAL PROPERTY PROTECTION	2.9
D) CURRENCY TRANSFERABILITY	4.2
E) CONVERTIBLE CURRENCY	4.2
F) ARBITRATION ACCESS	2.6
G) EXPROPRIATION GUARANTEES	3.5
H) LACK OF IMPORT RESTRICTIONS	3.4
I) GOVERNMENTAL RED TAPE	3.1
J) NATIONAL TREATMENT FOR FOREIGN INVESTORS	3.8
AVERAGE	3.4

Note: Figures indicate the importance of corresponding item in executives' decision on FDI.
Rating is given on a scale from 1.0 to 5.0; "the greater the figure,
the more important the item."
Source: Reproduced from Guisinger and McNulty (1996)

TABLE 4.6

IMPORTANCE OF INVESTMENT AGREEMENTS

	NUMBER OF FIRMS
NOT AWARE OF INVESTMENT TREATIES	4
LITTLE/NO IMPORTANCE	4
SOME IMPORTANCE	19
IMPORTANT	14
VERY IMPORTANT	3
WILL NOT INVEST WITHOUT TREATIES	2

Source: Reproduced from Guisinger and McNulty (1996)

international standards for expropriation (3.5), national treatment (3.3), freedom from performance requirements (3.2), arbitration provisions (3.1), and most-favored-nation treatment (2.9).

A MITI survey conducted in 1992 on 7,108 overseas affiliates of Japanese companies found that restrictions on equity participation (market access) and the entry of foreign personnel are the two most serious problems Japanese firms face in Asia (see Table 4.7). It is interesting to note that affiliates in ASEAN face more restrictions than do those in NIEs. This finding is consistent with the expectation that less developed countries tend to have stronger protectionist policies than more developed ones. This observation also explains smaller figures on the proportion of affiliates facing problems for the affiliates in North America and Europe as compared to Asia. However, it should be noted that Japanese firms face restrictions even in developed countries, indicating the need for liberalization in developed countries as well.

VI. CONCLUSION

Foreign direct investment (FDI) worldwide has grown with increasing rapidity since the 1980s. The rate of increase has been

TABLE 4.7

GOVERNMENT RESTRICTIONS FACING JAPANESE FIRMS
IN THE OVERSEAS HOST ECONOMIES:1992

(PERCENT)

	LOCATION OF AFFILIATES OF JAPANESE FIRMS				
	ASIA	ASEAN	NIES	NORTH AMERICA	EUROPE
RESTRICTION ON:					
TRANSFER OF PROFITS	3.5	3	3.2	1.7	1.9
RAISING FUNDS LOCALLY	12	16.8	4.5	8.9	2.7
EQUITY PARTICIPATION	17.7	33.3	3.9	2.2	1.3
ENTRY OF FOREIGN PERSONNEL	20.3	31.2	12.3	12.2	9
LOCAL PROCUREMENT	5.2	6.9	3	6	3.5
IMPORTS OF MATERIALS AND PARTS	9.8	11.1	7.1	4.5	2.6
EXPORTS (EXPORTS REQUIREMENTS)	12	16.5	5.7	1	0.5
TECHNOLOGY TRADE	3.8	6.3	1.7	1.5	0.5

Note: Figures indicate the percentage of surveyed firms facing the problem in total firms surveyed.
Source: Ministry of International Trade and Industry, Kaigai toshi Tokei Soran (Comprehensive Statistics on Foreign Investment by Japanese Firms), no. 5, 1994

particularly high for the APEC region, contributing notably to the rapid growth of East Asian economies and revitalizing the U.S. economy. One of the most important elements behind the initial increase in FDI was the liberalization of FDI policies. Foreign firms were attracted to East Asian economies because their business opportunities widened with FDI liberalization.

In spite of FDI liberalization policies in recent years, a significant number of restrictions on FDI still remain, mainly to protect certain sectors of national economies. Despite a common understanding that restrictions on FDI reduce economic growth by discouraging FDI inflow, it is difficult to remove them as the groups that are likely to be affected negatively by FDI liberalization have organized effectively against it.

Multilateral and regional FDI liberalization has an advantage over unilateral FDI liberalization, as the negative impact of liberalization tends to be smaller if it is carried out regionally or multilaterally. Thus, from a policy perspective, multilateral or regional FDI liberalization efforts should be supported. Specifically, any attempt to establish investment rules such as the TRIMs in the WTO, the MAI in the OECD, and the NBIP in APEC should be carried out.

The eventual goal of various multilateral and regional arrangements is to establish investment rules in the WTO, which has the largest membership. However, regional efforts such as those of APEC should be strongly encouraged for several reasons. First, an agreement may be achieved more easily when negotiations are carried out by a small group of like-minded countries. Indeed, the WTO appears to be moving slowly on investment issues. Second, APEC has an advantage over other multilateral or regional arrangements regarding their membership, including the WTO, since China and Taiwan, two important economies in East Asia, are not members of the WTO but are part of APEC. APEC has an advantage over the OECD as well since some increasingly important FDI suppliers and recipients in East Asia are members of APEC but not the OECD. The diversity in APEC can also be problematic, as agreement among the countries with diverse interests is difficult to achieve. For example, at present some developing members are not in favor of strengthening the NBIP mainly because of their concern that such measures would weaken their position vis-à-vis foreign firms. However, the fact that FDI-led growth has been realized in East Asia should make an agreement on FDI acceptable even to these members.

It should be noted that the nonbinding nature of the investment rules in APEC's NBIP, reflecting a principle of voluntary execution of its policies, has both positive and negative elements. The nonbinding nature makes it easier for members to accept very high standards while creating difficulties in enforcement. The issue of enforcement may be dealt with once countries realize the need to offer foreign investors an attractive environment to attain valuable FDI, such as ensuring market access and national treatment.

As long as economic growth continues in East Asia, FDI is likely to be attracted to the region, even without strictly binding FDI rules. However, a challenge will arise when economic growth in East Asia starts to decline. Under conditions of slower growth, countries tend to shift toward inward-looking protectionist policies. Needless to say, protectionist policies reduce FDI, which in turn would reduce economic growth. In order to avoid such an undesirable situation, binding FDI rules should be established. In order to achieve this, more research on the importance of investment rules for attracting FDI should be conducted and presented to policymakers in the APEC region.

NOTES

1. An earlier version was presented at the Second Workshop on APEC and Regime Creation in Asia and the Pacific, held at University of Washington, Seattle, August 13-15, 1996. The author acknowledges useful comments from Vinod Aggarwal, Charles Morrison, and other participants in the workshop.
2. In this paper, East Asia consists of the Asian NIEs (Hong Kong, Korea, Singapore and Taiwan), ASEAN4 (Indonesia, Malaysia, Philippines, and Thailand), and China.
3. The *World Investment Report*, an annual publication of UNCTAD, discusses the trends and developments of FDI. See also the WTO (1996) for recent developments in FDI and its impact on investing and receiving countries.
4. This discussion is based on figures for FDI outflow. Discrepancy between the figures for FDI outflow and inflow are likely to be due largely to differences in the timing of measurement and differences in the definition of FDI in various investing and receiving countries.
5. The FDI-intensity between regions i and j is computed as $(FDIij/FDIi.)/(FDI.j/(FDI..-FDI.i))$, where FDIij indicates FDI from region i to region j, and "." indicates the summation of all the countries comprising the investing world.
6. The discussion in this section draws on PECC (1995).
7. Technology-transfer requirements were discussed above. Performance requirements that violate the GATT rules were agreed to be removed at the

Uruguay Round. See section IV of this chapter for a more detailed discussion.

8. WTO (1996) provides a discussion on institutional frameworks regarding FDI.

9. Ruggiero (1996).

10. There are other regional/multilateral rules and codes on foreign direct investment: The U.N. Code of Conduct on Transnational Corporations, and the World Bank guidelines. See Bora (1993) and PECC (1995) for these and other agreements on FDI.

11. For the positions of developed and developing countries on FDI rules, see *The Economist,* October 19, 1996.

12. *The Economist,* October 19, 1996.

13. See, for example, Bora (1993).

14. Bora and Graham (1996) discuss these points in detail.

15. APEC Secretariat (1995), *Implementing the APEC Vision.*

16. APEC Secretariat (1995).

17. Bora and Graham (1996).

18. *APEC Economic Leaders' Declaration for Action,* Osaka, Japan, November 19, 1995.

19. *The Osaka Action Agenda,* the APEC Osaka meeting, November 16, 1995.

20. Asia-Pacific Economic Cooperation (1996).

21. Individual Action Plans by APEC members.

22. ABAC (1996).

23. Guisinger and McNulty (1996) report some results of the survey and present an interesting analysis of these results.

CHAPTER 5

INTELLECTUAL PROPERTY AND APEC

Sumner J. La Croix

I. INTRODUCTION[1]

The 1994 Uruguay Round Agreements represent another large step toward free international trade but a giant leap toward the creation of a viable worldwide regime governing intellectual property. Previous international accords governing intellectual property rights (IPRs), for example, the Paris Convention, the Berne Convention, the Treaty of Rome, the Madrid Agreement, and the Patent Cooperation Treaty, had focused on establishing national treatment for foreigners seeking to establish and enforce domestic IPRs. These accords failed to establish strong minimum standards for different types of intellectual property or to require effective enforcement procedures to remedy violations of foreigners' IPRs. The 1994 Uruguay Round Agreements went far beyond these earlier international IPR agreements, as its Trade-Related Aspects of Intellectual Property Rights (TRIPS) Agreement requires member countries to bring their IPR laws closer to the standards found in most OECD countries and to provide more effective private and public IPR enforcement mechanisms.[2]

The TRIPS Agreement represents the culmination of a 15–year campaign by the United States and the European Union for strengthened IPRs in developing countries, particularly in East and Southeast Asia. The developed world's renewed interest in IPRs was spurred by the rising consumption of IPR-intensive goods in rapidly growing developing countries and by the expanding volume of international trade in goods and services in the 1970s and 1980s. Alarmed at inroads by imports in long-established manufacturing industries, the United States reacted by taking measures to increase exports of goods in which the United States has a comparative advantage. Increasingly, these are IPR-intensive manufactures and creative and artistic works.[3] U.S. firms complained to the U.S. government that exports of these goods were being depressed by widespread imitation of patented U.S. technologies, copying of copyrighted creative works, and counterfeiting of well-known trademarks. Threatened with loss of access to the U.S. market if they did not adopt stronger IPR legislation, many developing countries in Asia significantly strengthened their IPRs in the late 1980s and early 1990s. Given the potential for further unilateral pressure by the United States with respect to IPRs, developing countries agreed to incorporate intellectual property provisions in the Uruguay Round Agreements in exchange for concessions from the developed countries. Thus, in the 1994 Uruguay Round Agreements, the developing countries acceded to the inclusion of the TRIPS Agreement in exchange for the gradual dismantling of the MultiFiber Arrangement, a complex system of textile quotas imposing significant welfare and income losses on developing countries.[4]

Since the conclusion of the Uruguay Round, developed and developing countries have started the process of upgrading their IPR laws and institutions to conform with TRIPS. The TRIPS Agreement allows signatories to retain distinctive registration and enforcement procedures as well as some important differences in substantive IPR law. The incomplete nature of the TRIPS Agreement leaves open the possibility that other global and regional IPR institutions may be able to fill a niche and improve global or regional welfare. Regional and global IPR institutions have four potentially important functions: (1) coordinating claims and rights across national IPR regimes; (2) harmonizing national IPR regimes; (3) setting minimum standards for national IPR regimes; and (4) creating transnational intellectual property laws and institutions.

Two *global* IPR treaties, the Patent Cooperation Treaty and the Madrid Agreement Concerning the International Registration of Marks, are designed to coordinate more fully national IPR institutions. Two *regional* IPR regimes, the European Patent Convention and the European Community Trade Mark, have moved beyond harmonizing national IPR regimes by establishing transnational IPR laws and institutions. An analysis of both the global and regional arrangements indicates that they are valuable complements to the TRIPS Agreement. This leads us to our main question: Could APEC be a vehicle for establishing similar IPR institutions in the Asia-Pacific region? Or, given APEC's aversion to institutionalization, is there an alternative role for APEC to play with respect to intellectual property issues?

The analysis in section II begins by outlining the major changes in Asia-Pacific IPRs since the early 1980s and summarizing the main provisions of the TRIPS Agreement. Section III considers how other global and regional institutions serve to coordinate, implement, and enforce IPRs. Section IV considers the interests of APEC members in establishing APEC institutions governing intellectual property and evaluates whether APEC proposals to coordinate, harmonize, and upgrade Asian intellectual property institutions would enhance world or regional welfare. Section V concludes the analysis with reflections on APEC's future role in creating viable IPR institutions in the Asia-Pacific region.

II. FROM UNILATERAL PRESSURE TO THE MULTILATERAL TRIPS AGREEMENT

Since the early 1980s, the United States has imposed strong pressure on countries with weak IPR laws and institutions through its "Special 301" amendments to U.S. trade law.[5] Using a number of designated threat levels—for example, countries could be placed on a "watch list," a "priority list," "designated" for such but not yet placed on it, and so forth—the United States threatened virtually all Asian countries with retaliatory trade sanctions unless they upgraded their IPR laws, institutions, and enforcement activities. From the U.S. perspective, problems included inadequate protection of patented chemicals and pharmaceuticals; copyrighted first-run films, videocassettes, sound recordings, and personal computer software; and a wide variety of entertainment and fashion trademarks. Some Asian governments also were lobbied by domestic interest groups standing to gain from stronger IPR laws. For example, Hong Kong's decision to strengthen enforcement of its copyright laws coincided with the rise of its popular music industry in the 1980s.

This international pressure, coupled with the increasing industrial and service orientation of most Asian economies, prompted some Asian countries to make major changes in their IPR laws, while others have proceeded more slowly.[6] Indonesia, for example, has extensively upgraded its IPR laws and institutions in the last decade, but its IPR laws and institutions still need extensive revision to meet TRIPS standards. Other Asian countries are finding changes in IPR laws difficult to undertake due to domestic pressures. The Philippines promised the United States in 1993 that it would strengthen its IPRs, but the Philippine legislature has continually balked at passing implementing legislation. India's upper house of Parliament has refused to endorse changes in patent laws to allow patenting of pharmaceutical products required by the TRIPS Agreement.

Despite the resistance to upgrading IPRs, by early 1995 most targeted Asian countries had brought their laws closer to TRIPS standards—but the focus of U.S. and European pressure had already shifted from stronger IPR standards to stronger enforcement of IPRs, especially of computer software and entertainment copyrights. Some Asian countries have responded by devoting more resources to enforcement. A few selected examples from the last few years serve to illustrate this trend. Singapore has prosecuted software pirates and raided electronic bulletin boards services that download copyrighted software. In Thailand, enforcement activities against software pirates have expanded in Bangkok and selected provinces, but illegal use of computer software remains extensive—an estimated 90 percent of computer software in use has been illegally copied, and government raids against retail software stores have had limited impact. After pressure from French fashion designers, Indonesia has cracked down on misappropriation of trademarks in the fashion industry. Many foreign corporations have taken advantage of changes in Asian IPR laws that reduce the cost of bringing private enforcement actions. The Walt Disney Company, for example, has threatened illegal users of its cartoon characters in Singapore and Indonesia with lawsuits unless they cease illegal uses and make a public apology to Disney and Indonesian consumers.

The unilateral pressure from the United States during the 1980s stemmed from soaring U.S. trade deficits and a recognition in government that U.S. comparative advantage was shifting toward IPR-intensive products.[7] Another reason for unilateral pressure from the United States was that international treaties coordinating and harmonizing national IPR regimes were relatively weak. The Paris Convention of 1883 covered inventions, trade names, trademarks, service marks, industrial designs, indications of source, and appellations of origin. Later conventions covered copyrights (Berne, 1886), sound recordings (Rome, 1961), and layout designs of integrated circuits (Washington, 1989). All four conventions are uniformly flawed by inadequate mechanisms to resolve disputes, and some fail to specify the most minimal standards of IPR protection. Attempts by the United Nation's World Intellectual Property Organization (WIPO) to remedy these difficulties were hampered by disputes between developing and developed countries that proved impossible to resolve in stand-alone negotiations.[8]

The mammoth 1994 Uruguay Round Agreements established the World Trade Organization (WTO) as a successor to the GATT and included a special annex with surprisingly strong provisions forcing nearly all countries to strengthen their IPR laws.[9] The Agreement on Trade-Related Aspects of Intellectual Property Rights (TRIPS) represents a dramatic breakthrough for worldwide international IPR agreements, as it specifies strong minimum standards for copyrights, patents, trade secrets, trade and service marks, and indicators of geographic appellation. By forcing WTO member countries to adopt strict minimum standards for establishing and enforcing IPRs, TRIPS forced extensive but not complete harmonization of national IPR regimes. A short summary of the central provisions of TRIPS follows.[10]

1. All WTO members must comply with the central provisions of the four major international IPR conventions (Paris, Berne, Rome, and Washington).

2. WTO members cannot exclude certain classes of products from being patented, but for a few exceptions stipulated in the treaty.

3. WTO members must provide patent protection for at least twenty years from the application filing date.

4. Patent holders no longer have an obligation to work their patent locally if they supply the market's demand for the good with imports.

5. All WTO members, regardless of their developing country status, must accept interim patent applications for pharmaceutical and agricultural chemicals.

6. WTO members must protect new plant varieties, either within their patent system or with a new intellectual property right.

7. The detailed enforcement procedures specified in the Agreement must be incorporated into each WTO member's national laws.

8. WTO members must adopt strict enforcement measures, including border controls, to prevent imports of counterfeit goods.

9. Compulsory licensing of trademarks and local linkage requirements are prohibited.

10. WTO members must provide copyright protection for computer programs and databases for a term of at least 50 years.

11. Each WTO member must establish a system for protecting trade secrets that meets specified minimum standards.

12. Original industrial designs must be protected for at least ten years.

13. Authors and their successors in title have the right to authorize or prohibit the commercial rental to the public of their copyrighted works.

14. Service marks as well as trademarks must be protected.

15. Commercial data submitted for regulatory approval of pharmaceutical or agricultural chemical products must be protected against unfair commercial use.

16. WTO members must protect geographical indications of origin.

17. Damages must be available as a remedy for violations of any intellectual property law. WTO members must have available criminal sanctions for willful trademark counterfeiting and illegal copying on a commercial scale.

18. All WTO members must adhere to all TRIPS provisions.

Developed countries were given until 1996 to comply with TRIPS, developing countries were given until 2000, and the least developed countries until 2005.

III. REGIONAL AND WORLDWIDE IPR INSTITUTIONS

The TRIPS Agreement forces WTO members to adopt measures that partially coordinate and harmonize their national IPR laws and institutions.[11] TRIPS leaves plenty of room for other regional and worldwide IPR institutions due to its incomplete IPR harmonization and coordination as well as its emphasis on national (rather than regional or international) IPR laws and institutions. Two global institutions, the Patent Cooperation Treaty and the Madrid Agreement, focus on coordinating priority dates for patent and trademark applications, respectively. Their purpose is to reduce the cost of operating national IPR registration systems by standardizing applications procedures and to reduce transaction costs incurred by creators of intellectual property who apply for IPRs in multiple countries. Both the Patent Cooperation Treaty and the Madrid Agreement create additional opportunities for creators of intellectual property by providing them with an option to delay making a final decision to file additional IPR applications beyond the home country while still maintaining a priority date in member countries.[12]

By contrast, two regional institutions, the European Patent Organization and the European Community Trademark, establish regional organizations to examine and grant patents and to review and register trademarks. These regional institutions reduce coordination costs across national institutions by providing intellectual property applicants with the option of transacting with a single regional institution rather than multiple national institutions. We review these four regional and global institutions below.

Patent Cooperation Treaty

The Patent Cooperation Treaty (PCT) entered into force in 1978. It established an international patent filing system among its 84 contracting states that relies on separate examinations of a single international patent application by each national patent office. The primary advantages to an applicant of using the PCT's provisions are that "(1) it preserves priority in multiple jurisdictions with a single filing and (2) it offers a period of up to thirty months in which to begin test marketing and/or production of protected products abroad, before incurring the expense of patent prosecution at the national stage."[13] In the language of economics, the PCT creates an *option* to apply for a patent in the designated countries. When more information about the product or process becomes available to the applicant, a decision can be made, up to the 30–month expiration date, to exercise the option or leave it unused. Another advantage of using the PCT's provisions is that the patent application undergoes an international search and preliminary examination at the national patent office where it is filed. This usually enables the other designated patent offices to speed their examination of the application. Note, however, that the PCT does not harmonize more substantive aspects of patent law such as procedures and standards relating to patent infringement. Use of the PCT has grown remarkably over the last ten years, rising from 7,095 international applications in 1985 to over 34,104 in 1994.

Madrid Agreement and Madrid Protocol

The Madrid Agreement Concerning the International Registration of Trademarks entered into force in 1892. It allows for trademarks registered in the national trademark offices of member countries to receive protection in each member country if the applicant files an international Madrid application. Unless a designated country refuses protection within one year, the mark is protected in all designated countries.[14] In response to a request by the applicant for international registration, the trademark registration is automatically registered at WIPO. In 1992, over 290,000 international Madrid registrations were in effect.

Forty-four countries belong to the Madrid Agreement, including major countries such as Germany, France, and Italy, but the

United States and Japan are not members.[15] Objections to the agreement include the long period of examination in the United States, the ease of striking down a trademark challenged in its home country, the use of French as the agreement's only official language, and the need for subsidization of foreign applicants by domestic applicants.[16]

To remedy objections to the Madrid Agreement posed by non-member countries, the Madrid Protocol was signed by 28 countries in June 1989. After nine countries ratified the Protocol, it began operations on April 1, 1996.[17] The Protocol closely follows the provisions of the Madrid Agreement, except for a few sections that were changed to resolve objections to the Madrid Agreement. The Protocol allows an international application to be based on a home country application rather than a home country registration; allows additional time to review the application in countries with long examination periods; waters down the "central attack" system; and adds English as an official language.[18] The main effect of the Protocol is to reduce coordination costs, in this case transaction costs incurred by trademark owners in registering, renewing, and transferring their marks in foreign countries. Like the Patent Cooperation Treaty, the Protocol does not harmonize more substantive aspects of trademark law, such as requirements for protection, standards for infringement, or penalties for violations of trademark law.

European Patent Convention

The United States has indicated that it supports the substantive provisions of the Madrid Protocol and has recently amended its trademark laws to reduce differences between U.S. and foreign trademark laws.[19] However, the United States is unlikely to enter the Protocol in its present form, as it objects to the EU being granted a vote separate from its member states on the Protocol's governing board. Observers expect that if the United States joins an amended Protocol, other countries, particularly in South America, will jump on the bandwagon.

Like the Madrid Protocol and the Patent Cooperation Treaty, the EPO allows substantial transaction cost savings to patent applicants who would have applied for patents in multiple EU countries. Unlike the Protocol and the PCT, the European Patent Convention "creates transnational substantive patent law."[20] It moves beyond the TRIPS goal of harmonizing *national* IPR regimes to the challenge of creating a single *international* IPR regime. The EPO sets the term for the patent, rules for inventorship, standards for patentability, and rules for claim interpretation.[21] For all intents and purposes, EPO patent law replaces patent examination by multiple European patent offices with examination by the centralized EPO bureaucracy, thereby substantially reducing the cost to an inventor of obtaining a patent in multiple EPO countries.

Fifty thousand annual applications are disproportionately from large firms. Because an EPO application is more costly than a single national application, firms generally apply when they otherwise would have applied for patents separately in three or four EPO countries.[22] Small firms have stated that they do not use EPO because a national application is usually sufficient.

Community Trademark

The European Union has established a Community Trademark that came into force in 1996. Registrants are awarded a trademark valid in each of the EU's 15 member states. The Community Trademark does not replace national trademark—it adds a new transnational trademark as an option for trademark registrants. The EU's new Office of Harmonization in the Internal Market (located in Alicante, Spain) has been taking applications for Community Trademarks since January 1, 1996 and has issued registrations since April 1, 1996.

The Community Trademark will be attractive to some trademark holders because it is valid in all EU states. The Madrid Agreement and Madrid Protocol are inadequate substitutes in many cases because only a subset of EU states are members. Moreover, unlike the Protocol, registration of a Community Trademark is open to all nationals from WTO member countries. The Community Trademark is quite similar to the Madrid Protocol in its potential to reduce transaction costs to trademark applicants, as only one application is required to register and renew the mark in all EU countries. Where the Community Trademark goes beyond the Madrid Protocol is in its emphasis on centralized examination of the application. National trademark offices submit search reports to the Harmonization Office, which makes an independent decision concerning the registrability of the mark. Appeals of the Harmonization Office's decision are also conducted by the EU's judiciary. In sum, though similar in its operation to the Madrid Protocol, the Community Trademark establishes transnational standards for trademark examination.

IV. APEC AND INTELLECTUAL PROPERTY

At the 1995 Osaka Summit, APEC leaders put forth two statements that specifically addressed IPR issues. The first statement involved pledges (see Table 5.1) by individual APEC countries of initial actions to be undertaken to quicken the formation of a free trade area, as discussed in the Bogor Declaration adopted at the 1994 APEC Summit. Some of the pledges involved IPRs and were, with few exceptions, not particularly valuable. Japan magnanimously offered to speed up its implementation of TRIPS by six weeks. The United States topped Japan's offer by agreeing to implement TRIPS on time (January 1, 1996)! Some developing economies offered to implement TRIPS one to three years ahead of the year 2000 deadline.

TABLE 5.1

INITIAL IPR LIBERALIZATION ACTIONS PLEDGED AT 1995 OSAKA APEC MEETING

MEMBER	INITIAL IPR ACTION
AUSTRALIA	None
BRUNEI	Amending Trade Marks Act, drafting copyright legislation, and reviewing patent system (currently a re-registration system) to ensure compliance with the TRIPS Agreement
CANADA	None
CHILE	None
HONG KONG	Accelerate implementation of the TRIPS Agreeement by 1996 (rather than the deadline of 2000 specified in the Agreement)
INDONESIA	None
JAPAN	Implement a "major portion" of the TRIPS Agreement before the greed date (January 1, 1996). To facilitate international trade in seeds and seedlings, Japan will provide aid to contribute to the establishment and extension of plant variety systems in nations where such systems have not been fully established.
KOREA	Proposed amendments to 9 IPR laws to National Assembly to speed implementation of TRIPS Agreement
MALAYSIA	None
MEXICO	None
NEW ZEALAND	TRIPS Agreement was implemented one year ahead of schedule
PNG	Assessing possibilities for establishing IPRs
PHILIPPINES	None
SINGAPORE	Implement TRIPS Agreement on January 1, 1999 rather than January 1, 2000
TAIWAN	None
THAILAND	Immediate effectiveness of new copyright legislation with respect to performers' right in accordance with TRIPS Agreement.Government is in the final stages of approving a bill to set up an Intellectual Property and International Trade Court.
USA	TRIPS Agreement to be fully implemented on January 1, 1996 (as required by TRIPS)
TAIWAN	None

Source: Ministry of Foreign Affairs, Japan. *The Economic Leaders Meeting: The Osaka Initial Actions*. Osaka, Japan, November 19, 1995.

The second statement, the Osaka Action Agenda, was concerned with the future implementation of the Bogor Declaration.[23] It pledged actions in 15 specific areas, one of which is IPRs. The leaders agreed that *each* APEC economy will:

a. ensure that IPRs are granted expeditiously;
b. ensure that adequate and effective civil and administrative procedures and remedies are available against infringement of IPRs; and
c. provide and expand bilateral technical cooperation in relations such as patent search and examination, computerization and human resources development for the implementation of the TRIPS Agreement and acceleration thereof.

The three measures to be undertaken separately by each country are relatively general. Measure (a) is closely related to measure (c)—until IPR offices in many developing APEC economies are modernized, expeditious processing of IPR applications is unlikely. And technical assistance to IPR offices in APEC developing economies to implement the TRIPS Agreement is already being provided by Germany, Japan, the United Kingdom, and the United States. Likewise, measure (b) is already required under the TRIPS Agreement. In sum, the three measures represent a reiteration of existing commitments in TRIPS and of existing technical assistance programs to speed implementation of TRIPS.

The APEC leaders also agreed to *collective* action, in which the APEC economies will cooperate to:

a. deepen the dialogue on intellectual property policy among APEC economies;
b. survey the current status of IPR protection in each APEC economy including the related statutes and corresponding jurisprudence, administrative guidelines, and activities of related organizations;

c. develop a contact point list of public and business/private sector experts on IPRs and a list of law enforcement officers, the latter list for the purpose of establishing a network to prevent cross-border flow of counterfeits;

d. exchange information on well-known trademarks as a first step in examining the possibility of establishing an APEC-wide trademark system;

e. exchange information on current IPRs administrative systems with a view to simplifying and standardizing administrative systems throughout the region;

f. study measures, including development of principles, for the effective enforcement of IPRs; and

g. implement fully the TRIPS Agreement no later than January 1, 2000, and examine ways to facilitate technical cooperation to this end.

Six of the seven measures requiring collective action constitute pledges of dialogue, information exchange, and timely TRIPS implementation. They place the APEC Secretariat in a familiar "middleman" role that it has regularly played in other functional areas, e.g., transportation and energy. APEC has already established an ad hoc working group to facilitate cooperation on intellectual property among member economies. Measure (d) is, however, a change from APEC's usual routine and merits more examination. By proposing to study the possibility of forming an APEC-wide trademark regime, the APEC economies have suddenly jumped to an explicit consideration of transnational regime building in the field of IPR. This is at variance with APEC's usual aversion to formal institution building.

At the 1996 Subic Bay APEC Summit, APEC members issued updated individual action plans. Member individual pledges once again focused on meeting TRIPS obligations ahead of schedule. Pledges of collective action under APEC's Committee on Trade and Investment were more noteworthy. The Collective Action Plan

(CAP) for IPRs outlined a series of surveys, studies, workshops, and training projects carried out in 1996 or planned for 1997. The intent was to improve understanding of IPR issues among APEC members and to provide technical cooperation to facilitate TRIPS implementation. APEC's individual and collective IPR plans raise two fundamental questions: What are the interests of APEC members with respect to APEC involvement in IPR matters, and is there a productive role for APEC to play with respect to IPRs?

The interests of APEC's members with respect to IPRs vary tremendously. The United States, a net exporter of intellectual property, is the only APEC member actively lobbying for higher IPR standards.[24] Most other APEC economies signed onto TRIPS with great reluctance and have little interest in using APEC to conclude IPR agreements that go beyond TRIPS. APEC's collective and individual pledges with respect to IPRs have therefore generally focused on implementing rather than extending TRIPS.[25] The emphasis on technical assistance, surveys, studies, and workshops in the 1996 CAP plan for IPRs reflects the U.S. interest in speeding TRIPS implementation as well as other members' interests in achieving TRIPS compliance at the least cost.

Looking beyond the particular interests of APEC members, is there a substantive role for APEC to play with respect to regional or global IPR institutions? We examine three possible roles for APEC. First, APEC could reduce coordination costs across member IPR regimes by taking measures to improve the efficiency of IPR offices in developing member economies. Technical assistance to these members would facilitate the adoption of more transparent and lower cost search and examination procedures, thereby bringing benefits to foreign applicants and to the home country.[26]

Second, APEC members could conclude a treaty that furthers coordination of IPRs across national regimes. Models for such "coordinating" treaties are the Patent Cooperation Treaty and the Madrid Protocol.[27] Both agreements are, however, global rather than regional agreements. Of course, given APEC's emphasis on open regionalism, any coordinating IPR institutions that it creates or facilitates should be global institutions, i.e., open to membership from any country. This leaves APEC with two main choices with respect to "coordinating" IPR measures: promote membership in existing global IPR institutions or create new global institutions that are superior to existing institutions.[28] Given APEC's general aversion to institutionalization, promoting membership in existing institutions could be a more realistic goal.

Promoting participation in the Patent Cooperation Treaty (PCT) could be a particularly productive role for APEC. As of July 1996, eight APEC members were not PCT contracting states: Malaysia, Thailand, Papua New Guinea, Indonesia, the Philippines, Taiwan, Hong Kong, and Chile. The large number of patent applications currently processed under the PCT signals that it has been highly successful in reducing transaction costs to patent applicants. An APEC declaration that all APEC members will be PCT contracting states by 2000, coupled with pledges of technical assistance to bring IPR institutions in new contracting states into compliance with PCT procedures, could benefit both the new contracting states and all applicants for patents in the Asia-Pacific region.

Promoting membership in the Madrid Protocol would also be a useful role for APEC. Among APEC members, only China had ratified the Protocol as of July 1996. Most APEC members would need to make only minor changes in their trademark laws to join; if most APEC members joined the Protocol, trademark owners from APEC members desiring registration in multiple APEC economies would encounter markedly reduced transaction costs associated with registration, renewal, and transfer of marks. An APEC commitment to the Protocol could prompt countries from other regions to join the Protocol, which would lead to a worldwide trademark regime to emerge rapidly. U.S. objection to the EU's vote on the Protocol's governing board, however, has not been resolved.

Finally, APEC members could conclude a treaty setting up an independent IPR regime that creates substantive transnational IPR law. The EPO, independent of the EU, is the model for such regimes.[29] A similar arrangement would allow APEC to facilitate the formation of an independent Asia-Pacific IPR institution. To preserve open regionalism, the new institution would also have to be open to membership of non-APEC countries.

An APEC-inspired, independent IPR institution could serve as a complement to other regional IPR-harmonizing institutions, such as the European Patent Organization. By creating additional regional regimes that further harmonize national IPRs, the costs of establishing and protecting IPRs in world markets would be significantly reduced.[30] The main barrier to APEC-wide IPR institutions is that there are significant differences in IPR law across APEC economies that would have to be resolved to implement a regional IPR-harmonizing institution. For example, Japanese patent law allows the patenting of relatively narrow inventions that represent only a small advance over current technologies, while U.S. patent law emphasizes the patenting of broader, more fundamental inventions. The Japanese system encourages cross-licensing of these narrow patents, while the U.S. system emphasizes exclusive control of broad technologies. To resolve the differences between these two patent systems would require extensive negotiation and fundamental changes in the patent systems of one or both countries. In sum, formation of regional institutions to harmonize patent law among APEC economies would be a daunting task, one that is unlikely to be accomplished unless it is embedded in a negotiating framework that facilitates compensation of losing countries. APEC's open regionalism and voluntary adherence make the WTO an obvious choice for this type of negotiation.

APEC is already studying the possibility of setting up an APEC trademark regime. Such a regime would, however, be plagued by the same problems as an APEC patent regime. One possible rationale for setting up an APEC trademark regime could be to place pressure on the Madrid Protocol to solve the problem of the

EU vote.[31] The success of such a venture would depend on whether the APEC "threat" of a competing international trademark system is perceived to be credible. For example, are preparatory measures being taken to formulate and implement the new regime and are APEC leaders committed to the new regime?[32] More importantly, the major U.S. objection to the Madrid Protocol, the EU vote, does not seem large enough to warrant such a large international effort. A better alternative to APEC involvement is for the United States and the European Union to resolve this issue and for the United States and other APEC members to join the revised Madrid Protocol.

V. CONCLUSION

APEC's involvement with IPRs has generally been limited to facilitating the implementation of the TRIPS Agreement. This paper has examined whether APEC has a role to play in stimulating additional IPR coordination and harmonization among its member economies. Coordination initiatives have the highest chance of success. A commitment by all APEC members to joining the Patent Cooperation Treaty and the Madrid Protocol should be a high priority. The PCT allows for considerable coordination across disparate national patent regimes and imposes few costs on economies joining the PCT. And the Madrid Protocol offers an excellent vehicle for taking the first step to an international trademark regime. APEC harmonization initiatives are less likely to generate political support within APEC, as many member economies are not supportive of the upgrading of national IPR laws and institutions mandated by TRIPS. APEC's current focus on technical assistance seems appropriate for a young organization that is still looking for tangible achievements and is averse to formal institutionalization. Further down the road, APEC may play a bigger role in creating transnational IPR harmonization. However, for such a regime to succeed, both Japan and the United States would have to make significant changes in their IPR institutions. As we noted earlier, such changes generally require compensation and are often best accomplished in the context of worldwide trade negotiations under the auspices of the WTO. More importantly, institutions that establish transnational law also require transnational methods for resolving disputes. Since APEC lacks formal dispute resolution institutions, such as an APEC Court of Justice, regimes involving IPR harmonization are unlikely to materialize until more fundamental efforts at regime building in APEC have come to fruition.

NOTES

1. Comments by Jay Dratler, Hugh Patrick, Natalia Tabatchnaia-Tamirisa, and participants in the two "Workshops on APEC and Regime Creation in Asia and the Pacific" were extremely helpful. All errors are, of course, my responsibility.
2. Agreement on Trade-Related Aspects of Intellectual Property Rights, Annex 1C to Agreement Establishing the World Trade Organization.
3. See Markusen, Melvin, Kaempfer, and Maskus (1995), chap. 14.
4. See Aggarwal (1985) for a full analysis of the politics and economics of the MultiFiber Arrangement. See Eby-Konan, La Croix, Roumasset, and Heinrich (1995) for a more extensive analysis of TRIPS.
5. See La Croix (1995) for a summary of the debate over whether it is in the interest of developing countries to adopt stronger IPRs. Helpman (1993) provides an excellent theoretical analysis of the issue, and La Croix (1992) considers the politics behind the decision to strengthen IPRs. La Croix (1992) emphasizes that the demand for patent protection is smaller in an agricultural economy than in an industrialized economy.
6. See La Croix (1994) for a discussion of recent changes in IPRs in the ASEAN countries.
7. The increasing electoral importance of California and its two IPR-intensive industries, Hollywood entertainment products and Silicon Valley software, is another important reason for the U.S. pressure.
8. Stand-alone, or single-issue negotiations between numerous countries often fail because there is no mechanism to compensate losers.
9. See Maskus and Eby-Konan (1994) and Maskus and Penubarti (1995) for analyses of the effect of stronger IPRs on foreign investment.
10. See Reichman (1994) and Primo Braga (1995) for extended discussions of TRIPS.

11. Two countries have fully "harmonized" their IPR laws and institutions when they are identical or have identical effects. On the other hand, two countries have fully "coordinated" their IPR laws when foreign intellectual property owners and applicants receive national treatment in both countries and have well-defined priority rights and options.

12. See Dixit and Pindyck (1994) for an analysis of the value of options in a wide variety of contexts. Since the Madrid Protocol and Madrid Agreement allow for an international trademark, they go beyond coordinating and harmonizing national IPR regimes by producing substantive transnational IPR law.

13. Dratler, §1.09[2]. The applicant receives a 20–month priority period if preliminary international examination is not selected. See also Cartiglia (1994).

14. See Samuels and Samuels (1993-1994) for an extended discussion of international trademark law.

15. Dratler, §1.09[2].

16. Samuels and Samuels (1993-1994, pp. 443-44).

17. China, Cuba, Denmark, Finland, Germany, Norway, Spain, Sweden, and the United Kingdom sent ratifications by April 1, 1996.

18. Samuels and Samuels (1993-1994, pp. 444-47).

19. The Trademark Law Revision Act of 1988, Pub. L. No. 100-667, 100th Cong., 2d. Sess., Tit. I, 102 Stat. 3935, 3935 (Nov. 16, 1988).

20. Dratler, §1.09[2].

21. The TRIPS agreement narrowed differences between the EPO and other major national patent systems, but EPO and U.S. law still differ with respect to the subject matter that can be protected by patents.

22. See Braendli, (1995, pp. 21-22). See also Lees (1995-1996).

23. See Ministry of Foreign Affairs, Japan. *The Osaka Action Agenda: Implementation of the Bogor Declaration*. Osaka, Japan, November 19, 1995, Section C, Item 7.

24. See Gruen, Bruce, and Prior (1996) for a discussion of which countries are net exporters and importers of patent rights.

25. APEC also provides a way for China to pledge "some" adherence to TRIPS despite not being a member of the WTO.

26. Some countries (e.g., India) do not have a computerized trademark registry. This complicates initial searches for trademark applicants and increases the number of submitted trademark applications that are in conflict with existing trademark registrations. A computerized search system could help to reduce the total number of applications submitted to trademark offices.

27. The Paris Convention and the Berne Convention could also be considered treaties coordinating, rather than harmonizing, national IPR institutions.

28. An alternative to the formation of new independent regional IPR institutions would be for APEC to encourage APEC members to join worldwide IPR institutions that harmonize national regimes. However, the TRIPS Agreement is now the major worldwide IPR harmonization institution, and

virtually all APEC members (with the exception of China, Taiwan, and Hong Kong) belong to the WTO and have pledged to adhere to it.

29. See Thompson (1993-1994) for a proposal to set up a North American patent office.

30. Bhagwati and Krueger (1995) have argued that regional institutions are likely to have the effect of retarding world welfare, while Summers (1991) and others have argued that regional institutions contribute to world welfare and to a more liberal world trading order.

31. In the language of game theory, the game's Nash equilibrium is "subgame" perfect.

32. A complicating development is that the decision to study an APEC trademark regime was followed in December 1995 by ASEAN's decision to explore the possibility of setting up an ASEAN trademark office and an ASEAN patent office. At the December 14-15, 1995 ASEAN leaders' summit in Bangkok, an "ASEAN Framework Agreement on Intellectual Property Cooperation" was approved. An ASEAN working group met in Chiang Rai, Thailand in February/March 1996 to develop plans to implement the Framework and more meetings are planned. Are ASEAN IPR institutions efficient from a global perspective or are they redundant given the existing institutions coordinating and harmonizing IPRs? There are several reasons for believing that an ASEAN Patent Organization (APO) modeled on the European Patent Organization could have the same success as the EPO. First, since no global patent institutions offer substantive transnational patent law, regional institutions like the EPO and APO, fill this gap and have the potential to create efficiency gains (if well-designed). Second, the biggest obstacle to establishing an APO would be developing standards for granting patents and examining patent applications. EPO standards and procedures could be adopted with only minor modifications. Third, ASEAN contributions have relatively similar patent laws and should not encounter major conflicts in harmonizing their laws or agreeing on substantive APO law. Finally, several ASEAN countries are working on upgrading their patent laws to meet TRIPS standards and could also use the opportunity to prepare for APO.

PART TWO

THE DOMESTIC POLITICAL CONTEXT

CHAPTER 6

AUSTRALIA AND APEC

John Ravenhill

I. THE CONTEXT

Australia might seem an unlikely champion of the Asia-Pacific Economic Cooperation (APEC) grouping. For much of the postwar period, successive Australian governments were unenthusiastic participants in multilateral trading arrangements. Canberra had resisted the provision in the General Agreement on Tariffs and Trade (GATT) that "no new preferences" should be created, as this was seen as undermining prospects for the resurrection of an imperial preferential trading area. Of equal import, Australian governments expressed frustration that GATT was far less ambitious in its provisions for commodity producers than the stillborn International Trade Organization; its failure to tackle nontariff barriers in the agricultural sphere adversely affected what was at the time the country's major export sector. The Department of Commerce and Agriculture asserted that the continued nontariff barriers faced by the country's major exports ensured that Australia enjoyed no true reciprocity for the obligations it had assumed in GATT.

Governments argued until the mid-1960s that Australia should be exempted from certain international trade obligations because of its heavy dependence on exports of primary products. Australia, they asserted, was a "middle zone" country, with an economic structure "midway" between developing and industrialized country status. Accordingly, Australia refused to bind its tariffs, played almost no role in multilateral negotiations on trade liberalization until the Tokyo Round, maintained (along with its Oceanic neighbor, New Zealand) the highest levels of tariffs on manufactured imports within the OECD, and attempted (until the formation of UNCTAD in 1964 cemented the North-South divide) to portray itself as the natural leader of primary commodity-exporting countries.

The proposal made by then-Prime Minister Bob Hawke to the Korean Business Association in Seoul in January 1989 that a meeting of ministers from throughout the region be held to assess the possibility of "creating a more formal intergovernmental vehicle of regional cooperation" reflected how much Australia's economic interests and official thinking had changed over the previous quarter of a century. During these years the Australian economy experienced simultaneous processes of internationalization, liberalization, and diversification—although not at the same rate. The trading patterns of few countries, industrialized or less developed, have changed as dramatically as that of Australia since the end of the 1950s, a consequence both of the loss of the UK market for agricultural products when Britain joined the EEC and of the rapid growth of the East Asian economies (Table 6.1). The Agreement on Commerce between Australia and Japan, signed in 1957, laid the foundations for Japan to become Australia's principal export market by the end of the following decade. Korea, Taiwan, the People's Republic of China and the ASEAN countries subsequently became increasingly important trading partners for Australia. By the end of the 1980s, the six ASEAN member states plus five Northeast Asian economies (China, Hong Kong, Japan, Korea, and Taiwan) together accounted for close to 55 percent of Australian merchandise exports.

TABLE 6.1

AUSTRALIA'S MAIN TRADING PARTNERS (%)

	UK	OTHER EC	JAPAN	SOUTH/ SOUTHEAST ASIA	USA
(A) EXPORTS					
1913	44.0	31.7	1.8	4.0	3.4
1919/20-21/2	50.3	14.6	4.5	6.1	9.7
1928/29-30/31	46.2	21.3	7.4	5.4	3.8
1937/38-38/39	52.0	11.6	3.6	3.0	10.2
1949/50	39.4	18.9	4.0	11.1	8.2
1959/60	26.4	18.7	14.4	8.4	8.1
1969/70	11.8	10.9	25.0	12.3	13.4
1979/80	5.0	9.3	26.9	13.0	10.8
1989/90	3.5	10.4	26.1	18.7	10.9
(B) IMPORTS					
1913	51.8	13.0	1.2	5.0	13.7
1919/20-21/2	45.9	3.3	3.6	6.7	21.5
1928/29-30/31	40.1	7.7	3.4	4.3	23.0
1937/38-38/39	40.1	6.5	4.4	3.0	15.0
1949/50	53.1	6.3	1.3	13.5	9.9
1959/60	35.7	11.7	4.5	11.3	16.2
1969/70	21.8	12.8	12.4	6.5	24.9
1979/80	10.2	13.4	15.6	12.4	22.1
1989/90	6.51	5.5	19.21	2.1	24.1

Source: For years 1913 to 1939, Dyster and Meredith (1990) and Commonwealth Bureau of Census and Statistics (Various); for subsequent years, Foster and Stewart (1991)

The Whitlam Labor government began a slow process of economic liberalization in 1973 with a 25 percent across-the-board cut in Australian tariffs. The liberalization process largely stalled during the conservative Fraser administration of 1975-1983, which flirted with populist economic policies, but was restarted with renewed vigor by the Labor governments after the 1983 election.

The Australian dollar was floated, financial markets deregulated, efforts were made to increase competition within the domestic economy, and unilateral tariff reductions were undertaken.

Of particular importance to the liberalization and internationalization processes was the manner in which changes in Australia's external economic relations, domestic economic reform, and dominant economic ideas were, and were seen to be, mutually reinforcing. Economic liberalization was perceived as essential if Australia was to capitalize on rapidly growing Asian markets.[1] The impetus for reform intensified in the mid-1980s as Australia's terms of trade collapsed (from 104 in 1979 to 1980 to 87.4 in 1986 to 1987 [where 1984 to 1985=100]). The traditional role of agricultural and mineral exports in sustaining a largely inefficient, domestically oriented manufacturing sector, the economic foundations of Australia's unique system of social protection,[2] appeared to be no longer viable—symbolized by a speech by then-Treasurer Paul Keating in 1985 when he warned that without significant structural reform Australia ran the risk of becoming a "banana republic." Meanwhile, the Keynesian consensus that had been dominant in the Australian bureaucracy for much of the postwar period disappeared, replaced by a commitment to the precepts of neoclassical economics, an economic philosophy that was endorsed by the Labor governments after 1983.[3] Increasingly, economists and government reports saw East Asian economies not only as "natural" economic partners for Australia, but also potential allies in international trade negotiations. Canberra was urged to redirect its trade policies towards the "Western Pacific."[4]

II. THE PRECIPITANTS

Australia's increasing enmeshment in the Asia-Pacific economy was the precondition for the APEC initiative, but the precipitating factors were developments in the multilateral trading system in the late 1980s—of particular import were the slow progress in the Uruguay Round (the impasse at the Montreal midterm review), the growth of regionalism in North America (the signature of the Canada–United States Free Trade Agreement) and in Europe (the negotiation of the Single Internal Market arrangements for 1992), and the increasing tendency by the United States to resort to bilateral pressure in its relations with Asia.

Canberra's nightmare scenario was the fragmentation of the world economy into three rival trading blocs organized around the dollar, the deutschmark and the yen. In none of these would Australia be a natural member. Although some commentators had proposed that Australia should seek to join a North American Free Trade Area, the long history of U.S. protection of agriculture against Australian imports, reinforced by the difficulties that Canadian primary products had experienced in entering U.S. markets, suggested that the prospects for Congressional approval of Australian membership in a North American-centered agreement were slight.[5] In any event, the North American market was of declining significance for Australia compared with the rapidly growing Asian economies. Yet the Australian government had little confidence that it would be accepted as a member of any East Asian regional grouping given the continued suspicion with which the predominantly European-settled country was viewed, particularly in some ASEAN member states. It was perhaps a sign of the desperation of the time that the president of the opposition Liberal Party suggested that Australia should seek membership in the European Community—an even less likely prospect than a link with North America. For Canberra, the sad reality is that Australia's "natural" region consists of New Zealand and the Pacific Islands, the first captured in the Australian New Zealand Closer Economic Relationship Trade Agreement (ANZCERTA), the second in the South Pacific Regional Trade and Economic Cooperation Agreement (SPARTECA).

Meanwhile, the increasing resort to unilateralism by administrations in Washington after September 1985 caused great alarm in

Canberra. Here the concern was less the possibility of an adverse impact on the Australian economy from American pressure on Canberra (although Australia had been identified in some of the USTR National Trade Estimate Reports on Foreign Trade Barriers as maintaining significant barriers to some U.S. exports, especially services, and to U.S. foreign investment in some sectors) than the potential damage to Australian export prospects in third markets where the United States was pushing for liberalization. The primary anxiety was the Japanese market where Australia competed with the United States not just in exports of agricultural products but also in some "sensitive" manufactures such as car parts. Canberra was also worried that U.S. bilateral pressure for market opening in other Asian markets, especially Korea, would lead to an increase in U.S. market share at Australian expense.

In trade disputes between East Asian countries and the United States, Canberra's sympathies lay entirely with East Asia. Anti-American sentiment was rife among trade officials given the difficulties that Australian primary producers had experienced in the entire postwar period in gaining access to the U.S. market and, more recently, the damage that the Export Enhancement Program had done to Australian agricultural exports. Since Australia was in the unusual situation of running large trade surpluses with Japan and most other East Asian economies, yet a large trade deficit (on a per capita basis, larger than that of the United States with Japan) with the United States, few officials had sympathy with U.S. complaints about access to East Asian markets—even though some Australian exporters of manufactures experienced similar access problems. And some evidence existed that previous bilateral pressures on Japan had increased the market share of American products at the expense of Australian exports.[6]

Clearly, Australia, which accounts for only slightly over 1 percent of world trade, was no potential hegemon. By itself, Australia had little power to affect outcomes in international trade negotiations. Bilateral negotiations held little prospect for achieving the objectives that Canberra sought. For a small economy like Australia's, the attractions of a rules-based international trading system are obvious. Not surprisingly, the government's first preference was for a strengthened system of world trading rules as proposed under the Uruguay Round. One lesson that the government had already learned from the Uruguay Round talks was the advantages to a small economy to be gained through coalition-building. The Cairns Group of Fair Traders in Agriculture had succeeded in attracting substantially more attention in the Uruguay Round than any of its fourteen members acting individually would have received. The Cairns Group had demonstrated that an activist middle power with a very capable foreign service would be able to exercise two forms of leadership: entrepreneurial leadership, based on bargaining skills that permit leaders to broker agreements that would otherwise elude participants; and intellectual leadership in which ideas are supplied that shape the attitudes of participants and thereby influence outcomes.[7] Under an activist foreign minister, Gareth Evans, Australia had concentrated its diplomatic efforts on a number of global and regional initiatives aimed at coalition-building and conflict resolution, a process that Evans described as "niche diplomacy."[8] Politicians and bureaucrats in Canberra believed that Australia, as a middle-ranking power, was better placed to take an initiative on Asia-Pacific economic cooperation than either of the two economic superpowers of the region, Japan and the United States.

Coalition-building in support of regional economic liberalization was intended to serve two purposes. The first preference was to reinforce the multilateral commitment to GATT—by attempting to tie the hands of two of the major players, Japan and the United States, and by creating a new bargaining chip to be deployed against the European Community. But if that outcome was not realized, coalition-building with states from East Asia at least offered a fallback position—a Western Pacific economic grouping—that might avoid the worst possible outcome from the

Australian perspective: a world of trading blocs from whose membership it would be excluded.[9]

The combination of evolving national interests coupled with perceptions of adverse developments in the global trading system explains Australia's interests and timing in launching the APEC initiative. It is notable, however, that Prime Minister Hawke's speech was a personal initiative that the Department of Foreign Affairs and Trade had not previously cleared. Neither the foreign minister nor the secretary of the department traveled with Hawke on this trip. The Foreign Minister was visiting Washington at the time; the first that he was reported to have heard of Hawke's APEC proposal was when he received an angry phone call from the U.S. State Department demanding to know why the United States had been omitted from the list of countries that Hawke had proposed as members.

To be sure, the Department of Foreign Affairs and Trade had recently been sounding out countries in the region on their views on a more institutionalized form of regional economic consultation / collaboration. Several proposals along these lines had been put forward from other sources in previous years.[10] And it may have been no coincidence that Hawke made his speech just a few days after the tenth Australia-Japan Ministerial Committee had met in Tokyo and agreed on a joint study of the effects of the Canada–United States Free Trade Area and EC 1992.[11] Japan's Ministry of International Trade and Industry was later to claim credit for the APEC idea, much to the annoyance of Prime Minister Hawke.[12]

Australian officials have confirmed some of the key elements of Funabashi's story: that MITI had earlier proposed a meeting of trade ministers from Asia-Pacific countries (including the United States), and that bureaucratic rivalry between MITI and *Gaimusho* officials prevented the idea from being taken further. When Hawke left Canberra for the Seoul visit, the speech prepared by officials of the Department of Foreign Affairs and Trade made no reference to an initiative for a new body to promote regional economic cooperation. And no consultation occurred with the Japanese government before Hawke's speech. Senior officials from the Department of Prime Minister and Cabinet, and from Hawke's own office, developed the APEC idea in Seoul itself. When the idea was conveyed back to Canberra, it was opposed by the Department of Foreign Affairs and Trade and by the Treasury. Nevertheless, Hawke raised the idea in a private meeting with South Korean President, Roh Tae Woo; when Roh was sympathetic, Hawke then went ahead with the public proposal.[13]

Not surprisingly, the manner in which the proposal was made gave the impression of ad hockery and policymaking on the run and may explain the confusion over which countries would be invited to participate in the proposed organization. In the months following the Seoul speech, the Secretary of the Department of Foreign Affairs and Trade, Richard Woolcott, was sent on a mission around East Asia to explain the Hawke initiative and to collect responses from potential partners.

III. WHY A NEW INSTITUTION?

The Australian government had no option but to engage in coalition-building if it was to have any realistic possibility of affecting outcomes in the multilateral trade regime. But why choose to attempt to construct a new institution? What would be the objectives and membership of the institution? And how, using Aggarwal's terminology, would it be nested within the existing multilateral trading framework?[14]

Although the timing of the Hawke speech may have taken the Department of Foreign Affairs and Trade by surprise, the content was consistent with ideas that had been put forward for some years by a group of influential Australian economists, including Stuart Harris, Andrew Elek, Peter Drysdale, and Ross Garnaut, who had combined academic and public service careers and had been active in PAFTAD and/or PECC. Some of the major themes developed by these economists placed emphasis on the emerging economic complementarities of the region (usually defined in static neoclassical conceptions of comparative advantage), on the importance of confidence building and respect for the significance that many Asian countries gave to consensus in diplomacy, on the need to strengthen the multilateral system and to avoid the construction of a closed trading bloc, on the need for greater transparency in intraregional trade, and on the advantages of liberalization on a nondiscriminatory basis and hence on hostility toward American unilateralism and toward the Bush administration's ideas of a "hub and spokes" model for regional trade agreements.[15]

Hawke suggested that the objective of a future regional organization would be "to develop a capacity for analysis and consultation on economic and social issues" and that there is merit "in the model provided, in a different context, by the OECD." In particular, he identified three tasks for the proposed organization: to improve the prospects for a successful conclusion to the Uruguay Round; to discuss obstacles to the growth of intraregional trade and explore the possibilities for liberalization; and to identify common economic interests and capitalize on regional economic complementarities.[16] From the beginning, no ambiguity existed in Australia's views on the appropriate relationship between the new institution and GATT. Hawke was explicit:

> I must stress that my support for a more formal vehicle for regional cooperation must not be interpreted as suggesting by code words the creation of a Pacific trading bloc. Australia's support for non-discriminatory multilateral trading solutions in the GATT framework is clear, long-standing and unambiguous. I have made it clear that a major priority of any regional effort would be the strengthening of the GATT system.[17]

Hawke's speech did not, however, indicate how the nesting of APEC within GATT was to be achieved. Only later did Australian officials advocate the concept of "open regionalism," a concept first put forward by Ippei Yamazawa in 1988[18] and subsequently taken up by Harris, Drysdale, and Garnaut in their writings.

Why the need for a new institution? Why not work informally through bilateral and existing multilateral bodies to break the impasse in the Uruguay Round? Or use an existing institution with broad regional membership, PECC, for the exchange of information on various dimensions of intraregional trade? The immediate Uruguay Round impasse was soon broken, leaving the emphasis in official Australian statements on the potential role that the proposed regional institution could play in promoting trade liberalization and in enhancing the transparency of intraregional trade. According to Hawke, the tripartite (government, business, and academic) membership of PECC prevented it from playing the role envisaged for the new institution:

> PECC's work has illuminated large areas of common interests within the region. But its informality, which has helped to broaden its membership, has also made it difficult for it to address policy issues which are properly the responsibility of governments system.[19]

The new institution, it was argued, would take advantage of the work done under PECC's auspices. Although the OECD was still cited as a model, this reference was more for the type of activities that it conducted than its institutional form. Australian officials were quick to point out that they envisaged an institution that had at most a very modest secretariat. National bureaucracies rather than a large international bureaucracy of the OECD type would undertake most of the support work. Besides the issue of cost, officials believed that a large institution would tend to minimize Australia's role. Stuart Harris noted that a permanent institution would institutionalize U.S. and Japanese dominance—to Australia's disadvantage.[20]

IV. MEMBERSHIP

Hawke listed ten countries on the Western Pacific Rim as potential members of the proposed institution: Australia, the then-six-member states of ASEAN, Japan, the Republic of Korea, and New Zealand. He insisted in his memoirs[21] that he had never intended to exclude the United States from the grouping, but such an interpretation sits uneasily with the content of his Seoul speech. This appeared to identify the United States as a source of problems in Pacific trade rather than as part of a solution. For instance, in referring to problems in the Uruguay Round and developments that were undermining GATT, Hawke pointed to the United States–Canada Free Trade Agreement. And in discussing obstacles to trade within the region, he made a thinly disguised attack on U.S. trade policies:

> Australia's view is that the essence of a properly functioning trading system is, of course, that countries should seek multilateral trade balance, not bilateral balance with all countries . . . where [trade] liberalization occurs, it must not be used to placate trade frictions being encountered with certain countries.[22]

Other Australian participants in the process have acknowledged that a deliberate decision was made to exclude the United States from the list of members proposed in the Seoul speech. Foreign Minister Gareth Evans stated that the exclusion was an effort to fire a "warning shot" across Washington's bows. Funabashi provides further discussion of official Australian attitudes towards U.S. membership and is correct in his assessment of Australian motives—not only did Canberra want to shift Washington away from its policy of unilateralism towards the region, but it also wanted to distance itself from the United States in its approach to Asia.[23]

It soon became apparent, however, that only Malaysia among the nine other states originally proposed for membership favored an organization that excluded the United States and that, after initial reluctance, Washington was keen to participate. A trans-Pacific organization therefore quickly became the preferred alternative. Canberra had no problems with extending the proposed membership to include the North American countries and the three Chinas—the PRC, Hong Kong, and Taiwan.

The Labor government, however, resisted further expansion of the grouping: it was lukewarm to Chilean membership, viewing Malaysian sponsorship of the South American country as an attempt to dilute the organization. The Labor government consistently opposed Indian membership (despite targeting India as a major potential market for Australian exports) and showed similar hostility toward Russian overtures. The Coalition government, elected in March 1996, initially appeared to be more sympathetic to an expansion of APEC. In its discussion of possible membership for India and Vietnam, its trade manifesto for the election asserted that "at an appropriate time, a Coalition Government would not oppose their participation."[24] By the time of the Manila summit, however, the Coalition had reverted to its predecessor's opposition to further immediate expansion of the grouping.

V. ISSUE LINKAGE

The Canberra consensus, to adapt John Williamson's shorthand description of the views of the Washington-based international financial institutions and the United States government, rested on a faith in the neoclassical argument that unilateral trade liberalization primarily benefits the country that is removing its trade barriers.

Accordingly, and consistent with the recommendations of the report from the prime minister's former economic adviser on Australia's domestic adjustment to the Northeast Asian "miracle,"[25] Australian proposals for APEC made no reference to adjustment assistance. Similarly, the government gave no consideration in the initial APEC proposals to offering special treatment for the less developed participants. The dominant economic orthodoxy portrayed GATT Part IV as a significant mistake that had delayed necessary reform and adjustment in less developed economies. Tariff rates in many East Asian countries were still high. The obvious gains from unilateral liberalization, especially in Indonesia, Malaysia, and Thailand, in the mid-1980s were seen as demonstrating the benefits to the local economies of further trade liberalization. Canberra thus was unwilling to engage in a strategy of tactical issue linkage to sell the APEC initiative to its proposed partners.

The Australian government's ideas of issue linkage were confined to the three areas of trade liberalization identified in the Hawke proposal. Unilateral liberalization would be linked to a diffuse reciprocity through a successful conclusion of the Uruguay Round. Greater transparency on intraregional trade would again link domestic freeing of trade with that undertaken elsewhere. And a significant incentive for several East Asian countries, liberalization under APEC's auspices would be accompanied by the expectation that the regional grouping would construct trade dispute resolution mechanisms that would inhibit the attempt by the United States to resort to aggressive bilateralism. To be sure, Canberra like other member states saw a host of other possible linkages arising from APEC: a means of encouraging a continuing U.S. security commitment to the region at a time when isolationist forces were on the rise in Congress; a bargaining chip in negotiations with the European Community, etc.[26] But Canberra's ideas on specific *substantive* linkages within the provisions of APEC itself were minimal; it was left to the Japanese to develop an explicit technical cooperation dimension to the body.

VI. DOMESTIC COALITION BUILDING

Once the Department of Foreign Affairs and Trade had determined that proposed member states in principle were supportive of a ministerial meeting to discuss the institutionalization of economic cooperation in the Asia-Pacific, the Australian initiative took on the characteristic of a no-lose proposition for the government. The possibility of humiliation, if the Canberra ministerial meeting in November 1989 failed to reach agreement in principle on further work on the creation of APEC, appeared slight. The government was able to portray its initiative as further evidence of the benefits of its activist foreign policy and of its commitment to a reorientation of Australia foreign policy to be more Asiacentric. As importantly, the initiative provided a second dimension to its commitment to domestic economic restructuring through liberalization: the foundation of APEC promised some reciprocity to Australian domestic economic interests for the unilateral tariff reductions that were being forced upon the domestic economy. And for the government, a commitment in a multilateral forum to trade liberalization further strengthened its hand vis-à-vis domestic interests that were seeking continued protection. For Prime Minister Hawke, the foundation of APEC was a personal diplomatic triumph at a time when his leadership was under challenge from within his own party. The Liberal/National party coalition, the largest opposition grouping in the Australian Parliament, which at that time was attempting to distinguish itself from the government by proposing even more hardline "economic rationalist" policies, had little option but to applaud the government's initiative. To have criticized it would have left the party vulnerable to accusations that it was backward-looking, failing to capitalize on the new opportunities offered by the growth of Asia, and unwilling to take initiatives to promote a successful outcome of the Uruguay Round.

As in most other democracies, foreign affairs rarely impinge on the voting preferences of the Australian electorate. Insofar as it was aware of APEC, the Australian public appeared to be supportive or, at worse, indifferent. The coverage that the government's initiative received in the media was almost uniformly favorable.

Nor did the government have concerns about serious opposition from organized domestic interests. The attitude of Australia's peak business organizations toward trade liberalization had changed dramatically in the 1970s and 1980s. Certainly, by the time of the APEC initiative they were enthusiastic proponents of free trade and saw APEC as a means of extracting some reciprocity from other states in the region for the unilateral freeing up of the Australian market that occurred in the 1980s. Similar enthusiasm came from the National Farmers' Federation, which hoped that APEC would accelerate the liberalization of agricultural markets in Northeast Asia in particular and also restrain the United States from continuing to subsidize its agricultural exports.

VII. AUSTRALIA AND THE FUTURE OF APEC

APEC continues to be regarded by the Australian government as the jewel in the crown of its activist foreign policy, a testimony to the effectiveness of entrepreneurial and intellectual leadership by a small economy. Hawke's successor as leader of the Australian Labor Party and prime minister, Paul Keating promoted APEC with even more vigor than Hawke himself. Even though APEC is closely identified with these two Labor prime ministers, bipartisan support for the grouping was demonstrated in the trade policy manifesto of the Coalition parties for the 1996 election, which asserted that "The Bogor Declaration of APEC leaders and the recent Osaka Declaration are major achievements welcomed by the Coalition."[27] On taking office, the Coalition government went further than the Labor Party in its commitment to APEC by appointing an ambassador to the grouping. The Coalition government in general, and its prime minister, John Howard, in particular are less preoccupied with foreign affairs than their Labor Party predecessors and less inclined to engage in foreign policy activism—which may affect the role that Australia plays within APEC.

Generally, APEC's evolution has been very much in accord with Australian preferences: an agreement on a goal for trade liberalization, working groups established to enhance transparency in intraregional trade and reduce transactions costs, and most of the support work for the grouping being done by national bureaucracies and/or PECC rather than by a large secretariat. Yet, as APEC's evolution has unfolded, so it has posed new dilemmas for Canberra.

Two of the most important of these arise from what Ravenhill termed "competing logics" of regionalism in the Asia-Pacific.[28] The first of these contrasts the Asian preference for *regionalism by declaration* with the "Western" (or in the words of the Malaysian representative on the APEC Eminent Person's Group, Noordin Sopiee, a "Cartesian") preference for *regionalism by treaty*. A lack of specificity in agreements is characteristic of the preference of many Asian countries for an informal, incremental, bottom-up approach to regional cooperation. In contrast is the "Western" preference for formal institutions established by contractual agreements. These competing logics are seen in the contrast between the dozen or so pages of the Singapore Declaration that established the ASEAN Free Trade Agreement (AFTA) and the more than 1,000 pages of the North American Free Trade Agreement. The Bogor Declaration is very much in the Asian tradition of lack of specificity about institutional design and agreement implementation, reminiscent of the lack of such content in the Singapore Declaration that led AFTA to be dubbed "Agree First, Talk After."[29] The lack of specificity not only deprives the regime of the potential advantages in constraining national behavior that come from monitoring, enforcement through sanctions, and the retaliation of others against non-cooperative behavior, but it also provides governments with grounds for dissent regarding the nature of the obligations to which they have agreed.

Asian objectives in trade negotiations appear to have been largely *agreement*-oriented, with a great deal of emphasis placed on reaching consensus (inevitably requiring some flexibility in interpretation and implementation of agreements). Generally, the Australian government—and certainly the academic economists who have played a leading role in shaping the Australian position—have been sympathetic to Asian concerns. This agreement-oriented approach stands in contrast to the emphasis in U.S. trade policy over the last decade, which has been very much *results*-oriented. As APEC moved into the second half of its first decade, however, increasing criticism was voiced in Australia of the lack of results to date. The Australian Chamber of Commerce and Industry complained that too much time was being spent on preparatory work rather than on the implementation of trade liberalization.[30] Similar criticisms were voiced by members of the academic community, ranging from arguments that APEC was merely another junket for bureaucrats[31] to those that suggested that APEC *itself* would do little to change the incentives for governments to engage in trade liberalization.[32]

A related problem arising from the lack of specificity in the Bogor Declaration was the question of how comprehensive APEC's program of trade liberalization would be. Domestic interest groups expressed increasing concern in the months leading up to the Osaka leaders' meeting that APEC's substitution of "comparability" for "reciprocity" and adoption of the notion of "concerted unilateralism" would permit countries to continue to practice selective protection. Causing particular anxiety was the suggestion by the Japanese government, supported by China and Korea, that agriculture be exempted as a "sensitive" sector from APEC's program of trade liberalization. The National Farmers' Federation, which had estimated that full liberalization of agricultural trade within the APEC grouping would generate a further $2.9 billion in export earnings for Australian agriculture and a further $1 billion for the food processing industry (to add to the 1994 total for "rural" exports to APEC countries of $11 billion), proposed that Prime Minister Keating should boycott the Osaka meeting should an attempt be made to exempt agriculture. The declaration at the Osaka summit papered over the divisions on agricultural products for a while. If, however, agricultural products do not figure on the future liberalization schedules of Northeast Asian countries, the likely outcome will be significant domestic pressures on the government either to withdraw from APEC or to insist on binding obligations.

The other clash of competing logics in APEC that has caused increasing divisions within the Australian bureaucracy and academic community is that between the economist's logic of unilateral liberalization on a nondiscriminatory basis[33] and the political scientist's logic (based on a Prisoners' Dilemma conception of trade liberalization) of conditional liberalization on the basis of reciprocity. The alternative logics envisage different mechanisms for liberalization and for rendering APEC compatible with the GATT/WTO. For adherents of the "Prisoners' Delight" formulation, the prescription is "concerted unilateralism" and "open regionalism" in which the benefits of trade liberalization within the region are extended on a nondiscriminatory basis to all WTO member states. The alternative logic, of using tariff concessions as a bargaining chip to induce reciprocity from other economies within APEC and from extraregional partners, suggests that the region should move toward a discriminatory bloc that is compatible with GATT/WTO requirements under the old Article XXIV provisions.

For the most part, Australian governments have accepted the argument put forward by the adherents of neoclassical theory that the major benefits from trade liberalization accrue to those economies that are reducing barriers to trade. Moreover, in the Asia-Pacific region, the more rapid growth of intraregional trade compared with that of extraregional trading partners has assured that other member economies have captured the majority of the benefits of tariff reductions by APEC countries. Elek estimated that 70 percent of the increase in the region's total trade had occurred with other economies of the region.[34]

The Coalition government elected in 1996, however, gave a new emphasis to the principle of reciprocity in its dealings with its trading partners, especially those in East Asia (reflecting both its populist inclinations and an ongoing domestic debate on the future of tariff policy for Australia's most highly protected industrial sectors). Reciprocity was given prominence in Australia's Individual Action Plan for the Manila summit in which the government made its commitment to review the general tariff level conditional on an assessment of progress in trade liberalization by other APEC economies.[35] The Coalition government did re-affirm, however, the commitment of its Labor predecessor to a process of nondiscriminatory liberalization within APEC.

The tensions between these competing logics continue to be played out within Canberra. With the successful completion of the Uruguay Round, the government has far fewer concerns about the possible fragmentation of the global economy into rival trading blocs. To date, little conflict has occurred between Australian promotion of APEC and its desire to be accepted in Asia; indeed, the two have gone hand in hand. But if Australia is perceived as siding with North American opinion in favor of a discriminatory trading bloc, and if the action plans of East Asian economies exclude sectors of interest to powerful domestic interest groups in Australia, then APEC may pose growing dilemmas for the Australian government both domestically and in its relations with its Asian neighbors.

NOTES

1. This argument was made persuasively by an official report, *Australia and the Northeast Asia Ascendancy,* by the prime minister's former Chief Economic Adviser (Garnaut, 1989). For comments see Ravenhill and Matthews (1991).
2. Castles (1988).

3. Pusey (1991); Whitwell (1986); Whitwell (1993).

4. Anderson *et al.* (1985).

5. Snape (1986).

6. George (1983).

7. These forms of leadership were identified by O. Young (1991). Prime Minister Hawke (1994, p. 432) claimed that "Cairns established Australia as an intelligent, relevant, hard-working nation whose views on the free-trade issue were well known and understood." Then Secretary of the Department of Foreign Affairs and Trade, Richard Woolcott, echoed these views: "We have not always been successful in the past in projecting our interests in international economic fora. But our experience with the Cairns Group has demonstrated that we can do so. We believe that the world is better off because of the contribution the Cairns Group of agricultural free-traders has made to reducing distortions in agricultural trade." See Woolcott, "Regional Economic Cooperation," *Australian Foreign Affairs and Trade: The Monthly Record* 60, 4 (April 1989) p. 122. For an assessment of the Cairns Group, see Higgott and Cooper (1990).

8. Evans and Grant (1991), p. 323.

9. As Hawke acknowledged in response to a Parliamentary question. *Australian Foreign Affairs and Trade: The Monthly Record* 61, 12 (December 1990), p. 874.

10. Former Japanese Prime Minister Nakasone had proposed a Pacific forum for economic and cultural cooperation in May 1988, described as a "Pacific OECD." Two months later, former Secretary of State George Shultz proposed a series of intergovernmental exchanges on sectoral issues as part of a "Pacific Basin Forum." In December 1988, Senator Bill Bradley suggested a Pacific Coalition on Trade and Development to press for liberalization of agricultural trade and to manage currency volatility with a membership of the Australia, Canada, Japan, Republic of Korea, Mexico, the Philippines, Thailand, and the United States. In early 1989, former Senator Alan Cranston introduced a resolution that called for a Pacific Basin Forum to promote economic and military cooperation in the region; the principal meeting was to be an annual leaders' summit. For details, see Evans and Grant (1991, p. 123). For a discussion of earlier proposals on Asia-Pacific economic cooperation, see Drysdale (1998).

11. Interestingly, the major institutional innovations in the Asia-Pacific region such as PAFTAD and PECC have all resulted from collaboration between Australia and Japan, on the Australian side often conducted under the umbrella of the Australia-Japan Research Centre at the Australian National University. To date, no detailed analytical study of this collaboration has been produced.

12. See Funabashi (1995).

13. Hawke's leadership was under challenge from within his own party at this time and Hawke frequently attempted to use foreign affairs to boost his stature. Never short of hubris, he claimed in his memoirs, "When I outlined

the APEC concept to Roh it was to a man who was prepared out of friendship and trust to discuss seriously any proposal I raised with him. It was yet another example of the importance of personal relations in the conduct of international affairs" (Hawke, 1994, p. 430). Greg Sheridan provides the "inside story" from the point of view of Australian participants in "How Hawke's idea took off," *The Weekend Australian,* January 6-7, 1996, p. 17.

14. Aggarwal (1985).
15. See, for example, Drysdale (1988; 1991; 1989; 1983); Elek (1992a; 1992b; 1995); Garnaut (1989; 1994; 1995); and Harris (1991; 1992).
16. Hawke (1989).
17. Hawke (1989, p. 7).
18. See Japanese Committee for Pacific Economic Cooperation (1988), chapter 5, "Trade and Industrial Adjustment."
19. Hawke (1989, p. 5).
20. Hawke (1989, p. 66).
21. Hawke (1989, p. 431).
22. Hawke (1989, p. 6).
23. Funabashi (1995, chap. 3).
24. Liberal and National Parties (1996, p. 13).
25. Garnaut (1989).
26. For a fuller discussion of the motives of member states, see Ravenhill (1995b).
27. Liberal and National Parties (1996, p. 14).
28. Ravenhill (1995b).
29. Ravenhill (1995c).
30. Australian Chamber of Commerce and Industry (1995).
31. Hughes (1991).
32. Fane (1995); Ravenhill (1996).
33. Termed by Drysdale and Garnaut (1993) the "Prisoners' Delight."
34. Elek (1992a).
35. "Tariff Cuts Fail to Open Export Doors: Moore," *The Australian,* November 8, 1996; "PM to Asia: We Won't Go It Alone on Tariff Cuts," *Australian Financial Review,* November 20, 1996.

CHAPTER 7

THE UNITED STATES AND APEC REGIME BUILDING

Richard W. Baker

I. INTRODUCTION[1]

This chapter considers the U.S. approach to Asia-Pacific economic cooperation as it has evolved over the period since 1989 in terms of this "institutional bargaining game" schema.[2] Principal questions that the United States and other actors must answer include whether or not to work through existing institutions, whether to establish a new institution, what type of new institution (multilateral or bilateral) might be established, what bargaining approaches to use (multilateral, bilateral, or unilateral), and what kinds of linkages to other issues might be employed in the process.

By way of background, several basic considerations heavily influence U.S. policymaking toward the Asia-Pacific region in general and therefore the U.S. approach to Asia-Pacific regionalism and APEC. First, fundamental U.S. objectives in the Asia-Pacific have been remarkably consistent over time. These can be summarized as: to secure economic access to the region; to spread value systems preferred by Americans; and to prevent domination of the region by other powers. These objectives have been manifested in various forms in different historical periods, according to the conditions of the times as well as U.S. national capabilities. The pursuit of economic access has varied from the opening of Japan in the mid-nineteenth century to the Open Door policy in China in the early twentieth century to auto parts and intellectual property rights in recent years. Values that have in one way or another been supported or propagated by U.S. policy have ranged from religion (protection of missionaries) to politics (national independence, democracy, and/or human rights) and economics (capitalism and free markets). And preventing domination of the region by others became the overwhelming consideration during both the Second World War and the Cold War periods. But all three objectives have been durable fixtures of American policy in the region, and they remain so today.

Second, since the end of the Second World War, U.S. policy in the region has been heavily influenced by America's status as a global superpower. Following the end of the Cold War, the focus on the confrontation with communism and the Soviet Union has given way to the more general and diffuse set of concerns of "the only remaining superpower." These global considerations have had at least two major effects on U.S. policy in the Asia-Pacific region. First, they have meant that throughout the post–Second World War period, U.S. policy has been subject to the distractions of responsibilities and crises elsewhere in the world. U.S. Asia policy has been embedded in global emphases such as anticommunism during the Cold War and human rights, an increasing theme in the post–Cold War period. And second, America's global involvements have meant varying but very real limits on the resources that the U.S. government could or would make available for this region. In the post–Cold War period, resource limitations have been compounded by a more general shift in national priorities toward domestic concerns and the associated debate over what America's international role should be and how it should be discharged. A number of voices in the ongoing debate argue strongly for a shift in priorities to domestic issues, at least as a prerequisite for any continuing global influence.[3]

The third fundamental feature of U.S. policy that is relevant to this discussion concerns the nature of the U.S. policymaking process. Power is so diffuse in the American political and governmental systems, and there are so many points of access and influence, that U.S. policy on complex issues is frequently only the sum of a variety of elements, some of which may even be mutually inconsistent. On noncentral and relatively complicated topics such as Asia-Pacific regional cooperation, which do not command frequent or intense attention from top policymakers, there is even more than the normal chance that multiple or conflicting agendas may be pursued by different actors in the process.

Despite the changing conditions and various internal debates, there is a general level of satisfaction within the U.S. government and political circles over the American political position in the Asia-Pacific region. However, there is less satisfaction with the U.S. economic position in the region and a corresponding tendency to push aggressively on economic matters. Most of this action takes place at the bilateral level, but there is also a desire to make APEC a tool for realization of U.S. economic interests.

II. THE U.S. AND THE FOUNDING OF APEC

The changed circumstances in the Asia-Pacific region and the potential for responding to the new circumstances by creating a new institution were recognized by many in American leadership circles in the latter years of the 1980s. The new conditions included the region's dynamic economic growth as well as the increasing intensity of economic relations among the Asian nations, and the adoption of market-oriented economic reforms in China plus the winding down of the global Cold War that removed what had been major obstacles to the formation of regionwide institutions in the

Asia-Pacific. As noted by John Ravenhill in his chapter on Australian policy, between mid-1988 and early 1989, Ronald Reagan's Secretary of State George Shultz and two important members of the U.S. Senate responded to these changed circumstances by calling for the creation of mechanisms for intergovernmental economic consultation in the region.[4] The views of these political leaders were shared and supported by a number of prominent figures within the American academic community as well as some Pacific-oriented business leaders who had been participating in the work of Pacific Economic Cooperation Conference and other regional forums.

However, the United States government took no formal initiatives to follow up or implement these suggestions for the establishment of an intergovernmental institution. Thus, when Australian Prime Minister Bob Hawke in his January 31, 1989 Seoul speech proposed that a ministerial meeting on the subject be held in Canberra later that year, the U.S. government under the newly inaugurated Bush administration was placed in the rather uncomfortable position of having to react to a proposal in whose development it had not been involved and in which it was not even included as a proposed invitee. One result was that the initial U.S. reaction to the Hawke proposal was restrained— if not skeptical. The State Department took the position, as later publicly articulated by Secretary of State James Baker in a June 26 speech to the Japan Society in New York, that the United States would await the response of the ASEAN countries before deciding whether or not to participate in the proposed Canberra meeting.

It is worth noting here that despite its precursors and the broadly favorable regional conditions, the timing of Hawke's proposal was problematic in a number of other respects for the Bush administration. Bush had been in office barely two weeks, had campaigned on a foreign policy platform that was far more skeptical of the prospects for change in the Soviet Union than

Reagan's had been and, therefore, was not initially inclined to sweeping post–Cold War thinking (although this attitude did change after only a few months). Economic reform was proceeding in China, but political reform seemed unlikely, a fact that was to be graphically demonstrated by the Tiananmen massacre in June, and the Bush administration remained opposed to multilateral approaches to political-security issues in the Asia-Pacific throughout its tenure in office. So the reserved response to the Hawke proposal was consistent with the broader perspective of the Bush administration at that time.

Nevertheless, there was never any serious question that, if the meeting proposed by the Australians materialized, the United States would want to participate. Secretary of State Baker indicated as much in his June 26 Japan Society speech, shortly before the ASEAN states endorsed the APEC proposal at their July meeting in Brunei.[5] And starting with the November 1989 meeting, the United States became one of the most active and supportive APEC members, participating intensively in developing APEC's program of work and (at the second ministerial in Singapore in 1990) offering to host the 1993 meeting.

III. U.S. INTERESTS AND OBJECTIVES

There are a number of possible rationales for American support of and participation in the establishment of a mechanism for economic dialogue and cooperation in the Asia-Pacific. Most of these rationales have been cited in one form or another in the literature and discussion of the subject. The major arguments are briefly enumerated below, though not necessarily in the order of their level of acceptance or impact.

At the conceptual or metaregime level, building an institutional framework for a regional community in the Asia-Pacific can contribute to long-term stability and order in this region.

This is particularly true given the relative absence of regionwide institutions in the Asia-Pacific compared with other areas such as Europe or the Americas. As a major stakeholder in the world order, the United States arguably has a strong interest in the building of a stable regional community in the Asia-Pacific. This position was widely shared among Asian specialists in the academic and policy-advisory communities.

The economists' argument for such institutions also applies. A regional economic institution has the potential of reducing transaction costs in American economic relationships with the region, through making available greater information, increasing transparency, the development of common standards, and the reduction of barriers to trade and investment. These aspects are of particular interest to the business community and those sectors of the bureaucracy that represent American business interests, though the degree of optimism that an Asia-Pacific institution such as APEC will actually produce results in these areas has varied widely, and some elements of the business community have been openly skeptical on this score.

A series of more specific arguments can be adduced in favor of American association with an Asia-Pacific regional economic institution. In the context of the GATT Uruguay Round negotiations, which were essentially stalemated at the time APEC was formed, an Asia-Pacific grouping could work to advance the round, particularly vis-à-vis the Europeans who were seen as the principal obstacle to a successful conclusion. An Asia-Pacific grouping was a double-edged instrument in this regard, as a lobby supporting a successful outcome of the round and as a possible alternative trade grouping (from which the Europeans might be excluded) should the round collapse. However hypothetical or even dubious as a practical matter this latter proposition may have been, many in APEC and in Europe believe it had a significant impact in persuading the Europeans to make the necessary concessions to conclude the round.[6]

Participation in APEC (and other regional institutions) establishes the United States as a member of the Asia-Pacific community and reinforces U.S. links with the region.[7] Most critically, it avoids U.S. exclusion from regional councils and loss of assured access to the resources and other opportunities offered by the region's dynamic growth. This argument relates directly to the fundamental American interest in maintaining economic access to the region, and it certainly underlay the Bush administration's concern over being omitted from the original Australian list. It also explains the initial U.S. hostility and continuing skepticism about Malaysian Prime Minister Mahathir's proposal for an Asians-only East Asian Economic Group or (later) Caucus.

In addition to ensuring access, participation in an institution such as APEC helps preserve broader American influence in the region. It provides opportunities to advocate the principles and economic models to which the United States subscribes and to contest domination by Japanese or other business value systems and practices.[8] Again, this argument harks back to historic American interests in projecting "American values" in this region.

The flip side to avoiding exclusion from the region is that institutional engagement in the Asia-Pacific can help fend off pressures from within the United States for withdrawal or a reduced presence in the region. In the post–Cold War context, these pressures are very real in both budgetary and political terms. Such institutional binding can both provide a concrete demonstration of the American stake in the region and complicate efforts to unravel American participation.

Related to the previous argument is the possibility that membership in APEC and other Asia-Pacific institutions could soften or even help resolve American economic disputes with the nations of the region.[9] It could also help constrain American tendencies toward unilateralism and excessively muscular approaches; as indicated by John Ravenhill, this thought was certainly in the minds of Australians and others.

IV. WHY A NEW INSTITUTION?

Clearly, as an invitee (and a somewhat belated one at that) to the founding meeting rather than a sponsor or organizer, the United States did not play an active role in the operative decision to propose a new institution for Asia-Pacific economic dialogue rather than working through existing institutions. However, the actual scenario was of little real consequence in this regard, because the very lack of existing institutions in the region made the establishment of a new institution in this case the logical—indeed, almost inevitable—course. Neither global institutions such as the GATT nor the U.N. (even its Asian regional subunit ESCAP) could effectively serve the purpose. PECC did have a regional scope, but while it had usefully pioneered regional economic dialogue and developed some helpful formulas (especially concerning participation by the "three Chinas"), as a nongovernmental institution with largely academic and business membership, it simply could not fill the need for an intergovernmental mechanism.[10]

In any event, the proposal to form a new institution was one that the Americans never questioned and of which they quickly became enthusiastic boosters.[11] Further, neither the Bush administration nor the successor Clinton administration saw any necessary conflict or inconsistency between APEC and the other existing institutions, whether global such as GATT, regional such as ASEAN or NAFTA, or bilateral such as America's security treaties in the region. Each of these institutions and levels had its value, and although the regional institutions could potentially serve as alternatives to the global institutions if the latter broke down, it was equally possible and considered more desirable that the various levels of institutions could reinforce each other. Indeed, one of the arguments for both NAFTA and APEC has been that it would be possible to take steps among smaller numbers of members at the regional level that were not yet possible within the global institutions, with the idea that this could pave the way for adoption of the same measures by global institutions and thus contribute to the creation of global regimes in these areas.[12]

V. DOMESTIC COALITION BUILDING

It is important to underline at the outset of this discussion that neither APEC nor Asia-Pacific regional policy as a whole is a particularly high-profile subject in the United States, even among the elite. Within the Asia-Pacific, bilateral economic or security issues such as those involving Japan, the Koreas, and China tend to overwhelm APEC as a priority for the top U.S. leaders. And finally, at a time of resource constraints and priority to domestic concerns, any new international policy initiative faces an uphill battle in the policymaking process as a whole. Nevertheless, American support and active participation in APEC have proceeded apace. The relevant question is why, and on the basis of what kind of coalition of domestic interests and actors.

Experts and Politicians

As in Australia and Japan, which were the two earliest players in this field, in the United States interest in the concept of Asia-Pacific regional institutions for economic cooperation and dialogue was originally largely confined to academic/expert circles and a few politicians. The involvement of the American intellectual community in Asia-Pacific regionalism dates to the earliest organized advocacy of regional economic cooperation, specifically the PAFTAD meetings of academic economic and trade specialists starting in the mid-1960s.

Among the early leading figures in this effort was Hugh Patrick, a participant in the PAFTAD meetings and the author, with Peter Drysdale of Australia, of a 1979 study of the potential for a regional trade organization. Academics and other experts formed the backbone of American participation in PECC starting in 1980.

The American intellectual community was a natural source of advocacy for a multilateral approach to the organization of the Asia-Pacific region and U.S. relations with that region. The academic community had been a stronghold of the internationalist, multilateral perspective since the early years of the post–Second World War period when the major elements of the postwar international order were put in place including the precursors of the European Union. The application of the same framework and metaregime to the Asia-Pacific region was thus a logical extension of this world view.

Given the extensive interchange, both of ideas and people, between the intellectual community and the American government, it was not surprising that the regionalist approach to the Asia-Pacific was picked up by some politicians and policymakers. Two recent, direct, and influential examples of connections between experts and politicians are Clinton's Assistant Secretary of State for East Asian and Pacific Affairs from 1993 through 1996, Winston Lord, and APEC Eminent Persons Group Chair (and former Treasury official) C. Fred Bergsten.

Lord was the author of the Clinton administration's embrace of multilateral cooperation as a central element of its policy in the Asia-Pacific region. He unveiled his approach in his first formal policy statement, his opening remarks at his confirmation hearing before the Senate Foreign Relations Committee on March 31, 1993. His statement was deliberately entitled "A New Pacific Community." As a practical matter, the new elements in Lord's presentation related to security policy more than economic policy, regarding which the United States was already solidly on the multilateral bandwagon, but it did upgrade the whole area of multilateralism as a fundamental element of the administration's approach to the region. Clinton subsequently adopted Lord's concept (and its label) as his own in speeches during his July 1993 trip to Asia.

Fred Bergsten, now head of the private Washington-based Institute for International Economics, was appointed as the American Eminent Person by the outgoing Bush administration. Bergsten first succeeded in gaining the chairmanship of the EPG. He then proceeded to engineer the highly ambitious proposal for "free trade in the Asia-Pacific region" by the year 2020.

Bergsten's vision was not only well out in front of most of the rest of the members of the EPG (as evidenced by the many qualifications and even contradictory language included in the first EPG report that laid out the basic concept), it was probably more ambitious than any position that the Clinton administration's policymakers in this field would have formulated or been able to sell on their own at that time. The degree to which it was coordinated with the administration remains unclear. However, the proposal was consistent with the overall regional policy framework, and the administration endorsed it and worked for its acceptance.

The Bureaucracy and Congress

At least in the American foreign affairs bureaucracy, as in the expert community outside government, by the late 1980s there was a predisposition on the part of many officials to support proposals for Asia-Pacific regional cooperation. Many in the foreign affairs and national security bureaucracy came to believe that the Bush administration's continuing resistance to broader proposals for Asia-Pacific cooperation, including in the security area, was shortsighted and risked missing a clear window of opportunity for change in this region following the end of the Cold War. This in turn helped provide the groundwork for the formulation and selling of a shift in policy under the Clinton administration.

A second point to note here is that policies and relationships that become embedded in the bureaucracy and the institutions of the U.S. government tend to have a permanence and a staying power beyond the interests of the groups or individuals who are originally responsible for putting them in place. The APEC process appears to have acquired an increasingly broad bureaucratic support base within the U.S. government. APEC ministerial and other committees now involve at least six cabinet-level agencies. The Department of State and the office of the U.S. Trade Representative are the central players in overall policy formation and coordination, but the Departments of Commerce, Treasury, Energy, Education, and Transportation also play roles in various substantive areas of APEC activity.

Beyond the small but influential group of experts and politicians, the two most critical elements in building a coalition in support of APEC are the Congress and the business community. Both have been problematic, but for different reasons.

To this day, other than a few individual members who are interested in Asia-Pacific affairs, there is no significant Congressional constituency for APEC. If anything, the overall sentiment in Congress has to be considered an obstacle to the kinds of initiatives and agreements that are likely to emerge from APEC. However, on the major issues in which an administration has favored liberalizing measures and agreements, the Congress has generally if sometimes reluctantly gone along.

Nevertheless, in the post–Cold War period, debates over international economic agreements have become increasingly more hard-fought and the margins of victory more narrow. Ratification of the NAFTA and Uruguay Round agreements under the Clinton administration were the latest and closest of these battles, and they featured the introduction of new issue areas (e.g., environmental and labor standards) that seemed likely to become a standard and complicating fixture in Congressional evaluation of future trade agreements. As a result, administration policy makers would have to give very careful consideration before engaging in any aspects of an APEC free trade plan that would have to be submitted to Congress.

Business

The ultimate measure of the value of an economic organization to the American government (or at least its political leadership) is how it plays with the business community. In the case of the Asia-Pacific and APEC, there is some ambivalence in this regard. The strong emphasis in the government's economic policy on export promotion has been reflected in policy toward APEC, which has been presented as a way to reduce barriers to market access. This, of course, appeals to American exporters, who are an influential sector of the business community. However, in keeping with their focus on the bottom line, these businesses are primarily interested in concrete results from the APEC process that will facilitate their own activities, not in the progress of APEC as an institution or regional "talk shop." Further, a substantial portion of American business is more interested in maintaining barriers to Asian imports that are seen as undercutting domestic industry, and this group is more likely to oppose than to endorse the kinds of liberalizing measures being developed by and through APEC.

From the start, some American businessmen have been involved in promoting Asia-Pacific regional economic cooperation. American business participated in both the explicitly business-oriented Pacific Basin Economic Council (PBEC), founded in 1967, and the tripartite PECC, established in 1980. However, the American committees of both PBEC and PECC had persistent problems of funding and recruitment of participation by prominent business leaders.

The American business community as a whole took a similarly detached attitude toward APEC in the first years following its founding in 1989. As long as the discussions at APEC ministerials were largely confined to general exchanges and organizational questions—and despite the consistent support given in APEC statements to trade liberalization and successful completion of the

GATT Uruguay Round—these deliberations had little immediate significance for the American business audience.

This situation began to change with the American-hosted APEC ministerial in Seattle in 1993 and the associated first meeting of APEC leaders initiated by the Clinton administration. The administration made a conscious effort to attract American business leaders to Seattle at the time of the APEC meetings. These meetings also featured the first report of the APEC Eminent Persons Group, with its call for the adoption of free trade in the region as APEC's long-term goal.

The 1994 APEC meetings in Indonesia and the 1995 meetings in Japan, with their respective agreements on the objective of free trade in the region by 2020, saw further increases in interest and attendance by American business. The U.S. administration's objectives for the Osaka meeting placed particularly high priority on steps that would be seen by American business as having immediate, practical value in such areas as customs procedures, harmonized standards, and the like. The U.S. delegation to the Osaka meeting spent considerable time briefing U.S. business representatives on the meetings. At the 1996 Manila APEC meetings, the United States put highest priority on one specific objective that was of direct interest to important American business interests—obtaining APEC endorsement for the conclusion at upcoming meetings of the World Trade Organization of an Information Technology Agreement (ITA) to eliminate tariffs on computers and telecommunications equipment. With President Clinton again in attendance at Manila, this objective was achieved.

At the same time, overall interest within the American business community in the dynamic Asia-Pacific economies appears to be steadily increasing. One measure is expanding membership in the U.S. national committee of the regional business organization PBEC. Corporate membership in the U.S. committee grew from 50 at the start of 1996 to 65 in July. The new members include heavyweight firms from a variety of fields, such as Bank of America and Goldman Sachs in finance, Exxon in energy, Pfizer in pharmaceuticals, and Procter and Gamble, Goodrich, and United Technologies in other areas of manufacturing. Although the Asia Pacific is attracting more interest on the part of American business, the business jury on APEC must be considered still out, pending more tangible results of the APEC process.

VII. BARGAINING ROUTES AND STRATEGIES

Another key factor in American policy and behavior in the region is reflected both in the view of most of the other potential participants in APEC that American membership is essential to the enterprise and in the hope of many that the new institution might help restrain unilateral American actions toward its major trading partners in the region. Following the typology set out by Vinod Aggarwal in chapter 2, the United States can make effective use of multilateral, bilateral, and unilateral bargaining routes and tools, and institutional or ad hoc settings, separately or in combination. The desire to preserve flexibility in the choice of tools and approaches has exerted a powerful influence on policymaking with respect to Asia-Pacific regional cooperation. The channeling of the U.S. reaction to the initial Hawke proposal for APEC was probably fairly typical in this regard. It included bilateral exchanges with major public deference to the views of existing subregional multilateral groups (ASEAN) and ultimate active participation in the deliberations of the broader Canberra meeting.

In the general area of international economic policy, the Bush administration pursued a mixed approach. While it consistently pushed for a global trade agreement in the GATT Uruguay Round, it also initiated and concluded first the bilateral Canada–United States Trade Agreement and then the regional NAFTA. Similarly, the Bush administration's policy toward Asia-Pacific regional cooperation as a whole remained uneven. Secretary of State Baker's major contribution to the articulation of a broad regional policy spoke of a "hub and spoke" architecture, with the United States staying firmly in the role of hub.[13] In early 1992, when the new Australian Prime Minister, Paul Keating, who had been in office for only about a month, proposed that it was time to hold a summit meeting of APEC leaders, the public response of the Bush administration was polite but noncommittal, and no action was taken.[14] During the 1992 presidential election campaign, Bush announced that in a second term he would pursue free trade agreements with a number of Asian nations. But it was clear that these were intended to be bilateral, not regional or even multilateral agreements. The Bush administration strategy toward international trade negotiations was pithily summarized by a middle-level trade official shortly after Bush's Detroit speech on export promotion: "We will take trade liberalization where we can find it"—i.e., globally, regionally, or bilaterally.[15]

Finally, it is also important to note that other events and interests in the Asia-Pacific region were a far greater and more continuous focus of attention for the Bush administration than questions of regional cooperation. The Tiananmen massacre in June 1989 and the subsequent near-freeze in United States–China relations were one continuing preoccupation. The trade deficit with Japan was another, ultimately leading to Bush's ill-starred visit to the region in early 1992, which was recast as essentially a trade promotion exercise with the president playing the role of door-opener for the Big Three American auto makers.

When Clinton came to power, he also emphasized that his administration would use a combination of global, regional, and bilateral/unilateral approaches to pursue America's international economic objectives. The early, aggressive posture taken by Clinton trade negotiator Mickey Kantor toward Japan confirmed the administration's intent to make muscular use of bilateral and, if necessary, unilateral instruments. By contrast with the Bush administration, however, the Clinton administration's policy for the Asia-

Pacific region from the start embraced regional cooperation and multilateralism as a major objective. Winston Lord's "New Pacific Community" initiative became the centerpiece of the administration's declaratory policy in the region. Following the Seattle meeting, the administration's East Asian policy team continued to pursue the regional cooperation track. It lobbied hard for the adoption at the November 1994 meetings in Indonesia of the objective of regional free trade proposed by the Eminent Persons Group and largely conceived by Fred Bergsten, however, the ultimate acceptance of the proposal at the Bogor meeting probably owed more to the support and diplomacy of host President Suharto than to U.S. persuasiveness.[16]

Clinton administration officials worked assiduously through a grueling round of preparatory meetings in 1995 to ensure that the Osaka APEC meetings sustained the momentum of the process or at least avoided high-profile setbacks or stalemate. The prospects for Osaka were considered problematic virtually from the start, for several reasons. These included the inherent difficulty of putting a specific timetable and action plan to Bogor's sweeping but highly general statement of objectives, the weakness of the Murayama government in Japan, which as host of the meeting bore the brunt of preparing the agenda and negotiating an agreed outcome, and the fact that many of the other APEC members did not fully share either the Bogor/Bergsten long-term vision or the American government's view that specific, significant "down payments" were a necessary first step.

The Osaka meeting was ultimately regarded as a success, if only because all of the serious differences were at least papered over and the feared breakdown did not occur. This outcome benefited from a significant assist from the Indonesian president, who did not want to see his accomplishment at Bogor tarnished through lack of follow-up, and from skillful Japanese "Asian-style" diplomacy. But the American delegation could and did claim some credit, despite the fact that the budgetary stalemate in Washington and temporary closedown of the U.S. government prevented Clinton from attending, and the lack of resources or Congressional negotiating authority prevented the United States from putting on the table any significant "down payments" of its own.

At the 1996 APEC meetings in the Philippines, the major objective in the trade liberalization area was for each member to present its own detailed schedule for meeting the free trade timetable. The Manila meetings did not feature significant breakthroughs on any of the issues left hanging at Osaka, and the detailed action plans did not contain any major new initiatives beyond existing commitments made in the Uruguay Round or previously made as part of national regulatory changes. Endorsement of the ITA was seen by the Americans as the most significant positive achievement. However, breakdowns and confrontations were again avoided, and marginal progress was made on the action plans and in several other areas—confirming that the APEC process was now entering a less dramatic but necessary phase of detailed follow-up work consolidating and implementing the broad agreements that had been made at the earlier meetings.

Barring some new turn of events, the consolidation phase could be lengthy. Under these circumstances, one question increasingly raised in connection with the annual APEC meeting cycles is how long—and how—the meetings can continue to provide sufficient substance and opportunities for visible leadership and accomplishments by the leaders to hold their interest and keep them attending.

Despite the continuing work and progress on multilateral regional cooperation, following the high-profile 1993 Seattle summit, the first Clinton administration's relations with Asia were largely dominated by tensions with China and Japan and heavy reliance on unilateral action and bilateral negotiations. The administration had come to office with positions on relations with both countries that had been formulated during the campaign and that were designed primarily to distinguish Clinton from Bush and to appeal to various party and domestic constituencies. In the case of Japan, there was the promise of a tougher posture in negotiations on reducing the trade deficit, including insistence that agreements provide for "measurable results." Even more difficult, and ultimately costly to the administration, was its linkage of most-favored-nation trade status for China with its human-rights performance. Successive confrontations triggered by these two issues tended to overshadow the administration's broader regional policy.

An additional liability for the Clinton administration in its efforts to support the APEC process has been the continuing lack of government resources available for investment in the effort. Particularly by contrast with Japan, which at the Osaka APEC meeting was able to pledge $100 million for APEC technical and development activities, the United States currently has virtually no program funds to invest in APEC activities. This makes it difficult for the United States to implement even its previous APEC initiatives, including the APEC Leaders' Education Initiative, in an effective way, and virtually precludes new initiatives that could influence the direction in which APEC's future agenda and activities develop.

The second Clinton administration seems likely to continue to pursue an essentially two-track approach to Asia-Pacific economic policy. There will continue to be strong political incentives for high-profile advocacy of American economic interests through direct (bilateral/unilateral) action. But pursuit of the multilateral track of regionwide trade liberalization through APEC will also continue, within the limits set by other demands on the time and attention of the top policymakers and by continuing resource constraints.

VII. ISSUE LINKAGES

The United States was hardly in a position to press for linkages in connection with the original establishment of APEC. As previously noted, its primary concern was to be included, and from that position it would have been inappropriate to make too many or explicit demands. If anything, in the initial phase the Bush administration was most interested in avoiding one type of linkage— between the discussion of economic and trade issues and discussion of security issues in a regional forum. But the Americans clearly realized that they could resist this linkage from within the forum more effectively than if they did not participate. The administration was successful in structuring APEC to focus exclusively on an explicitly economic and in some cases highly technical work agenda.[17]

Like virtually all of the other potential participants, the United States saw the APEC enterprise as consistent with and supportive of (and thus linked with) the higher-priority goal of a successful conclusion of the GATT Uruguay Round, and the APEC instrument did prove helpful (particularly at the Seattle meeting) in pushing the GATT negotiations to completion. In this case, however, the actual linkage was somewhat inverse: the only influence the linkage could have on the Europeans was the implied threat that APEC could become an alternative to the GATT mechanism. But the real threat involved was not so much that APEC would or could actually become an effective substitute trade negotiation vehicle as that failure of the round could deprive the Europeans of the benefits of the GATT system.

Another area of asserted linkage in the establishment of APEC that involves the United States is more complicated. This is the hope mentioned by John Ravenhill that APEC would restrain U.S. conduct in pursuing its bilateral differences with its major Asian trade partners, especially unilateral U.S. actions that were seen as having the potential to cause wider economic disruptions in the region. In terms of the Aggarwal typology (see chapter 2, Figure 2.4), this would be a "nested substantive" linkage although perhaps only an indirect one (i.e., not made an explicit condition of other areas of economic cooperation within APEC). As noted in the discussion of U.S. objectives earlier in this chapter, it is easier for

Americans to make (and accept) the case that APEC might help reduce conflicts with Asian countries by promoting economic structures and practices in the other member countries that are compatible with the American system and American economic values. This form of "linkage" is rather indirect and long term. However, there are some respects in which APEC agreements may more directly constrain U.S. conduct—for example, the Osaka principle that there should be a "standstill" in trade restrictions. Provisions such as this could serve to discipline U.S. conduct in certain areas and could supply arguments to participants in internal U.S. policy debates. The ultimate nature and extent of such linkages remain to be seen.

With APEC now an established entity working on a substantive agenda, one area in which the Americans have clearly identified linkage (also substantive and nested) is the question of whether trade liberalization measures undertaken within APEC are to be extended to nonmembers on an unconditional basis. Such unconditionality is the essence of the "open regionalism" concept formulated to distinguish APEC from a traditional customs union or free trade area, and also to ensure the compatibility (nesting) of APEC with the GATT/WTO global trade regime. However, from the American perspective, such unconditionality opens the possibility of "free-riding" by other trading nations, especially the European Union, which shows no disposition to grant similar unconditional access to nonmembers.

Another issue with continuing linkage potential is membership. The United States agreed with Australia and all the major APEC players in the first rounds that admission of China was linked to the simultaneous admission of Hong Kong and Taiwan, following the formula (members are economies rather than states) established by PECC. Further, U.S. sponsorship of Mexican membership in APEC was indirectly (but substantively) linked to the question of how comfortably APEC and NAFTA could relate to each other and "nest" within the global GATT/WTO framework.

The practical reality of this substantive linkage meant that there was never any serious doubt that Mexico would gain admission. With Mexican membership accepted, all of NAFTA was now included under the APEC umbrella. Regarding further expansion of membership, the United States has been more ambivalent, but often, as in the case of Chile, is in an awkward position, recognizing the institutional difficulties of further rapid expansion but politically reluctant to oppose the candidacy. The moratorium on further new members after 1994 suited the United States very well in this regard, but this formula only postponed the issue. The Manila meeting agreed that decisions on new members would be announced in 1998 (and become effective in 1999), and further expansion at that time seems inevitable as does U.S. acquiescence if not active support.

VIII. CONCLUSION

Other chapters have set out the many questions hanging over APEC's future and the relatively heavy agenda of issues and differences that need to be resolved if the organization is to consolidate its position as the premier regional economic institution and have a tangible impact on future economic relations and growth. Many of these questions will be answered only over a considerable period of time and through a complex and unpredictable bargaining process. However, in keeping with the purpose of this project to explore the various options as well as the roles and strategies of the principal actors in terms of regime-creation in APEC, the U.S. record to date and its likely continuing approach can be briefly summarized.

The diffuseness of U.S. interests and the American political system have meant that at the national level, there is little concentrated or continuous attention to the Asia-Pacific region, to regional cooperation in general, or to specific institutions such as APEC and the issues associated with them. To date, a virtual handful of experts and politicians have been the key figures in developing and sustaining a supportive approach to the establishment and evolution of APEC. The core group and its related support network are slowly growing, but they cannot be expected to command significantly greater influence or higher priority on the national political agenda any time soon.

Partly as a result of the first factor, U.S. policy toward economic cooperation in this region has been frequently reactive, heavily affected by domestic political considerations, and has often contained conflicting elements. The combination of America's superpower status and its political system (which is prone to overestimate the country's power to achieve specific outcomes in the international arena) leads to a constant tendency toward unilateralism in American policies and bargaining strategies. Specific issues between the United States and other major Asia-Pacific countries have caused its behavior in recent years to be frequently perceived as disruptive to regional harmony and even endangering the possibilities of building a stronger and more institutionalized regional community, and this condition too seems likely to persist for the foreseeable future. Nevertheless, there has also been room for important initiatives by Americans affecting APEC. Those initiatives have generally involved substantial consultations and coalition-building efforts, and the overall American attitude toward regional economic cooperation and APEC has become progressively more enthusiastic over time.

Despite the diffuseness of the policy process and the multiplicity and sometimes conflicting nature of American objectives and strategies, it is possible to identify a core American approach to regime building in APEC and to argue that the U.S. government has been reasonably successful to date in this approach. The United States has not been interested in a regional economic regime for its own sake, but rather in building regional arrangements that advance compliance with international regimes and that support increased American access to global markets. APEC is seen as a potentially helpful instrument in this regard. To help APEC play this role effectively, American participants have supported institutional consolidation and strengthening of APEC through steps such as the establishment of the secretariat, with reasonable if not complete success. The United States has also consistently emphasized the importance of trade in APEC's agenda, succeeding in making this APEC's central focus in its first years, and will be able to maintain this as a major area of activity in the future. The initiation of the leaders' meetings gave APEC a platform for top-level dialogue and initiatives and a forum in which the American president (when he attends) and his agenda will inevitably play key roles. Most broadly, U.S. membership in APEC has helped ensure that the United States is a part of the basic concept of an Asia-Pacific region. This has both advanced and protected the core American interest in continued access and engagement in the region, and reflects and institutionalizes the continuing reality of the importance of the United States to Asia.

Finally, to end on a more speculative note, over the longer term APEC is likely to have a cumulative impact both on private American interests and on government policies. Thus the more institutionalized and regularized APEC becomes, and the more it actually accomplishes in liberalizing trade and investment conditions in the Asia-Pacific, the more attention and support it will gain from the groups in America that really matter in this area. As this happens, broad American policy and strategy in the region can be expected to give correspondingly higher priority to the interests of—and the U.S. stake in—APEC as well as the rest of the emerging network of regional institutions.

NOTES

1. The author gratefully acknowledges the many helpful comments on a previous version of this paper from Dr. Han Feng and other participants at the January 1996 workshop of this project, as well as additional significant contributions by Charles Morrison to the development of the present paper.

Responsibility for the judgments and any errors of fact of course remains with the author.

2. See chapter 2 (Aggarwal 1998a) in this volume.
3. See Paarlberg (1995); Clarke and Clad (1995).
4. Indeed, similar proposals had been made in the late 1970s as part of the wave of interest in Asia-Pacific cooperation that led to the foundation of the nongovernmental Pacific Economic Cooperation Conference in 1980.
5. Funabashi (1995, p. 64).
6. Funabashi (1995, p. 107).
7. See, for example, Morrison (1994, pp. 66-67).
8. Preeg (1990, pp. 24-25).
9. See, for example, Bergsten (1994, p. 22).
10. Indeed, PECC itself had been urging the establishment of an intergovernmental forum, partly in order to have a governmental counterpart to lobby and work with (see Baker 1994, p. 133).
11. The major issues in this regard had more to do with the type of institution, its membership, and other structural and operational details, and in these areas the Americans were more supportive of having a strong, formally structured institution than were many of the Asian members.
12. Bergsten (1994, pp. 23-24).
13. *Foreign Affairs* (Spring 1991).
14. The inaction was apparently due in part to concern that such a meeting might get into regional security and arms control issues that the Bush team did not want to discuss (*Pacific Research* 1992).
15. Lavin (1992).
16. Funabashi (1995, pp. 89-93). Whether the goal was ultimately realistic or not, it was also true that since the United States was already one of the most open economies in APEC, it would presumably profit significantly from the removal of trade barriers by the rest of the APEC membership.
17. Somewhat ironically, however, with the advent of the APEC summits under the Clinton administration, the United States has begun to see—and even occasionally to advocate openly—the potential utility of these meetings for the discussion of broader political and even security questions.

CHAPTER 8

JAPAN'S APPROACH TO APEC AND REGIME CREATION IN THE ASIA-PACIFIC

Yoshinobu Yamamoto and Tsutomu Kikuchi

I. INTRODUCTION

Throughout the postwar era, Japan has been reluctant to participate in discriminatory regional arrangements that might have a
negative impact on global free trade agreements.[1] It has been a firm
belief among Japanese political, business, and academic communities that, as a global trading nation, Japan must place the highest
priority on maintaining the stable development of international
regimes such as GATT. A free and open trading system supported
by GATT is believed to be indispensable to Japan's economic
welfare. This belief was further enhanced by Japan's unhappy
experience of discrimination following its membership in GATT.[2]

The Japanese have taken consistently negative attitudes
toward any regional integration schemes that were potentially
discriminatory. In fact, Japan has historically fought against
potential and real threats to the nondiscrimination principle of
the GATT system.[3] Thus, when some academics and former
senior government officials such as Kiyoshi Kojima and Saburo

Okita proposed the creation of a Pacific Free Trade Area (PAFTA) and the Organization of Pacific Trade and Development (PAFTAD) in the 1960s and 1970s, this was done with the intention of reconciling regional and global arrangements. The three primary aims of those efforts were: (1) to counterbalance the formation and consolidation of European integration; (2) to contain American protectionism; and (3) to provide collective leadership to maintain the global liberal economic order. Contrary to the idea of mercantilist blocs, these aims reflected a strong commitment to globalism manifested in the GATT system. No regional economic integration scheme with external discrimination has ever been supported as a governmental policy by any successive Japanese administrations.

Japanese trade and investment liberalization has been pursued at two levels: (1) the multilateral level through GATT; and (2) the bilateral level, especially through relations with the United States under strong pressure from Washington.[4] In this context, the provision of the benefits of liberalization measures to all countries (not exclusively to the United States) in a nondiscriminatory way reflects Japan's firm commitment to the nondiscrimination principle of GATT.[5]

With the fluctuation of the global economic system caused by huge imbalances, the frequent use of unilateral measures by the United States, and the dramatic increase of FDI by Japanese enterprises in the Asian economies since the mid-1980s, Japan began to pay more attention to regional arrangements as instruments to enhance the global system, to moderate pressures from Washington, and to enhance the industrial infrastructure of the Asian countries.

In spite of its deep-seated reluctance to engage in discriminatory regional arrangements, some common perceptions are now emerging in Japan that regional arrangements will serve more as "nesting" instruments to supplement rather than enhance global mechanisms.[6]

II. TIDING OVER AN EMERGING CRISIS OF THE GLOBAL ECONOMIC ORDER

Responding to the Global Imbalance—MITI and the Birth of APEC

There have been different views regarding who deserves credit for the birth of APEC in 1989. Some Japanese Ministry of International Trade and Industry (MITI) officials claim that credit should be given to MITI rather than to Australian Prime Minister Hawke. Let us briefly discuss the background behind the Japanese proposal to set up a ministerial conference dealing with Asia-Pacific Economic Cooperation in order to examine MITI's role in the creation of APEC. There were three major reasons for the ministerial conference: (1) an emerging feeling of crisis about the future of the global trading system; (2) pressure from Washington; and (3) private sector interest in Asia.

MITI took the lead because of a concern over the huge imbalance in the world economy caused primarily by the huge U.S. trade deficit and the corresponding accumulated debt, debt issues in the developing countries, and the increasing trade surplus enjoyed by Germany, Japan, and other Asian economies. Although there were many efforts to sustain the international economy such as the G5/G7 summits, the GATT Uruguay Round of multilateral trade negotiations in 1986, and regional endeavors to revitalize economies through the strengthening of regional trade arrangements such as the EC, the above-listed imbalances continued to endanger the smooth maintenance of the world economy as a whole. Without rectifying the imbalances, the international financial system was vulnerable to instability and there was a danger of emerging protectionism. The "Black Monday" incident in October 1987 was a clear market signal that the imbalance would not be sustainable.[7] Japan's response to Asia-Pacific cooperation was reconsidered in this context.

From the perspective of the Asia-Pacific, two aims had to be realized simultaneously: (1) to reduce the trade deficit with the

United States (to decrease dependence of the Asian economies upon the U.S. market); and (2) to maintain a steady increase of exports from the Asian economies to sustain economic growth. To realize both, Japan had first to increase its capacity to absorb more exports from other Asian economies. The other Asian economies were in turn also expected to increase their capacity to absorb exports and to improve their industrial infrastructure. The dramatic increase of Japanese foreign direct investment in Southeast Asian economies after the Plaza Accords revealed these obstructions to the Japanese establishment of region wide production networks.

Thus, MITI took the initiative to establish networks for the "horizontal division of labor" in the Asia-Pacific region through its integrated use of overseas development aid (ODA), trade, and investment. This policy manifested itself in the so-called New Asian Industrial Development (AID) Plan. As the 1988 MITI White Paper pointed out, Japan's role was to promote the horizontal division of labor in Asia and to reduce Asia's dependence upon the U.S. market.

The New AID Plan called on Japan to recycle its surplus to the Asian developing countries in the form of investment to extend more aid and technical cooperation to its Asian neighbors. This policy was also expected to contribute to the construction of horizontal division of labor networks in the region, which had been actively pursued by Japanese enterprises.

MITI's plan on regional economic cooperation, which called for the construction of an international division of labor through more imports, more ODA, and more FDI, was shared by other government agencies such as the Economic Planning Agency (EPA). In fact, in the newly announced five-year economic plan (1988-1992) entitled *Sekai to tomoni ikiru Nihon* (Japan Living with the World) released in May 1988, the EPA emphasized that Japan should promote "comprehensive economic cooperation by combining and integrating ODA, FDI, and trade."[8]

The Ministry of Foreign Affairs (MFA), a bureaucratic rival of MITI, also seemed to accept MITI's thinking about Japan's economic policy toward Asia. In the new Fourth ODA Plan (1988-1992) released in June 1988, the MFA pointed out the importance of continuing to promote technical cooperation and coordination with private sector activities in order to enhance the industrial foundation of developing countries (especially those in Asia).[9]

In February 1988, nearly one year before the Hawke speech in Korea, an informal study group on Asia-Pacific trade and development headed by then-director Yoshihiro Sakamoto of the International Department of MITI was established. The purpose of this group was to study the possibility of creating a new regional cooperation framework that would enhance the industrial foundation of the Asian developing nations and in doing so rectify the huge trade imbalances among Asian-Pacific nations.

Given the political sensitivities that the trade imbalance created in U.S. domestic politics, from the perspective of MITI, the huge trade imbalance had to be rectified as soon as possible. Without such action, the United States would likely have taken more aggressive unilateral and protectionist measures to rectify the imbalance and thus jeopardize the future of the international trading system.[10] The increasing U.S. reliance on unilateral measures and the conclusion of the Canada–United States Free Trade Agreement in 1989 demonstrated a new inward-looking disposition on the part of the United States, thereby diluting the basic foundation of the GATT.

Following the interim report presented by Sakamoto's study group, MITI established a special committee on promoting Asia-Pacific Economic Cooperation in September 1988.[11] The pressing task, they argued, was to enhance the function of Asian economies as "absorbers," thereby lightening the surplus burden taken on by the United States.

In turn, however, there remained serious obstacles before Asia could become such an "absorbing" growth center. These included export reliance upon the U.S. market and the narrow industrial foundation as well as the lack of mature transportation systems, financial systems, and information networks. Thus the committee judged that Asian economies had to enhance infrastructures to develop their huge economic potentials.

The committee argued in its report that given deepening interdependence among the regional economies, regional cooperation would be needed in order to solve such problems. Rejecting the idea of an "Asian version of OECD" because of the region's huge diversity, the committee recommended a ministerial meeting devoted to trade and industry in which all regional economies had common interests.[12]

MITI's emphasis on enhancing the industrial foundation of the developing countries reflected the changing patterns of Japan's economic relations with the rest of Asia. Encouraged by appreciation of the yen, many Japanese companies began to establish production networks around the region.[13] Enhancing industrial infrastructure through regional cooperation was expected to contribute to an international division of labor that strengthened Japanese enterprises as well as those of the developing countries.

The committee argued that even though in the early stages of an international division of labor market forces could be left to their devices, some consultative framework would be required to coordinate systems of "borderless" manufacturing, capital, technology, and information to eliminate barriers that hinder trade and investment activities and to harmonize microeconomics policies. The ministerial forum was also expected to serve as a regional framework to contain U.S. unilateralism, such as the threat of retaliation under the Super 301 of the 1974 Trade Act, through putting a regional constraint on U.S. behavior.[14]

The committee's cautious, gradualist approach was reflected in its four principles for regional cooperation.[15] These were quite similar to those developed in the Pacific Economic Cooperation Conference (PECC). They are:

1. *Gradual development in multiple dimensions.* The report emphasized that Asia-Pacific cooperation should cover trade, investment, technology, infrastructure, and so forth. At the early
   stage of development, cooperative activities should start on
   issues of mutual interest and proceed gradually.
2. *Mutual respect and equal participation.* All economies should
   participate on an equal basis.
3. *Promotion of cooperation on multilevels.* Asia-Pacific cooperation should complement existing bilateral cooperation mechanisms such as ANZCERTA and multilateral forums such as
   GATT, and should remain flexible.
4. *Importance of market mechanisms and the role of the private sector.*
   Asia-Pacific cooperation will provide an overall framework for
   policy coordination among the regional countries to enhance
   the role of market mechanisms and the private sector.[16]

MITI's idea of regional cooperation was in a sense colored by
Japan's traditional policies of the successive administrations that
had emphasized aspects of development cooperation with the rest
of Asia. But it was also a new development in which development
cooperation was closely connected with enhancing the absorption capacity of the Asian developing economies to rectify huge
trade imbalances between Asian economies and especially the
United States.

The Foreign Ministry: A Cautious Observer

The MFA reacted negatively to MITI's initiative to set up a
ministerial meeting for promoting regional cooperation.[17] Its perceptions and attitudes toward regional economic cooperation were
primarily based on its experiences at forum activities such as PECC
in which the MFA had been involved in for nearly ten years.[18]

Since its establishment, PECC, with full recognition of the
region's diversity, had given great emphasis to selecting specific

areas of mutual interests and building consensus among the parties concerned. The group had emphasized "what is feasible" rather than "what is desirable." PECC had encouraged informal communication among members, thereby avoiding the rigid management that comes with tight institutionalization.

To sum up, the PECC process reflected intense efforts to create a new type of cooperative framework to enhance confidence-building among the diverse economies, in which dialogue and communication were more important than organizational structures. The main function of PECC was to diffuse information, thereby contributing to establishing norms and principles for regional cooperation.

Based upon this experience, the Ministry of Foreign Affairs felt that regional cooperation had not yet taken root firmly in the region. Therefore, it criticized MITI's neglect of neighboring states' concerns regarding Japanese economic domination.[19] MFA believed that Asia still needed to build confidence through informal dialogue and also thought that it would be difficult to solve membership issues, such as the "three Chinas," in a governmental forum. Therefore, MFA insisted that for the time being, APEC should be carried out through nongovernmental organizations such as PECC.

In addition, MFA felt that APEC should cover not only trade-related issues but also more comprehensive issues such as energy, environment, food, development assistance, and technology transfer. Furthermore, as the government organization responsible for regional cooperation since the late 1970s, MFA could not accept the idea that only trade ministers would represent respective governments.[20] The negative attitude of MFA toward a governmental forum was expressed clearly by Australian special envoy Richard Woolcott when he came to Japan to obtain support for Hawke's proposal.

In June 1989, U.S. Secretary of State James Baker expressed the willingness to join a more institutionalized governmental forum for regional cooperation. This greatly contributed to a change in the attitudes of MFA officials. Baker's formulation was more acceptable to the MFA for two main reasons. First, there was an acknowledged role for the Foreign Ministry. Second, the proposed regional cooperation agenda focused on a broad range of issues rather than specifying only trade and investment-related measures.

III. THE JAPANESE APPROACH TO APEC

Stalemate in the GATT Uruguay Round of Negotiations and the Emergence of Regional Arrangements

Since the first ministerial meeting in 1989 in Canberra, Japan has been cautious not to create confrontation between the developed and developing countries within APEC, especially given the skepticism expressed by the ASEAN countries toward APEC, symbolized in the "Kuching Agreement." The Japanese approach to APEC has been characterized by its emphasis on development cooperation to establish stable economic foundations in the developing countries. In fact, from the beginning of APEC, Japan has tried to place items on the APEC agenda that seemed more acceptable to the developing countries, especially to ASEAN members. Most of the issues taken up by the respective APEC work programs are those in which the developing countries have interests.[21]

APEC concentrated on those issues promising a high likelihood of cooperation. To prevent polarization, members have adopted a decision-making process based on consensus. Indeed, APEC has placed a higher priority on creating an atmosphere of cooperation and on promoting confidence-building among the members than on solving immediate economic problems. Generally speaking, these processes have been well suited to the Japanese preference for confidence-building and development cooperation as the two most important agenda items for regional cooperation and steady progress towards institutionalization.

In spite of the rising concern of the Foreign Ministry regarding MITI's increasing role in the APEC process, there exists a common understanding in Japan concerning the basic modalities of regional cooperation. For example, the report of the "Round Table on Japan and the Asia-Pacific Region in the 21st Century" commissioned by then-Prime Minister Miyazawa pointed out that for the region to continue to enjoy economic growth in line with MITI's New Aid Plan, Japan had to continue to: (1) persist in its efforts to increase imports of manufactured goods to promote a horizontal division of labor among the regional countries; and (2) further expand the process of direct investment and technology transfer to them.[22] At the same time, the stalemate in GATT's negotiations and the ensuing anxieties over the future of the multilateral free trading system pushed many countries in the direction of economic regionalism. It was feared that GATT might be less effective than it had been in the past.

Although Japan supported the idea that APEC demonstrate collective willingness to complete the Uruguay Round as soon as possible, the Japanese commitment to economic regionalism did not change. Since the Asian economies are dependent on European and American markets, Asia could not have a completely self-contained economic system even with an appropriate division of labor.[23]

Thus it was commonly understood that Japan should not consent to a regionalism that incorporated discriminatory measures. Any attempt to introduce regionalism to the area should adhere to the following basic principles: (1) regional cooperation should be nonexclusive, nondiscriminatory, and open in nature; (2) it should be compatible with GATT; and (3) it should not harm the interests of third-party countries.[24] In this context, APEC was regarded as an important forum not for deeper regional institutional integration but for looser policy coordination at the regional level through the exchange of views and information on structural adjustment, economic cooperation, technology transfer, and other related issues.

The APEC ministerial and informal summit meetings, held at Seattle and Bogor in 1993 and 1994 respectively, however, marked significant milestones as APEC moved to transform itself from a loose consultative body into an organization with concrete goals and a timetable. At Seattle, it was agreed that trade and investment liberalization, facilitation, and development cooperation would be the three pillars of the APEC process. Both meetings indicated a move by APEC toward institutionalizing Asia-Pacific cooperation, or rather a shift in priority from the discussion process itself to actual policy implementation. In spite of these developments, the basic rationale of APEC for Japan did not change during this period. There remained a fairly strong consensus among government, business and academic circles in Japan about how APEC should develop in the future.

First, it should be institutionalized gradually, paying due attention to the wide diversity of the member economies. For the time being, at least, it should be a consultative body, not a formalized regional integration scheme. The rapid development of Asian countries has occurred without any regionwide institutional framework of economic liberalization. Asian governments liberalized their economies mainly on a voluntary basis. Therefore, many Japanese experts have argued that the "natural market mechanism," as opposed to an institutional framework, should be an essential factor in Asian development.[25]

Some Japanese experts have argued that customs unions and free trade agreements would be appropriate for those nations that have lost economic dynamism and vitality.[26] They have also pointed out that through international structural changes of the last decade, some mechanisms to promote voluntary liberalization have been built into the region, particularly in the developing countries. Therefore, some "liberalization competition" to enhance their international competitiveness would be continued in this region even without any institutionalized regional framework. There has been a belief that given a relatively high rate of protection in the Asian economies and the pressing need of the Asian economies to attract foreign direct investment, there remains much room for further unilateral liberalization in the Asian economies. Thus, the concept of "Open Economic Association," has been more acceptable in Japan than more formalized regional economic integration schemes have been.[27]

Second, APEC should maintain its guiding principle of "open regionalism." This means that liberalization measures taken within APEC should be unconditionally applied to non-APEC members. APEC should avoid discriminatory measures not only among its members but also among nonmembers. Japanese ministers who attended the successive APEC ministerial meetings have emphasized this point explicitly.

There have been few in Japan who have supported the argument that discriminatory regional liberalization measures be used as bargaining instruments to put pressure on other regional arrangements to take more outward-oriented positions. The Japanese worry much more about the possibility of severe competition among discriminatory regional economic arrangements. They would prefer a scenario in which Europe would free-ride on APEC while maintaining its current trade restrictions against North America and Asia.

Third, development cooperation should be one of the major items on the agenda of APEC. Trade and investment liberalization through APEC is clearly important, but it should not be the only focal point since many of the regional countries continue to suffer from a shortage of industrial infrastructure. Despite the bureaucratic rivalries mentioned earlier, there has been a consensus that development cooperation is one of the major issues for regional cooperation.[28]

From these perspectives, the Seattle meeting indicated that a serious chasm might emerge among the members over the basic modalities of APEC, as was shown in conflicting views on Clinton's reference to a "Pacific Community." It was in this context that the

Japanese Foreign Minister Tsutomu Hata made a remark at the Seattle meeting containing the five basic principles to be respected by all the members. They were: (1) due attention to the different stage of development and diversity of each member; (2) gradualism with consensus and consultation rather than negotiation; (3) consistency with GATT; (4) open regionalism and unconditional provision on an MFN basis; and (5) intensive consultation and dialogue with nonmembers.[29]

Japan and Liberalization in the APEC framework

At Bogor in 1994, the leaders of the member economies agreed to create a "free and open economic area" by the year 2020. The task of formulating an "Action Agenda" to implement this vision was left to Japan as the next host nation. The task was truly tremendous and difficult to manage for Japan, given conflicting views among APEC members about the institutional form and functions of APEC. Also, given the unstable Japanese domestic political situation caused by the realignments of major political forces, it was even more difficult to touch on politically sensitive issues such as the opening of the domestic rice market.

Through efforts to build consensus not only among APEC's members but also among domestic interest groups, Japan demonstrated a strong commitment to the principles that were finally included in the Action Agenda. There still remain historically deep-rooted anxieties in more structured and mutually bound regional cooperation mechanisms. Preferences for a global approach and "soft" regional arrangements still exist in various parts of Japan. The Japanese Diplomatic Bluebook of 1996 emphasizes, for the first time in an extensive manner, the importance of regional mechanisms such as APEC and ARF (ASEAN Regional Forum) to enhance global mechanisms such as the United Nations and GATT/WTO. It also suggests that multiplex and multilayered mechanisms at bilateral, regional, and global levels alike will provide the basic foundations for global peace and stability.[30] The MITI 1996 annual report also pointed out the importance of APEC to promote further trade and investment liberalization as well as development cooperation.[31] In a sense, the APEC meetings held in Bogor and Osaka played a catalytic role in consolidating Japan's basic position toward APEC's goals of liberalization, facilitation, and cooperation.

Today, many are beginning to recognize that regional economic arrangements are more effective than GATT/WTO because of their flexibility. Regional arrangements could also act as negotiating laboratories for new issues that have not yet advanced on the multilateral trade agenda. Regional arrangements can broaden and deepen GATT/WTO trade reform and, in so doing, provide useful models for strengthening multilateral arrangements. Furthermore, regional cooperation addresses the central question facing Japan— whether Japan is capable of radically deregulating the domestic economic system that many observers believe is necessary in order to cope with economic globalization and megacompetition. This recognition is shared by an increasing number of government officials as well as business leaders and academics.

By combining development and technical cooperation objectives, APEC can more effectively facilitate liberalization than instruments available at the WTO level. In order to further promote liberalization at the APEC level, then, it is vital for APEC liberalization to "nest" itself within broader liberalization developments at the WTO level. Simultaneously, further liberalization at the WTO level is expected to encourage further liberalization at the APEC level. Both WTO and APEC must be understood and developed as mutually reinforcing processes for liberalization to be established on a solid foundation.[32]

Although all members presented their respective individual action programs at the APEC Manila meeting, Japan is not optimistic about the future of APEC liberalization. The APEC style of liberalization, which is based on voluntarism, may not produce and sustain an incentive strong enough to promote the substantial liberalization process envisioned by the year 2020. Given the "fatigue of liberalization" experienced by the developing economies after the completion of the GATT Uruguay Round negotiations and the protectionist measures in some of the APEC economies, the political obstacles alone are formidable. This accounts for the cautious attitudes among the developing economies toward initiating a new round of multilateral negotiations under the auspices of the WTO and the introduction of the protectionist "national car" plan of the Indonesian government.

The best scenario for Japan is that APEC would develop in accordance with the visions laid out at Bogor and Osaka, which would contribute to strengthening the existing global mechanisms as well as encouraging Japanese domestic economic liberalization. However, there exists much uncertainty over whether APEC will develop in accordance with these visions. We cannot deny the possibility that APEC will be ineffective, especially regarding trade and investment liberalization. For example, there is serious contention over how to apply the principle of compatibility in the actual process of liberalization. In fact, there is concern among senior government officials about the future prospects of liberalization based on the principle of voluntarism, which many believe is not conducive to producing the minimum common liberalization sufficient to maintain economic dynamism in the region. Many participants believe that the most that can be expected is some possibility of negotiations taking place among the like-minded governments.[33]

However, it is not clear what policy measures Japan should take if the APEC liberalization process should stall in the future. Even though many Japanese specialists are well aware of the argument that the APEC liberalization process must eventually take the form of "APEC minus X," the majority of Japanese policy makers still consider that consensus must be the basic principle of APEC and that APEC should go along with the "slowest" liberalizing economy in the region.

The Private Sector's Involvement in the APEC Process

Given the wide range of regional business activities among the Japanese companies, the establishment of APEC provides a good opportunity for Japanese business organizations to voice their concerns in an intergovernmental process. They are working to eliminate regulatory barriers in the belief that these efforts will spur further Japanese investment in the region and accelerate the expansion of trade. Their major interests are, of course, to rectify various trade and investment-related bottlenecks through regional cooperation. They have presented various policy recommendations to the government on issues of trade and investment liberalization and facilitation.

The establishment of the APEC Business Advisory Council (ABAC) as a full-fledged partner to provide business advice served as a catalyst for further involvement of the Japanese business sector in the APEC policy process. ABAC believes that no other regional economic grouping has recognized the need to integrate business views in the policy process or attached as much significance to the role of business. Japanese business has a major stake in APEC's success as the major beneficiary of freer trade and investment.

For the Japanese business sector, infrastructure development is the key to realizing sustainable development in the region. However, the current scale of official development assistance is wholly inadequate for supplying the immense capital required for infrastructure. More private sector investment will be indispensable in the coming years. Except for electric power plants, the capital returns on infrastructure projects tend to be low, undercutting their attractiveness to private capital. It is therefore necessary for host governments and aid agencies to establish investment facilitation measures that can encourage flows of private capital into large-scale projects. If APEC successfully forms guidelines on this issue, the opportunities for Japanese companies to invest in infrastructure development will greatly improve.[34]

As an international organization, APEC accords an unprecedented level of discretion and independence to its members. With its unique structure and ambitious goals, APEC's future course of action will depend to a large extent on how "peer pressure" works to facilitate further liberalization. The Japanese business sector is expected to put such pressures on the participants in the APEC process.

It should be noted, at the same time, that there is still uncertainty over whether Japanese business organizations will be able to overcome their internal differences and organizational rivalries to present a common unified position on specific issues. In fact, although Japanese business leaders are quite active in such forums as the ABAC, it is quite difficult to prioritize various recommendations presented by different business organizations.[35]

IV. CONCLUSION

APEC as a regime can be described in the following way: The principles—the most important goals of APEC—are liberalization, facilitation, and economic cooperation, even though the relative weights among them have shifted over the years and have been perceived differently by individual members. The basic norm—the rule guiding behavior—is that APEC is a consultative body based on voluntarism (i.e., concerted unilateral action). Rather than hard negotiations, its aim is confidence-building based on the concept of "open regionalism" and consistency with GATT/WTO. The set of principles declared at the Osaka meeting, including compatibility and comprehensiveness, can be considered a set of concrete norms or rules established to achieve liberalization in trade and investment.

The actual outputs of the regime are individual commitments of liberalization and facilitation measures as well as varied projects of economic and technical cooperation. Since one of the basic principles of APEC is voluntarism, there are no strong mechanisms to promote either the implementation or enforcement of commitments. Constant review among the members and peer pressure by both governmental and private sectors are the primary mechanisms.

Japanese interests in APEC were, at least at the beginning, reactive in the sense that Japan tried to utilize APEC as a means of avoiding or resolving the external pressures arising from its huge external surplus while simultaneously trying to maintain the stability of the economic order in the Asia-Pacific region as well as in the entire global economy.

Japan has also pursued its traditional policies of economic cooperation within the APEC context. The basic characteristics of the Japanese style in forging APEC have been rather low-key and modest efforts due partly to historical experience during the last war. The major Japanese aim, at least on the surface, has not been to maximize market access for the domestic private sector, even though Japan benefited from the trade and investment expansion in the region. Japan could not be aggressive in the pursuit of market access given its huge trade surplus vis-à-vis most of the APEC member economies. However, we may argue that, as a result, Japan has been successful in penetrating the Asia-Pacific region and expanding its economic presence through participation in the APEC regime-building process. In this sense, while Japan has played the usual role of reactive state, it has been successful in economic expansion in this region.

We argue that the above mentioned characteristics of APEC as a regime have been consistent with Japanese basic interests and that Japan has been contributing to the establishment of such a regime, as exemplified by the five principles for cooperation presented by Foreign Minister Tsutomu Hata. However, some Japanese policymakers, officials, and academics alike have begun to have doubts as to how much the APEC liberalization can proceed in the future, given the current set of principles of APEC.

But they themselves do not seem to have clear alternative ideas. They do not advocate that APEC be transformed into a free trade agreement. The most probable scenario is that if APEC becomes unable to prevent member countries from becoming protectionist, Japan would have to resort to the WTO rules. This indicates a clear preference for Japan to "nest" APEC within the parameters of global accords.[36]

NOTES

1. Today more than 100 regional economic integration schemes are registered in the GATT/WTO. Japan is one of the few countries that does not belong to any of them.
2. Japan entered GATT in 1955 after serious efforts to participate in the global economy. At the time of entry, more than 30 nations applied Article 35 of GATT to Japan. Japan had not been given the unconditional most-favored-nation treatment. It was not until 1976 that the last nation to apply Article 35 lifted that restriction.
3. For example, in the Tokyo Round negotiations, Japan waged battles against the European move to introduce the selective safeguard system into GATT. In the Uruguay Round negotiations, it seems to us that one of Japan's major objectives was to contain U.S. unilateral measures such as Article 301 of the Trade Act of 1974. Another objective was to check newly emerging regional economic integration schemes with external discrimination such as CUFTA and NAFTA. To the Japanese, both appear to be a violation of the universal nondiscrimination principle of the GATT.
4. Japan's investment liberalization began in the early 1960s when Japan joined OECD, separately from Japan's response to pressures from Washington.
5. Japan's continued strong support for the MFN principle and its consistently critical attitude toward discriminatory trade principle has been appreciated by the GATT system itself. See Yoko Sazanami (1993, p. 7).
6. See, for example, Hiroaki (1993, pp. 18-25).
7. Minister's Office, MITI (1988, pp. 18-25).
8. Kikakucho (1988, p. 26).
9. MFA (1988).
10. The trade deficit of the United States with Asia reached its historic peak in 1988.
11. More than two dozen business leaders, former senior government officials, and academics were members of this committee.
12. It should be noted that the U.S. participation in the ministerial meeting was assumed to be indispensable because of its deepened relations with Asia, though the committee's report did not mention membership explicitly.

13. From 1987 on, Japanese FDI in the ASEAN countries has risen dramatically. In the years prior to the Plaza Accord, Japan had invested about $900 million annually in the ASEAN countries. After a slight drop in 1986, Japanese FDI increased sharply, peaking at $4.6 billion in 1989. During the four years from 1988 to 1991, Japan invested over $15 billion in the ASEAN countries. ASEAN Promotion Centre on Trade, Investment, and Tourism (1987, 1991, 1992).

14. Trade policy disputes will continue to occur. Accordingly, there is an urgent need for a more rational approach to settling disputes. The idea to set up an APEC Dispute Mediation Service, which was contained in the Osaka Action Agenda, reflected Japan's concern over trade disputes.

15. Ajia-Taiheiyo Kyouryoku Suisin Kondarkai (1989).

16. Based upon the above consideration, the committee presented a large number of projects to be promoted through regional cooperation.

17. On the bureaucratic rivalry between the Foreign Ministry and the MITI, see Yoichi Funabashi (1995).

18. In the government, MITI has been in charge of the PBEC (Pacific Basin Economic Commission), a business-based, regionwide organization established in 1967. As a result, MITI has been virtually uninvolved in any PECC activity.

19. *Asahi Shimbun,* November 9, 1989.

20. Interview with the senior officials of the Foreign Ministry.

21. *Asahi Shimbun,* November 11, 1989.

22. The Round Table Report, December 1992.

23. 23.. The Round Table Report, December 1992, p. 17.

24. The Round Table Report, December 1992, p. 18.

25. Watanabe (1994).

26. The Japan Forum on International Relations (1994).

27. See Ippei Yamazawa (1992).

28. This was reflected in the fact that APEC has fallen under the jurisdiction of economies of the developing countries division of the Economic Bureau in the Foreign Ministry.

29. Speech by Foreign Minister Tsutomu Hata at the APEC Ministerial Meeting in Seattle, Ministry of Foreign Affairs of Japan.

30. *Gaikō Seisyo* (Diplomatic Bluebook) (1996, pp. 11-21).

31. *Tsuusho Hakusyo* (Annual Report of MITI) (1996, pp. 59-90).

32. Ippei Yamazawa (1997, pp. 20-31).

33. Speech by Mr. Toshinori Shigeie, Deputy Secretary-General, Economic Affairs Bureau, MFA, on December 2, 1996, Sekai Keizai Hyoron, February 1997, p. 15. Mr. Shigeie represented the Japanese government at the APEC SOMs.

34. Developing infrastructure is a pressing task for the developing countries. However, it is impossible to finance infrastructure development plans solely through public funds. In order to facilitate further allocation of private funds to infrastructure projects, investment risks have to be shared by the

public agencies. MITI is eager to expand Japanese export credit schemes to cover the private investment to infrastructure projects in the developing countries. Article 21 in the APEC Leaders Statement announced at Subic reflects MITI's eagerness in this area.

35. In Japan, the activities of ABAC are supported by a consortium compromising seven major economic organizations such as *Keidanren*. Most of the major business organizations have their own committee to compile opinions of the member companies.

36. See chapter 2 (Aggarwal 1998a) in this volume.

CHAPTER 9

CHINA AND APEC

Zhang Yunling

I. INTRODUCTION

On November 25, 1996, APEC leaders declared their commitment to free trade and investment in Subic. Building on the 1993 Seattle meeting, the Bogor Declaration of 1994 set the timetable for APEC's commitment "to achieve the goal of free and open trade and investment no later than the year 2010 for developed economies and developing economies no later than the year 2020."[1] The Osaka Action Agenda embodies the will of member states to carry out this commitment and MAPA (Manila Action Plan Agenda) shows their determination to make it a reality. This process contributes not only to achieving free trade and investment in the Asia-Pacific region but also "to increasing the momentum of community building in the region."[2]

Since China was accepted as a member in 1991, it has taken an active role in APEC and formulated an aggressive policy. Chinese officials have attended all of APEC's ministerial and senior official meetings. President Jiang Zemin has participated personally in every informal meeting and has always supported the programs and statements of the leaders. China clearly understands that its major economic relations and interests lie in the Asia-Pacific region. The progress of APEC promises significant benefits.

However, APEC provides not only opportunities and interests but also challenges. China is well on its way to reforming and opening its markets. Nevertheless, China needs time for fundamental economic and social transformation. China hopes that the international community will grant it the necessary time and space to learn, readjust, and change in order to meet increasing challenges that arise with integration into the international and regional trade and economic systems.

China's Increasing Economic Importance in the Region

The integration of the Asia-Pacific economies has been enhanced by the increasing share of trade and investment in the region. Two new trends are significant: (1) inter-Asian trade continues to rise— from 34 to 40 percent in 1990 to 50 percent in 1995; and (2) trade from the east coast of the Pacific, particularly North America, has been increasing to the west coast of the Pacific, East Asia. For example, East Asian markets are becoming significantly more important to the United States as the share of U.S. trade with East Asian countries reached 35 percent in 1993 and is projected to reach 38 percent by 2003—more than twice that of trade with Western Europe.[3]

China was previously marginal in the Asia-Pacific region economy but has recently become a major player. The Chinese have recorded high growth rates since the 1980s. The average growth rate was 9.9 percent in the years 1981-1990, 11 percent in the years 1991-1994, and may reach 8 to 9 percent in the years 1994-2003. This growth illustrates how China's share and influence in the regional economy has strengthened and is likely to increase. Due to its dynamism, China has become a principal engine for the economic growth of the Asia-Pacific region. China's foreign trade has grown fast—more than 15 percent annually in the last two decades. A growing share of Chinese imports is coming from the Asia-Pacific region and plays an increasing role in supporting the recovery and high growth of the economies of Taiwan, Hong Kong, Korea, Singapore, and Australia. It seems that dependence on China for growth of export markets is unlikely to be reduced in the future.[4] Still, China itself faces many challenges. The most serious challenge is how to make domestic market changes smoothly while simultaneously meeting the pace of increasing integration with the Asia-Pacific economies as well as the world market.

China Needs Time to Catch Up

China is undertaking two fundamental transitions: (1) from a developing country into an industrialized country; and (2) from a command economy to a market economy. As a developing country, China needs time to catch up to compete with others. China has achieved great progress since adopting policies of economic reform and market opening to the outside world. However, a majority of China's industrial sectors is still far from being competitive. According to a recent study, the general level of China's industrial technology lags behind advanced countries by 20 to 30 years. For example, the general level of technology of the automobile, steel (with a few exceptions, such as Bao Gang Steel in Shanghai), and railway transportation industries currently matches the level of the United States in the 1960s. Management of these industries is even worse.[5] Therefore, not only is it necessary to support and protect some infant industries, especially the automobile, computer, and telecommunication industries, but it is also imperative to improve the state of knowledge and skills through education and training.

To Manage the Smooth Transition

The central challenge is to manage the transition towards a socialist market system from the old planned economy. The biggest obstacle lies in reforming state-owned enterprises. Following the government's new policy of "focusing on the large ones [industrial sectors] and decentralizing the small ones," reforms are speeding up. The aim of the reforms is to make state-owned enterprises more efficient and competitive. But it is important to understand that these reforms are not just a simple matter of changing the ownership or management system. The government has to keep a balance between efficiency and employment. The public sector employs approximately 100 million people. According to some estimates, as many as one-third of them are unnecessary, but all of them rely on the government for social services such as pension, health care, and housing.

Furthermore, the state-owned enterprises are facing three serious challenges in their own domestic market: 1) strong competition from the non-state sector, which enjoys advantages such as lower tax burdens and social costs; 2) increasing competition from joint ventures with international corporations whose products are sold on the domestic market; and 3) steadily intensifying competition from imported products. These challenges add to the pressures on the government to consider the many domestic difficulties in carrying out market liberalization. The State Economic and Trade Commission, which is responsible for domestic industrial restructuring, development, and coordinating action plans related to the APEC action agenda, has received increasing pressures not to "give up" the domestic market to foreign companies and to take effective protectionist measures. China continues to face challenges from increasing sales and investment of multinationals in the domestic market as well as from pressures to liberalize. China has to find an effective way to enhance its competitive ability while protecting its market.

In the end, the success of Chinese economic development will depend on an open system. Foreign trade has played a significant role in the Chinese economy, with its share of GDP as high as 40 percent (export 21 percent, import 19 percent) (see Table 9.1).

TABLE 9.1

SHARE OF FOREIGN TRADE IN GDP (%)

YEAR	1978	1980	1985	1990	1993	1994	1995
TOTAL	9.8	12.6	22.3	30.0	32.7	45.4	40.1
EXPORT	4.6	6.9	9.0	16.1	15.3	23.2	21.2

Source: *China Statistical Yearbook*, 1995, 1996

More importantly, almost half of the foreign trade is through foreign firms and joint ventures in China, which demonstrates a very high percentage of direct integration of the economy with the world market.[6] China must keep its economy open despite the many domestic pressures that it will continue to face in the future due to foreign trade and FDI.

II. CHINA'S INTEREST IN APEC

APEC is a natural result of the increasing integration and interdependence among economies in the region. From the idea of a Pacific Free Trade Area in 1965 to the establishment of the Pacific Basin Economic Council (PBEC) in 1967 and the Pacific Economic Cooperation Council (PECC) in 1980, these efforts paved the way for the creation of APEC in 1989. APEC has provided opportunities for the first time in history for countries on both sides of the Pacific to sit together in one pan-regional framework and for the benefit of their economic development and interests. As pointed out in the chairman's statement during the first ministerial meeting during November 6-7, 1989 in Canberra, "the increasing interdependence of regional economies indicates a need for effective consultations among regional decision makers to help strengthen the multilateral trading system and enhance the prospects for success in the Uruguay round; to provide an opportunity to assess prospects for, and obstacles to, increased trade and investment flows within the Asia-Pacific region, and to identify the range of practical common interests."[7] Although APEC is designed to meet the needs and interests of the Asia-Pacific region, such recognition is difficult for China.

A Changed Attitude toward the Outside World

What were the motives behind China's decision to join APEC? The simple answer is that China needs APEC. The Chinese economy was basically closed to the outside world in the prereform period. Very limited foreign trade at that time explains China's minimal interest in considering the development and change occurring in other parts of the world economy. This also made China suspicious of any regional cooperative activities since they were perceived to be hostile. One example is China's strong criticism of the original creation of the European Common Market. The policy of reform and opening to the outside world that started in 1978 has drastically changed the structure of the Chinese economy and its relation to the outside world. Foreign trade has grown faster than the other sectors and has led to a significantly expanding share of the domestic economy. The value of China's import and export has grown from U.S. $20.6 billion in 1978 to U.S. $281 billion in 1995 and the annual growth rate has been as high as 15 percent. Foreign direct investment (FDI), along with foreign trade, plays a crucial role in the dynamic growth of the Chinese economy. Total FDI flows to China reached U.S. $135 billion in 1995. This included approximately 120,000 foreign funded enterprises, with a total work force of 16 million.[8] These developments have led China to make linkages and participate in the regional economy.

China has shown consistent interest in the activities of Asia-Pacific cooperation since becoming engaged in the activities of PECC in the early 1980s. China sent its first delegation to the fifth PECC general meeting in November 1986 and expressed interest in strengthening its economic ties with the pacific region. Now is the perfect opportunity for China to show its clear support by participating directly in the regional forum. Even though China was excluded from the original founding members, it supports "creating a more formal intergovernmental vehicle of regional cooperation through the formation of APEC," proposed by the former Australian Prime Minister Robert Hawke. This was probably due to the effect of the Tiananmen event in 1989. However, in Chairman Evans's summary statement of the first ministerial meeting of APEC during November 6-7, 1989, he "noted the importance of the People's Republic of China and the economies of Hong Kong and Taiwan to future prosperity of the Asia-Pacific region," and it was agreed that it would be desirable to consider further involvement of these three economies in the process of Asia Pacific Economic Cooperation.[9] China, together with Taiwan and Hong Kong as economic regions, were soon accepted as members of APEC in 1991. This was praised as "a positive development in Asia-Pacific economic cooperation" by Chinese Foreign Minister Qian Qichen.[10] It is a tremendous breakthrough for China to allow Hong Kong and Taiwan to have the status of independent economies and equal member in a regional economic forum that is designed to facilitate deeper integration among member countries.

Focusing on the Asia-Pacific Market

China understands that it belongs to the Asia-Pacific region since over 75 percent of its foreign trade and more than 90 percent of the foreign capital inflow come from this region (see Tables 9.2 and 9.3). Japan, the United States, and Hong Kong are the three largest trade partners and the major source of FDI in China. However, the importance of other new partners, like South Korea and ASEAN countries, is growing. For example, South Korea's trade and direct investment to China have increased significantly in recent years. On the other hand, the importance of China's economy to the other countries of the region is also growing since China is considered to be the "locomotive for the region" due to its high economic growth

TABLE 9.2

CHINA'S TRADE WITH ASIA-PACIFIC REGION

(IN BILLIONS OF U.S. DOLLARS)

	1990		1991		1992		1993		1994	
	VOL.	%	VOL.	%	VOL.	%	VOL.	%	VOL.	%
TOTAL	115.4		135.6		165.5		195.7		236.7	
ASIA*	73.6	63.8	90.9	67.0	110.1	66.5	115.2	58.9	142.2	60.1
JAPAN	16.6	14.4	20.3	14.9	25.4	15.3	39.0	20.0	47.9	20.2
US	11.8	10.2	14.2	10.4	17.5	10.6	27.7	14.1	35.4	15.0

*Including Japan
Source: *China Statistical Yearbook,* 1992, 1993, 1994, 1995

rates.[11] Increasing imports from China has become an important factor in maintaining high economic growth.

Regionalization in the Asia-Pacific is a natural result of open structures. One of the striking features of East Asian economic success is a continuous process of unilateral market liberalization (i.e., principles of nondiscrimination). China has achieved great success through its policies of economic reform and opening to the outside world. However, China faces challenges and competition from other Asia-Pacific countries, especially members of ASEAN. It is a strategic choice for China to join APEC, not only to meet these challenges but also to take advantage of opportunities. ASEAN has moved ahead in its internal liberalization through establishing an ASEAN Free Trade Area (AFTA). AFTA's stated objective is to enhance ASEAN's attractiveness as an investment location and market. China takes this challenge very seriously.

Witnessing the progress of regional integration, China does not want to miss the boat. As the largest developing economy, China no doubt will benefit immensely from trade and investment liberalization. This, of course, does not mean that China holds no reservations about APEC. China fears that developed members, especially the United States, may dominate APEC. Zhu Shoushen, for example, warned that it is important to prevent APEC from possible domina-

TABLE 9.3

CAPITAL FLOW TO CHINA (IN BILLION U.S. DOLLARS)

	1990		1991		1992		1993		1994	
	TOTAL	FDI	TOTAL	FDI	TOTAL	FDI	TOTAL	FDI	TOTAL	FDI
TOTAL	10.3	2.7	11.6	4.4	19.2	11.0	39.0	27.5	43.2	33.8
ASIA*	5.8	2.7	5.4	3.8	13.4	10.1	29.3	24.0	29.6	28.5
JAPAN	3.0	0.5	2.8	2.6	8.4	7.7	18.9	17.4	19.8	19.8
EUROPE	4.5	0.2	2.2	0.3	2.1	0.3	3.0	0.8	4.1	1.7
US	0.6	0.5	0.5	0.3	0.6	0.5	2.7	2.1	3.0	2.5

*including Japan and Hong Kong
Source: *China Statistical Yearbook*, 1992, 1993, 1994, 1995

tion by developed groups.[12] Suspicions are widespread among Chinese economists as well as policy makers that the primary U.S. interest in APEC is to open up the markets of Asian members. This provides China with the incentive to promote a "two wheels' process" (i.e., a parallel process of trade and investment liberalization as well as economic and technical cooperation). As one might expect, China has been insisting that developed members should contribute more in an effort to help developing members catch up and to compensate for the costs of liberalization.[13]

III. KEEPING APEC FLEXIBLE

Opening the market to the outside world is a natural part of China's economic development. However, China does not want the market to open too quickly since it is still a large developing country with very low per capita income. In addition, it is still on the difficult road of transition from a planned economic system to a market system. Although China wants to be a part of the international trade and investment system, China needs more time and room to reform and change. Regarding integration into APEC, China wants a more unilateral and gradual method. China supports the continuous progress of APEC, but it does not want to have a strong organization with mandatory powers that can force it to change beyond its ability and desire.

What China Wants

China considers the following principles most desirable for APEC:

1. Voluntary and unilateral efforts of member economies, not mandatory directives or hard negotiations. Consultations and commitments, rather than binding agreements, should be insisted upon. China insists that APEC be an open and flexible forum rather than a closed and institutionalized economic group.
2. Consideration for the divergent developmental conditions of the members. APEC should allow flexibility for member economies to have the freedom to arrange action plans within the timetable.
3. Equality, equity, and mutual benefit. It is vital to avoid discrimination, which means that liberalization of trade and investment should serve all member economies.
4. Economic and technical cooperation should be strengthened along with liberalization and the facilitation of trade and investment.

President Jiang Zemin put forward four principles for economic cooperation during the Seattle meeting: "mutual respect, equality and mutual benefit, opening up to each other, as well as common prosperity."[14] During the Jakarta informal summit meeting in November 1994, five more principles were mentioned: (1) mutual respect and consultative consensus; (2) gradual progress and stable development; (3) opening to each other and nondiscrimination; (4) comprehensive cooperation and mutual benefit; and (5) reducing the development gap and common prosperity.

The above points were reemphasized during the Osaka summit meeting and further summarized as "the APEC approach" during the Subic meeting. They clearly reflect China's general stand on its participation in APEC activities.

China is not alone in insisting on these principles. ASEAN set out the basis of its participation in APEC in early 1990, known as the Kuching Consensus, in which the principles of mutual benefit, diversity, an open system, a consultative forum, and gradualism were stressed.[15] In fact, these principles are well reflected in major documents of the APEC leaders' meetings. For example, the Seoul APEC Declaration of 1991 clearly reflected concern for these principles in the mode of APEC operation.[16]

Institution-building is an irreversible trend of APEC development. In general, China seems to accept this trend. But what China really wants is for this trend to progress gradually while taking into consideration the very different conditions of the member economies. To China, institution building does not mean that APEC becomes a superorganization with the power to arrange regional affairs. More specifically, China rejects the intention to include political, especially security issues on APEC's agenda since China worries that this may turn APEC in the wrong direction, such as possibly becoming a U.S.-dominated "community."

The Positive Role of APEC

APEC is a process through which China can participate and change. In fact, APEC has already played a positive role in promoting change and reform in China. For example, China announced major new moves in slashing import tariffs on 4,000 items by 30 percent beginning in April 1996. Among the measures made by China at the Osaka meeting were: (1) giving up close to 170 kinds of import quotas, licenses, and control measures; (2) allowing for some experiments in joint ventures in the foreign trade sector; and (3) opening some retail businesses to foreign investors. China's action showed how unilateral and voluntary liberalization could work in APEC.

One may ask whether China would have taken these measures if there were no APEC; the answer is no. This "down payment" reflects at least two clear dimensions: (1) it shows China's intention to support APEC; and (2) it illustrates how the APEC agenda has pressured China to take some "significant actions." The big package of measures was perceived as "a significant decision" made by the Chinese government to show its willingness to follow APEC's process of liberalization. On the other hand, China might have also intended to show the United States that it could make tremendous progress in multilateral cooperation even without the hard negotiations that have characterized past attempts to enter the GATT/WTO. The current down payment greatly exceeds the commitments made by China during the negotiations for GATT entry. International participation will play an important role in giving China the opportunity to learn and will also pressure China to change. But China enjoys keeping the initiative in its own hands.

Many may remain suspicious of the effectiveness of APEC's "soft approach" of unilateral and voluntary liberalization and facilitation of free trade and investment in the Asia-Pacific region. However, the result of the Osaka meeting has led leaders such as Australian Prime Minister Paul Keating to become more confident about the future: "Judging by the packages we got today, it's going to get us to the target dates and get us there very adequately." Prime Minister Mahathir is also warming to APEC, stating that: "I am quite sure APEC is going to play an ever-increasing role in the development of the economies in the Asia-Pacific region as well as in the world. Whether people like it or not, APEC is going to grow."[17]

APEC is already on the track toward the goal of trade and investment liberalization and facilitation. The free-trade-by-2020 objective is reflected in the Action Agenda passed at the Osaka meeting as well as the nonbinding action plans of individual member economies presented at Subic. APEC seems to have its own approach to regional integration. These mechanisms include: (a) concerted unilateral actions based on the needs of the economic development for member economies and agreed-upon guiding principles and targets; (b) collective actions coordinated by all member economies ranging from tariff database and investment guidebooks to training and business visas; and (c) regular monitoring and review of the implementation of principles, targets, and commitments.

There are, of course, some dangers to this "soft approach." One possible danger is that those who need to do more may offer to do less, which makes the lists of the actions inequitable. Another danger is that each member chooses the easy reforms first, and the momentum weakens when there are no easy reforms left to choose. The challenge is to strike a balance between the pace of liberalization and the benefits among the developing and developed members, whose markets are generally more open than those of the developing economies. It is important to gather enough evidence to convince the policymakers of all participants, especially major developed economies, like the United States, that APEC can overcome the difficulties inherent in a soft approach and move forward quickly. Due to the different stages and levels of market liberalization, equal contribution cannot be expected by member countries. According to Hadi Soesastro, "For some time to come East Asia should continue forcefully with its own liberalization without worrying about applying the principle of comparability to U.S. liberalization efforts. East Asia should allow the U.S. to essentially free-ride, that is to do nothing for a number of years to come." This may be logical since the U.S. economy "is already much more open than many East Asian economies."[18] However, not only China but also some other developing members feel that they will lose more and gain less from liberalization and facilitation of the trade and investment if the developed members do not take significant actions, and especially if development cooperation fails to reduce the development gaps among member economies. The real test is whether all members can guarantee their progress in moving their plans into action after 1997. China has promised that it will reduce its tariff rate to 15 percent by 2000. Nevertheless, this leaves China with the highest tariff rate of all members. China will certainly face pressures to speed up the process of opening its markets in the future.

China Hopes for Open Subregionalism

A strong driving force for progress in reaching APEC's goals is the development of subregional organizations to promote trade and investment liberalization. ASEAN has established the goal of a free trade zone by 2003, and it is well ahead of schedule as its member nations have agreed to reduce tariffs to 0-5 percent for most of their goods by 2000. AFTA does not intend to become exclusive. The Philippine government proposed that AFTA be open to APEC members. NAFTA, approved by Canada, Mexico, and the United States in 1993, is another driving force in removing barriers to trade, investment, and other economic factors flows. However, the result of this internal liberalization will not extend directly to nonmembers given NAFTA's exclusive nature. On the one hand, these subregional groupings pressure APEC to move forward so APEC does not lose attractiveness. On the other hand, APEC itself may be a bridge to link these subregional organizations together and to make sure they are consistent with the principle of "open regionalism" and to encourage the extension of internal benefits to others. China is among the few in APEC who do not belong to any subregional organizations. It is crucial to keep the subregionalism open. The progress and success of APEC rely heavily on the continuous prosperity of member economies, especially the East Asian economies. In turn, progress in APEC will surely support the dynamism of economic growth.

IV. MEETING CHALLENGES

The integration of Asia-Pacific economies has been enhanced by an increasing share of intraregional trade and investment. As noted earlier, two new trends stand out. First, intra-Asian trade is continuing to rise, and second, trade from the east coast of the Pacific, noticeably North America, has been more and more dependent on the west coast of the Pacific, East Asia.[19]

China's economic importance used to be marginal in the Asia-Pacific region. But China has become a major player in the Asia-Pacific regional economy since recording high growth rates for nearly two decades. A growing share of Chinese imports coming from the Asia-Pacific region plays an increasing role in supporting the recovery and high growth of the economies of Taiwan, Hong Kong, Korea, and Singapore, as well as Australia. It seems that dependence on China for growth of export markets is unlikely to be reduced in the future.[20] However, China is facing new challenges. The most serious challenge is managing the changes to its domestic market in a smooth way while at the same time meeting the pace of increasing integration with the liberalization pressures of the global market.

Tariff Reduction

The dynamism of the Chinese economy is based on an open system. Total imports and exports have increased from U.S. $20.6 billion in 1978 to U.S. $237 billion in 1994, and to U.S. $280 billion in 1995. Following increasing integration of the Chinese economy into the regional and world markets, China's market needs to be opened to the others. In the past, China has protected its domestic market with high tariffs. This is no longer useful. China has to take active steps to reduce tariffs as well as nontariff measures. In 1995 alone, China reduced tariffs on 3,200 import

TABLE 9.4

TARIFF RATES BEFORE AND AFTER THE OSAKA ACTION

(SELECTED, NEW TARIFF FROM APRIL 1,1996)

	1	2	3	4	5	6	7	8	9	10
BEFORE	5%	15%	20%	20%	30%	45%	50%	60%	65%	150%
AFTER	2%	12%	10%	15%	20%	20%	40%	40%	55%	120%

Note: 1-airplane and helicopter parts; 2-portable radios and telephones; 3-pitch; 4-newsprint; 5-stylus printers; 6-unbleached plain-weave cotton; 7-household refrigerators; 8-women's shirts; 9-apple juice; 10-gasoline-powered sedans.

Source: *International Business Monthly,* Complete list of latest import tariffs, 1996.

goods and cleared up import quotas and licenses on 367 items. Significant steps were taken in 1996 with President Jiang Zemin's announcement of a 30 percent reduction of tariffs on 4,000 import items during the Osaka meeting, which is considered to be the most important step in opening the market since 1978 (see Table 9.4). In fact, the real reduction starting from April 1, 1996 turned out to be 35 percent, which exceeds the figure given in Jiang's announcement. Thus China's average import tariff rate has come down from 35.9 percent to 23 percent. However, compared to the other members of APEC, China's tariff rates are still among the highest. China has to speed up the reduction of tariff rates.

According to the action plan presented during the Manila APEC meeting in 1996, China's average tariff rate will be reduced to around 15 percent by 2000, 10 percent by 2010 and 5 percent by 2020. This timetable may be too ambitious. On the other hand, some argue that China can do more in the first two periods because China's real tariff level is much lower than the nominal rate. Due to the large amount of "policy reduction," the real tariff level has significantly come down. For example, real collected tariff rates conducted by the Custom is only 2.9 percent in 1994 if calculated on the basis of real tariff revenue to real imports (real tariff income U.S. $3.3 billion, import U.S. $115.7 billion) (see Table 9.5). This suggests that the negative impact on the Chinese economy would not be very significant if China took major steps to reduce the tariff level.

TABLE 9.5

NOMINAL TARIFF AND REAL CUSTOM COLLECTED RATE (1993-1995)

	TARIFF RATE (1) %	TARIFF INCOME (BILLION U.S. $)	IMPORT VALUE (BILLION U.S. $)	REAL RATE (2) %
1993	36.4	4.51	103.9	4.3
1994	35.9	3.32	115.7	2.9
1995	35.3	3.48	132.0	2.7

Note: (1) nominal tariff rate; (2) real collected rate.
Source: *China Statistical Yearbook,* 1994,1995, Customs Statistical data

Some sectors, however, still require high tariffs because of China's low competitive ability, and many tariff reductions have been carried out by the local authorities for their own immediate interests. Of course, high tariffs have negative consequences as well. One example is the increase of smuggling. In 1995 alone, the amount of smuggled goods seized by Chinese Customs reached U.S. $1 billion. Large amounts of smuggled goods with very low prices have had a significant negative impact on China's domestic market and production. The real problem is that there is no other alternative besides high tariffs to protect low efficient industries.

Reducing Nontariff Measures

Nontariff measures (NTMs) are primarily used in China's import control system by direct administrative arrangements. The most quantitative measures are import quotas, import licenses, and direct import controls. China has reduced NTMs significantly in recent years. About 1,000 different kinds of NTMs were cut during 1992-1995. The NTM rate in China's total imports was about 46 percent (in value) in 1992, and it will be cut down to about 21 percent in 1997 according to the memorandum on market access made between China and the United States. There are now only about 400 kinds of import goods that still fall under NTMs. Further reforms of the NTM system will be done in the future. The real challenge of the reform is how to make the system transparent and unified. There are still too many internal regulations.

Investment Liberalization

Foreign direct investment (FDI) into China has increased noticeably to more than U.S. $130 billion through 1995. China has become the second largest recipient country of FDI after the United States in the world. Total value produced by FDI enterprises is around U.S. $50 billion in 1994, which accounts for 13 percent of total industrial output in China. FDI has played a strong role in opening and integrating the Chinese market to the world market. What is conspicuous is that 37 percent of China's exports and 46 percent of China's imports are through FDI enterprises.[21] This is due to China's liberal policy regarding FDI. China has fewer restrictions to FDI than many of APEC's other members in terms of ownership laws and reinvestment of profit requirements. However, China still has many restrictions to FDI, mainly in the service sectors.

The government has begun to open the financial sector to foreign investors on an experimental basis. Foreign banks and accounting companies are allowed to open branches in 13 coastal cities and 14 inland cities to do Renminbi business. Shanghai and Guangzhou are open to foreign security companies. Since 1992, foreign investors have been allowed to invest in retail businesses in five major cities including Beijing, Tianjing, and Shanghai. In Pudong and Shanghai, some joint ventures are also permitted to do foreign trade. One important step in this liberalization process would be the implementation of the principle of national treatment in the tax system, as well as other regulations. The reform of China's service sector has many difficulties. The most important of those is that domestic companies are not very competitive. The liberalization process has to be done in a gradual way. APEC has agreed on nonbinding principles for investment liberalization.

Some members desire to make these nonbinding principles into binding ones. China would oppose any attempt to make these principles binding, though it may support efforts to strengthen the effectiveness of nonbinding principles through collective actions within the framework of APEC.

APEC and WTO

China failed to join GATT, and great difficulties have been met in accepting China as a member of the WTO. China insists that it has already met the necessary conditions of WTO as a developing country, while the United States argues that China is still far from meeting the basic requirements for WTO membership. In addition, it is argued that China should be treated as a developed country. Initially, China did not expect to wait too long to join GATT/WTO, but now it has become more realistic while maintaining a consistent interest in joining the WTO. China probably needs more time and room to readjust and reform its own economy. Thus, a delayed membership would serve its interest in maintaining a smooth transition. However, China understands that the debate between the major powers over "entry first" or "change first" will probably last for some time even though most developed countries, including the United States, seem to have reached a consensus on the importance of China's early entry.

It is true that China should not be treated as an ordinary country because of its size and impact on the others. But it is also important to judge its overall success in adapting itself to the international system. Compared with the WTO, China seems to like the "APEC approach" more since it is more flexible and unilateral in managing trade and investment liberalization. According to the timetable set out by the Bogor Declaration, China has more than 20 years before 2020 to liberalize its trade and investment market fully. China stated in 1995 during the second Senior Official Meeting of APEC that it would implement the Uruguay

Round agreement selectively even though it is not yet a member of WTO. The United States has strongly pressured APEC to play a role of "WTO plus" by promoting the process of WTO. China does not like this idea, but it will probably accept the effort if it is on a voluntary basis. WTO membership is important to China's interest. APEC is not an alternative to WTO for China. However, APEC does provide an alternative way for China to participate and change in a more flexible manner and to play a role in the international arena without legally binding itself to agreements that it is not yet sure are in its interests.

NOTES

1. See selected APEC Secretariat Documents, 1989-1994, especially APEC Secretariat (1995, pp. 2, 5).
2. Soesastro (1994a, p. 23).
3. Noland (1995, p. 15).
4. PECC, Pacific Economic Development Report (1995, p. 12).
5. Li Jingwen (1995, p. 342).
6. *China Statistical Yearbook* (1996).
7. Selected APEC Documents, 1989-1994 (1995); APEC Secretariat (1994, p. 37).
8. *Beijing Review,* Vol. 39, No. 12 (1996, p. 12).
9. Selected APEC Documents, 1989-1994 (1995, p. 42).
10. See Yang Guanqun (1994, p. 3).
11. PECC, Pacific Economic Development Report (1995, p. 9).
12. See Zhu Shoushen, "Suggestions for policy reflections to Osaka meeting," *International Business,* October 28, 1995.
13. Suggestion made from a research report submitted by APEC Study Center, Nankai University.
14. *People's Daily,* November 21, 1993.
15. See "Implementing the APEC Bogor Declaration," Australia-Japan Research Centre (1995, p. 15).
16. Selected APEC Documents, 1989-1994, APEC Secretariat (1995, p. 61).
17. Frank Ching, "APEC moving along 'Asian Way,'" *Far Eastern Economic Review,* December 7 (1995, p. 48).
18. Soesastro (1994a, p. 23).
19. Noland (1995, p. 15).
20. PECC (1995, p. 12).
21. *Foreign Investment in China,* No. 8 (1995, p. 7).

CHAPTER 10

POLITICAL-MILITARY DYNAMICS AND THE NESTING OF REGIMES: AN ANALYSIS OF APEC, THE WTO, AND PROSPECTS FOR COOPERATION IN THE ASIA-PACIFIC

Joseph M. Grieco

I. INTRODUCTION[1]

This chapter seeks to estimate whether and why the countries that constitute the Asia-Pacific Economic Cooperation forum (APEC) have sought to make their regional trade liberalization program consistent with the multilateral trade order as articulated by the World Trade Organization (WTO).[2] The APEC members have worked, in Vinod Aggarwal's terms, to "nest" APEC within the framework of the WTO.[3] The essay provides a sense of the ways in which this goal has been operationalized and the (high) degree to which that goal has been achieved to date.[4]

The chapter then raises questions about the significance of and prospects for the APEC liberalization program. The process by which the APEC countries are pursuing liberalization in the region is not based on formal, binding commitments. Instead, the members are pursuing liberalization by offering one another nonbinding announcements of unilateral liberalization measures. This process of unilateral nonbinding announcements, it is suggested below, may not yield significant levels of liberalization among the APEC members beyond that already stipulated by the Uruguay Round, and it may actually engender disagreements among major trading partners in the region.

The third section of this chapter seeks to understand why APEC's regional liberalization program is designed to be consistent with the WTO and why it faces limited prospects as an actual generator of liberalization in the Asia-Pacific. It suggests, in the first place, that the emphasis of APEC on WTO consistency is reflective of American preferences. It suggests further that APEC's constrained potential for effective liberalization or institutional development may be due to the fact that while APEC may be highly consistent with the WTO, and thus is nested "vertically" in a broader, universal regime "above" that forum, it is not well nested in a network of robust political and security arrangements spanning the Pacific Ocean. Thus, APEC does not have the advantage of having a strong "horizontal" nesting support system similar, most notably, to that of the European Union in Western Europe. This key difference regarding supportive noneconomic regimes across the two regions is the result, the section finally suggests, of differences in the geo-military circumstances that obtained at the outset of the Cold War in Western Europe and East Asia. These geo-military differences set the countries in the two areas on highly different trajectories regarding regionalism and institutionalized economic cooperation, trajectories that are still in evidence today.

II. ROBUST "VERTICAL" NESTING: AN ANALYSIS OF THE OSAKA SUMMIT RESULTS

Building on high-level meetings since 1989, especially an informal meeting of national leaders in Seattle in November 1993, the APEC members committed themselves to a program of trade and financial liberalization at the meeting of APEC leaders in November 1994, at Bogor, Indonesia.[5] In what came to be known as the Bogor Declaration, the APEC members said they were "determined to demonstrate APEC's leadership in fostering further global trade and investment liberalization," announced that they had established the specific goal of "free and open trade and investment" among the advanced APEC members by the year 2010 and all APEC members by 2020, and indicated that they had directed their "ministers and officials to immediately begin preparing detailed proposals" toward this end.[6] A year of consultations and negotiations followed, and these produced a package of announcements and agreements that were agreed to by the APEC members at a key meeting of national leaders and economic ministers in November 1995 in Osaka, Japan.

The Osaka package includes three main elements. First and most generally, there is an "APEC Economic Leaders' Declaration for Action," which reiterates the Bogor Declaration's stated purpose of APEC as being the attainment of free trade and investment in the Asia-Pacific by 2010 for the industrialized economies and 2020 for the developing members in APEC.[7] In addition, APEC members put forward at their ministerial meeting a more detailed and programmatic "Osaka Action Agenda: Implementation of the Bogor Declaration."[8] Finally, and in keeping with an agreement among APEC members that each would place a "down payment" on its medium-term efforts to promote liberalization in the region, each member put forward a list of unilateral technical measures to be undertaken, and these were listed in a document, "The Osaka Initial Actions."[9]

The first two parts of the Osaka package—the Declaration for Action and the Action Agenda—contain important trade and financial policy commitments undertaken collectively by the APEC membership. Consequently, they may shed light on the question of whether APEC is being designed in such a way as to be nested in the WTO multilateral order. In particular, we can first ask whether such nesting is prominent among the *objectives* posited by these two parts of the Osaka package. Second, we may determine if the *principles* that inform the two parts of the package are posited in ways that take into account the WTO or other international regimes. Finally, we may inquire if the *specific joint undertakings* included in these two parts of the package are supportive of or at least consistent with WTO rights and obligations.

The APEC members' objectives—the outcomes they wish to bring about—clearly indicate a commitment on the part of those countries to embed the APEC liberalization program in the WTO multilateral trade regime. For example, in the "Declaration for Action" the APEC leaders say that "We emphasize our resolute opposition to an inward-looking trading bloc that would divert from the pursuit of global free trade, and we commit ourselves to firmly maintaining open regional cooperation." They then go on to stress that "We reaffirm our determination to see APEC take the lead in strengthening the open multilateral trading system."[10]

Similar attention to the WTO as the guiding framework for APEC's activities can be observed in regard to the *principles* enunciated by the Osaka package, and especially the Action Agenda. To begin, in laying out the first section of the Action Agenda—on "general principles" to be used to guide APEC's liberalization efforts—the agenda states that the first is to be "comprehensiveness" (that is, the liberalization process will address "all impediments to achieving the long-term goal of free and open trade and investment"). It then goes on to posit as the second principle the requirement of "WTO-consistency"—that is, "The liberalization and facilitation measures undertaken in the context of the APEC Action Agenda will be WTO-consistent."[11] Moreover, the Action Agenda specifies in its second major section a "framework for liberalization and facilitation," and notes that in addition to the preparation of a national "action plan" aimed at unilateral liberalization, each APEC member would work to buttress the multilateral trading system "by participating actively and positively in multilateral negotiations and exploring the possibility of taking joint initiatives under the WTO."[12]

Finally and most interestingly, the Action Agenda turns in its third main section to lay out "actions in specific areas," and in doing so makes it plain that APEC's operational action plan has been designed with the multilateral trade order uppermost in mind. The agenda lays out a plan for joint action by APEC members in fifteen areas, including tariffs, nontariff measures, services, investment, standards, customs procedures, intellectual property, government procurement, rules of origin, and dispute mediation. For each of these fifteen areas, the agenda specifies an objective, guidelines for action, and a specification of expected collective action by the APEC members. Throughout the articulation of such objectives, guidelines, and expectations regarding collective action, the agenda turns to the WTO or other multilateral regimes for direct guidance as to what the APEC members will try to achieve in regard to liberalization or the manner in which they should proceed to try to achieve their goals.

For example, the Action Agenda specifies as a guideline the point that each APEC member will "contribute positively to the WTO negotiations on trade in services," and "expand commitments under the General Agreement on Trade in Services (GATS) on market access and national treatment and eliminate MFN exemption where appropriate."[13] Similarly, the Action Agenda specifies that "APEC economies will "progressively reduce or eliminate exceptions and restrictions to achieve the above objective, using as an initial framework the WTO Agreement, the APEC Non-Binding Investment Principles, any other international agreements relevant to that economy, and any commonly agreed guidelines developed in APEC."[14] The Action Agenda also stipulates that each APEC member will, by the year 2000, "harmonize customs valuation systems by adopting or abiding by the principles" of the Agreement on Implementation of Article VII under the auspices of the revised (1994) General Agreement on Tariffs and Trade and, again by 2000, "protect intellectual property rights by adopting or abiding by the principles of the GATT's new Agreement on Trade-Related Aspects of Intellectual Property Rights (the TRIPS Agreement)."[15] In regard to rules of origin, the agenda states that each member will "align its respective rules of origin with international harmonized rules of origin to be adopted as a result of the WTO/WCO process."[16] Finally, the Action Agenda has a separate section devoted to the Uruguay Round, and by virtue of it each APEC member commits itself to "ensure full and effective implementation of the Uruguay Round outcomes within the agreed time frame in a manner fully consistent with the letter and the spirit of the WTO Agreement," and each further agrees that it "will, on a voluntary basis, accelerate the implementation of Uruguay Round outcomes and deepen and broaden these."[17]

In cases in which the WTO does not have direct jurisdiction over some element of the Action Agenda liberalization program but another multilateral regime is active, the agenda directs APEC members to give attention to the rules and practices of the larger arrangement and thus continues with the practice of nesting APEC in some larger international regime. For example, in telecommunications the Action Agenda commits APEC members to "conform, where appropriate, to the Guidelines for Trade in International Value-Added Network Services (IVANS) by 1998," and in transportation the agenda states that APEC members will "promote the implementation of International Civil Aviation Organization and International Maritime Organization standards, regulations, and safety measures."[18] With respect to investment issues, the agenda stipulates that APEC members will "establish, in the short term, a dialogue process with the Organization for Economic Cooperation and Development (OECD) and other international fora involved in global and regional investment issues."[19] In the key area of standards, the agenda posits that members will "align APEC economies' mandatory and voluntary standards with international standards," and commits them to participate in such international bodies as the International Organization for Standardization, the International Electrotechnical Commission, and the Codex Alimentarious Commission.[20] Finally, in regard to dispute mediation, the Action Agenda commits members to "accede where appropriate by 1997 to international agreements for the settlement of disputes between governments and private entities such as the Convention on the Settlement of Investment Disputes between States and Nationals of Other States," and to "accede where appropriate by 1997 to the Convention on the Recognition and Enforcement of Foreign Arbitral Awards."[21]

Thus, in regard to the objectives, principles, and operational undertakings of its members, APEC's liberalization program as articulated by the Osaka package has clearly been designed to be shaped, informed, and constrained by WTO and other international economic regimes—in other words, to be nested "upward" in the larger multilateral trade order.[22] APEC, in other words, is clearly geared to open regionalism and has been carefully and explicitly designed to be nested in the larger, multilateral trade order.

III. APEC'S PROBLEMATIC PROSPECTS

The APEC members are not seeking to construct a formal regime either for coordinated, mutually agreed regional tariff cuts or for a common external tariff—as has been accomplished by the European Union and is now the main goal of Mercosur. There is, therefore, no effort by APEC to establish rules of origin particular to the Asia-Pacific—as is the case of NAFTA with regard to trade among the North American countries. And there appears to be no interest among the members in establishing a common policy in sectors such as agriculture or advanced technology or monetary affairs—as is the case of the European Union.

What, then, is the goal of APEC? As Funabashi points out, the APEC members are seeking to construct a liberalization program based on a process of "concerted unilateral action."[23] Through this process APEC members essentially have met together and have made unilateral, nonbinding commitments to open their markets. In addition, any liberalization of commerce that is achieved by the APEC process of concerted unilateral action is supposed to result in "open regionalism." APEC's private support body, the Eminent Persons Group, suggested in August 1994 that open regionalism consist of the extension of APEC liberalization measures either on an individual or collective basis, and either on a reciprocal or nonreciprocal (that is, most-favored-nation) basis.[24]

There are at least three reasons to believe that this approach is unlikely to produce a substantial increase in liberalization of economic relations in the Pacific Basin. The first concerns the basis for APEC members' commitments under the concerted unilateral action process. As noted in the previous section, in searching for unilateral actions to contribute to the APEC liberalization process, the APEC members have turned to their Uruguay Round commitments. For the most part, they have agreed to implement those commitments somewhat more quickly than called for under the terms of the Uruguay Round agreement itself.[25] There are exceptions: for example, Australia announced at Osaka that it would extend its coverage of services under the new General Agreement on Trade in Services to five new sectors.[26] On the other hand, Canada appears to have included in its list of initial actions reductions in tariffs that occurred outside the framework of the APEC process (that is, they had come into effect during the spring and summer of 1995, well before the Osaka meetings in November), and Japan announced as an Osaka initial action decisions made in April to open Japanese markets.[27] In other words, instead of APEC serving as a focal point for *new* unilateral commitments, the Osaka meetings served in substantial measure as a site for the rearticulation of Uruguay Round commitments or of actions already selected by the APEC member.[28]

Second, there are many ways in which the APEC strategy of concerted unilateral action could generate disagreements rather than greater comity and trust in the Pacific Basin. For example, if the APEC members stay with concerted unilateral action, the likelihood is that some members over time will feel that others are benefiting disproportionately from the APEC process. Further, if commitments are made but are voluntary in character, it is likely that members will believe that partners have undertaken obligations regarding liberalization but will be unable to raise concerns if they believe these obligations are not being discharged fully or faithfully. That could very well promote mutual frustration and recriminations.

Third, on the particular issues of intellectual property and customs valuation, it will be recalled from the discussion above that the Osaka Action Agenda commits signatories to promote progress in those areas "by adopting or abiding by the principles" of agreements on them under the auspices of the WTO. Presumably this clause foresees instances in which an APEC member does not adopt the agreement in question (which is clearly the case with China, which has not yet been admitted to the WTO), and in such situations the country is expected at least to act as though it were in compliance with the principles of that agreement. However, from the viewpoint of an APEC member seeking redress if it believes that a partner has not behaved in accord with those agreements, there is a qualitative difference between circumstances in which that partner has complied with the first or the second parts of that clause in the Osaka Agenda. If it has adhered to the former, then the aggrieved party can turn to the WTO's dispute settlement body; if it has elected to adhere to the latter, then the aggrieved party has no recourse under the WTO. Again, this element of APEC is as likely to generate conflict as cooperation in the Pacific Basin.

Thus it is difficult to see how APEC will result in significant new economic liberalization within the Asia-Pacific. Moreover, APEC's "open regionalism" strategy may create new tensions in world commercial relations. According to APEC's Eminent Persons Group, "open regionalism" means that members will have the *option* of extending any new APEC liberalization measures achieved to nonmembers on an unconditional, most-favored-nation basis. However, C. Fred Bergsten, chair of the Eminent Persons Group, suggested in December 1994 that in his view, any such liberalization in fact "will probably [be] offered to the rest of the world *on a reciprocal basis*." Bergsten made it clear that the bargaining context of such reciprocal extension of new liberalization measures will be on the basis of a very strong APEC. That is, for nonmembers who receive an APEC offer of reciprocal liberalization, "that's like the offer from the Mafia: it's an offer you can't refuse because you can't be blocked out preferentially from half the world economy."[29] The problem with this approach is that it underestimates the bargaining capabilities of at least one group outside APEC, namely the European Union. The latter might respond to pressures from APEC for mutual exchanges of liberalization measures by refusing further progress in the WTO unless it receives satisfaction on the issues raised by APEC liberalization agreements. Hence, APEC liberalization might complicate rather than facilitate world trade liberalization.

In sum, it is not clear that APEC will be effective in bringing about a net increase in openness in the Asia-Pacific region. There is also the possibility that the weakness of the APEC process for generating undertakings by member countries in regard to economic liberalization might sow the seeds of new trade disputes in the region. There is even the possibility that APEC's operative understanding of "open regionalism"—namely reciprocity—will hurt world trade liberalization. In any event, the likelihood that APEC might in fact so harm the world trade system is very small, for APEC is now and is likely to remain a very weak forum. This raises the question, addressed in the next section, of why APEC is so weak as an institution and as a means toward liberalization in the Asia-Pacific.

IV. APEC'S WEAKNESS:
THE IMPACT AND SOURCES OF STUNTED "HORIZONTAL" NESTING

Two questions may be derived from the discussion above. First, why is there so much effort by APEC to ensure that any Asia-Pacific liberalization effort be consistent with the WTO multilateral trade order? Second, why are the Asia-Pacific countries pursuing such a modest strategy of commercial and financial liberalization as entailed by concerted unilateralism? In respect to the first question, I would like to stress the role of the United States and its concerns about an alternative that was put forward to Asia-Pacific economic diplomacy in the early 1990s, namely an effort to construct a uniquely East Asian approach to economic regionalism; in regard to the second, I would like to stress the impact of the absence of a broader network of regional arrangements into which APEC could be nested.

In the first place, why is APEC so committed to consistency with the WTO? At least one major cause has clearly been the insistence by the United States government that APEC contribute to rather than detract from WTO-sponsored global trade liberalization. At least in part this U.S. insistence that APEC so reinforce the WTO appears to be a reaction on the part of the United States to Malaysian proposals in the early 1990s that the East Asia countries establish their own trade bloc, an East Asian Economic Group (EAEG) and, in later formulations, an East Asian Economic Caucus (EAEC). American officials in the early 1990s specifically voiced their concern that these two proposed arrangements would promote closure of Asian markets to the United States, and would do so because it would be decisively influenced by Japan. As one news report indicated, "Despite claims to the contrary, U.S. officials say, Mahathir's proposed East Asian Economic Group (EAEG) could—in a worst-case scenario—develop into a protectionist bloc prone to shedding traditional values of open markets," and it went on to specify that "The obvious tendency would be to emulate the Japanese model of development through industrial policy, managed trade and mercantilism, a model that draws vociferous complaints of unfairness from the West." The United States wanted to counter this prospect of a closed, Japan-dominated East Asian arrangement with APEC: an American official was quoted as saying about APEC, "Our goal is to get all these countries into the camp of open markets rather than see them take the Japanese approach of more managed trade."[30]

American power and preferences thus have ensured that APEC is embedded vertically in the world trade order. At the same time, as discussed above, APEC is likely to be remarkably limited in its impact on actual economic trends in the region. One cause for this weak character of APEC is that the members do not have at their disposal a range of cooperative institutions into which APEC can be situated, or horizontally nested. Indeed, what Barry Buzan and Gerald Segal say about the East Asian countries in the security field can be extended to Australia, New Zealand, and the countries of the Americas that are involved in APEC: they suggest, "Perhaps the most alarming aspect of East Asian security is the virtual absence of effective multilateralism." They go on to say that "What is distinctive about Asia is its combination of several industrialized societies with a regional international society so impoverished in its development that it compares poorly with even Africa and the Middle East."[31]

Just as the absence of broader intergovernmental arrangements and networks creates an unfavorable context for the construction of an Asia-Pacific economic regime, so too the absence of a significant network of societal linkages spanning East Asia and the Americas makes the formation of such agreements more difficult and doubtful. In Western Europe the creation and operation of the European Community served as a catalyst to the formation of transnational business and professional coalitions interested in and affected by community policies, and there is evidence that these transnational communities in turn have played at least a modest role in facilitating and even prompting the further development of the community.[32] The situation in East Asia and the Asia-Pacific area has been markedly less favorable: while there are some very weak trans-Pacific bodies that bring together individuals from business, government, and academia, these appear to be less robust than in Western Europe.

Moreover, in light of the absence of institutionalization of relations among the Asia-Pacific countries and the low level of transnational relationships in the region, the countries in that part of the world may have made less progress in developing the trust and habits of cooperation that now characterize Western Europe. In this sense one might suggest that the East Asian states enjoy a lower level of "social capital" than is the case in Western Europe or even the Americas.[33] One key symptom of this less favorable context for cooperation in the Asia-Pacific region is that compared to the reconciliation achieved by Germany and its neighbors in Europe, there has been a markedly lower level of reconciliation between Japan and its neighbors regarding the atrocities committed by Japanese forces during World War II.

Thus APEC's limited ambitions and capabilities may be related to the already low level of institutionalization that characterizes the Asia-Pacific region. This of course raises the question of why East Asia and, more broadly, the Asia-Pacific region are characterized by such a modest level of robust institutions and are plagued by a weak web of transgovernmental and transnational relationships. Again, there are many possible causes, but one that has been particularly important concerns the differences in the geo-military circumstances of the early Cold War in East Asia and Western Europe.[34]

In Western Europe there was great reluctance in the first years after World War II on the part of Germany's neighbors to envision full German participation in the European economy. Moreover, as John Ikenberry emphasizes, the United States sought immediately after World War II to help construct a genuinely multilateral ("one-world") economic order to be based on the Bretton Woods negotiations and the talks on the ill-fated International Trade Organization. As competition between the United States and the Soviet Union intensified, however, the United States turned to a European "third force" option. That is, the United States abandoned full world multilateralism and sought to promote the development of a strong Western Europe closely linked to America through the Bretton Woods agreements (and the fallback to the ITO, the General Agreement on Tariffs and Trade, or GATT) and able to contribute to its own defense against possible Soviet political or military pressures. Hence the United States turned to the Truman Doctrine of 1947 and the North Atlantic Treaty of 1949 in the military field, and in economic matters it formulated the Marshall Plan of 1948 together with its main European operating entity, the Organization for European Economic Cooperation (OEEC), as well as the European Payments Union (EPU), founded in 1950.[35]

In pursuing this "third force" option, the fundamental problem for the United States and its West European allies was crystal clear: the Soviets enjoyed massive conventional military superiority; there was no way the United States could commit sufficient ground troops to offset that superiority; while nuclear weapons *might* ensure deterrence, this became less credible as the Soviets developed a nuclear arsenal; and finally, there was one and only one Western European state that could contribute decisively to Western conventional security—the Federal Republic of Germany.[36]

That last fact, of course, created profound misgivings in Germany's World War II victims, and especially in France. The solution to which the West Europeans turned, and for which the United States gave decisively important support, was to allow

Germany to rebuild its economy, and later its armed forces, within the framework of regional institutions.[37] In this way, Germany's neighbors believed, German power would be shared with and managed by its Western European partners, and Germany's partners would be able to cooperate with but not be dominated by that key country.[38] The West German government was highly attracted to this approach insofar as it permitted reindustrialization and a larger voice in European affairs.[39] The institutions for this strategy in the economic domain were of course the European Coal and Steel Community and, later, the European Economic Community; and in the security domain they were the North Atlantic Treaty Organization (after the proposal for a European Defense Community was defeated by the French parliament in 1954) and, to a lesser degree, the Western European Union.[40]

As the Cold War commenced in East Asia in the late–1940s, the United States shifted its attention in regard to Japan from democratization and decartelization to economic recovery.[41] As a part of that "new course" strategy the United States sought to encourage the reestablishment of trade between Japan and its East and Southeast Asian countries (with the notable exception of China).[42] And, as in Western Europe, the United States initially favored the establishment of regional economic institutions involving Japan as the Cold War intensified in that part of the world in the early-to-mid-1950s. For example, Burton Kaufman reports that as a part of its containment strategy in Asia in the wake of the Korean War and the French defeat in Indochina, President Eisenhower and Secretary of State John Foster Dulles expressed in late 1954 the view that Japan was the key U.S. ally in the region and that it was essential to support it by fostering closer economic ties between that country and Southeast Asia. Further, Kaufman reports that in October 1954, U.S. foreign aid chief Harold Stassen proposed to Asian countries participating in the Colombo Plan that they band together to establish an organization similar to the OEEC in Europe, and the Eisenhower administration sought from 1954 through 1956 to obtain approximately $200 million from Congress to be distributed through such an Asian regional aid arrangement.[43] However, even before Congress declined to provide the Eisenhower administration the resources for an Asian development fund, thirteen Asian countries met in May 1955 in Simla, India to discuss how that proposed U.S. aid could be employed, and these countries formally rejected the idea that they should form a regional organization to dispense the resources.[44] The problem, Kaufman reports, was Japan: "With memories of World War II fresh in their minds, the countries of the region were reluctant to establish commercial relations with their former captors," and in addition, "they feared that their own interests would be dwarfed by an economically resurgent Japan supported by the United States."[45]

Given that the United States was pursuing a controversial embargo of China and that most countries in the region were averse to reestablishing economic ties with Japan, the United States supported Japan through direct assistance and military procurement and by sponsoring that country's acceptance into the GATT. The latter was accomplished in 1955. However, almost half of the GATT's membership at that time invoked safeguard provisions of the treaty against their new partner.[46] American policy then turned to the further opening of the U.S. market to Japanese goods, as well as the continuation of massive U.S. military orders that had begun with the outbreak of the Korean war in June 1950.[47] Thus, while the United States sought to promote Asian regionalism in the early-to-mid-1950s, Japan's potential partners rejected this option. They, as with Germany's partners in Western Europe, were extremely fearful and suspicious of Japan. But unlike Germany's European partners, they could not overcome that fear and suspicion and undertake the construction of regional economic ties with their former oppressor.

This difference in outcomes surely was due in part to the fact that Germany was not so far ahead of its European partners economically as was true of Japan in comparison with its Asian neighbors. But in addition, such countries as South Korea and the Philippines did not need Japanese military support in the early-to-mid-1950s, and the United States did not believe it needed Japan to help support these countries.[48] As noted above, the geo-military situation in Western Europe served in part to catalyze an interest on the part of Germany and its neighbors to construct European institutions as a way of managing the reconstitution of German power. For the noncommunist countries of East Asia, American hegemonic power was seemingly sufficient to maintain their security, and there was little interest in security ties with Japan.[49] Moreover, while the United States saw German conventional military reentry into the European power equation as vital to its strategy for the Continent, the United States was able to devise for Japan a key role in America's Asian strategy—most importantly permitting the establishment of huge American air and naval bases in Japan on the basis of the U.S.–Japan Security Treaty of 1952—without requiring that country to be a part of formal arrangements with its Asian neighbors.[50]

In sum, while constraints on American power led the United States in the early-to-mid-1950s actively to promote regional institutionalization in Western Europe, American military and economic hegemony in East Asia in the mid-1950s made such institutionalization unnecessary in that area of the world.[51] What this may have meant by the early 1990s was that the East Asian countries were ill-positioned not only to work among themselves—as might have been entailed in the ill-fated EAEG/EAEC proposals—but also to move forward aggressively in a larger Asia-Pacific project such as APEC.

V. CONCLUSION

At least three conclusions can be derived from the preceding discussion. First, the concept of nesting may provide insights into two different phenomena. On the one hand, the general concept of nesting helps us to think about whether a particular agreement among nations may be consciously embedded or situated "vertically" in a larger, functionally similar international regime. In the present discussion, there was clearly an effort—largely successful—by APEC members to make their liberalization efforts not just consistent with but informed and shaped by the larger WTO regime. On the other hand, we may also ask whether and to what degree an agreement among countries in one issue-area is nested "horizontally" in a broader web or pattern of agreements among those countries in other issue-areas.

Second, the discussion above suggests that in terms of relative impact on the prospects for any given arrangement among a set of countries, horizontal nesting may be more important than vertical nesting. The absence of a broader fabric of regional cooperation into which APEC could be embedded may well be hampering that particular experiment in regional economic liberalization. Moreover, while Japan's problematic relationships with its neighbors and the absence of strong regimes linking Asia-Pacific countries have been the key inhibitors of successful institutionalization in the Asia-Pacific region to date, new developments in the region might make institutionalization even less likely in the future. This is because there is another rising economic power in that part of the world. That country may have the capacity to surpass Japan and perhaps even to approach the United States in world economic matters. It also has domestic structural conditions and foreign policy goals and practices that are not likely to attract neighbors to closer, formalized relationships in either the economic or the political-military domain. That country, of course, is China.[52] If China continues on its present course—in particular, the use of force to deter independence by Taiwan and to buttress its claims to the potentially resource-rich South China Sea—then it will eventually come into direct military competition with its neighbors and, ultimately, the United States. That would destroy any effort at broad-based regional economic cooperation.

Finally, the discussion above underlines the core view of the realist perspective that political-military conditions often decisively affect the economic relationships that states may wish to pursue and be able to attain. In the present case, the intersection of the Cold War in Europe and NATO's need for a German military contribution to manage that conflict helped to bring about the initiation and flourishing of West European institutionalized cooperation in the economic realm. In contrast, the onset of the Cold War in the Asia-Pacific and the United States' capacity to carry out that struggle on its own probably doomed institutionalized economic cooperation among countries in that part of the world. Thus we see again that political-military realities often shape international economic relationships among nations.

NOTES

1. I thank Peter Feaver for suggesting that I seek to connect current trends in regionalism to U.S. political-military decisions during the early years of the Cold War, Ajin Choi and Imke Risopp-Nickelson for their assistance in the preparation of this essay, and Vinod Aggarwal and Paolo Guerrieri for their comments on an earlier draft of the paper.
2. The World Trade Organization is the more robust successor to the General Agreement on Tariffs and Trade (GATT), which when negotiated was intended to be only an interim accord while a broader International Trade Organization (ITO) was negotiated, but with the failure of the ITO in 1952 it became the basis for world commercial diplomacy. The WTO was created as a part of the Uruguay Round of multilateral trade negotiations, which was held under the auspices of the GATT and was completed in April 1994. For a helpful overview of the WTO charter and its relationship to the old GATT, see Jackson (1994).
3. See Vinod K. Aggarwal (1985). Aggarwal uses his nesting logic to reach the conclusion that APEC has been an extremely weak regime; see Aggarwal (1994), especially p. 51.

4. See chapter 2 (Aggarwal 1998a, p. 2) in this volume.
5. Two recent overviews of APEC's development are provided by Gary Hufbauer and Jeffrey Schott (1995, pp. 37-45) and Yoichi Funabashi (1995).
6. See United States Embassy in Indonesia (1994, pp. 4, 7).
7. Japanese Ministry of Foreign Affairs (1995) "APEC Economic Leaders' Declaration for Action," p. 1.
8. See Japanese Ministry of Foreign Affairs (1995), "The Osaka Action Agenda: Implementation of the Bogor Declaration."
9. See Japanese Ministry of Foreign Affairs (1995), "The Osaka Initial Actions."
10. "Declaration for Action," p. 2.
11. "Action Agenda," p. 1.
12. "Action Agenda," p. 3.
13. "Action Agenda," p. 6.
14. "Action Agenda," p. 8.
15. "Action Agenda," p. 11; see also pp. 12-13.
16. "Action Agenda," p. 16.
17. "Action Agenda," p. 18; these are listed in "Osaka Initial Actions."
18. "Action Agenda," p. 6.
19. "Action Agenda," p. 8.
20. "Action Agenda," p. 9.
21. "Action Agenda," p. 17.
22. This same reliance by APEC upon the WTO can be observed in the APEC annual summit that was held in Manila in November 1996. There the APEC member countries basically agreed to press at the WTO ministerial meeting scheduled for December of that year in Singapore for a WTO-wide agreement aimed at the liberalization of trade in information-industry products. For reporting on the Manila APEC summit, see Edward Luce and Guy de Jonquières (1996) "Clinton in Drive for IT Trade Pact" and "Confusion Greets Clinton's Big Deal," and Todd S. Purdum (1996) "At Asian Meeting, Support for Free Trade," and "APEC's Lost Opportunity."
23. Funabashi (1995, pp. 96-98).
24. See Asia-Pacific Economic Cooperation Secretariat (1994, pp. 29-30); C. Fred Bergsten (1994) "APEC: The Bogor Declaration and the Path Ahead," and Vinod Aggarwal (1995, pp. 45-47).
25. See, for example, Japan's commitments in "Initial Actions," p. 9.
26. "Initial Actions," p. 2.
27. See "Initial Actions," pp. 4, 9.
28. For a similar assessment of the results of the Osaka summit, see "Trade in the Pacific: No Action, No Agenda," Economist, November 25, 1995, pp. 75-76.
29. APEC Secretariat (1995c, p. 3).
30. Schoenberger (1991).
31. Buzan and Segal (1994, 15).

32. See, in the legal domain, Burley and Mattli (1993, pp. 41-76); also see Cameron (1992, pp. 48-51).

33. In this I am drawing upon the insights of Miles Kahler, who, basing his analysis on Robert Putnam's work on social capital, makes the important point that the Pacific region as a whole is characterized by a low level of interstate social capital: see Kahler (1994), 29-30; and Putnam, Leonardi, and Nanetti (1993).

34. I develop this argument further in Joseph M. Grieco (forthcoming 1998). In doing so I have benefited from the work of Benjamin Cohen and Robert Gilpin, who both have emphasized that U.S. national security policy at the outset of the Cold War fundamentally shaped U.S. preferences as it reshaped the post–World War II international economic order: see Benjamin J. Cohen (1974) and Robert Gilpin (1975). For an important recent investigation of the manner in which alliance relations drive commercial integration, see Joanne Gowa (1994).

35. G. John Ikenberry (1989, pp. 375-400).

36. On the centrality of West German conventional forces to NATO strategy, see Wolfram F. Hanrieder (1989, pp. 40-42).

37. See Geoffrey Warner (1993, pp. 319-29); Klaus Schwabe (1995, pp. 115-35) and Gustav Schmidt (1995, pp. 137-74).

38. The idea that institutionalization served as a postwar strategy by which France and other European countries sought to limit and channel German power was articulated in Hans Morgenthau's discussion of the European Coal and Steel Community in the second edition of his *Politics Among Nations* (1958, pp. 497-98), and his discussion of the European Communities in the third edition (1966, pp. 531-34).

39. On the point that West German Chancellor Konrad Adenauer recognized that Germany's partners needed that country's conventional capabilities, and that this approach afforded the new West Germany state important political and diplomatic opportunities, see Hanrieder (1989, pp. 9, 38-39).

40. For additional analyses of early postwar European economic cooperation in which the problem of managing German power is a focus of attention, see Michael Hogan (1987), especially p. 64; and Gillingham (1991, pp. 174, 364-66). On West European efforts—themselves prompted by significant U.S. pressure to bring about German rearmament—to build a uniquely European defense entity between 1950 and 1954 that would include but constrain Germany, the failure of that effort, and the subsequent admission of Germany into NATO at the end of 1954, see Willis (1968, pp. 130-97).

41. From an interesting comparison of Germany and Japan in the early Cold War, see James R. Kurth (1989, p. 36).

42. See William S. Borden (1984, pp. 109-42).

43. Kaufman (1990, pp. 106-7).

44. Kaufman (1990, p. 115).

45. Kaufman (1990, p. 115).

46. On the importance assigned in 1955 by the Eisenhower Administration to obtaining Japan's acceptance by a reluctant GATT membership, see Borden (1984, pp. 179-80).

47. On the vital role of U.S. military orders in Japan's economic recovery in 1950 and 1951, see Borden (1984, pp. 143-49); Kaufman (1990, pp. 116-17); and Richard B. Finn (1992, pp. 267-79).

48. See Barry Buzan (1995a, pp. 29-31). Finn points out that the outbreak of the Korean War did lead to a decision by General MacArthur, as supreme commander of the Allied powers in Japan, to bring about a limited rearmament of Japan; however, these forces had no power-projection capability; see Finn (1992, pp. 263-66).

49. On this point, see Donald Crone (1993, p. 507).

50. For a helpful discussion of the negotiation of the United States–Japan security treaty, as well as Japan's peace treaty with the United States and other allied powers, see Finn (1992, pp. 270-312).

51. For this argument in regard to Asia, see Crone (1993, pp. 501-25).

52. On the remarkable economic performance of China in recent years, see Nicholas R. Lardy (1994, pp. 14-25, 29-35). On the problems that the international community may encounter in accommodating growing Chinese power, see Aaron L. Friedberg (1993-1994, pp. 5-33); Richard K. Betts (1993-1994, pp. 34-77); and Gerald Segal (1996, pp. 107-35).

NESTING NAFTA IN APEC: THE POLITICAL ECONOMY OF OPEN SUBREGIONALISM

Maxwell A. Cameron

I. INTRODUCTION[1]

A major test of the strength of the Asia Pacific Economic Cooperation (APEC) forum will be its ability to regulate interaction among subregional trading arrangements (SRTAs). The importance of reconciling APEC with SRTAs is suggested by the fact that the members of one SRTA, the North American Free Trade Agreement (NAFTA), accounts for half of APEC's output.[2] The future of the General Agreement on Tariffs and Trade (GATT) and its newly formed successor, the World Trade Organization (WTO), crucially depends on how regional arrangements like NAFTA and APEC are reconciled with each other and within the larger GATT regime. Successful nesting of these institutions will be a factor in determining whether the GATT will, to use Robert Z. Lawrence's (1991) apt metaphor, stumble or build upon regional blocks in its efforts to enhance multilateral economic integration.

A number of proposals have been put forward to reconcile APEC with SRTAs, the most detailed of which have come from an advisory body, the Eminent Persons Group (EPG), chaired by C. Fred Bergsten.[3] The EPG's last recommendation, before being disbanded in 1995, was that SRTA reconciliation be consistent with "open subregionalism." In essence, this means that SRTAs should be nested in APEC in the same way that APEC is nested in the GATT.

APEC is nested in the broader world trading system in accordance with the concept of open regionalism. APEC fosters the reduction of barriers to goods, services, and capital among its members in a manner consistent with the GATT and WTO. In Bergsten's view, open regionalism leads to "a steady ratcheting up of trade liberalization between the regional and global levels."[4] Open subregionalism refers to the application of the principle of open regionalism to the acceleration of liberalization or linkage among SRTAs; it would avert the formation of exclusive and discriminatory trading blocs. What are the prospects for nesting NAFTA within APEC according to this or some other formula?

This chapter reviews the EPG's proposal for "open subregionalism," and raises critical questions about the ambiguities inherent in this formula. It then draws upon the theory developed by Vinod Aggarwal[5] to identify the issues involved in efforts to strengthen connections between the North American and Asia-Pacific trade regimes. The chapter explores a variety of ways in which actors might link issues in their attempts to nest NAFTA in APEC, as well as the kinds of bargaining routes they might follow. Finally it traces structural conflict between the Asia-Pacific and the North American regions to interactions rooted in contrasting tastes, technology, and social organization.

II. NESTING NAFTA IN APEC: THE PROPOSAL FOR OPEN SUBREGIONALISM

The three reports of the EPG outline possible mechanisms for reconciling APEC and SRTAs like NAFTA. In its First Report, the EPG outlined the possibility of a variety of SRTAs "harmonized within the arrangements of APEC itself."[6] It rejected the idea of NAFTA accession as a model for linking the two arrangements on the grounds that "it would create new discrimination within the region, at least for the long transition period; generate divisive strains as countries jockeyed for position in the queue (or decided not to do so); and impose a North American model on Asia."[7] In short, APEC sought to avoid the sort of discrimination and competition that would result in a U.S.-dominated process.

In its Second Report,[8] the EPG noted continuing interest in NAFTA-APEC links in part stimulated by the negotiation of NAFTA, the Association of Southeast Asian Nations (ASEAN) agreed to create an ASEAN Free Trade Area (AFTA) by the year 2003. Singapore and Thailand subsequently announced a joint study of AFTA-NAFTA links, and Singapore expressed an interest in joining NAFTA. Many of the ASEAN countries feared the expansion of NAFTA into a fully fledged FTAA would lead to a loss of their comparative advantage as low wage economies exporting into the North American market.[9]

The EPG reiterated its concerns about discrimination and division and added another objection to NAFTA accession: it could "create new entrenched interests that would resist broader liberalization and hence impede APEC-wide (or global) agreements."[10] The EPG noted that its recommendation that APEC leaders "move promptly to launch the APEC-wide initiatives proposed in this Report is reinforced by the need to accommodate the subregional groupings into the broader APEC arrangement."[11] Thus the proliferation of SRTAs, in the context of the ongoing Most-Favored-Nation liberalization, provided a powerful stimulus to APEC leading up to the Seattle summit.

The Third Report[12] of the EPG was written after the conclusion of the Uruguay Round, and it contains the most careful thinking to date about the interrelationship between APEC and SRTAs. If the creation of the WTO weakens the argument that SRTAs will create "new entrenched interests," this is not acknowledged in the report.

However, the EPG reiterated its objections to NAFTA accession for Asian countries,[13] and it began to spell out in greater detail the issues and policy options raised by linking SRTAs within APEC.

The EPG argued that the Bogor Declaration of free and open trade and investment in the region by 2010 and 2020 resolves the issue in the longer term.[14] As countries implement their Bogor commitments, they will eliminate the need for preferential rules of origin. However, this does not address the issue of institutional nesting: how should SRTAs link up, for example, AFTA-NAFTA?

Any linkages between SRTAs could increase the margins of preference between members and nonmembers, possibly leading to trade diversion as well as deflecting the attention of trade officials from the larger regional and global processes. The GATT provides only loose guidance on these issues, despite the progress of the Uruguay Round. In the absence of any clear precedent or blueprint, the EPG proposed that "linkage must be fully consistent with the WTO,"[15] and "any new SRTA initiatives within APEC be promptly submitted to the WTO for confirmation that they meet these test and for surveillance of their performance in practice."[16]

The EPG further recommended that liberalization of SRTAs and linkups between them should be pursued in a manner consistent with the principles of "open subregionalism."[17] These principles are spelled out in a "nonmutually exclusive four-part formula:"[18] (1) linkage should be unilateral and based on MFN to the maximum extent possible; (2) linkage should be accompanied by a statement of intent to reduce barriers to other APEC countries; (3) linkage should be accompanied by willingness to extend concessions on a reciprocal basis to other APEC members; (4) individual SRTA members can unilaterally extend their SRTA commitments to non-APEC countries on a conditional or unconditional (thus MFN) basis. As an example, NAFTA could extend its current margin of preference to AFTA countries, and to other APEC countries as a group on a reciprocal basis or unilaterally on a conditional or unconditional basis.[19]

Finally, the Third Report of the EPG discussed the prospect of an FTAA. It concluded that the FTAA should be WTO consistent, embrace open subregionalism, avoid restrictive rules of origin, support the WTO in order to reduce newly created margins of preference, and aim to harmonize the two agreements through the pursuit of global free trade.

The EPG's analysis leaves important issues unresolved. First, without enforcement mechanisms, how will failure to comply with principles of "open subregionalism" be ensured? APEC is a weak regime, lacking mechanisms to constrain national actions and resolve tensions related to SRTAs. The APEC dog cannot wag the NAFTA tail.

Second, without competition or discrimination, how will trade and investment liberalization be achieved? Global economic integration is partly driven by a process of competitive liberalization in which countries compete with one another for market access and foreign capital. Competitive liberalization often results in preferential agreements designed to ensure that the benefits of economic integration accrue to the parties to the agreement. The unilateral extension of preferences beyond the initial parties to an agreement would diminish margins of preference and thereby weaken the incentive to join, undermine the inducement of policy reform, and slacken the competition for foreign capital. In short, any weakening of the margins of preferences would undermine competitive liberalization.

Third, why should North American trade policymakers accept the idea of "open subregionalism" for NAFTA and the FTAA, given that the explicit purpose of the principle is to avoid a "U.S.-dominated process" in Asia? Open subregionalism, by discouraging the creation of margins of preference and discrimination, constrains United States trade policy. Unless implemented on a conditional basis, it would give the rest of the world a free ride on Asia-Pacific liberalization and thereby weaken pressures to bring other regions to the bargaining table in Geneva.

Finally, NAFTA and APEC are nested differently within the GATT/WTO regime. Whereas NAFTA, as a formal FTA, can be defended by appealing to the GATT provision that permits exceptions to the principles of nondiscrimination, APEC seeks to be nondiscriminatory and thus "WTO-consistent." This seemingly subtle difference reflects a fundamental contrast in approaches to economic integration. Analyzing NAFTA helps one understand the liberalization process in North America and Asia-Pacific and provides a basis for assessing the prospects for nesting NAFTA in APEC.

III. THE CREATION OF NAFTA

This chapter builds upon an extensive literature on institution building in North America.[20] It focuses on issues relevant to the reconciliation of NAFTA and APEC, such as trade and investment diversion and the shift of U.S. trade policy preferences from multilateralism to regionalism.[21]

International shocks—the decline in oil prices and rise of interest rates in 1982—provided the initial stimulus for Mexico's trade policy transformation. The need to negotiate with international banks and creditors and implement orthodox macroeconomic stabilization policies contributed to the rise of a technocratic elite with an outward-oriented growth strategy.[22] The new economic ideology was also designed to reinforce domestic coalition stability by strengthening business-state relations.

The requirements of non-oil exports within the new strategy increased the costs of isolation from multilateral and bilateral regimes. During the 1970s, when Mexico became a major oil exporter, it was possible to remain outside the GATT. The need to expand manufactured exports after 1982, however, increased the costs of uncertain access to the U.S. market. Moreover, the United States was able to link debt and trade to increase its leverage over

Mexico and punish what it considered Mexico's free-riding on the liberal international trading regime.[23]

Mexican technocrats pursued a variety of bargaining routes: they first negotiated an ad hoc bilateral accord (the 1985 Understanding on Subsidies and Countervailing Duties) and then signed a protocol of accession to the GATT in 1986. The low payoff from these negotiations led to the 1990 decision to negotiate a comprehensive regional trade agreement that would send a powerful signal to the international community that domestic reforms were permanent in order to attract massive inflows of foreign capital.[24]

The decision to pursue a comprehensive agreement was further influenced by international developments, including the negotiation of FTAs between the United States and Canada and the United States and Israel, the slow pace of the Uruguay Round, the Europe '92 project, and the fall of the Berlin Wall. The lesson drawn from these events by Mexico's technocrats was that the United States was open to bilateral bargaining, multilateralism offered a poor payoff, and Mexico's ability to attract foreign capital was threatened by regionalism. The electoral debacle of 1988 added urgency to the market reforms implemented by President Carlos Salinas de Gortari during his tenure (1988-1994).

The Mexican initiative was welcomed in Washington largely because United States policymakers realized they could use bilateral bargaining to achieve results among a small club of nations impossible in the larger multilateral arena. United States policymakers were particularly concerned by the rise of aggressively export-oriented states in East Asia, which, in Washington's view, were insufficiently committed to a liberal international trading system. Behind this concern was the persistent U.S. trade deficit with Asia, and Japan in particular, which led to pressures for unilateralism from the United States Congress. Indeed, some officials saw NAFTA as a way of emulating Japanese success. As President Salinas said, "Japan's success has been owed in part to its incorporation of its neighbors into production processes in a way that goes beyond mere trade relations . . . [A] free trade agreement between our countries could be the answer to this extraordinary challenge."[25]

NAFTA reshaped state-society and external relations in North America. The 1,000-page agreement was negotiated from June 1991 until August 1992 and then ratified in each country's domestic legislature prior to implementation on January 1, 1994. The agreement intrudes into the domain of domestic policymakers, especially in Mexico. It covers most goods traded by the three countries—including sensitive tariff items like agriculture, textiles and apparel, and automobiles and auto parts, energy—as well as services such as banking and insurance, transportation, and telecommunications. It also covers diverse trade-related issues such as intellectual property rights, investment rules, government procurement, technical standards, and mechanisms for dispute resolution. In many of these areas, NAFTA goes well beyond the scope and depth of the GATT, ostensibly setting precedents for future multilateral negotiations.[26]

The NAFTA negotiators—especially the Canadians—were strongly committed to GATT norms and jurisprudence, and they went to considerable lengths to ensure consistency with GATT. In December 1991, amidst NAFTA negotiations, the Draft Final Act of the Uruguay Round became available. Consequently, entire chapters mirror the results of the Uruguay Round.[27]

In some areas, such as labor and environmental issues, NAFTA exceeds the scope of the GATT. NAFTA offered U.S. firms an opportunity to become more competitive regionally and globally by rationalizing production on a continental scale. Access to a low-cost region would allow firms to compete with low cost competitors in Asia and elsewhere. This opportunity naturally implied a threat to the wages and working conditions of North American workers, who feared job losses, downward pressure on wages, and social dumping. Environmentalists feared that polluting firms would shift production to Mexico to avoid the more adequately enforced environmental regulations in the United States and

Canada. To assuage these fears, newly elected President Bill Clinton insisted on negotiating supplemental agreements on labor and environmental standards in the summer of 1993.

The NAFTA metaregime embodies liberal principles and norms. It is, as Aggarwal notes, "a classic free trade agreement—the standard exception to the MFN [Most Favored Nation] norm of the GATT."[28] Article 24 of the GATT allows exceptions to the MFN obligations for FTAs that remove "substantially all" trade among members and do not erect new barriers to third parties, and NAFTA meets these criteria. At the same time, it contains restrictive rules of origin, especially in certain sensitive sectors, safeguards and snapback provisions, and long phase-in periods for certain products. A vague accession clause is nominally open to all countries, but it does not specify procedures for joining and gives a veto to current members. These features bring the agreement closer to "liberal protectionism."[29]

Examples of liberal protectionism are found in the rules of origin in textiles and automobiles. The lack of a common external tariff in FTAs creates an incentive for third countries to export into the country with the lowest tariffs and then use that country as an export platform to gain access to the markets of other countries. To prevent that from occurring, FTAs generally contain provisions that determine what goods can legitimately be considered to have originated from within the region. The main NAFTA rule of origin is that goods wholly produced or obtained in North America are eligible for preferential treatment under NAFTA. The same treatment is given to goods that contain nonoriginating materials that have undergone a sufficient transformation (measured in terms of changes in tariff classifications) to be considered originating in the region. For certain sensitive sectors, goods must contain a certain percentage of North American content or contain a specified component. The latter case applies to textiles and automobiles.

In the case of textiles, NAFTA stipulates that preferential treatment will be granted only to those textile and apparel products that are produced from yarn or fibers produced in North America. Hufbauer and Schott argue that this rule "sets a high water mark for protective rules of origin."[30] The main consequence of this rule is to make it more costly to source for fabrics and yarns outside of the North American region. At the same time, Mexico was granted immediate liberalization of U.S. import quotas for Mexican textile and apparel products. It is obvious that high rules of origin were the price Mexico had to pay for the elimination of quotas. The United States negotiators understood that textile jobs were moving offshore to Asia; hence they were receptive to the Mexican argument that it was better to encourage U.S. industries to integrate with a country like Mexico that imported from the United States than to low wage Asian countries that import less from the United States. In short, investment diversion was part of the argument made to support higher rules of origin.

In the case of automobiles, the rules of origin stipulate that autos must contain a certain level of North American content to qualify for preferential treatment. Here again, high rules of origin were a major demand of the U.S. industry, mainly the Big Three auto producers. "Not only did the Big Three want better access to the fast-growing Mexican market, they also wanted to ensure that their Japanese competitors would not use Mexico as a ready-made 'export platform.'"[31] Automotive rules of origin were raised to 62.5 percent, and the method of calculating regional content was clarified. The final deal reflected a bargaining process in which Asian interests paid the price for satisfying U.S. industry demands. Mexico had to sacrifice its clear interest in attracting new investments from Asia and elsewhere in order to reach an agreement that would ensure the integration of its auto industry (especially the parts producers) with the U.S. industry. To get the guarantees it needed for domestic parts producers, Mexico had to accept higher rules of origin. Similar examples of "liberal protectionism" can be found in NAFTA, including computers, televisions, and financial services.

IV. RECONCILING NAFTA AND APEC

The major externalities for the Asia-Pacific resulting from North American economic integration were trade and investment diversion and the uncertainty caused by the apparent flagging of U.S. commitment to multilateralism. Although trade diversion caused by NAFTA was projected to be slight,[32] high rules of origin in certain sectors—such as textiles and automobiles—directly affected Asian interests. The purpose of these rules was to ensure the benefits of liberalization accrued to NAFTA members, not the rest of the world.

Investment diversion, while hard to measure, was expected to be more significant than the trade effects of NAFTA.[33] Investment diversion would result from the signaling and "confidence enhancement" effects of locking in domestic Mexican policy reforms. In the area of investment, the key reforms included the liberalization of investment restrictions, the creation of a mechanism for the resolution of disputes between investors and NAFTA states, and the establishment of rules on expropriation. Fears of investment diversion were diminished, however, after the Mexican financial meltdown of 1994-1995.[34]

Beyond immediate concerns of trade and investment diversion, many Asian countries feared that American and European support for multilateralism was being diverted to regional arrangements that threatened the export-oriented growth strategies of the Asia-Pacific.[35] The rapid succession in which the Canada–United States FTA and the NAFTA were negotiated seemed to indicate that the United States was less interested in maintaining the liberal international trading system based on the GATT and more concerned with demonstrating that it had bilateral alternatives in case the GATT failed. As a bilateral alternative, NAFTA not only excluded Asia: it seemed directed against Asia.[36]

In response to these externalities, a number of bargaining routes were explored by Asia-Pacific nations. The initial APEC proposal made by Australian Prime Minister Bob Hawke in 1989 was partly motivated by the perception of growing regionalism in North America following the negotiation of the Canada–United States FTA.[37] However, as APEC expanded to encompass all three NAFTA countries, the choice of bargaining routes became more complex.

The Malaysian proposal for a East Asian Economic Group opted for reduced linkages between Asia and the Americas, creating an alternative trading arrangement in Asia to offset the risk of regionalism and the collapse of multilateralism.[38] This was strenuously opposed by the North American members of APEC and abandoned on behalf of the more benign notion of an East Asian Economic Caucus.

The accession of East Asian countries to NAFTA was another possible bargaining route, one that attracted the interest of Singapore and Thailand. In this approach, NAFTA could be extended to single Asian countries or groups like AFTA. In the latter case, the SRTA would be nested within the NAFTA through substantive linkages. Singapore and Thailand played the role of defectors in a stag hunt game: they would undermine a collective Asian solution in an effort to avoid being shut out in a world of rival mercantile blocs. This option was strongly criticized by the EPG, which proposed an alternative: that NAFTA be substantively nested in APEC.

However, to nest NAFTA in APEC would require APEC to become more of a conventional preferential trade agreement under Article 24 of the GATT. Only such a solution would address the North American objection that open regionalism would give a free ride to Europe and other nonmember countries, weakening pressures on them to bargain in Geneva. Bergsten outlined the U.S. concern: "Nonmembers would have no incentive to negotiate multilaterally if they could simply sit back and receive the benefits of APEC liberalization without making concessions of their own. The use of 'temporary conditional MFN' uses the negotiating leverage available to APEC because of its large economic weight to obtain maximum liberalization around the world."[39]

The formula of open subregionalism explicitly permitted individual SRTA members to extend their SRTA commitments to non-APEC countries on a conditional basis. NAFTA countries could extend NAFTA preferences to all APEC countries on a conditional basis and remain faithful to open subregionalism. Only by offering NAFTA preferences on a conditional basis would North America be able to encourage an accelerated liberalization in the Asia-Pacific without giving the Europeans a free ride. Over time, the gradual elimination of tariffs through the implementation of the Uruguay Round would make these rules progressively less trade distorting.

If NAFTA was to be nested in APEC in such a manner, it would be necessary for APEC to become an FTA and adopt rules of origin. As William James notes, NAFTA rules of origin could be: (1) replaced by a single harmonized set of APEC rules of origin; (2) negotiated among existing SRTAs; or (3) adopted by expanding NAFTA to encompass APEC members. The first solution would be the one most consistent with the spirit of the EPG's proposal for nesting NAFTA in APEC, and would possibly result in the most liberal rules. The third solution was explicitly rejected by the EPG on the grounds that it would divide Asia and intensify pressures to respond with measures to exclude North America. The second solution would be an intermediate compromise, but policymakers in Washington have little interest in harmonizing discriminatory rules.

Nevertheless, there are political challenges inherent in turning APEC into an FTA. In the first place, support for new trade initiatives in the United States Congress would be weak, especially given tensions with Japan. Second, there is little business momentum behind APEC in the United States, and strong opposition could be expected from those North American producers facing competition from Asian imports. Third, many policymakers would see the further Asia-Pacific integration as part of a tactical effort to constrain U.S. trade policy.

Above all, common rules of origin with APEC would, in essence, undermine U.S. discrimination against Japan and other

Asia-Pacific countries with which it has a trade deficit. Common APEC rules of origin would help address the problem of European free-riding on APEC liberalization efforts but not the U.S. perception of "unfair" trading practices by Japan and other East Asian nations. Common rules of origin would partially undo the U.S. strategy designed to confront the challenge of Asian competition.

Finally, any effort to formalize APEC would immediately confront the problem of linking trade and labor and environmental standards. There are contrasting views on the role of labor standards and environmental regulations in trade policy.

Canadian and U.S. policymakers argued during the negotiation of the Canada–United States FTA that there was no linkage between trade and labor or environmental issues. Republican members of the United States Congress and some policymakers in developing countries argue that efforts to link trade with labor and the environment are merely a new form of protectionism. In their view, the linkages are tactical, not substantive.

Environmentalists and trade unionists argue that growth through trade does not guarantee either rising wages or environmental protection. Rather, they project a downward harmonization of labor and environmental standards as countries liberalize their trade policies. In this view, the efforts to link trade with labor and environmental standards are substantive.

Even when actors agree that there is a substantive connection between trade and labor and environmental standards, they may differ on whether labor and environmental issues should be linked hierarchically to trade. Malaysia's trade minister, for example, argued that social clauses should not be linked to trade because they are more appropriately dealt with in the International Labor Office. Some environmentalists fear that linkage strategies will undermine environmental protection by subordinating environmental regulations to commercial jurisprudence. In their view, attacks on "disguised protectionism" mask an effort to straightjacket environmental initiatives. Disagreement over whether the supplemental agreements on labor and the environment are optional for new members held up U.S. consideration of Chilean accession to the NAFTA, and it is likely that the same issues would be raised in any negotiations to turn APEC into a formal FTA.

The idea of nesting NAFTA in APEC in a substantive way raises serious problems. If the two are nested in a tactical way, tensions are likely to persist. In the next section the underlying differences in the political economy of Asia-Pacific and North America are compared to help understand why many Asian countries have resisted efforts to institutionalize APEC into a formal agreement.

V. COMPARING ECONOMIC INTEGRATION IN ASIA AND THE AMERICAS

Structural conflict between the Asia-Pacific and the North American regions is rooted not only in occasional macroeconomic imbalances but also in microeconomic differences at the level of the firm and business networks, individual tastes, preferences, propensities to save, the scope and nature of government intervention, and patterns of social organization. Although this chapter has focused on institutional issues, there are sharp underlying differences in the political economies of the Western Hemisphere and Asia-Pacific regions that help account for the different approaches to regional integration.[40] These differences will play a role in any future effort to nest NAFTA in APEC.

Efforts to create more formal trade agreements between North America and Asia-Pacific may raise major problems. Unlike the GATT regime, which provided considerable scope for domestic autonomy in designing economic policy, a more formal free trade regime linking North American with the Asia-Pacific would be likely to constrain domestic policy. Asia-Pacific countries have little incentive to undertake such reforms, and the United States has less structural power to promote them in Asia than it does in the Western Hemisphere.

NAFTA is characterized by enormous asymmetries of power, as well as dramatic differences in levels of overall economic and human development. The recent economic performance of the NAFTA countries has been modest at best: all are heavily indebted, and their respective levels of savings and investment as a percent of GNP are comparatively low. The Asia-Pacific region is even more heterogeneous than North America. However, a cluster of Asian economies—Japan, the four tigers of East Asia, plus Malaysia, Thailand, and Indonesia—exhibit a high level of economic dynamism. These nations have rates of savings and investment significantly above those of North America, indicating solid prospects for sustained growth, despite the financial crisis of 1997-1998.

The model for economic development of the Asia-Pacific region has not sacrificed equity. The most dynamic economies of Asia exhibit "a remarkable mix of regionally concentrated and sustained high growth combined with low and declining levels of income inequality."[41] None of the Asian countries have the sort of inequitable distributions characteristic of Latin American countries like Mexico or Peru, largely because of agrarian reform in the postwar period.[42]

Robust social institutions and sustained investments in human capital characterize a number of the emerging Asian NICs.[43] Small but activist states have played a key role in the promotion of export-oriented industrial transformation.[44] The Japanese model contrasts with the United States model (widely emulated in Latin America) of low savings, high levels of consumption and debt, reliance on abundant natural resources, and a more pluralist political system.

Trade and investment flows demonstrate extreme patterns of dependence within North America. Mexico and Canada export three quarters of their goods and services within the North American region. Although the importance of the U.S. market for the East Asian NICs increased until the late 1980s,[45] it has since declined and none of the Asian nations are as reliant on the United

States or any other market as Canada or Mexico.[46] Similarly, with regard to foreign direct investment, both Mexico and Canada receive over 60 percent of their FDI flows from the United States. The Asian country that receives the most FDI from North America is the Philippines, which gets nearly half its FDI from the United States. None of the other Asian cases comes remotely close to the level of dependence of Canada or Mexico.

NAFTA as an institution reflects these structural asymmetries in the distribution of capabilities in North America. The United States used the enormous structural power of its massive market in bilateral negotiations with Canada and Mexico to extract concessions and create a regime that reflects U.S. interests in areas like intellectual property protection, liberal investment rules, and trade in financial and other services. Facing obstacles to progress on this agenda in the MTN, the United States sought to use the Canada-United States FTA and NAFTA negotiations to achieve results by engaging in power-based bargaining and specific reciprocity.

NAFTA imposes a strong laissez-faire, market driven policy framework on the countries of North America.[47] It does not recognize norms of development, and it sharply restricts the ability of states to regulate business. The approach to negotiations stressed formal contractual obligations and specific targets. Little attention was given to problems of domestic adjustment.[48] NAFTA embodies an approach to trade that emphasizes securing markets through contractual arrangements over conquering markets by domestic policies to enhance competitiveness.[49]

In marked contrast to NAFTA, APEC bargaining has tended to reflect the more diffuse distribution of economic and political capabilities in the Asia-Pacific region. No single player has an overwhelming influence over the terms of the evolving trade and investment arrangements. Different groups of countries are given responsibility for developing different issue-areas in APEC. There is strong adherence to diffuse reciprocity, and some observers have noted that regionalism in the Asia-Pacific region involves a "greater reliance on forms of persuasion emanating from the development—often by smaller actors in the system—of significant technical, intellectual, and entrepreneurial skills rather than on what we might call the structural, or power-driven, bases of international leadership associated with hegemony."[50]

APEC may be more consistent with the dirigiste policies that have been essential to the success of Japan and East Asian countries.[51] The emphasis on flexibility, cooperation, and different timetables is a weak but significant recognition of developmental norms consistent with the Asian development experience.[52] The purpose of APEC is not to secure markets contractually but to ensure that they remain open to conquest and penetration as the dynamism of the region continues.

Tensions between North America and the Asia-Pacific region—such as the 1995 dispute over the automotive sector—are unlikely to diminish. Moreover, disputes between the United States and Japan are likely to revolve around domestic differences in tastes, patterns of consumption, levels of savings, and other domestic differences—not tariffs or quotas.[53] The United States has responded to this fundamental problem by using national controls—such as Section 301 of the 1988 U.S. Trade Act—and pursuing a variety of bargaining routes, including results-oriented bilateral negotiations, multilateral pressures. Japan has resisted U.S. pressure, expressing concern that NAFTA must not become a "North American fortress," and has become more proactive in pursuing economic activity in Asia through APEC and other fora.[54]

An example of the interplay of political rivalries and the evolution of economic institutions came at the APEC summit in Osaka. United States Trade Representative Mickey Kantor proposed that NAFTA and ASEAN countries should begin an "informal dialogue" to align the two agreements. Meanwhile, Japanese minister of international trade and industry Ryutaro Hasimoto courted closer economic ties with Chile and Mexico.[55]

VI. CONCLUSION

This chapter began with the question: can NAFTA and APEC be reconciled? The answer prescribed by the Eminent Persons Group was that the two institutions should be substantively nested through open subregionalism. The assessment of this chapter is that open subregionalism provides an improbable formula for the reconciliation of NAFTA and APEC.

The main objections to open subregionalism are: the lack of enforcement mechanisms, undermining of competitive liberalization, incompatibility with U.S. interests, and differences in the nesting of APEC and NAFTA in the GATT. The lack of enforcement of open subregionalism implies that any reconciliation effort will be only as stable as its ability to serve the interests of the most powerful players. From this it follows that any incompatibility between the principle of open subregionalism and U.S. interests is likely to be a major stumbling block in progress toward nesting NAFTA in APEC.

A major problem with open subregionalism from a U.S. perspective is that it is inconsistent with competitive liberalization. Above all, the United States seeks to retain the flexibility necessary to use preferential agreements to promote and shape economic integration in accordance with its interests. It has been successful in using its considerable structural power to push for liberalization by countries in the Western Hemisphere that need access to its market and capital. Most of the countries in the Western Hemisphere are engaged in an intense competitive struggle for foreign investment.[56] It is not in the interest of the United States to ignore the opportunity to exploit this competition to advance its interests in the Western Hemisphere.

One way of addressing the U.S. concern that open regionalism gives a free ride to nonmembers in APEC liberalization is to make APEC a formal FTA. This arrangement would change the way

APEC is nested in GATT, making it more like NAFTA. APEC rules of origin could then be used to discriminate against nonmembers, thus sustaining the pressure for global trade liberalization. However, this would not resolve U.S. conflicts with countries within APEC—especially Japan—that are rooted in structural problems such as the persistent U.S. trade deficit.

In short, open subregionalism would constrain U.S. interests in the Western Hemisphere without resolving problems in the United States–Japan bilateral relationship. The United States may promote both NAFTA and APEC as institutions loosely nested in a tactical way in order to encourage regional and global trade and investment liberalization simultaneously. Participation in APEC encourages Asia-Pacific liberalization and demonstrates U.S. commitment to the region. Extension of NAFTA to other countries in the Western Hemisphere is likely to foster a continuing dynamic of competitive liberalization advantageous to Washington. Policymakers in the United States are unlikely to be concerned that NAFTA and APEC represent contrasting models of economic integration.

The tension between regionalism and multilateralism will not be resolved in the near future, and efforts to square this circle will yield few benefits. The underlying differences between Asia-Pacific and Western Hemispheric countries will become increasingly conspicuous sources of tension even as the world moves toward a more integrated global system. The analytical focus on institutional nesting will reveal the interaction between structural, cognitive, strategic, and domestic factors in the evolution of the global political economy and explain how these tensions are managed.

NOTES

1. This chapter benefited from the comments of participants in two workshops on "APEC and Regime Creation in Asia and the Pacific," held at the East-West Center, Honolulu, Hawaii, January 11-13, 1996, and at the East-West Center, Seattle, Washington, August 13-15, 1996. I am especially grateful to Paolo Guerrieri. Quinn Goretzky provided research assistance. Maureen

Appel Molot and Lisa North also made helpful suggestions on an earlier draft.

2. APEC Secretariat (1995c, p. 30).
3. APEC Secretariat (1995c); Bergsten (1994, pp. 20, 23); and APEC Secretariat (1993).
4. Bergsten (1994, pp. 20, 23).
5. See chapter 2 (Aggarwal, 1998a) in this volume.
6. APEC Secretariat (1993, p. 32).
7. APEC Secretariat (1993, p. 32).
8. APEC Secretariat (1994c).
9. Mehmet (1994-1995, p. 65).
10. APEC Secretariat (1994, p. 47).
11. APEC Secretariat (1994, p. 47).
12. APEC Secretariat (1995c).
13. APEC Secretariat (1995c, p. 30).
14. APEC Secretariat (1995c, p. 30).
15. APEC Secretariat (1995c, p. 33).
16. APEC Secretariat, (1995c, p. 34).
17. APEC Secretariat (1995c, section iv).
18. APEC Secretariat (1995c, p. 34).
19. APEC Secretariat (1995c, p. 35).
20. For recent reviews, see Grinspun and Cameron (1996); Brunelle and Deblock (1995); Pastor (1994).
21. See Morrison (1995) and Rudner (1992, 1995).
22. Centeno (1994).
23. Cameron (1996, pp. 433-36).
24. Cameron (1997).
25. Grimm (1991, p. 4).
26. Cameron (1997).
27. Appleton (1994, p. 21).
28. Aggarwal (1995, p. 56).
29. Aggarwal (1995, p. 57).
30. Hufbauer and Schott (1993, p. 44).
31. Hufbauer and Schott (1993, p. 37).
32. Morrison (1995, pp. 106-9).
33. Morrison, (1995, pp. 109-10).
34. Cameron and Aggarwal (1996).
35. Rudner (1993, p. 139).
36. Morrison (1995, p. 111).
37. See chapter 6 (Ravenhill, 1998) in this volume.
38. Rudner (1993, pp. 144-45).
39. Bergsten (1994, p. 23).
40. See Wade (1992) and Fishlow (1989).
41. Helliwell (1995, p. 5).
42. Cameron and North (1996).

43. Helliwell (1995).
44. Evans (1992); Fajnzylber (1990a, 1990b); Gereffi and Wyman (1990).
45. Gereffi (1989, p. 99).
46. APEC Secretariat (1994, p. 24).
47. Grinspun and Cameron (1993).
48. Grinspun and Cameron (1994, pp. 29-30).
49. Fajnzylber (1990b, pp. 324-25).
50. Higgot et. al. (1990, p. 825).
51. Kim and Leipziger (1993).
52. APEC Secretariat (1995, p. 3).
53. Lawrence (1994, p. 229).
54. Dobson (1995, pp. 3-6).
55. Oxford Analytica (1995, p. A9).
56. Cameron and Tomlin (1995, pp. 140-44).

CHAPTER 12

ASEAN AND INSTITUTIONAL NESTING IN THE ASIA-PACIFIC: LEADING FROM BEHIND IN APEC

Michael G. Plummer

I. INTRODUCTION[1]

Formal regional economic integration is relatively new to modern Asia. In fact, while proposals to create an Asian free-trade area had been tabled as early as the late 1960s, serious debate regarding the benefits and costs of such a scheme was conspicuously absent from the economic literature until the late 1980s. Since then, various configurations of preferential trading arrangements in Asia have been considered and the debate has created considerable controversy in academia and government circles.

Although there currently exists no regionwide economic cooperation agreement, the Association of Southeast Asian Nations (ASEAN) was ostensibly created to foster cooperation in a variety of areas, including economics. However, formal economic integration was not stressed de facto until the Third Summit (December 1987). Many in fact would argue that serious steps toward real economic integration were not taken until the Fourth Summit (January 1992), at which point ASEAN committed itself to creating a free-trade area. Since then, ASEAN has taken a number of additional steps towards closer economic integration, including an expansion of product coverage, liberalization of nontariff barriers, creation of a dispute-settlement mechanism, common investment codes, and closer economic harmonization.

A number of contributing factors can be ascribed to the change in attitude toward economic cooperation in ASEAN over the past eight years, including developments exogenous to ASEAN (e.g., real or perceived protectionism in the West, the creation and enhancement of trading blocs in some of ASEAN's most important markets, competition from emerging markets for investment flows and in labor-intensive goods markets) and those coming from within ASEAN itself (e.g., domestic economic reform, unilateral liberalization of trade and investment, etc.). But certainly a key factor in the creation of the ASEAN Free-Trade Area (AFTA), its expansion to include its seventh member state, Vietnam, and plans to accept other Indochinese countries, as well as the recent trend of speeding up implementation and deepening cooperation in AFTA, has been the agreement to form the Asia-Pacific Economic Cooperation (APEC) forum in November 1989.

APEC includes ASEAN's most important political and economic partners and, in fact, its greatest competitors. For example, ASEAN conducts approximately three-fourths of its trade with APEC countries, and its share of ASEAN investment flows is even higher.[2] The ASEAN Regional Forum (ARF), which is the first Asia-Pacific regional organization to discuss security issues between major (and minor) member states in a systematic manner, is dominated by APEC member states. APEC even appears to be emerging as an important vehicle through which the region's actors are uniting to apply pressure in global fora, such as the World Trade Organization (WTO).[3]

In sum, APEC is of great relevance to the future of ASEAN economic cooperation. Yet it is not yet clear to what extent—and in which direction—APEC will affect ASEAN economic cooperation. On the one hand, APEC could produce competitive forces that tend to dilute ASEAN and eventually render it redundant, which is currently the most salient fear of ASEAN leaders. On the other hand, it might serve to complement ASEAN economic integration by "pushing" ASEAN toward higher levels of integration while at the same time opening up markets and reducing transactions costs in doing business with regional nonpartners.

This chapter attempts to consider how the institutional nesting of ASEAN within APEC will affect both subregional and regional cooperation. The chapter takes an exclusively economic track and in this sense distinguishes itself from other contributions in this volume. Hence it begins with a discussion of some of the major theoretical issues relevant to economic regionalism in the Asia-Pacific, followed by rather detailed analysis of how "open regionalism" is being played out in ASEAN through AFTA (Section III), the East Asian Economic Caucus (EAEC) (Section IV), and APEC (Section V). Section VI offers some concluding remarks on the future of institutional "nesting" in the Asia-Pacific region.[4] It is argued that ASEAN will continue to influence the direction of APEC heavily as it moves toward formal economic integration, in essence "leading from behind." In addition, the direction of APEC has and will continue to have important implications for the future of ASEAN economic cooperation.

II. A BIT OF THEORY APPLIED TO ASIA-PACIFIC REGIONALISM

Although divisions and controversy exist, a strong majority of academic economists are wedded to the idea that open trade and investment flows constitute a "first best" policy ideal to which nations states should aspire. This is because unimpeded trade and investment flows allow for maximum efficiency by reducing international transactions, allowing for specialization in comparative advantage industries, and providing optimal "dynamic" gains through greater economies of scale, technology transfer, productivity spillovers from greater interaction with the international marketplace, and the like. Even today, when economists dispute the merits of regional economic integration, the debate usually boils down to the question of whether or not regionalism serves as a step toward international free trade (argued by "regionalists") or away from it.

The major critique of the regional approach to global liberalization is that there is no guarantee that a discriminatory trading bloc would be outward-looking. Moreover, it could constitute a competing institution within the global framework that could risk the segmentation of the General Agreement on Tariffs and Trade (GATT)/WTO system, i.e., as competing rather than complementary institutions. And since economists concur that nondiscriminatory international trade maximizes efficiency and hence global welfare, regionalism is considered detrimental to multilateral liberalization. In fact, if the goal of the regional trading arrangement is to promote internal industries at the expense of other countries (e.g., earlier initiatives in Latin America and Africa), this would be the case. However, regionalism as an expanded form of import substitution has never worked; inward-looking blocs have always been either short-lived or ineffectual. Regionalists would argue that endogenous processes eventually push the trading bloc toward greater liberalization or hasten its demise.[5] In this sense, regionalism is "second best" static but "first best" dynamic.

Nowhere is this process clearer than in the movement toward regionalism in the Asia-Pacific region. Regional cooperation initiatives attracting the interest of Pacific Asian economies have been motivated by the need to enhance international competitiveness and interact more effectively with the global economy. Hence, while at a superficial level it may appear potentially disturbing to free-trade economists to hear of new economic cooperation initiatives in the region developing outside the auspices of the GATT/WTO, strong forces are at work that will ensure that each of these arrangements are open to the international marketplace.

In essence, this strong outward orientation of Asia-Pacific economies in general and ASEAN in particular finds its ideological roots in neoclassical economics and is the driving force behind unilateral, plurilateral, and global policy stances. Hence, economic efficiency constitutes what we might call the economic foundation of the ASEAN "metaregime" discussed by Aggarwal in chapter 2 of this volume.[6]

III. ASEAN ECONOMIC INTEGRATION

Established in 1967 by the Bangkok Declaration, ASEAN was initially formed with political goals in mind, i.e., to present a united front in light of instability in Indochina and China (Cultural Revolution), the British withdrawal "East of the Suez," and fears of changes in U.S. policy toward Southeast Asia. However, the regional organization always had economic cooperation as one of its goals, with its original architects stressing the need for regional "resource pooling and market sharing." The first noticeable economic initiatives began in the mid-1970s with the first two ASEAN summits, but ensuing trade and industrial cooperation programs were quite modest and, in fact, reflected the import-substitution bias of most of their member states.

As noted above, in the late 1980s, economic cooperation in ASEAN took a quantum leap forward for a number of reasons. First, with a stable and reforming China, the end to the Vietnamese occupation of Cambodia (and its desire to pursue economic liberalization itself), and a much more "confident" region, the political imperatives became less dominating, though clearly they continue to be an important part of ASEAN. Second, and most important for our purposes, there was a fundamental transformation of the economic dimensions of the ASEAN metaregime; domestic economic policies of the ASEAN countries shifted from import-substitution to export promotion.[7] The focus on economic policy became one of enhancing internal economic efficiency, promoting nontraditional exports (especially manufactures), and tapping the benefits of the international marketplace. Importantly, economic growth and liberalization in the ASEAN countries attracted large inflows of direct foreign investment (DFI), first from Japan and then from the Asian NIEs. Hence, domestic economic reform started a process of liberalization that rapidly accelerated, bolstered by international exposure and an increased presence of foreign investors. Third, trends in the global marketplace made ASEAN rethink its somewhat lethargic approach to economic integration. The "deepening" and "widening" of economic integration in Europe (e.g., the Single Market Program in the late 1980s, Economic and Monetary Union, the European Economic Area, new arrangements with newly liberated Eastern European countries, etc.), the Canada–United States Free-Trade Area (1989), the North American Free-Trade Area (1994), and the associated trade and investment diversion that would follow threatened the outward-looking economic development strategies that ASEAN had recently embraced. Moreover, the increased use of nontariff barriers; protectionism associated with politically sensitive issues, such as trade and the environment, labor issues, and human rights; and the first two failures to conclude the Uruguay Round in December 1990 and 1992 exacerbated the problem. While ASEAN economic integration could not possibly be a substitute for access to external markets, it could serve to enhance the competitiveness of the region as well as increase bargaining power with the newly emerging blocs.

Note that the ASEAN economic miracle cannot be attributed to regional economic cooperation but rather to domestic economic reform. By the late 1980s, existing regional cooperation in trade and industry had been improved and developed to be more private-sector-friendly, but it is unlikely that they stimulated trade or even much DFI.[8] Still, the desire for peace and stability in the region suggested the need for ASEAN, which helped strengthen dialogue, compromise, and cooperation. Could political cooperation have been possible without an economic dimension? Possibly, but it is doubtful. First, an important aspect of ASEAN's identity is its shared experience as a developing region. Economic cooperation, therefore, was thought to be necessary, even if it were to develop slowly. The myriad ASEAN meetings led to a great deal of interaction and forms of cooperation. Second, the slow pace of economic integration clearly testified to the reality that the economic dimension was more important in terms of "form," i.e., to give "cover" for political discussions before the First ASEAN Summit in Bali (1976).[9] Third, there is an important demonstration effect evident in growth experiences of developing countries, and the successes of more outward-oriented developing strategies in liberalizing ASEAN economies become more evident with frequent interaction. In fact, from an economic perspective, it may be that such liberalization is actually a *threat* to other countries. This is not true in the case of trade, which is the focus of most economic analysis and therefore, receives the most attention in the economic literature. Typically, liberalization of barriers to trade generates greater welfare benefits to the liberalizing economy but also boosts the welfare of partner countries who find that their exports to that market increase and, possibly, import prices fall. On the other hand, liberalization of barriers to *direct foreign investment* (DFI) could lead to a diversion of global capital toward the liberalizing region at the expense of stagnant countries (Petri 1997 demonstrates this using a computational general equilibrium model). In sum, ASEAN as a regional institution may not have *caused* the secular shift in economic growth, but it did contribute and certainly gave it an important push through its effects on ASEAN policy formation and, to a lesser extent, trade and investment. With deeper forms of economic integration in the works, it may be that the importance of ASEAN economic integration in contributing to the engine of regional growth will increase.

The decision to create AFTA at the Fourth Summit in January 1992 was a milestone in regional economic cooperation. Subsequent amendments to the AFTA, which was originally restrictive and long-term, rendered it comprehensive and shortened the time horizon to ten years. The mechanism to be used to harmonize tariffs within ASEAN is the Common External Preferential Tariff (CEPT), which will bring internal tariffs down to 0-5 percent. The ASEAN leaders have also committed themselves or have tabled initiatives related to other (higher) forms of economic cooperation in "nonborder areas," such as those pertaining to trade facilitation, an advanced investment code, agreements on intellectual property protection, attempts at creating closer mechanisms to present a unified stance in other international fora, a services agreement, means to minimize economic conflict (including areas under the broad rubric of competition policy), and greater product harmonization.

The increasingly ambitious nature of AFTA is indicative of how free-trade areas tend to create liberalization processes that force the grouping to aspire to ever-higher levels of economic integration. In the case of ASEAN, however, external liberalization of trade policies really came before AFTA itself and, in effect, were important determinants of AFTA. In essence, AFTA was in part a manifestation of the overall liberalization policies of the ASEAN countries.

Hence, it is not surprising that AFTA is unabashedly outward-looking in its orientation. In 1994, approximately one-fourth of ASEAN trade was intraregional, and even this figure is deceptive, as much of this trade is entrepôt in nature and flows through Singapore; if Singapore is excluded, the figure falls to about 5 percent.[10] If AFTA were to create a "fortress," trade diversion would clearly be high and trade creation fairly minimal (the economies are competitive but not necessarily complementary). Hence, an inward-looking bloc in ASEAN would be disruptive and antithetical to the original purpose: to create an integrated region in which regional transaction costs would be minimal and, hence, a cost-effective vertical division of labor would be possible. Therefore, a major goal of AFTA is to attract DFI—not so much for capital but for technology transfer, access to foreign markets, etc.—and this is why it is often referred to as more of an investment pact than a trade pact.[11] This orientation reflects the important role of foreign investors and their local partners as not only potent domestic constituencies but also *desired* constituencies in the region from the viewpoint of the metaregime.

Moreover, AFTA has embraced "open regionalism" in its purest form: ASEAN countries are choosing to "multilateralize" regional tariff reductions, thereby precluding trade diversion and bolstering the liberalization process. Singapore and Indonesia have already agreed to do this, and the AFTA agreement itself encourages it through special arrangements under the CEPT. Further, economic integration in ASEAN has been a powerful motivation for Vietnam's economic reform program. In July 1995, Vietnam joined ASEAN and agreed to accede to AFTA (with complete liberalization by 2006); Laos is slated to join by 1998; and Cambodia and Myanmar will likely follow in the medium term.

Table 12.1 gives some *prima facie* evidence of impressive trade liberalization during the period of increased economic cooperation in ASEAN at a disaggregated level. We choose two time periods; the first is the mid-1980s (1984-1987), at which point ASEAN economic cooperation essentially ebbed, and the most recent year for which these data are available (1991-1993), i.e., after the Third (1987) and Fourth (1992) Summits at which regional "deepening" took place. We can only suggest that deeper forms of economic integration were consistent with external liberalization, without any pretense to causality. Arguably, they are both reflections of the outward-oriented nature of the ASEAN metaregime and as such cannot be separated.

In Table 12.1, Singapore stands out as the most open country, with virtually no tariff barriers in both periods. However, a number of nontariff barriers (NTBs) were in existence in the first period and all but abolished in the second. For example, NTB coverage averaged 52 percent of all product lines in chemicals for the 1984-1987 period, but by the early 1990s these had all been abolished. With respect to the other countries (except the Philippines, for

TABLE 12.1

CHANGES IN SELECTED ASIAN DEVELOPING COUNTRY PROTECTION LEVELS
MAJOR SECTORS
(WEIGHTED AVERAGE, PERCENTAGES)

	MEAN TARIFF RATES			NTM INCIDENCE		
	1984-87	1988-90	1991-93	1984-87	1988-90	1991-93
SINGAPORE						
PRIMARY PRODUCTS	0.7	1.9	1.9	12.6	3.3	2.1
MANUFACTURING	1.4	1.9	1.9	12.8	0.2	0
ALL	1.2	1.9	1.9	12.9	1.3	0.7
INDONESIA						
PRIMARY PRODUCTS	10.4	9.1	8.5	98.4	14.9	11.2
MANUFACTURING	21.7	22.6	14.7	89.8	10.8	5.3
ALL	18.2	18	12.6	92.5	12.1	7.3
MALAYSIA						
PRIMARY PRODUCTS	6.4	5.4	5.3	6.3	1.6	1.6
MANUFACTURING	17.7	14.5	14.1	9.1	8	7
ALL	14.7	11.5	11.2	8.2	6	5.1
THAILAND						
PRIMARY PRODUCTS	16.5	31.5	26.4	28.6	12.1	12
MANUFACTURING	30.4	40.9	41.6	16.3	3.7	6.2
ALL	26.9	38	36.9	20.2	6.5	8.2

NOTES:
*Asian developing countries were selected on the basis of data availability.
Sources: UNCTAD, *Director of Import Regimes, Part 1: Monitoring Import Regimes* (New York: UN, 1994); MITI; *1996 Report on the WTO Consistency of Trade Policies by Major Trading Partners* (MITI, 1996).

which data were not available), economic liberalization in Indonesia is clearly the most impressive, with mean tariffs in manufacturing (all products) falling from 23 percent (18.2 percent) to 15 percent (12.6 percent) and NTBs falling from 90 percent (92.5 percent) to 5 percent (7.3 percent). Liberalization essentially took place across the board, but the transportation sector appears to have been opened the most, with tariffs falling from 40 percent to 7 percent over the time period and nontariff barriers being phased out almost completely. Malaysian tariffs and NTBs were consistently low over this period, and while tariff and NTBs each fell by over 20 percent on average, the marginal changes were small. In some ways, Thailand is the exception to the rule; average tariffs actually increased over this period from 30 percent to 40 percent in manufactures. However, some of these changes were obviously the "tariffication" and rationalization of nontariff barriers, which fell from an average of 20 percent to 8 percent. Thailand has become a fairly "transparent" market to the extent that businesspeople consider it relatively easy to tap.[12]

In sum, AFTA is enhancing economic liberalization throughout Southeast Asia in a manner consistent with global liberalization and one that would not have been possible without a regional approach, at least within the slated time horizon. In ASEAN, it is in no country's interest to pay more for its imports because of trade diversion; this is arguably the main force behind the multilateralization of CEPT cuts. Moreover, the desire for increased DFI is determining to no small degree the pace and direction of economic integration.[13]

IV. ASEAN AND THE EAST ASIAN ECONOMIC CAUCUS

There currently exists no formal regional trade bloc in the Asia-Pacific; however, market-driven economic integration in the region has been taking place at a rapid pace. For examples, Tables 12.2-12.3 give matrices of bilateral exports shares for APEC and European Union (EU) member states for 1994 and 1980, respectively. Intra-APEC exports have increased from 57 percent to 73 percent over the past 15 years; this implies that APEC trades more with itself than does the EU (whose intraregional trade comes to about two-thirds). This same trend is also in evidence in China, Japan, Hong Kong, and South Korea, and ASEAN member states.

TABLE 12.2

EXPORTS—1994—PERCENTAGE

EXPORTER	TOTAL EXPORTS (US$ BN)	DESTINATION										
		US	CAN.	MEX.	CHE	JPN	AUSL	NZ	HK	SK	TW	SING.
US	476.00	0.00	0.22	0.10	0.01	0.11	0.02	0.00	0.02	0.04	0.03	0.02
CAN.	163.00	0.82	0.00	0.00	0.00	0.04	0.00	0.00	0.00	0.01	0.00	0.00
MEX.	61.88	0.85	0.02	0.00	0.00	0.02	0.00	0.00	0.00	0.00	0.00	0.00
CHE	11.06	0.16	0.01	0.02	0.00	0.18	0.00	0.00	0.00	0.05	0.05	0.00
JPN	395.00	0.30	0.01	0.01	0.00	0.00	0.02	0.00	0.06	0.06	0.06	0.05
AUSL	42.02	0.07	0.02	0.00	0.00	0.25	0.00	0.06	0.04	0.07	0.05	0.03
NZ	11.63	0.11	0.02	0.01	0.00	0.16	0.20	0.00	0.03	0.05	0.03	0.01
HK	28.74	0.28	0.02	0.00	0.00	0.05	0.01	0.00	0.00	0.01	0.03	0.06
SK	95.44	0.22	0.01	0.01	0.00	0.14	0.01	0.00	0.08	0.00	0.03	0.04
SING.	96.59	0.19	0.01	0.00	0.00	0.07	0.02	0.00	0.09	0.03	0.04	0.00
INDO.(1)	39.91	0.15	0.01	0.00	0.00	0.27	0.02	0.00	0.03	0.06	0.04	0.10
MAL.	58.73	0.21	0.01	0.01	0.00	0.12	0.02	0.00	0.05	0.03	0.03	0.21
PHIL.	13.09	0.40	0.01	0.00	0.00	0.15	0.01	0.00	0.05	0.02	0.03	0.05
THAI.(2)	37.08	0.22	0.01	0.00	0.00	0.17	0.01	0.00	0.05	0.01	0.02	0.12
CHN	121.00	0.18	0.01	0.00	0.00	0.18	0.01	0.00	0.27	0.04	0.02	0.02
FRN	233.00	0.07	0.01	0.01	0.00	0.02	0.00	0.00	0.01	0.01	0.01	0.01
GER.	423.00	0.08	0.01	0.01	0.00	0.03	0.01	0.00	0.01	0.01	0.01	0.01
BELUX	137.00	0.05	0.00	0.00	0.00	0.01	0.00	0.00	0.01	0.00	0.01	0.00
NETH.	146.00	0.04	0.00	0.00	0.00	0.01	0.00	0.00	0.01	0.00	0.01	0.00
ITALY	190.00	0.08	0.01	0.00	0.00	0.02	0.01	0.00	0.02	0.01	0.01	0.01
UK	200.00	0.13	0.01	0.00	0.00	0.02	0.01	0.00	0.02	0.01	0.01	0.01
DEN.	39.83	0.05	0.00	0.00	0.00	0.04	0.01	0.00	0.01	0.01	0.00	0.00
IRE.	29.90	0.08	0.01	0.00	0.00	0.03	0.01	0.00	0.00	0.00	0.00	0.01
SPN	72.87	0.05	0.01	0.02	0.00	0.01	0.00	0.00	0.01	0.01	0.00	0.00
GCE(2)	8.78	0.04	0.00	0.00	0.00	0.01	0.00	0.00	0.00	0.00	0.00	0.00
PORT.(2)	15.42	0.04	0.01	0.00	0.00	0.01	0.00	0.00	0.00	0.00	0.00	0.00
SWD	61.24	0.08	0.01	0.00	0.00	0.03	0.01	0.00	0.01	0.01	0.01	0.01
FND	29.79	0.07	0.01	0.00	0.00	0.02	0.01	0.00	0.01	0.01	0.00	0.01
AUS(2)	40.14	0.03	0.01	0.00	0.00	0.02	0.00	0.00	0.01	0.00	0.00	0.00
BZL(2)	43.36	0.21	0.01	0.02	0.02	0.06	0.01	0.00	0.01	0.01	0.01	0.01
ARG	15.80	0.11	0.00	0.02	0.06	0.03	0.00	0.00	0.01	0.00	0.01	0.00
EAEC		0.25	0.01	0.01	0.00	0.08	0.02	0.00	0.09	0.04	0.04	0.06
APEC(3)	1651.16	0.25	0.07	0.03	0.00	0.09	0.02	0.00	0.06	0.04	0.03	0.04
EU15	1626.97	0.07	0.01	0.01	0.00	0.02	0.01	0.00	0.01	0.01	0.01	0.01
ASEAN(4)	245.39	0.20	0.01	0.00	0.00	0.13	0.02	0.00	0.06	0.03	0.03	0.09

TABLE 12.2

EXPORTS—1994—PERCENTAGE (CONTINUED)

EXPORTER	TOTAL EXPORTS (US$ BN)	DESTINATION										
		Indo.	Mal.	Phil.	Thai.	CHN	Viet.	FRN	Ger.	BeLu	Neth.	Italy
US	476.00	0.01	0.01	0.01	0.01	0.02	0.00	0.03	0.04	0.02	0.03	0.01
CAN.	163.00	0.00	0.00	0.00	0.00	0.01	0.00	0.01	0.01	0.01	0.01	0.01
MEX.	61.88	0.00	0.00	0.00	0.00	0.00	0.00	0.01	0.01	0.00	0.00	0.00
CHE	11.06	0.01	0.00	0.00	0.01	0.01	0.00	0.04	0.04	0.02	0.03	0.03
JPN	395.00	0.02	0.03	0.01	0.04	0.05	0.00	0.01	0.05	0.01	0.02	0.01
AUSL	42.02	0.03	0.03	0.01	0.02	0.05	0.00	0.01	0.02	0.01	0.01	0.02
NZ	11.63	0.01	0.02	0.01	0.01	0.03	0.00	0.01	0.03	0.01	0.01	0.01
HK	28.74	0.01	0.01	0.01	0.01	0.27	0.00	0.01	0.06	0.00	0.02	0.01
SK	95.44	0.03	0.02	0.01	0.02	0.06	0.01	0.01	0.05	0.00	0.01	0.01
SING.	96.59	0.00	0.20	0.02	0.06	0.02	0.01	0.01	0.04	0.00	0.03	0.01
INDO.(1)	39.91	0.00	0.02	0.01	0.01	0.03	0.01	0.01	0.03	0.01	0.03	0.02
MAL.	58.73	0.01	0.00	0.01	0.04	0.03	0.00	0.01	0.03	0.01	0.02	0.01
PHIL.	13.09	0.01	0.02	0.00	0.03	0.01	0.00	0.01	0.05	0.01	0.04	0.01
THAI.(2)	37.08	0.01	0.03	0.01	0.00	0.01	0.00	0.02	0.04	0.02	0.03	0.01
CHN	121.00	0.01	0.01	0.00	0.01	0.00	0.00	0.01	0.04	0.01	0.02	0.01
FRN	233.00	0.00	0.00	0.00	0.00	0.01	0.00	0.00	0.17	0.09	0.05	0.09
GER.	423.00	0.01	0.00	0.00	0.01	0.01	0.00	0.12	0.00	0.07	0.07	0.08
BELUX	137.00	0.00	0.00	0.00	0.00	0.01	0.00	0.19	0.21	0.00	0.13	0.05
NETH.	146.00	0.00	0.00	0.00	0.00	0.00	0.00	0.10	0.26	0.12	0.00	0.05
ITALY	190.00	0.00	0.00	0.00	0.00	0.01	0.00	0.13	0.19	0.03	0.03	0.00
UK	200.00	0.00	0.01	0.00	0.01	0.01	0.00	0.10	0.13	0.05	0.07	0.05
DEN.	39.83	0.00	0.00	0.00	0.00	0.00	0.00	0.05	0.21	0.02	0.04	0.04
IRE.	29.90	0.00	0.01	0.00	0.00	0.00	0.00	0.09	0.14	0.04	0.06	0.04
SPN	72.87	0.00	0.00	0.00	0.00	0.01	0.00	0.20	0.14	0.03	0.04	0.09
GCE(2)	8.78	0.00	0.00	0.00	0.00	0.01	0.00	0.06	0.24	0.02	0.02	0.13
PORT.(2)	15.42	0.00	0.00	0.00	0.00	0.00	0.00	0.15	0.20	0.04	0.05	0.03
SWD	61.24	0.00	0.01	0.00	0.01	0.02	0.00	0.05	0.13	0.05	0.05	0.04
FND	29.79	0.00	0.01	0.00	0.01	0.01	0.00	0.05	0.13	0.02	0.05	0.03
AUS(2)	40.14	0.01	0.00	0.00	0.00	0.01	0.00	0.04	0.39	0.02	0.03	0.08
BZL(2)	43.36	0.01	0.00	0.01	0.01	0.02	0.00	0.02	0.05	0.03	0.07	0.04
ARG	15.80	0.01	0.01	0.00	0.00	0.01	0.00	0.01	0.04	0.01	0.07	0.04
EAEC		0.01	0.04	0.01	0.03	0.04	0.00	0.01	0.04	0.01	0.02	0.01
APEC(3)	1651.16	0.01	0.03	0.01	0.02	0.03	0.00	0.02	0.04	0.01	0.02	0.01
EU15	1626.97	0.00	0.00	0.00	0.00	0.01	0.00	0.10	0.14	0.06	0.06	0.06
ASEAN(4)	245.39	0.00	0.09	0.01	0.03	0.02	0.01	0.01	0.04	0.01	0.03	0.01

TABLE 12.2

EXPORTS—1994—PERCENTAGE (CONTINUED)

EXPORTER	TOTAL EXPORTS (US$ BN)	DESTINATION										
		UK	Den.	Ire.	SPN	GCE	Port.	SWD	FND	AUS	BZL	ARG
US	476.00	0.05	0.00	0.01	0.01	0.00	0.00	0.01	0.00	0.00	0.02	0.01
CAN.	163.00	0.01	0.00	0.00	0.00	0.00	0.00	0.00	0.00	0.00	0.00	0.00
MEX.	61.88	0.00	0.00	0.00	0.01	0.00	0.00	0.00	0.00	0.00	0.01	0.00
CHE	11.06	0.04	0.00	0.00	0.02	0.00	0.00	0.01	0.00	0.00	0.06	0.06
JPN	395.00	0.03	0.00	0.00	0.01	0.00	0.00	0.00	0.00	0.00	0.00	0.00
AUSL	42.02	0.04	0.00	0.00	0.00	0.00	0.00	0.00	0.00	0.00	0.00	0.00
NZ	11.63	0.06	0.00	0.00	0.00	0.00	0.00	0.00	0.00	0.00	0.00	0.00
HK	28.74	0.05	0.00	0.00	0.00	0.00	0.00	0.00	0.00	0.00	0.00	0.00
SK	95.44	0.02	0.00	0.00	0.01	0.00	0.00	0.00	0.00	0.00	0.01	0.00
SING.	96.59	0.03	0.00	0.01	0.00	0.00	0.00	0.00	0.00	0.00	0.00	0.00
INDO.(1)	39.91	0.03	0.00	0.00	0.01	0.00	0.00	0.00	0.00	0.00	0.00	0.00
MAL.	58.73	0.04	0.00	0.00	0.00	0.00	0.00	0.00	0.00	0.00	0.00	0.00
PHIL.	13.09	0.04	0.00	0.00	0.00	0.00	0.00	0.00	0.00	0.00	0.00	0.00
THAI.(2)	37.08	0.03	0.00	0.00	0.01	0.00	0.00	0.00	0.00	0.00	0.00	0.00
CHN	121.00	0.02	0.00	0.00	0.01	0.00	0.00	0.00	0.00	0.00	0.00	0.00
FRN	233.00	0.10	0.01	0.01	0.07	0.01	0.01	0.01	0.00	0.01	0.00	0.00
GER.	423.00	0.08	0.02	0.00	0.03	0.01	0.01	0.02	0.01	0.06	0.01	0.00
BELUX	137.00	0.08	0.01	0.00	0.03	0.01	0.01	0.01	0.00	0.01	0.00	0.00
NETH.	146.00	0.09	0.01	0.01	0.02	0.01	0.01	0.01	0.01	0.01	0.00	0.00
ITALY	190.00	0.06	0.01	0.00	0.05	0.02	0.01	0.01	0.00	0.02	0.01	0.01
UK	200.00	0.00	0.01	0.05	0.04	0.01	0.01	0.03	0.01	0.01	0.00	0.00
DEN.	39.83	0.08	0.00	0.00	0.02	0.01	0.01	0.10	0.02	0.01	0.00	0.00
IRE.	29.90	0.27	0.01	0.00	0.02	0.01	0.01	0.02	0.01	0.01	0.00	0.00
SPN	72.87	0.08	0.01	0.00	0.00	0.01	0.08	0.01	0.00	0.01	0.00	0.01
GCE(2)	8.78	0.06	0.01	0.00	0.02	0.00	0.00	0.01	0.01	0.01	0.01	0.00
PORT.(2)	15.42	0.11	0.02	0.00	0.15	0.01	0.00	0.03	0.01	0.01	0.00	0.00
SWD	61.24	0.10	0.07	0.01	0.02	0.01	0.00	0.00	0.05	0.01	0.01	0.00
FND	29.79	0.10	0.03	0.00	0.02	0.01	0.00	0.11	0.00	0.01	0.00	0.00
AUS(2)	40.14	0.03	0.01	0.00	0.02	0.01	0.00	0.01	0.01	0.00	0.00	0.00
BZL(2)	43.36	0.03	0.01	0.00	0.02	0.00	0.01	0.00	0.00	0.00	0.00	0.10
ARG	15.80	0.01	0.01	0.00	0.04	0.00	0.00	0.00	0.00	0.00	0.23	0.00
EAEC		0.03	0.00	0.00	0.01	0.00	0.00	0.00	0.00	0.00	0.00	0.00
APEC(3)	1651.16	0.03	0.00	0.00	0.01	0.00	0.00	0.00	0.00	0.00	0.01	0.00
EU15	1626.97	0.08	0.01	0.01	0.04	0.01	0.01	0.02	0.01	0.02	0.01	0.00
ASEAN(4)	245.39	0.03	0.00	0.00	0.01	0.00	0.00	0.00	0.00	0.00	0.00	0.00

Notes:
(1) data for East Timor was added to Indonesia
(2) 1993 data used for Thailand, Greece, Portugal, Austria, and Brazil
(3) APEC: missing Papua New Guinea and Brunei, as well as Taiwan in the "exporter" aggregate.

TABLE 12.2

EXPORTS—1994—PERCENTAGE (CONTINUED)

EXPORTER	TOTAL EXPORTS (US$ BN)	DESTINATION					SUM(5)
		SWIT	EAEC	APEC(3)	EU15	ASEAN(4)	
US	476.00	0.01	0.24	0.63	0.21	0.06	0.87
CAN.	163.00	0.00	0.08	0.91	0.05	0.01	0.97
MEX.	61.88	0.00	0.02	0.90	0.04	0.00	0.96
CHE	11.06	0.00	0.28	0.51	0.23	0.03	0.86
JPN	395.00	0.01	0.33	0.74	0.16	0.15	0.91
AUSL	42.02	0.00	0.53	0.74	0.12	0.13	0.87
NZ	11.63	0.00	0.33	0.70	0.15	0.07	0.85
HK	28.74	0.01	0.43	0.77	0.17	0.10	0.95
SK	95.44	0.00	0.42	0.70	0.12	0.13	0.84
SING.	96.59	0.01	0.49	0.74	0.13	0.28	0.90
INDO.(1)	39.91	0.00	0.55	0.76	0.15	0.14	0.92
MAL.	58.73	0.00	0.50	0.77	0.14	0.27	0.92
PHIL.	13.09	0.00	0.34	0.79	0.17	0.10	0.97
THAI.(2)	37.08	0.01	0.41	0.68	0.17	0.16	0.86
CHN	121.00	0.00	0.54	0.76	0.13	0.06	0.90
FRN	233.00	0.04	0.07	0.16	0.63	0.02	0.84
GER.	423.00	0.05	0.09	0.20	0.58	0.03	0.84
BELUX	137.00	0.02	0.05	0.11	0.75	0.01	0.89
NETH.	146.00	0.02	0.04	0.09	0.71	0.01	0.81
ITALY	190.00	0.04	0.08	0.19	0.57	0.02	0.81
UK	200.00	0.02	0.09	0.26	0.56	0.03	0.85
DEN.	39.83	0.02	0.07	0.14	0.59	0.01	0.75
IRE.	29.90	0.02	0.06	0.17	0.73	0.01	0.92
SPN	72.87	0.01	0.05	0.14	0.71	0.01	0.87
GCE(2)	8.78	0.01	0.03	0.08	0.59	0.01	0.69
PORT.(2)	15.42	0.02	0.02	0.08	0.80	0.00	0.90
SWD	61.24	0.02	0.09	0.21	0.59	0.03	0.82
FND	29.79	0.01	0.09	0.19	0.57	0.03	0.78
AUS(2)	40.14	0.06	0.05	0.10	0.66	0.02	0.82
BZL(2)	43.36	0.01	0.13	0.41	0.28	0.03	0.79
ARG	15.80	0.00	0.08	0.29	0.25	0.02	0.78
EAEC		0.00	0.41	0.74	0.15	0.16	0.90
APEC(3)	1651.16	0.01	0.32	0.73	0.15	0.11	0.90
EU15	1626.97	0.03	0.07	0.17	0.62	0.02	0.84
ASEAN(4)	245.39	0.00	0.48	0.74	0.15	0.23	0.91

(4) ASEAN includes Indonesia, Malaysia, Singapore, Thailand, Philippines, and Vietnam; except Vietnam is absent in the "exporter" aggregate

(5) SUM is the total for all countries shown in this table

Source: United Nations, Commodity Trade Statistics, Various Years

TABLE 12.3

EXPORTS—1980—PERCENTAGE

EXPORTER	TOTAL EXPORTS (US$ BN)	DESTINATION										
		US	CAN.	MEX.	CHE	JPN	AUSL	NZ	HK	SK	TW	SING.
US	213.00	0.00	0.15	0.07	0.01	0.10	0.02	0.00	0.01	0.02	0.02	0.01
CAN.	63.11	0.63	0.00	0.01	0.00	0.06	0.01	0.00	0.00	0.01	0.00	0.00
MEX.	15.44	0.65	0.01	0.00	0.00	0.05	0.00	0.00	0.00	0.00	0.00	0.00
CHE(1)	3.58	0.19	0.02	0.01	0.00	0.12	0.00	0.00	0.00	0.01	0.01	0.00
JPN	130.00	0.24	0.02	0.01	0.00	0.00	0.03	0.01	0.04	0.04	0.04	0.03
AUSL	21.28	0.10	0.02	0.00	0.00	0.25	0.00	0.04	0.01	0.02	0.02	0.02
NZ	5.26	0.13	0.02	0.01	0.00	0.13	0.13	0.00	0.01	0.01	0.01	0.02
HK	13.67	0.33	0.03	0.00	0.00	0.03	0.03	0.00	0.00	0.00	0.01	0.03
SK	17.45	0.26	0.02	0.00	0.00	0.17	0.01	0.00	0.05	0.00	0.01	0.02
SING.	19.38	0.13	0.01	0.00	0.00	0.08	0.04	0.02	0.08	0.02	0.02	0.00
INDO.(2)	21.91	0.20	0.00	0.00	0.00	0.49	0.02	0.00	0.01	0.01	0.02	0.11
MAL.	12.94	0.16	0.00	0.00	0.00	0.23	0.01	0.00	0.02	0.02	0.02	0.19
PHIL.	5.75	0.28	0.01	0.00	0.00	0.26	0.02	0.00	0.03	0.04	0.02	0.02
THAI.	6.37	0.13	0.00	0.00	0.00	0.15	0.01	0.00	0.05	0.01	0.01	0.07
CHN	NA	NA	NA	NA	NA	NA	NA	NA	NA	NA	NA	NA
FRN	111.00	0.04	0.01	0.00	0.00	0.01	0.00	0.00	0.00	0.00	0.00	0.00
GER.(3)	192.00	0.06	0.01	0.01	0.00	0.01	0.01	0.00	0.00	0.00	0.00	0.00
BELUX	63.97	0.03	0.00	0.00	0.00	0.00	0.00	0.00	0.01	0.00	0.00	0.00
NETH.	73.87	0.03	0.00	0.00	0.00	0.00	0.00	0.00	0.00	0.00	0.00	0.00
ITALY	77.64	0.05	0.01	0.00	0.00	0.01	0.01	0.00	0.00	0.00	0.00	0.00
UK	114.00	0.10	0.02	0.00	0.00	0.01	0.02	0.01	0.01	0.00	0.00	0.01
DEN.	16.41	0.04	0.01	0.00	0.00	0.02	0.00	0.00	0.00	0.00	0.00	0.00
IRE.	8.47	0.05	0.02	0.01	0.00	0.00	0.01	0.00	0.00	0.00	0.00	0.00
SPN	20.83	0.05	0.01	0.02	0.01	0.01	0.00	0.00	0.00	0.00	0.00	0.00
GCE	5.14	0.06	0.00	0.00	0.00	0.00	0.00	0.00	0.00	0.00	0.00	0.00
PORT.	4.63	0.06	0.01	0.00	0.00	0.01	0.00	0.00	0.00	0.00	0.00	0.00
SWD	30.79	0.05	0.01	0.01	0.00	0.01	0.01	0.00	0.00	0.00	0.00	0.01
FND	14.14	0.03	0.00	0.00	0.00	0.01	0.01	0.00	0.00	0.00	0.00	0.00
AUS	17.48	0.02	0.00	0.00	0.00	0.01	0.00	0.00	0.00	0.00	0.00	0.00
BZL	20.13	0.17	0.01	0.02	0.02	0.06	0.00	0.00	0.00	0.00	0.00	0.00
ARG	8.02	0.09	0.01	0.02	0.03	0.03	0.00	0.00	0.00	0.00	0.00	0.00
EAEC		0.23	0.02	0.01	0.00	0.09	0.02	0.01	0.03	0.03	0.03	0.04
APEC(4)	549.13	0.19	0.07	0.03	0.00	0.10	0.02	0.01	0.02	0.02	0.02	0.02
EU15	750.36	0.05	0.01	0.00	0.00	0.01	0.01	0.00	0.00	0.00	0.00	0.00
ASEAN(5)	66.34	0.17	0.00	0.00	0.00	0.27	0.02	0.01	0.04	0.02	0.02	0.08

TABLE 12.3

EXPORTS—1980—PERCENTAGE (CONTINUED)

EXPORTER	TOTAL EXPORTS (US$ BN)	DESTINATION										
		INDO.	MAL.	PHIL.	THAI.	CHN	VIET.	FRN	GER.	BELU	NETH.	ITALY
US	213.00	0.01	0.01	0.01	0.01	0.02	0.00	0.03	0.05	0.03	0.04	0.03
CAN.	63.11	0.00	0.00	0.00	0.00	0.01	0.00	0.01	0.02	0.01	0.02	0.01
MEX.	15.44	0.00	0.00	0.00	0.00	0.01	0.00	0.04	0.02	0.00	0.00	0.01
CHE(1)	3.58	0.00	0.00	0.00	0.00	0.02	0.00	0.04	0.11	0.03	0.04	0.05
JPN	130.00	0.03	0.02	0.01	0.01	0.04	0.00	0.02	0.05	0.01	0.02	0.01
AUSL	21.28	0.02	0.02	0.01	0.01	0.04	0.00	0.02	0.02	0.01	0.01	0.02
NZ	5.26	0.01	0.01	0.01	0.01	0.03	0.00	0.02	0.03	0.01	0.02	0.02
HK	13.67	0.00	0.01	0.01	0.01	0.02	0.00	0.02	0.11	0.01	0.02	0.02
SK	17.45	0.02	0.01	0.01	0.01	0.00	0.00	0.02	0.05	0.01	0.02	0.01
SING.	19.38	0.00	0.15	0.01	0.04	0.02	0.00	0.02	0.03	0.00	0.02	0.01
INDO.(2)	21.91	0.00	0.00	0.01	0.00	0.00	0.00	0.01	0.02	0.00	0.02	0.01
MAL.	12.94	0.00	0.00	0.02	0.01	0.02	0.00	0.02	0.04	0.01	0.06	0.02
PHIL.	5.75	0.02	0.02	0.00	0.01	0.01	0.00	0.02	0.05	0.01	0.06	0.01
THAI.	6.37	0.04	0.05	0.00	0.00	0.02	0.00	0.02	0.04	0.03	0.14	0.02
CHN	NA	NA	NA	NA	NA	NA	NA	NA	NA	NA	NA	NA
FRN	111.00	0.00	0.00	0.00	0.00	0.00	0.00	0.00	0.16	0.09	0.05	0.13
GER.(3)	192.00	0.00	0.00	0.00	0.00	0.01	0.00	0.13	0.00	0.08	0.10	0.09
BELUX	63.97	0.00	0.00	0.00	0.00	0.00	0.00	0.20	0.22	0.00	0.15	0.06
NETH.	73.87	0.01	0.00	0.00	0.00	0.00	0.00	0.11	0.30	0.15	0.00	0.06
ITALY	77.64	0.00	0.00	0.00	0.00	0.00	0.00	0.15	0.18	0.03	0.04	0.00
UK	114.00	0.00	0.00	0.00	0.00	0.00	0.00	0.07	0.11	0.05	0.08	0.04
DEN.	16.41	0.00	0.00	0.00	0.00	0.00	0.00	0.05	0.19	0.02	0.04	0.05
IRE.	8.47	0.00	0.00	0.00	0.00	0.00	0.00	0.08	0.10	0.05	0.05	0.03
SPN	20.83	0.00	0.00	0.00	0.00	0.00	0.00	0.17	0.10	0.03	0.04	0.08
GCE	5.14	0.00	0.00	0.00	0.00	0.00	0.01	0.07	0.19	0.02	0.06	0.10
PORT.	4.63	0.00	0.00	0.00	0.00	0.00	0.00	0.10	0.14	0.03	0.05	0.06
SWD	30.79	0.00	0.01	0.00	0.00	0.00	0.00	0.06	0.13	0.03	0.05	0.04
FND	14.14	0.00	0.00	0.00	0.00	0.01	0.00	0.05	0.11	0.01	0.04	0.02
AUS	17.48	0.00	0.00	0.00	0.00	0.00	0.00	0.03	0.32	0.02	0.03	0.11
BZL	20.13	0.00	0.00	0.00	0.00	0.00	0.00	0.04	0.07	0.02	0.06	0.05
ARG	8.02	0.00	0.00	0.00	0.00	0.02	0.00	0.02	0.06	0.01	0.09	0.06
EAEC		0.02	0.02	0.01	0.01	0.03	0.00	0.02	0.05	0.01	0.02	0.01
APEC(4)	549.13	0.01	0.01	0.01	0.01	0.02	0.00	0.02	0.04	0.02	0.03	0.02
EU15	750.36	0.00	0.00	0.00	0.00	0.00	0.00	0.10	0.13	0.06	0.07	0.07
ASEAN(5)	66.34	0.01	0.05	0.01	0.02	0.01	0.00	0.01	0.03	0.01	0.04	0.01

TABLE 12.3

EXPORTS—1980—PERCENTAGE (CONTINUED)

EXPORTER	TOTAL EXPORTS (US$ BN)	DESTINATION										
		UK	DEN.	IRE.	SPN	GCE	PORT.	SWD	FND	AUS	BZL	ARG
US	213.00	0.05	0.00	0.00	0.02	0.00	0.00	0.01	0.00	0.00	0.02	0.01
CAN.	63.11	0.04	0.00	0.00	0.00	0.00	0.00	0.00	0.00	0.00	0.01	0.00
MEX.	15.44	0.01	0.00	0.00	0.08	0.00	0.00	0.00	0.00	0.00	0.03	0.00
CHE(1)	3.58	0.06	0.00	0.00	0.02	0.00	0.00	0.01	0.00	0.00	0.09	0.04
JPN	130.00	0.03	0.00	0.00	0.01	0.00	0.00	0.01	0.00	0.00	0.01	0.01
AUSL	21.28	0.04	0.00	0.00	0.00	0.00	0.00	0.00	0.00	0.00	0.00	0.00
NZ	5.26	0.13	0.00	0.00	0.00	0.01	0.00	0.00	0.00	0.00	0.00	0.00
HK	13.67	0.10	0.01	0.00	0.01	0.00	0.00	0.01	0.00	0.01	0.00	0.01
SK	17.45	0.03	0.00	0.00	0.01	0.00	0.00	0.01	0.00	0.00	0.00	0.00
SING.	19.38	0.03	0.00	0.00	0.00	0.01	0.00	0.00	0.00	0.00	0.00	0.00
INDO.(2)	21.91	0.01	0.00	0.00	0.00	0.00	0.00	0.00	0.00	0.00	0.01	0.00
MAL.	12.94	0.03	0.00	0.00	0.01	0.00	0.00	0.00	0.00	0.00	0.00	0.00
PHIL.	5.75	0.03	0.00	0.00	0.00	0.00	0.00	0.00	0.00	0.00	0.00	0.00
THAI.	6.37	0.02	0.00	0.00	0.00	0.00	0.00	0.00	0.00	0.00	0.00	0.00
CHN	NA	NA	NA	NA	NA	NA	NA	NA	NA	NA	NA	NA
FRN	111.00	0.07	0.01	0.00	0.03	0.01	0.01	0.01	0.00	0.01	0.01	0.00
GER.(3)	192.00	0.06	0.02	0.00	0.02	0.01	0.01	0.03	0.01	0.06	0.01	0.01
BELUX	63.97	0.08	0.01	0.00	0.01	0.00	0.00	0.02	0.00	0.01	0.00	0.00
NETH.	73.87	0.08	0.02	0.00	0.01	0.01	0.00	0.02	0.01	0.01	0.00	0.00
ITALY	77.64	0.06	0.01	0.00	0.02	0.02	0.01	0.01	0.00	0.03	0.01	0.01
UK	114.00	0.00	0.02	0.05	0.02	0.00	0.01	0.03	0.01	0.01	0.00	0.00
DEN.	16.41	0.14	0.00	0.01	0.01	0.01	0.00	0.13	0.02	0.01	0.00	0.00
IRE.	8.47	0.43	0.01	0.00	0.01	0.00	0.00	0.01	0.00	0.00	0.00	0.00
SPN	20.83	0.07	0.01	0.00	0.00	0.01	0.03	0.01	0.00	0.00	0.01	0.02
GCE	5.14	0.04	0.01	0.00	0.01	0.00	0.00	0.00	0.00	0.01	0.00	0.00
PORT.	4.63	0.15	0.02	0.00	0.04	0.00	0.00	0.04	0.01	0.01	0.01	0.00
SWD	30.79	0.10	0.08	0.01	0.01	0.00	0.01	0.00	0.06	0.01	0.00	0.00
FND	14.14	0.11	0.03	0.01	0.01	0.01	0.00	0.17	0.00	0.01	0.00	0.00
AUS	17.48	0.04	0.01	0.00	0.01	0.01	0.00	0.03	0.01	0.00	0.00	0.00
BZL	20.13	0.03	0.01	0.00	0.03	0.01	0.01	0.01	0.00	0.00	0.00	0.05
ARG	8.02	0.03	0.01	0.00	0.02	0.00	0.01	0.00	0.00	0.00	0.10	0.00
EAEC		0.03	0.00	0.00	0.00	0.00	0.00	0.01	0.00	0.00	0.01	0.01
APEC(4)	549.13	0.04	0.00	0.00	0.01	0.00	0.00	0.01	0.00	0.00	0.01	0.01
EU15	750.36	0.07	0.02	0.01	0.02	0.01	0.01	0.03	0.01	0.02	0.01	0.00
ASEAN(5)	66.34	0.02	0.00	0.00	0.00	0.00	0.00	0.00	0.00	0.00	0.00	0.00

Notes:
(1) 1982 data used for Chile
(2) data for East Timor was added to Indonesia
(3) East Germany Import Data Unavailable

TABLE 12.3

EXPORTS—1980—PERCENTAGE (CONTINUED)

EXPORTER	TOTAL EXPORTS (US$ BN)	DESTINATION					
		SWIT	EAEC	APEC(4)	EU15	ASEAN(5)	SUM(6)
US	213.00	0.01	0.19	0.46	0.27	0.04	0.78
CAN.	63.11	0.00	0.09	0.74	0.13	0.01	0.89
MEX.	15.44	0.00	0.06	0.72	0.16	0.00	0.91
CHE(1)	3.58	0.01	0.15	0.38	0.35	0.01	0.88
JPN	130.00	0.01	0.22	0.56	0.15	0.10	0.74
AUSL	21.28	0.00	0.40	0.59	0.13	0.08	0.73
NZ	5.26	0.00	0.25	0.55	0.24	0.06	0.79
HK	13.67	0.02	0.12	0.52	0.31	0.05	0.87
SK	17.45	0.00	0.28	0.60	0.16	0.07	0.78
SING.	19.38	0.00	0.40	0.61	0.13	0.21	0.75
INDO.(2)	21.91	0.00	0.64	0.87	0.07	0.13	0.95
MAL.	12.94	0.00	0.51	0.71	0.18	0.22	0.90
PHIL.	5.75	0.00	0.41	0.73	0.18	0.07	0.92
THAI.	6.37	0.02	0.39	0.54	0.27	0.16	0.84
CHN	NA	NA	NA	NA	NA	NA	NA
FRN	111.00	0.04	0.03	0.09	0.57	0.01	0.72
GER.(3)	192.00	0.05	0.04	0.12	0.58	0.01	0.80
BELUX	63.97	0.03	0.02	0.07	0.75	0.01	0.87
NETH.	73.87	0.02	0.02	0.06	0.75	0.01	0.85
ITALY	77.64	0.04	0.03	0.10	0.55	0.01	0.72
UK	114.00	0.06	0.05	0.18	0.47	0.02	0.75
DEN.	16.41	0.02	0.03	0.09	0.55	0.01	0.79
IRE.	8.47	0.01	0.01	0.10	0.77	0.00	0.89
SPN	20.83	0.02	0.03	0.12	0.53	0.01	0.70
GCE	5.14	0.01	0.02	0.08	0.50	0.01	0.60
PORT.	4.63	0.04	0.02	0.09	0.61	0.01	0.81
SWD	30.79	0.02	0.04	0.12	0.59	0.02	0.75
FND	14.14	0.02	0.02	0.07	0.42	0.01	0.68
AUS	17.48	0.08	0.02	0.05	0.58	0.01	0.74
BZL	20.13	0.01	0.08	0.32	0.32	0.01	0.70
ARG	8.02	0.01	0.06	0.20	0.31	0.00	0.61
EAEC		0.01	0.30	0.61	0.15	0.11	0.79
APEC(4)	549.13	0.01	0.23	0.57	0.20	0.07	0.80
EU15	750.36	0.04	0.03	0.11	0.59	0.01	0.77
ASEAN(5)	66.34	0.00	0.50	0.72	0.14	0.17	0.87

(4) APEC: missing Papua New Guinea and Brunei, as well as Taiwan and China in the "exporter" aggregate
(5) ASEAN includes Indonesia, Malaysia, Singapore, Thailand, Philippines, and Vietnam; except Vietnam is absent in the "exporter" aggregate
(6) SUM is the total for all countries shown in this table
Source: United Nations, Commodity Trade Statistics, Various Years

In fact, as can be seen in Tables 12.4-12.5, if exports are normalized by the importance of trading partners in global trade (an index that has been called a "gravity coefficient" or "double-density" measure),[14] one finds that the "bias" in favor of trade between EAEC countries is strong, coming to 1.92 in 1994, and suggesting that EAEC members trade twice as much as one would expect.[15] This compares with 1.63 in the case of APEC and 1.69 in the case of the EU. While these figures are no doubt inflated by the entrepôt trade in the EAEC, particularly among the ASEAN countries, they do imply that regional integration within Asia is high, with or without North America or Oceania.

In December 1990, Prime Minister Mahathir of Malaysia called for the creation of an "East Asian Economic Grouping" (EAEG), to include all countries in East and Southeast Asia. As it was presented, the EAEG was to be a formal preferential trading area in reaction to "exclusionism" in the West, i.e., economic integration in Europe and North America, as well as the failure to push through the Uruguay Round. The concept has evolved and now receives general, albeit ambivalent, support from its proposed members who have stressed that it will be consistent with GATT/WTO and parallel to APEC. At the Fourth ASEAN Summit, the ASEAN heads-of-state decided to transform the EAEG into a milder "East Asian Economic Caucus."

The reason for the transformation of the EAEG into an EAEC is significant for our purposes, for it shows that ASEAN countries do not intend to create a discriminatory trade bloc regardless of any political motives. In particular, any regional grouping should not exclude critical economic partners, such as the United States. Instead, the EAEC is now being considered more as a framework for economic dialogue as well as a potential "warning" that Asia has its own options should the United States decide to close itself off or create discriminatory trading blocs. As such U.S. policies are extremely unlikely, the EAEC might be thought of as unimportant.

TABLE 12.4

EXPORTS—1994—DOUBLE DENSITIES

EXPORTER	DESTINATION											
	US	CAN.	MEX.	CHE	JPN	AUSL	NZ	HK	SK	SING.	INDO.	MAL.
US	0.00	6.26	5.47	2.12	1.68	1.63	1.11	0.51	1.53	1.02	0.78	1.01
CAN.	5.09	0.00	0.25	0.54	0.68	0.35	0.22	0.11	0.41	0.07	0.28	0.10
MEX.	5.28	0.72	0.00	1.28	0.25	0.07	0.04	0.07	0.03	0.05	0.08	0.01
CHE	0.96	0.18	0.98	0.00	2.79	0.27	0.20	0.08	2.24	0.21	1.07	0.27
JPN	1.87	0.43	0.57	0.91	0.00	1.82	1.39	1.71	2.57	2.06	2.58	2.28
AUSL	0.46	0.54	0.18	0.74	3.94	0.00	22.33	0.95	2.87	1.40	4.54	2.08
NZ	0.69	0.51	0.52	1.18	2.51	16.14	0.00	0.70	2.10	0.55	1.67	1.47
HK	1.71	0.54	0.26	0.25	0.74	0.95	0.52	0.00	0.40	2.30	0.75	0.93
SK	1.34	0.42	0.72	1.63	2.20	1.07	0.59	2.15	0.00	1.77	3.54	1.18
SING.	1.16	0.18	0.11	0.30	1.10	1.95	1.17	2.29	1.10	0.00	0.00	14.44
INDO.(1)	0.90	0.23	0.19	0.46	4.28	1.46	0.46	0.86	2.71	4.21	0.00	1.36
MAL.	1.31	0.27	0.35	0.26	1.87	1.28	1.62	1.21	1.17	8.64	1.62	0.00
PHIL.	2.45	0.43	0.16	0.49	2.39	0.86	0.49	1.28	0.89	1.95	0.71	1.20
THAI.(2)	1.34	0.40	0.13	0.20	2.66	1.14	0.60	1.38	0.52	4.99	0.72	2.05
CHN	1.10	0.33	0.09	0.90	2.79	1.02	0.56	7.03	1.52	0.88	1.16	0.68
FRN	0.44	0.20	0.31	0.58	0.31	0.37	0.22	0.26	0.30	0.26	0.43	0.34
GER.	0.49	0.19	0.35	0.51	0.41	0.57	0.37	0.22	0.45	0.28	0.69	0.36
BELUX	0.31	0.12	0.14	0.39	0.21	0.29	0.23	0.23	0.16	0.17	0.22	0.16
NETH.	0.23	0.11	0.08	0.31	0.14	0.30	0.23	0.14	0.17	0.20	0.34	0.13
ITALY	0.48	0.27	0.26	0.66	0.33	0.57	0.37	0.43	0.39	0.31	0.45	0.22
UK	0.81	0.42	0.16	0.44	0.35	1.20	1.12	0.46	0.31	0.56	0.37	0.72
DEN.	0.30	0.14	0.18	0.45	0.58	0.42	0.34	0.20	0.33	0.19	0.21	0.13
IRE.	0.53	0.27	0.15	0.40	0.52	0.48	0.31	0.13	0.16	0.27	0.06	0.39
SPN	0.31	0.17	1.00	1.90	0.21	0.31	0.18	0.18	0.32	0.20	0.28	0.08
GCE(2)	0.28	0.14	0.11	0.04	0.14	0.38	0.12	0.07	0.11	0.06	0.16	0.02
PORT.(2)	0.27	0.23	0.03	0.24	0.12	0.22	0.19	0.05	0.04	0.06	0.00	0.13
SWD	0.50	0.32	0.21	0.59	0.42	1.10	0.81	0.17	0.36	0.37	0.47	0.48
FND	0.44	0.19	0.10	0.71	0.32	1.04	0.46	0.31	0.57	0.39	0.46	0.38
AUS(2)	0.20	0.18	0.11	0.33	0.24	0.29	0.17	0.15	0.20	0.12	0.70	0.15
BZL(2)	1.28	0.33	1.29	8.80	0.93	0.48	0.27	0.23	0.61	0.30	0.67	0.36
ARG	0.67	0.13	0.92	24.13	0.44	0.24	0.31	0.34	0.13	0.14	0.89	0.61
EAEC(6)	1.53	0.37	0.40	0.80	1.23	1.52	1.06	2.40	1.72	2.30	1.86	3.01
APEC(3)	1.54	2.05	1.83	1.17	1.35	1.44	1.48	1.48	1.51	1.58	1.39	1.98
EU15	0.46	0.22	0.27	0.56	0.33	0.57	0.42	0.27	0.33	0.29	0.45	0.33
ASEAN(4)	1.25	0.26	0.19	0.31	2.11	1.53	1.04	1.61	1.28	3.61	0.53	6.28

TABLE 12.4

EXPORTS—1994—DOUBLE DENSITIES (CONTINUED)

EXPORTER	DESTINATION											
	PHIL.	THAI.	CHN	FRN	GER.	BELU	NETH.	ITALY	UK	DEN.	IRE.	SPN
US	1.47	0.90	0.71	0.48	0.43	0.74	0.89	0.37	0.93	0.31	1.08	0.44
CAN.	0.16	0.17	0.38	0.11	0.11	0.20	0.18	0.15	0.25	0.06	0.13	0.08
MEX.	0.02	0.03	0.03	0.16	0.07	0.15	0.00	0.03	0.08	0.04	0.30	0.64
CHE	0.93	0.94	0.44	0.67	0.49	0.62	0.87	0.82	0.73	0.23	0.04	0.92
JPN	2.79	3.44	1.74	0.25	0.51	0.35	0.69	0.22	0.62	0.27	0.72	0.25
AUSL	2.27	1.74	1.77	0.23	0.18	0.25	0.40	0.51	0.71	0.13	0.14	0.23
NZ	1.84	1.00	1.06	0.21	0.30	0.40	0.21	0.38	1.18	0.25	0.14	0.21
HK	2.45	1.05	10.08	0.24	0.65	0.08	0.70	0.16	0.89	0.53	0.35	0.17
SK	2.37	1.78	2.38	0.20	0.51	0.15	0.38	0.21	0.36	0.23	0.13	0.31
SING.	3.05	5.14	0.80	0.25	0.40	0.17	0.87	0.19	0.52	0.16	1.23	0.18
INDO.(1)	1.71	0.93	1.22	0.20	0.36	0.35	1.09	0.43	0.50	0.34	0.16	0.53
MAL.	1.95	3.49	1.21	0.25	0.37	0.43	0.76	0.19	0.73	0.24	0.61	0.20
PHIL.	0.00	2.56	0.46	0.26	0.54	0.25	1.29	0.18	0.75	0.22	0.27	0.19
THAI.(2)	0.99	0.00	0.53	0.39	0.45	0.53	1.02	0.32	0.61	0.38	0.08	0.34
CHN	0.74	0.89	0.00	0.22	0.44	0.23	0.61	0.34	0.38	0.27	0.12	0.30
FRN	0.27	0.36	0.34	0.00	1.94	2.96	1.52	2.44	1.88	1.10	1.04	3.32
GER.	0.37	0.60	0.55	2.24	0.00	2.27	2.45	1.96	1.53	2.31	0.77	1.49
BELUX	0.15	0.44	0.25	3.55	2.37	0.00	4.32	1.34	1.61	1.17	0.70	1.40
NETH.	0.22	0.26	0.14	1.79	2.95	4.18	0.00	1.26	1.65	1.86	0.89	1.06
ITALY	0.22	0.37	0.44	2.44	2.15	1.01	0.94	0.00	1.24	1.05	0.59	2.18
UK	0.50	0.52	0.23	1.86	1.44	1.82	2.31	1.30	0.00	1.68	8.86	1.75
DEN.	0.19	0.38	0.15	0.92	2.35	0.56	1.18	0.96	1.46	0.00	0.77	0.77
IRE.	0.23	0.12	0.04	1.74	1.60	1.33	1.91	0.99	5.26	1.47	0.00	1.11
SPN	0.15	0.22	0.40	3.77	1.61	1.01	1.37	2.39	1.56	0.80	0.73	0.00
GCE(2)	0.06	0.32	0.18	1.16	2.68	0.51	0.82	3.43	1.09	0.94	0.35	0.80
PORT.(2)	0.03	0.09	0.07	2.82	2.21	1.19	1.70	0.78	2.18	2.68	0.68	6.76
SWD	0.21	0.61	0.61	0.95	1.49	1.66	1.73	0.98	1.95	8.67	1.13	0.89
FND	0.51	0.65	0.54	0.91	1.47	0.71	1.62	0.75	1.93	4.24	0.77	1.03
AUS(2)	0.14	0.37	0.29	0.83	4.41	0.64	0.97	2.05	0.63	1.10	0.34	0.97
BZL(2)	0.94	0.82	0.70	0.39	0.53	1.06	2.32	0.99	0.52	0.67	0.46	0.76
ARG	0.18	0.17	0.52	0.25	0.43	0.33	2.44	1.07	0.27	1.12	0.08	1.74
EAEC(6)	2.26	2.75	1.61	0.24	0.48	0.30	0.71	0.24	0.56	0.27	0.55	0.26
APEC(3)	1.73	1.81	1.16	0.30	0.40	0.41	0.68	0.27	0.63	0.25	0.64	0.31
EU15	0.29	0.44	0.37	1.88	1.56	1.92	1.88	1.52	1.45	1.88	1.77	1.73
ASEAN(4)	2.09	3.15	0.91	0.27	0.40	0.32	0.92	0.25	0.59	0.25	0.68	0.27

Notes: * Formula used to calculate double-density ratio was (Xij/Xiw)/(Ijw/Iw)
(1) data for East Timor was added to Indonesia
(2) 1993 data used for Thailand, Greece, Portugal, Austria, and Brazil
(3) APEC: missing Papua New Guinea and Brunei, as well as Taiwan in the "exporter" aggregate

TABLE 12.4

EXPORTS—1994—DOUBLE DENSITIES (CONTINUED)

EXPORTER	GCE	PORT.	SWD	FND	AUS	BZL	ARG	EAEC(6)	APEC(3)	EU15	ASEAN(4)
									DESTINATION		
US	0.32	0.38	0.42	0.39	0.24	2.50	1.74	1.14	1.40	0.56	1.01
CAN.	0.07	0.07	0.09	0.11	0.11	0.68	0.15	0.35	2.04	0.14	0.13
MEX.	0.02	0.17	0.03	0.01	0.01	0.96	0.79	0.10	2.02	0.12	0.04
CHE	0.68	0.19	0.48	0.64	0.07	8.70	11.33	1.30	1.14	0.63	0.52
JPN	0.29	0.33	0.31	0.46	0.28	0.74	0.34	1.53	1.66	0.42	2.51
AUSL	0.05	0.10	0.16	0.51	0.03	0.73	0.31	2.49	1.66	0.32	2.12
NZ	0.66	0.24	0.19	0.07	0.07	0.19	0.32	1.56	1.56	0.40	1.11
HK	0.12	0.10	0.31	0.50	0.36	0.41	0.23	2.01	1.72	0.46	1.64
SK	0.33	0.32	0.30	0.16	0.18	1.38	0.98	1.94	1.56	0.32	2.09
SING.	0.33	0.10	0.13	0.26	0.17	0.39	0.38	2.28	1.65	0.37	4.61
INDO.(1)	0.30	0.18	0.10	0.14	0.10	0.30	0.22	2.56	1.71	0.40	2.36
MAL.	0.13	0.13	0.18	0.11	0.09	0.55	0.19	2.32	1.73	0.39	4.41
PHIL.	0.11	0.06	0.11	0.27	0.10	0.11	0.11	1.57	1.77	0.45	1.65
THAI.(2)	0.23	0.35	0.30	0.29	0.26	0.17	0.17	1.91	1.51	0.47	2.64
CHN	0.21	0.11	0.34	0.24	0.11	0.47	0.47	2.51	1.70	0.35	0.90
FRN	1.35	2.63	0.95	0.64	0.96	0.65	0.92	0.31	0.36	1.71	0.33
GER.	1.55	1.47	1.85	1.44	5.09	1.16	0.59	0.40	0.44	1.57	0.42
BELUX	1.11	1.44	1.09	0.77	0.91	0.43	0.28	0.22	0.25	2.05	0.22
NETH.	1.81	1.19	1.20	1.04	0.98	0.37	0.25	0.17	0.20	1.92	0.21
ITALY	3.35	2.38	0.75	0.73	2.16	1.52	1.46	0.37	0.42	1.55	0.32
UK	1.29	1.64	2.09	1.80	0.69	0.62	0.34	0.41	0.58	1.53	0.57
DEN.	1.35	0.88	8.09	4.17	0.85	0.36	0.37	0.33	0.31	1.59	0.23
IRE.	0.96	0.75	1.98	1.37	0.65	0.38	0.19	0.27	0.37	1.98	0.24
SPN	1.74	13.61	0.63	0.63	0.73	0.77	2.44	0.23	0.31	1.92	0.18
GCE(2)	0.00	0.73	0.80	0.96	1.26	0.85	0.19	0.12	0.19	1.60	0.11
PORT.(2)	0.98	0.00	2.11	1.81	1.03	0.61	0.17	0.08	0.17	2.17	0.07
SWD	1.08	0.81	0.00	8.72	1.22	0.91	0.66	0.40	0.46	1.61	0.44
FND	1.06	0.87	8.78	0.00	0.90	0.56	0.51	0.41	0.42	1.54	0.46
AUS(2)	0.94	0.85	1.15	0.95	0.00	0.29	0.27	0.23	0.22	1.78	0.25
BZL(2)	0.83	1.23	0.33	0.51	0.20	0.00	18.81	0.62	0.93	0.76	0.50
ARG	0.88	0.59	0.11	0.07	0.03	36.07	0.00	0.37	0.65	0.67	0.34
EAEC(6)	0.27	0.24	0.27	0.33	0.21	0.66	0.40	1.92	1.66	0.39	2.56
APEC(3)	0.25	0.26	0.28	0.32	0.20	1.26	0.85	1.48	1.63	0.41	1.74
EU15	1.62	2.18	1.64	1.46	2.11	0.83	0.71	0.33	0.39	1.69	0.35
ASEAN(4)	0.25	0.15	0.16	0.21	0.15	0.37	0.26	2.24	1.66	0.40	3.74

(4) ASEAN includes Indonesia, Malaysia, Singapore, Thailand, Philippines, and Vietnam; except Vietnam is absent in the "exporter" aggregate
(5) SUM is the total for all countries shown in this table
(6) EAEC includes all the ASEAN countries plus China, Japan, Hong Kong, and South Korea
Sources: United Nations, Commodity Trade Statistics, Various Years IMF, International Financial Statistics

TABLE 12.5

EXPORTS—1980—DOUBLE DENSITIES

EXPORTER	DESTINATION											
	US	CAN.	MEX.	CHE	JPN	AUSL	NZ	HK	SK	SING.	INDO.	MAL.
US	0.00	5.22	6.92	4.02	1.35	1.89	0.99	1.07	1.83	1.14	1.19	1.11
CAN.	4.98	0.00	0.66	0.98	0.83	0.89	0.55	0.20	0.60	0.21	0.53	0.24
MEX.	5.15	0.26	0.00	1.12	0.67	0.05	0.02	0.00	0.09	0.01	0.11	0.02
CHE(1)	1.52	0.51	0.63	0.00	1.69	0.20	0.03	0.00	0.97	0.14	0.66	0.05
JPN	1.92	0.64	0.95	2.28	0.00	2.59	1.86	3.27	3.66	2.44	4.84	2.91
AUSL	0.78	0.68	0.16	0.58	3.55	0.00	15.95	1.28	1.96	1.92	3.01	4.04
NZ	1.03	0.76	0.67	0.13	1.82	12.70	0.00	1.33	0.97	1.26	2.71	2.51
HK	2.61	0.89	0.23	2.07	0.48	2.83	1.31	0.00	0.30	2.16	0.84	1.28
SK	2.08	0.67	0.26	2.25	2.43	1.31	0.57	4.22	0.00	1.25	3.79	1.92
SING.	1.00	0.23	0.22	0.45	1.13	4.00	6.47	6.90	1.33	0.00	NA	27.55
INDO.(2)	1.55	0.04	0.07	0.00	6.94	1.54	1.66	0.62	1.19	9.31	0.00	0.50
MAL.	1.29	0.17	0.06	0.15	3.22	1.42	1.44	1.68	1.79	15.70	0.48	0.00
PHIL.	2.18	0.38	0.30	0.13	3.73	1.68	0.27	2.92	3.12	1.53	3.39	3.00
THAI.	1.01	0.12	0.00	0.28	2.16	1.04	0.25	4.44	0.65	6.05	6.68	8.27
CHN	NA	NA	NA	NA	NA	NA	NA	NA	NA	NA	NA	NA
FRN	0.35	0.21	0.50	1.10	0.14	0.27	0.12	0.22	0.11	0.24	0.39	0.31
GER.(3)	0.48	0.21	0.64	0.92	0.16	0.59	0.30	0.26	0.24	0.30	0.57	0.44
BELUX	0.27	0.10	0.41	0.46	0.07	0.23	0.11	0.54	0.31	0.16	0.19	0.16
NETH.	0.20	0.09	0.14	0.44	0.06	0.28	0.31	0.16	0.08	0.22	1.15	0.16
ITALY	0.42	0.21	0.46	0.91	0.13	0.58	0.25	0.31	0.12	0.22	0.21	0.27
UK	0.75	0.53	0.39	0.73	0.17	1.64	1.82	0.99	0.18	0.55	0.42	0.83
DEN.	0.35	0.20	0.15	0.69	0.24	0.39	0.35	0.23	0.12	0.21	0.10	0.36
IRE.	0.42	0.62	0.82	0.44	0.07	0.59	0.17	0.08	0.03	0.13	0.04	0.22
SPN	0.42	0.24	2.05	4.62	0.18	0.30	0.22	0.16	0.10	0.20	0.43	0.11
GCE(2)	0.45	0.15	0.11	0.00	0.07	0.36	0.04	0.02	0.20	0.08	0.00	0.01
PORT.(2)	0.45	0.32	0.08	0.75	0.13	0.36	0.22	0.14	0.03	0.08	0.03	0.37
SWD	0.42	0.38	0.58	0.59	0.16	1.04	0.39	0.19	0.12	0.69	0.35	1.01
FND	0.25	0.16	0.30	0.15	0.09	0.97	0.13	0.08	0.06	0.11	0.34	0.19
AUS(2)	0.17	0.16	0.15	0.37	0.11	0.28	0.16	0.11	0.23	0.12	0.21	0.10
BZL(2)	1.37	0.41	2.35	14.35	0.86	0.48	0.22	0.15	0.16	0.21	0.37	0.11
ARG	0.71	0.18	1.52	17.39	0.37	0.08	0.04	0.24	0.08	0.05	0.13	0.11
EAEC(7)	1.81	0.52	0.61	1.66	1.32	2.39	1.99	3.13	2.54	3.62	3.41	4.59
APEC(4)	1.51	2.28	3.03	2.41	1.35	1.95	1.89	1.80	1.93	2.05	2.08	2.54
EU15	0.43	0.25	0.50	0.87	0.14	0.64	0.48	0.37	0.17	0.30	0.46	0.40
ASEAN(5)	1.34	0.16	0.13	0.20	3.78	2.20	2.77	3.23	1.46	6.85	1.03	9.27

TABLE 12.5

EXPORTS—1994—DOUBLE DENSITIES (CONTINUED)

EXPORTER	DESTINATION											
	PHIL.	THAI.	CHN	FRN	GER.	BELU	NETH.	ITALY	UK	DEN.	IRE.	SPN
US	2.20	1.06	1.74	0.50	0.54	0.82	1.02	0.51	0.88	0.39	0.68	0.89
CAN.	0.36	0.40	1.16	0.20	0.21	0.32	0.49	0.27	0.66	0.12	0.27	0.18
MEX.	0.09	0.01	0.62	0.55	0.21	0.14	0.13	0.13	0.10	0.01	0.02	4.66
CHE(1)	0.17	0.16	1.71	0.60	1.21	0.70	0.93	0.99	0.94	0.01	0.13	1.41
JPN	3.07	3.08	3.86	0.23	0.48	0.30	0.41	0.15	0.47	0.34	0.30	0.30
AUSL	1.93	1.49	3.61	0.26	0.25	0.28	0.30	0.41	0.71	0.09	0.07	0.20
NZ	3.34	1.34	3.01	0.32	0.27	0.27	0.44	0.34	2.24	0.13	0.29	0.22
HK	2.55	1.23	2.33	0.30	1.16	0.24	0.59	0.35	1.66	0.61	0.23	0.47
SK	2.04	1.96	0.00	0.25	0.53	0.22	0.51	0.26	0.55	0.35	0.22	0.29
SING.	3.36	9.11	1.57	0.32	0.32	0.14	0.49	0.26	0.43	0.17	0.09	0.25
INDO.(2)	1.97	0.33	0.00	0.08	0.19	0.03	0.49	0.23	0.11	0.19	0.01	0.09
MAL.	3.61	3.03	1.65	0.26	0.39	0.24	1.54	0.32	0.46	0.17	0.14	0.33
PHIL.	0.00	2.28	0.77	0.24	0.48	0.17	1.63	0.23	0.42	0.26	0.08	0.26
THAI.	0.76	0.00	1.92	0.25	0.45	0.70	3.47	0.40	0.32	0.35	0.02	0.13
CHN	NA	NA	NA	NA	NA	NA	NA	NA	NA	NA	NA	NA
FRN	0.19	0.19	0.27	0.00	1.73	2.59	1.23	2.52	1.16	0.71	0.86	1.66
GER.(3)	0.34	0.40	0.59	1.96	0.00	2.16	2.44	1.72	1.08	1.95	0.67	0.88
BELUX	0.16	0.16	0.16	2.88	2.29	0.00	3.93	1.12	1.39	1.23	0.54	0.56
NETH.	0.21	0.22	0.20	1.55	3.20	4.17	0.00	1.16	1.32	1.92	0.74	0.61
ITALY	0.34	0.34	0.33	2.23	1.96	0.92	0.95	0.00	1.02	0.71	0.48	1.17
UK	0.42	0.38	0.34	1.10	1.12	1.47	2.01	0.77	0.00	2.14	9.60	0.88
DEN.	0.38	0.68	0.26	0.75	2.05	0.53	0.94	1.03	2.37	0.00	0.93	0.51
IRE.	0.22	0.14	0.03	1.14	1.03	1.39	1.40	0.62	7.13	0.75	0.00	0.69
SPN	0.07	0.10	0.31	2.43	1.10	0.74	0.98	1.57	1.17	0.54	0.58	0.00
GCE(2)	0.03	0.06	0.25	1.09	2.00	0.50	1.46	1.95	0.69	0.90	0.18	0.32
PORT.(2)	0.05	0.49	0.07	1.54	1.45	0.86	1.21	1.18	2.47	1.82	0.62	2.12
SWD	0.29	0.58	0.27	0.86	1.34	0.90	1.23	0.77	1.66	8.66	0.97	0.70
FND	0.68	0.43	0.55	0.67	1.18	0.40	1.10	0.48	1.88	3.56	1.08	0.51
AUS(2)	0.24	0.22	0.49	0.51	3.41	0.42	0.67	2.20	0.61	1.17	0.29	0.39
BZL(2)	1.01	0.22	0.35	0.60	0.75	0.49	1.46	0.98	0.46	0.66	0.19	1.51
ARG	0.02	0.12	2.33	0.34	0.59	0.21	2.29	1.30	0.42	0.99	0.04	1.36
EAEC(7)	2.77	3.02	2.65	0.23	0.48	0.26	0.62	0.21	0.51	0.31	0.22	0.28
APEC(4)	2.15	1.78	2.10	0.35	0.46	0.48	0.74	0.34	0.68	0.30	0.40	0.63
EU15	0.29	0.32	0.36	1.47	1.41	1.78	1.71	1.33	1.10	1.79	2.03	0.91
ASEAN(5)	2.41	3.56	1.03	0.22	0.32	0.18	1.08	0.27	0.32	0.20	0.06	0.20

Notes:
* Formula used to calculate double-density ratio was (Xij/Xiw)/(Ijw/Iw)
(1) 1982 data used for Chile
(2) data for East Timor was added to Indonesia
(3) East Germany Import Data Unavailable
(4) APEC: missing Papua New Guinea and Brunei, as well as Taiwan and China in the "exporter" aggregate

TABLE 12.5

EXPORTS—1994—DOUBLE DENSITIES (CONTINUED)

EXPORTER	DESTINATION										
	GCE	PORT.	SWD	FND	AUS	BZL	ARG	EAEC(7)	APEC(4)	EU15	ASEAN(5)
US	0.73	0.90	0.48	0.30	0.16	1.59	2.15	1.49	1.49	0.63	1.27
CAN.	0.33	0.29	0.22	0.19	0.07	0.96	0.57	0.72	2.43	0.30	0.32
MEX.	0.04	0.08	0.07	0.03	0.00	2.06	0.51	0.45	2.35	0.38	0.04
CHE(1)	0.76	0.14	0.68	0.24	0.05	6.83	7.84	1.23	1.23	0.83	0.22
JPN	0.78	0.43	0.36	0.38	0.25	0.68	1.44	1.73	1.84	0.34	3.14
AUSL	0.15	0.18	0.17	0.03	0.01	0.11	0.62	3.22	1.92	0.31	2.46
NZ	1.64	0.22	0.08	0.08	0.03	0.01	0.22	1.99	1.79	0.57	2.01
HK	0.24	0.11	0.84	0.35	0.60	0.07	1.14	0.92	1.71	0.72	1.70
SK	0.86	0.09	0.43	0.19	0.27	0.02	0.83	2.27	1.96	0.38	2.02
SING.	1.12	0.22	0.17	0.05	0.05	0.31	0.45	3.18	1.99	0.30	6.55
INDO.(2)	0.03	0.08	0.02	0.00	0.00	0.50	0.00	5.09	2.86	0.15	3.92
MAL.	0.12	0.19	0.18	0.02	0.03	0.10	0.19	4.04	2.33	0.42	6.96
PHIL.	0.10	0.09	0.18	0.10	0.07	0.32	0.03	3.23	2.39	0.42	2.04
THAI.	0.06	0.03	0.24	0.10	0.07	0.30	0.01	3.10	1.78	0.62	5.00
CHN	NA	NA	NA	NA	NA	NA	NA	NA	NA	NA	NA
FRN	1.98	1.49	0.77	0.50	0.68	0.50	0.73	0.20	0.28	1.34	0.28
GER.(3)	2.02	1.27	1.71	1.20	4.45	0.63	1.22	0.28	0.39	1.35	0.39
BELUX	0.80	0.96	0.97	0.46	0.62	0.18	0.37	0.17	0.22	1.75	0.17
NETH.	1.24	0.90	1.04	0.67	0.77	0.22	0.46	0.17	0.18	1.77	0.37
ITALY	2.87	1.39	0.63	0.50	2.16	0.40	1.52	0.21	0.32	1.29	0.28
UK	0.87	1.69	1.96	1.35	0.46	0.35	0.66	0.37	0.60	1.10	0.54
DEN.	1.03	0.70	7.46	2.68	0.75	0.11	0.45	0.28	0.30	1.28	0.34
IRE.	0.72	0.53	0.72	0.57	0.40	0.09	0.25	0.09	0.32	1.81	0.14
SPN	1.03	5.79	0.59	0.51	0.30	0.69	3.36	0.20	0.38	1.24	0.19
GCE(2)	0.00	0.77	0.27	0.33	0.48	0.02	0.05	0.16	0.25	1.18	0.30
PORT.(2)	0.58	0.00	2.65	1.79	0.93	0.89	0.28	0.14	0.30	1.43	0.18
SWD	0.88	1.53	0.00	7.95	1.12	0.38	0.80	0.31	0.40	1.39	0.67
FND	1.09	0.71	9.75	0.00	0.60	0.31	0.85	0.18	0.24	0.98	0.29
AUS(2)	1.48	0.70	1.51	1.17	0.00	0.17	0.64	0.18	0.18	1.37	0.17
BZL(2)	1.12	1.62	0.58	0.44	0.27	0.00	10.14	0.63	1.04	0.74	0.33
ARG	0.92	1.12	0.16	0.31	0.07	7.54	0.00	0.45	0.64	0.73	0.09
EAEC(7)	0.64	0.30	0.33	0.26	0.21	0.49	1.00	2.38	1.99	0.36	3.57
APEC(4)	0.61	0.52	0.36	0.25	0.16	1.04	1.41	1.81	1.85	0.46	2.13
EU15	1.58	1.40	1.52	1.19	1.76	0.42	0.93	0.25	0.35	1.37	0.36
ASEAN(5)	0.37	0.14	0.13	0.04	0.03	0.33	0.17	3.97	2.36	0.32	5.22

(5) ASEAN includes Indonesia, Malaysia, Singapore, Thailand, Philippines, and Vietnam; except Vietnam is absent in the "exporter" aggregate

(6) SUM is the total for all countries shown in this table

(7) EAEC includes all the ASEAN countries plus China, Japan, Hong Kong, and South Korea

Sources: United Nations, Commodity Trade Statistics, Various Years IMF, International Financial Statistics

However, there are at least two reasons why it may remain significant in both substance and symbol.

First, although such U.S. policies are improbable, it is not so unlikely that the United States will continue to press issues that threaten, harass, or embarrass ASEAN countries. These issues often develop through domestic pressure groups within the United States (e.g., unions, environmental and human-rights organizations), and these agents can often produce policy uncertainty. The existence of the EAEC suggests that any political chips to be gained domestically through controversial policy stances will have to be weighted against the costs associated with countermeasures taken by the EAEC as a group.

Second, it would appear that the EAEC is being used as part of a system of negotiation between greater "poles" in the international marketplace.[16] For example, the first Asia-Europe Meeting (ASEM) was attended by members of the EAEC and the EU; North America, Australia, and New Zealand were excluded.[17] In recent years, there have been discussions of creating a Free-Trade Area of the Americas (FTAA) and a "Transatlantic Free Trade Area"; combined with APEC, this left out only an Asia-Europe link to complete the circle. While ASEM has a very weak and uncertain agenda, the composition of the grouping suggests that it may be used as a potential threat to developments in other regional groupings.

Nevertheless, the EAEC in itself cannot be considered as a potential inward-looking trade bloc. Any implicit "threat" posed by EAEC is there only as a means to ensure that other areas will not look inwardly, and in this sense it serves as a (weak) reflection of the ASEAN and APEC (discussed below) metaregimes. Hence, to the extent that the EAEC is a "vital" organization, it is being nested safely within APEC.

V. ASEAN AND ASIA-PACIFIC ECONOMIC COOPERATION

While developing East Asia is not interested in creating its own inward-looking trade bloc to the exclusion of its major markets, a regional cooperation agreement that did include them (i.e., Japan and the United States) and would not overtly discriminate against the rest of the world (especially the EU) would be consistent with the economic development goals of the region. This is why APEC has taken shape so quickly. However, the APEC "forum" has been turned into an 18–member organization representing all major Pacific Rim markets, complete with a secretariat (in Singapore), a number of working committees and task forces, and an annual summit of APEC heads of state. At the 1994 Summit in Bogor (Indonesia), APEC leaders dedicated themselves to the creation of a region of "free and open trade and investment in the Asia-Pacific no later than 2010 in the case of industrialized economies and 2020 in the case of developing economies."[18]

Unlike all other major regional economic cooperation agreements, liberalization within APEC is envisioned to be explicitly outward-looking—that is, all APEC members have agreed to embrace "open regionalism," which apparently means either (1) the circumvention of trade/investment diversion upon liberalization by not requiring external reciprocity (e.g., through the "MFN-ization" of tariff cuts within APEC); or (2) reciprocity with liberalization but without excluding nonmembers from participating (e.g., a discriminatory free-trade area within APEC that allows the EU to negotiate a reciprocal agreement with APEC, thereby allowing outside countries to participate in APEC liberalization). Either way, regional economic cooperation within APEC will be necessarily open, not just as a predicted outcome of a free-trade area (as argued in this paper), but explicitly as a quid pro quo for economic integration. For example, ASEAN countries, which constitute the core of APEC, agreed in 1991 to the "Kuching Consensus," in which the organization stated that APEC should be open and actually remain a consultative group.[19]

The Kuching Consensus is also significant in that it expressed implicitly ASEAN concerns that APEC may develop too quickly and possibly in directions in which it was not completely comfortable. In particular, there was—and still is—the fear that APEC will end up diluting ASEAN economic integration under AFTA. In part, this is because AFTA was created when the political situation of the time suggested that the regional organization may become less cohesive as external threats disappeared. The choice of closer economic integration as the "new phase" of ASEAN was deemed important for the organization's political survival; should APEC overshadow the importance of ASEAN economic integration—and the greater economic integration with non-ASEAN APEC economies suggests that this could easily be the case—this could pose a threat to ASEAN itself. In fact, initiatives toward closer economic integration in APEC going well beyond that envisioned by the Kuching Consensus have influenced ASEAN to "deepen" and "hasten" economic integration as a means of keeping ahead of APEC.

Another ASEAN concern with APEC relates to its relationships with Japan and the United States. The major push of Japanese DFI into ASEAN in the mid-to-late 1980s, together with its place as the most important source of ASEAN development assistance, imports, and number three in terms of exports (after the United States and the EU), was cause for some concern in the region. ASEAN countries do not want to expose themselves to one "dominant" developed country, particularly Japan. In addition, U.S. policies toward ASEAN are often perceived to be unpredictable, heavy-handed, and intrusive. For example, the use of the Super 301 clause of the U.S. Omnibus Trade and Competitiveness Pact; complaints regarding competition policies in ASEAN and intellectual property protection; and insistence on the inclusion of politically sensitive issues considered to be outside the domain of international negotiations (and certainly inapplicable to trade and investment discussions) have caused ASEAN countries to be wary of a strong U.S. agenda in APEC. The U.S. attitudes toward the EAEC (discussed below) also created some mistrust in certain ASEAN countries (or at least in Malaysia).

Thus, while ASEAN countries do accept U.S. and Japanese participation in APEC as very important, they would like guard against developments that could serve to impede ASEAN objectives in APEC. In this sense, ambiguities surrounding "open regionalism" may be intentional.

Despite the complicated political dimensions to ASEAN involvement in APEC, it is clear that ASEAN and other APEC-member states intend to keep APEC consistent with outward-oriented development strategies, consistent with the region's metaregime. The APEC Economic Leaders' Declaration of Action from the Osaka meeting in November 1995 stressed that:

> We emphasize our resolute opposition to an inward-looking trading bloc that would divert from the pursuit of global free trade, and we commit ourselves to firmly maintaining open regional cooperation. We reaffirm our determination to see APEC take the lead in strengthening the open multilateral system. Ensuring that APEC remains consistent with the WTO agreement, we will achieve trade and investment liberalization progressively. (Point 4, November 19).

In fact, the ultimate form of regional economic integration within APEC is far from clear. While declarations from APEC leaders seem to suggest that the "voluntary, concerted" push to open trade and investment will be multilateralized (for example, the Osaka agreement to "deepen and broaden the outcome of the Uruguay Round" through acceleration of tariff reductions, early implementation of WTO agreements, etc.), it is likely that political imperatives (especially in the United States) will eventually require reciprocity. APEC's merely becoming the "Pacific Chapter of the WTO" might please many economists but could be difficult to pass through parliaments.[20] However, if a regional arrangement within APEC emerges, leading to some trade and investment diversion, the organization cannot become a "fortress," and at the minimum, the unilateral liberalization supported by the APEC process will ensure that external trade creation should be more than enough to compensate for any (Vinerian) trade diversion effects. Moreover, as additional countries strive to join APEC (e.g., Russia, some South American and South Asian countries, and Indochina), they will have to liberalize their economies in order to be candidates. This application process will probably speed up ongoing liberalization programs in these countries.

VI. OPEN REGIONALISM AND THE NESTING OF ASEAN IN APEC

From the above analysis it is clear that to date, ASEAN has had a critical impact on the institutional development of APEC. First, without ASEAN there can be no APEC. APEC seemed at first to be an extension of the ASEAN Post–Ministerial Conference, at which its member states meet with dialogue partners to discuss matters of mutual concern (in the past, this usually meant development aid). ASEAN constitutes the core of APEC; this is recognized, for example, in the institutional arrangement to rotate the chair of APEC such that an ASEAN member state will be host every other year. Economic cooperation within APEC will move forward only if ASEAN member states are not opposed. EAEC, created and supported by ASEAN, serves as a constant implicit or explicit threat to developed countries in APEC (except, of course, Japan). While the commitments of APEC have gone well beyond those considered appropriate in the Kuching Consensus, it is important to note that formal economic integration in APEC remains mostly in words rather than deeds. The famous APEC "action plan" that was to be developed in Osaka was pushed forward to the Manila meeting in 1996, where the Manila Action Plan for APEC (MAPA) was negotiated.[21] In Manila, the Philippines stressed the need to focus on issues of more direct concern to developing countries in APEC (read: ASEAN), including development cooperation, technology transfer, and human resources development. This led to new initiatives under the "Eco-Tech" framework. Moreover, it would appear that "open regionalism" within APEC will remain "voluntary" and as such will probably move slowly. This is the ASEAN way.

Second, the preoccupation with "open regionalism" within APEC reflects the ASEAN approach to economic development and regionalism. ASEAN economic integration has proceeded only as its member states have been bringing down unilaterally trade and investment barriers, even multilateralizing CEPT cuts in AFTA. This is not how NAFTA or, arguably, Closer Economic Relations (between Australia and New Zealand) work; they—like the EU— are preferential trading arrangements without any specific reference to "open regionalism," though even these arrangement are on the whole "open" (with a few sectoral exceptions).

In turn, APEC has been important in influencing the direction of ASEAN economic cooperation in general and AFTA in particular. For example, at the September 1995 ASEAN Economic Ministers (AEM) meeting, the sultan of Brunei announced various "deepening" and speeding-up liberalization measures in AFTA in light of competition from other free-trade areas.[22] This is a clear reference to developments in APEC. In addition, the AEM began to discuss additional supporting measures for AFTA (e.g., through "action plans" in transportation, communications, and infrastructural development), possible harmonization policies, and even trade in services. Most—if not all—of these items are currently being discussed in various APEC working groups, as well as in the GATT/ WTO. Such "competition" with APEC appears to be healthy and in fact has helped strengthen ASEAN economic cooperation.

On the other hand, ASEAN does not seem to have used deepening economic cooperation in the region as a means to present joint positions in APEC. Why is this? It could be due to divergent economic and other policy interests. If this is so, then it would appear that perhaps APEC is diluting ASEAN and could potentially hurt subregional institutional development. But this need not be the case. While ASEAN countries might have different preferences for various initiatives within APEC, what has been decided so far is not inconsistent with the interests of any individual ASEAN country. Also, the time line for economic integration is sufficiently long (25 years) to go beyond the "policy time horizons" of contemporary leaders. Thus a strong ASEAN caucus in APEC is not yet needed. Besides, APEC faces major hurdles that will keep integration focused on "first best" and noncontroversial initiatives, a natural tendency in the world's most heterogeneous region in terms of economic and political structures. If possible "dilution" will occur only if the United States and China agree to give themselves reciprocal free access to each other's markets, then it will be easy for ASEAN leaders to postpone action without deleterious consequences.

We have discussed above what ASEAN does not want out of APEC—a discriminatory trading regime, a grouping that reduces the importance of ASEAN, or a means to exert greater U.S. influence in unacceptable areas—without considering the motivations of individual member states. And there does exist diversity on a variety of issues in the region; for example, the Philippines is less concerned about "sensitive" political issues, while Malaysia and Indonesia place them as high priorities on the negative list. Singapore favors total free trade whereas Thailand has been reticent in this regard. Nevertheless, deeper ASEAN economic integration through AFTA was possible only as the ASEAN metaregime changed—i.e., when all ASEAN countries became convinced in the importance of outward-oriented development policies and more competitive domestic economic environments. Hence, at this basic level, ASEAN countries do strive for the same goals.

In particular, ASEAN countries will continue to use APEC to further their own agenda of opening of trade and investment in the region and, from a political perspective, keeping the United States engaged (though not dominant) in the region. APEC is an economic arrangement, and its initiatives can help promote ASEAN economic development through trade and investment liberalization and facilitation, promotion of technology transfer in environmental and other areas, reducing transactions costs of doing business, and encouraging more effective development assistance through Eco-Tech and in other fora. It will also be possible for ASEAN to use APEC as a means of pushing liberalization at the global level; for example, the United States was able to do this successfully at the Manila 1996 Summit, when a (more or less) united front at APEC was forged in information technology products and used at the WTO ministerial meeting in Singapore 1996 to negotiate successfully an arrangement encompassing 90 percent of information-technology markets. As ASEAN is small but potentially powerful within APEC, it should in the future be able to adopt the same sort of strategy.

While ASEAN countries are often criticized in the West for their desire to keep economic cooperation voluntary and informal (the "Asian way"), to some extent ASEAN countries would like to strengthen APEC rules in certain areas, though it does not appear that ASEAN would like to see such rules formalized. In particular, ASEAN would like to see greater restrictions on what should and should not be appropriate for discussion in APEC; security issues, for example, would most likely be handled best at the ARF, though informal discussions at the APEC heads-of-state meetings would obviously be useful. Trade restrictions would be fair game; labor organization restrictions, territorial disputes, "constructive engagement," and certain environment questions should be anathema. Malaysia has been the most vocal in opposing these areas, but it has general support from ASEAN—and some other APEC countries—in this regard.

In sum, ASEAN can be successfully "nested" in APEC. Moreover, this has already been the case and it is highly likely that it will be in the future. But perhaps more importantly, APEC will continue to be "nested" in ASEAN in that the subregional organization is playing a central role in molding the direction of APEC to be consistent with the goals of ASEAN economic cooperation.

NOTES

1. The author revised this chapter while visiting at the Research Institute of Economics and Business Administration, Kobe University. He would like to thank participants at the "APEC and Regime Creation in Asia and the Pacific," East-West Center, January 11-13, 1996, and Charles Morrison in particular, for extremely useful comments. In addition, he would like to acknowledge the excellent research assistance of Jason Eis and Shino Kuwahara.

2. United Nations, Commodity Trade Statistics, various issues and U.N. (1995).

3. A recent example of this was the decision reached at the Manila APEC Summit Meeting in 1996 to push for free trade in information technology products at the WTO Ministerial Meeting in Singapore in December 1996.

4. Aggarwal (1998a).

5. See, for example, Petri and Plummer (1996).

6. Aggarwal (1998a).

7. The reasons for this shift are many, but there can be no doubt that the collapse of commodity prices, unsustainable fiscal deficits, external debt problems, and widespread belief in the bankruptcy of import substitution played important roles (see, for example, World Bank [1993c] for a detailed discussion). In addition, the successful economic development of the Asian NIEs through export promotion had an important demonstrative effect. Moreover, as intraregional trade as a share of total trade was low in ASEAN and based on inter-industry transactions, there was no large "threat" of vinerian trade creation (though economists would have welcomed this).

8. The Preferential Trading Arrangement (PTA) had deepened margins of preference to 60 percent and began to take an across-the-board approach to liberalization rather than a product-by-product one, but exclusion lists and implementation problems prevented trade expansion. The industrial cooperation programs (ASEAN Industrial Projects, ASEAN Industrial Complementarity, ASEAN Industrial Joint Ventures) were generally improved, but the effect was extremely modest, with only 3 AIPs, 2 AICs, and about 23 (much smaller) AIJVs in existence (as of 1996).

9. Morrison (1997).

10. United Nations, Commodity Trade Statistics, various issues.

11. Ariff (1996).

12. See, for example, Hill (1996).

13. "Growth Triangles," of which only one currently exists in any substantial form (Johor-Singapore-Riau) but many more are being discussed, constitute

another form of economic cooperation among the ASEAN countries. They have been created exclusively to enhance DFI flows to the region on a nondiscriminatory basis.

14. The double-density measure is calculated by dividing the share of bilateral exports (or imports or exports + imports) to a country by that country's share in receiving total global exports. A double-density measure of 5.47 in the case of U.S. exports to Mexico suggests that the United States exports almost 5½ times what one would expect given Mexico's importance as a destination of world exports. Hence, there is a strong trade "bias" in favor of Mexico from the U.S. perspective.

15. However, this bias has decreased from 2.03 in 1986; Frankel (1993) uses a related result to suggest that the EAEC was not a "natural" economic bloc, as the bias is decreasing.

16. See, for example, Abe and Plummer (1996).

17. However, as the next ASEM will be held in the UK, the possibility that Australia and New Zealand will be allowed to attend is greater.

18. Summary taken from *APEC Economic Leaders' Declaration of Action,* Osaka, Japan, November 19, 1995.

19. Obviously, the Kuching Consensus has been surpassed by events, as APEC has developed into more than a consultative group. However, ASEAN has insisted that APEC remain "open," leaving the interpretation of exactly what this means ambiguous. No doubt it relates not only to the ASEAN prior of outward-oriented regional policies, but also to the ASEAN political stance of not exposing itself too much to dominance by any one country (e.g., the United States) or group of developed countries.

20. For example, speeding up and extending Uruguay Round commitments through APEC might be criticized even if other APEC members follow suit. This is because groups like the EU would benefit from the concessions without having to bargain away their own trade barriers, thereby provoking charges of "free-riding" and given-away "chips" that could otherwise be used for negotiations with the Europeans.

21. MAPA is an extremely long document (its 2,000 or so pages are accessible from the APEC web-site) but as with the Osaka Action Plan, not much progress was made in reaching the Bogor vision except in terms of speeding up Uruguay Round liberalization and offering liberalization packages that had already been promised or that were being promoted for reasons not necessarily associated with APEC.

22. *ASEAN Update,* October 1995.

PART FOUR:

INSTITUTIONAL MODELS FOR APEC

CHAPTER 13

APEC AND REGIME CREATION IN THE ASIA-PACIFIC: THE OECD MODEL?

Sylvia Ostry

I. INTRODUCTION

If Europe can be said to have an institutional surplus (most prominently but by no means solely the European Union and NATO), the Asia-Pacific clearly has an institutional deficit. While a number of international nongovernmental organizations (INGOs) have been established, ASEAN, the Association of Southeast Asian Nations, is the only prominent intergovernmental organization. By European standards, ASEAN is a noninstitutionalized institution that functions through meetings organized by intergovernmental committees and a modest secretariat. In between these two extremes of Europe and Asia is the North American landscape, with the recently established North American Free Trade Agreement (NAFTA) and the regional security institution, the Organization of American States (OAS). NAFTA has a secretariat in each member country, a secretariat for environment and labor matters, a ministerial-level commission, a large number of committees and working groups mandated by the commission, and a complex dispute-settlement mechanism to enforce the extensive set of negotiated rules. Thus, while the institutional density of NAFTA is far less than the European model, it is significantly greater, especially in terms of binding, transparent rules, than any Asian organization.

Since the creation of the Asia-Pacific Economic Cooperation (APEC) in 1989 and the creation of a small secretariat in 1993, there has been a growing interest in the question of institution-building in East Asia. Many explanations, both geopolitical and cultural, have been proffered for the historical Asian institutional deficit. Changes signaled by APEC's creation, it is argued, prompt the exploration of institutional alternatives (e.g., the OECD) to provide guidelines for promising policy options. Indeed, before the formal launch of APEC in early 1989, Australian Prime Minister Bob Hawke referred to the OECD as a possible model for a new Pacific multilateral forum,[1] echoing an earlier suggestion for an Organization for Pacific Economic Cooperation and Development (OPTAD) put forward at the first Pacific Trade and Development (PAFTAD) Conference in 1968.[2]

So is the OECD a relevant model for the new noun? This chapter will explore that question first by highlighting the main features of the origins of the OECD in order to compare them with those of the origins of APEC. The stark contrast between these background conditions will then be assessed in the final section on the policy implications for the future evolution of an Asia-Pacific OECD through APEC.

Before turning to this discussion, however, a caveat is in order. The international regime literature, which provides the contextual framework for much of the analysis of institutions, often extends to the political domain the basic optimizing assumptions of economic theory. In the present author's view, the real world of political economy is too messy for optimizing calibration, even at the margin. The role of accident, error, individual actors, and inadequate information almost always ensures that the unintended consequences of policy outweigh the specified objectives. Moreover, the objectives of the major actors—the nation states—are neither static nor given but reflect domestic interests and a range of contextual factors that are in continuing flux. Even in the case of the Marshall Plan (which spawned the OECD), the overriding objectives so carefully negotiated and spelled out were certainly attained, but just as certainly the Marshall Plan produced results of great importance that were not predicted—or predictable. In the case of APEC, in which an essential feature is the lack of information about the objectives of the key players and the complex dynamics of the relationships among the major actors, the law of unintended consequences is likely to reign supreme.

II. THE MARSHALL PLAN AND THE OECD

By 1961 Western European growth was buoyant, not only (indeed, not primarily) because of the Marshall Plan but because of technology transfer, high investment, and growth-friendly domestic policies fostered by the Organization for European Economic Cooperation (OEEC). Thus it was decided to create the Organization for Economic Cooperation and Development (OECD) as a permanent institution to continue these activities. Understanding the OECD's institutional genesis requires an examination of its provenance in the Marshall Plan.

The Marshall Plan: The Initiation

This section will highlight the basic causal variables that gave rise to the Marshall Plan. Essentially there are two somewhat conflicting views of its origin: the consensual hegemon versus the cold warrior. Can the system be effectively adapted in the absence of an unchallengeable leader or hegemon? Or will hegemonic decline and the end of the Cold War inevitably lead to a destruction of the regime? The most optimistic appraisal is that the postwar order built by the United States was not imposed on the convergence club but rather reflected a unique "consensual hegemony" based on shared views ("embedded liberalism"), essentially a commitment to international rules that were compatible with a government's domestic objectives. Thus these shared views are durable and can be adapted to ongoing change in the world economy and polity.

For some purposes, however, it could be argued that the debate is irrelevant. As noted above, in analytic models that function on the notion that governments pursue fixed single-focus or "rational" objectives, the models, mental or formal, the complexities of the policymaking process, and the role of error and accident, are impounded in the requirement that all other things remain equal. If one evaluates the Marshall Plan in terms of one aspect of the outcome—its contribution to the creation of the "convergence club" of the major OECD countries who by the 1970s had by and large converged in technological capabilities, capital per worker, education levels, and managerial capacity—it can be argued that the Marshall Plan success was a bit of an unwelcome surprise to some Americans: too true to be good, to borrow from George Bernard Shaw. And there was another surprise. While the OECD countries all chose capitalism and rejected communism, it became clearer over time that capitalism came in a variety of brands. There weren't just two systems—capitalism and communism—but a range of variants, with structural differences that affected openness to trade, investment and technology. These two unexpected outcomes have shaped the evolution of U.S. trade policy and, of course, APEC.

Thus the Cold War was the "shock" that provided the initial impetus for the Marshall Plan and hence the OECD. But the subsequent evolution of the OECD and the other postwar international institutions reflected the unique characteristics of U.S. hegemony. The creation of the OECD and the GATT, which will be discussed shortly, was based less on the analysis of the benefits of free trade than on "the most elemental concerns: war and peace and the need for allies to be economically prosperous."[3] With the decline in relative economic dominance that began in the 1970s, the issue of "unfairness"—a word with powerful resonance in the United States—became a defining parameter of American trade policy. Indeed, the first overt and dramatic manifestation of policies stemming from this feeling was the Nixon-Connally actions in 1971, which marked the beginning of the end of the Bretton Woods system of fixed exchange rates. As one analyst remarked: "Not far below the surface was the feeling—tapped by Nixon and Connally—that the United States is carrying an unfairly large share of the burdens of maintaining security in the world and is somehow made a victim of the others in international trade."[4]

Thus the nesting of the economic and security issues were key systemic factors that led to an economic institutional architecture and a security institution, NATO.[5] The objective in both cases was the creation of comprehensive global security that embraced both the economic and political domains. But as the economic (and later the security) context changed, the obvious problem of how to control free-riders was bound to arise and to change policy purpose and practice.

Another significant aspect of the background factors that influenced American policy leading to the Marshall Plan was domestic. U.S. business, far more efficient than any potential competitors in Europe, saw enticing opportunities in a stable and more open European markets. The terms of Marshall Plan aid clearly involved trade and payments liberalization, albeit initially only within Europe, and market primacy in domestic policy. U.S. business approved the policy as "the sweetest deal."[6] Strict conditionality for the use of Marshall aid was negotiated bilaterally, and for the most part the terms reflected the views of the U.S. business community. The conditionality was much tougher than that envisaged under Bretton Woods arrangements.

Early action was undertaken toward the dismantling of restrictions among the European members in trade and payments. This resulted in the 1950 institution of the European Payments Union (EPU) and the Code of Liberalization of trade. Unlike its prewar policy stance, the United States. demanded no reciprocity in this liberalization effort. But American business supported this position as a preliminary measure to full liberalization. Thus the promise of American access to a more prosperous Europe enabled the American government to give up its traditional demand for reciprocity in trade negotiations under the EPU. (Decades later, this and other similar policy decisions rekindled the more deep-seated views of unfairness.)

While American labor was not quite so fervent in its support, the lingering effects of the New Deal were sufficient to forestall serious opposition. And as is clear from the Marshall Plan's Technology Assistance program,[7] efforts were made from the outset to engage unions in OEEC activity. In addition, a Business and Industry Advisory Committee (BIAC) and a Trade Union Advisory Committee (TUAC) were established. So the politics of consensus in the U.S. context were skillfully handled by the American planners.

Finally, it is necessary to explore the issue of cognitive factors or "norms." Did the United States and the Western Europeans share a set of principles, implicit or explicit, that facilitated the creation of not only the OEEC/OECD but, indeed, the entire postwar architecture of international cooperation? While a full analysis of the postwar architecture would lead us too far afield, it is important to examine the trade issue and briefly review the origins of the GATT and the demise of the International Trade Organization (ITO) to demonstrate the elusiveness of the notion of shared norms. At one level the postwar elites did share similar views on the objectives of international cooperation, but when these broad principles had to be applied to the construction of an institution, cognitive consensus gave way to cognitive dissonance.

The United States took the leading role in building a new trading system. Cordell Hull, Roosevelt's Secretary of State, had reversed the long-standing protectionist policy of the United States in 1934 by the passage of the Reciprocal Trade Agreements Act (RTAA), which authorized the president to negotiate tariff reductions with foreign states on a nondiscriminatory basis. Hull was convinced that freer international trade was essential to U.S. prosperity, world recovery, and the maintenance of world peace. From 1934 on, Hull's vision became "the core mythology" of American foreign policy.[8]

The other major actor in the design of the postwar institutions, the United Kingdom, was also strongly influenced by the memory of the 1930s. British Lord Keynes and American Harry Dexter White, the fathers of Bretton Woods, saw the beggar-thy-neighbor devaluations as pernicious as the tariff wars of the 1930s. They agreed that a stable rule-based payments system required a stable rule-based trading system, and vice versa. But they were unable to agree on the architectonic principles to construct such a system because politics and competing domestic lobbies differed in the two countries. The trade negotiations thus followed a separate track.

The disagreement between the British and Americans concerned two fundamental issues, nondiscrimination, or the most-favored-nation (MFN) rule and the extent and nature of "escape clauses" to permit temporary import barriers for protection of the domestic economy. The British wanted to maintain their system of preferential treatment of commonwealth countries for political reasons. And as stated in their 1944 White Paper on Employment Policy, they regarded the maintenance of full employment and the creation of the welfare state as more important than free trade. While there were some Americans, especially Keynesian academics, who shared that view, it was not the prevailing view of the elites. As Jacob Viner noted,

the zeal of the United States for the elimination of special and flexible controls over foreign trade is in large part explained by the absence of any prospect that the United States will in the near future devise or accept a significant program for stabilization of employment or for the planning of investment, the confidence prevailing in this country that our competitive position in foreign trade and the exchange position in foreign trade and the exchange position of the American dollar will continue to be strong, and the availability of the cache of gold at Fort Knox to tide us over even a prolonged and substantial adverse balance of payments if perchance it should occur.[9]

The separate trade negotiations between the United States and the United Kingdom began in 1943. It was not until the end of 1945—well after Bretton Woods—that a document was released in Washington that included, among a number of proposals, a charter for an International Trade Organization (ITO) and the GATT, a subset of the broader institution. After several preparatory meetings and extensive negotiations, the ITO charter was presented in 1948 at a meeting in Havana.

The charter of the ITO reflected the many compromises negotiated during the preparatory process. But all the compromise and difficult negotiations leading to agreement in Havana were overtaken by events. At the time of the Havana meeting, the Marshall Plan was launched. The trade and payments liberalization of the OEEC, based on discrimination against the United States, settled the issue of nondiscrimination without debate. The ITO was not ratified after Havana by any country because all were waiting for the leader to ratify first. Since the president required another extension of negotiating authority in 1949, he decided not to send the ITO to Congress that year. However, opposition was building from many quarters—and support from few. In addition, the Korean War had started, and interest in global cooperation had waned. Truman judged there was virtually no chance of approval of the Havana charter and decided not to seek Congressional approval.

The basis for the judgment seems pretty plausible: no strong support (except among academics and some bureaucrats) but lots of strong opposition. Why did Bretton Woods get by Congress? And the Marshall Plan? The fact that there was no strong opposition seems to be the answer. Bretton Woods was about money and the dollar, and Americans were worried about the Cold War, not the dollar. There was little opposition to the Cold War. But the domestic coalition for the ITO was too weak, the proposal had too many loopholes, and satisfied no one entirely, especially not labor unions who feared import penetration. But the most effective business opposition was not based on this fear. As Diebold explains: "Their objection was that the Charter would do little to remove the trade barriers set up by foreign countries and might even strengthen some of them. Moreover, the businessmen who took this view usually believed that the Charter went too far in subordinating the international commitments of signatory countries to the requirements— real or imagined—of national economic plans and policies."[10]

What lay at the heart of the opposition of powerful business lobbies was a rejection of the idea that there can be many variants of market systems, with different institutional arrangements including different mixes of government and business roles. The support for trade liberalization by many U.S. business groups, was based on support for access to foreign markets which were seen as less open than those of the United States, in large part because of government intrusiveness.

Despite this opposition, American leadership in the trade arena did not fail with the death of the ITO. It was American initiative that launched the GATT negotiations in Geneva in 1947 as a prelude to Havana. Since GATT was much narrower in coverage and because the commitments contained in the agreement were less binding, it did not elicit the widespread opposition of the ITO. Its weakness was its strength—at least at the outset.

But over time the essential compromises embedded in the GATT came to erode the structure. The numerous "escapes" from negotiated commitments to liberalization created new forms of protectionism to counter "unfair" trade in the form of the rules on antidumping and countervailing subsidies and contributed to the increasing "legalization" of trade policy. A number of provisions protected agriculture from liberalization, adding to the American concern with unfairness—especially vis-à-vis the European Common Agricultural Policy (ECAP). At the most fundamental level, the consensus in the GATT rules and the exceptions masked significant differences on the basic issue of the nature and extent of government intervention. With the reduction of border barriers, these domestic differences became the focus of U.S. trade policy. Systemic differences, some of which significantly affected the contestability of markets, created a new form of international divisiveness—system friction—which was most obvious in American-Japanese relations in the 1980s. The broadly shared views on the objective of reducing the border barriers of the 1930s had far less relevance to the problems of "domestic impediments" to market access. This contrast between the "shallow integration" focus of the GATT norms and the "deeper integration" of today's policy focus is essential to any discussion of the institutional nature of APEC. But before turning to APEC, an exposition of the institutional character of the OECD will be presented.

III. THE OECD: METAREGIME AND INSTITUTION

The OECD mandate reflected the major objectives of the Western powers led by the United States, i.e., essentially the objectives of the postwar consensus were (1) economic growth, (2) a rising standard of living, and (3) multilateral liberalization of trade.[11] These objectives (the metaregime of the institution), however, were expressed in terms of the world economy and not just the member countries. The Euro-American hegemonic "vision" of

OECD spanned the globe. Its emphasis on multilateralism was an oblique reference to the preferential arrangement for the EC, reluctantly sanctioned by the United States in the GATT, to further the primary foreign and security policy objectives of the State Department.[12] Thus the metaregime of the OECD exemplified the global vision of comprehensive security.

In addition to these overall objectives, the convention spelled out several other policy priorities for member countries to pursue "both individually and jointly" including science, technology, and training programmes. This surprising emphasis on "innovation" policies stemmed from two sources: the remarkable success of a little-known aspect of the Marshall Plan, the Technical Assistance Program, and the priority placed by the European members of the OECD on closing the "technology gap" with the United States.[13] The Europeans fully understood the importance of technology transfer as an engine of growth. American businesses were obviously convinced that given their overwhelming lead in productivity, they need not fear any challenge from new competitors and could only benefit from a reconstructed Europe. But there were more subtle reasons reflecting the unique nature of American hegemony. Commenting on the "voluntary contribution" of American know-how, Raymond Aron notes:

> The American propensity to consider their own system exemplary, proved most fortunate for the European and Japanese economies; the productivity missions which toured the United States, and the closely knit relationships which sprang up on both sides of the Atlantic, had beneficial repercussions on the Old Continent. The Americans, by virtue of their philosophy, considered it a matter of course to teach others the secret of their own success. As the predominant economy, the United States had the advantage from its partners' point of view, of believing in freedom and communication rather than secrecy and bureaucracy.[14]

The Americans were equally generous in technology transfer to Japan, where a similar program was launched.

Another surprisingly forward-looking inclusion in the OECD mandate was the environment. While not specifically cited as an objective in the original convention, because studies on various aspects of pollution were carried out under the general scientific research program, this work was formalized by the creation of an Environment Committee and Directorate in 1970. This is but one example of the flexibility of the institution and its broad substantive scope.

The substantive scope of the OECD is the broadest of any postwar institution. There are secretariat resources that provide information and analysis for macro- and microeconomic policy-making; trade; aid to developing countries; financial regulation; labor market and social policies; industrial, energy, and agricultural policies; science, technology, innovation, and education; public administration; and statistics. In addition to producing biannual forecasts, the OECD prepares annual reports on the performance of each member country, which include policy recommendations to enhance growth, trade liberalization, innovation, and so on. Because of the broad array of analytic capacity and the flexibility of the institution, it is easier to promote policy dialogue in the OECD than in national capitals on cross-cutting issues, such as technology and jobs, trade and labor standards, trade and the environment, competition policy and market access, financial regulation and innovation by small and medium-sized enterprises, globalization, and regulatory reform, to name but a few recent examples.

The flexibility, and hence adaptability, of the OECD as an institution is a key characteristic that will be discussed further in this section. The OECD itself is, in a very important sense, not a rules-based institution—i.e., it does not administer rules (unlike the Bretton Woods institutions and the GATT/WTO). Rather it helps to secure adherence to rules and the need to foster changes in rules by its mode of operation, which involves:

1. regular meetings of senior officials from capitals, which may include academics and representatives of nongovernmental institutions as appropriate;
2. annual meetings of ministers from finance, trade and foreign affairs;
3. issue-specific meetings of ministers from the range of departments covered by the scope of the institution;
4. in all the meetings, information and policy-analytic studies are provided to promote the diffusion of knowledge both internationally and in national capitals; the review of economic activity to enhance domestic policy performance; to encourage international policy cooperation, coordination, and continuous monitoring by means of information, debate, and peer group pressure; to highlight new issues for national and international policy consideration; to encourage policy dialogue within capitals and the main international economic institutions (Bretton Woods; the WTO; the U.N. and its agencies).

Thus the OECD exploits its strategic assets:

1. soft power (knowledge and networks that create the means to influence policy decision making)
2. diffusion networks of key actors, both governmental and nongovernmental (business, labor, NGOs, academics, etc.).

The absence of rules or hard power (power of the nation state to make and enforce policy) is essential to this performance since the diffusion of knowledge rests on a degree of informality in discussion and debate, an informality lacking in more formal rules-based institutions. The absence of rules also enhances flexibility and adaptability, whereas inertia dominates the decision-making process in more formal institutions. (And of course, the smaller size of the OECD is also important: larger institutions need to create smaller subgroups to improve their operations, and this is often very difficult, as the creation of the IMF Interim Committee demonstrates). But access to hard power via a network of officials and ministers is also essential. A brief account of the role of the OECD in the Uruguay Round illustrates this soft power/networking aspect of the institution.

The negotiation to launch the Uruguay Round negotiation took almost as long as the entire Tokyo Round of the 1970s. A U.S. call for new negotiations dated back to 1981, and the Uruguay Round was launched in 1986 and finally concluded in 1994. The extraordinary difficulty in both initiating and completing the round stemmed essentially from two fundamental factors: the nearly insuperable problem of finishing the unfinished business of past negotiations, most of all agriculture; and the equally contentious issue of introducing quite new agenda items, especially trade in services. The role of the OECD was to further the negotiations on negotiations. Because of U.S. and EU influence, a high priority was assigned to comprehensive analytical studies on the key issues, especially agriculture, for which new measures of protectionism were devised. Studies on the impact of protectionism on growth and inflation, the distorting effects of agricultural protectionism, the beneficial impact of liberalizing trade in services, etc., were in the OECD and widely disseminated in member countries in order to raise public awareness and assist politicians who wanted an external counterweight to protectionist lobbying.

But knowledge diffusion was only half the strategy. From 1981, when the Americans became increasingly concerned about the increasing protectionist fervor of the Congress, a hard power network was established that included the OECD; the Quadrilateral Trade Ministers created by the United States that included the EU, Japan, and Canada; the Economic Summit; and the (now defunct) policy committee of the GATT, the Consultative Group of 18 (CG18), which included India and Brazil. The analytic resources of the OECD were deployed through a series of linked meetings: senior officials in OECD committees; Quadrilateral Trade Ministers; OECD ministers and, at the pinnacle, the summit of heads of government. The link to the GATT was the CG18 and ad hoc informal meetings convened by member country representatives. The coordination of each step of the strategy—analytical studies, planning and linking committee, ministerial, and summit agendas; information flows to and from GATT headquarters in Geneva—was the responsibility of senior officials in national capitals. But the OECD role as a generator of information, a forum for discussion and the exercise of peer group pressure, was a key element in the design and implementation of strategy. The element of continuity was essential. A permanent venue and a permanent knowledge infrastructure were essential to the monitoring of policy commitments, which are usually presented in very generalized form.

In summary, then, the OECD as an institution includes a broad metaregime of basic principles and a combination of strategic assets: a knowledge infrastructure in the form of a secretariat; a meeting infrastructure for knowledge diffusion, debate, peer group pressure, strategic planning, and continuing monitoring of policy performance; and a hard power network for policymaking. All these assets are deployed to reduce the transactions costs of policymaking. The OECD can thus be seen as a "parallel substantive" institution with respect to the GATT/WTO that prevented direct conflicts between the two organizations and enhanced the effectiveness of both through an efficient division of labor.

It would have been far more difficult to pursue the Uruguay Round negotiating-for-negotiations strategy bilaterally. Further, peer group pressure is a valuable tool in both constraining opponents and rallying supporters, often through issue-specific, variable-geography coalitions. For example, in the Uruguay Round strategy, the OECD includes Canada, Australia, and New Zealand, all members of the Cairns Group established by Australia to promote agricultural trade reform. All this said, it is not possible to evaluate the contribution of the OECD—or indeed, any such institution. It may be that the best judgment would be Churchill's: it was better than any other alternative available to promote the OECD's founding mission of multilateral liberalization. Let's now turn to a very different alternative—APEC as noninstitution with a millennial vision. Could it morph into an OECD?

IV. ASIAN-PACIFIC OECD?

The Asia-Pacific region is unique in many respects other than its institutional deficit characteristic. Most relevant is the extraordinary diversity of culture, language, legal systems, stages of development, and political governance arrangements. Even in the Western Hemisphere, which includes countries of widely different levels of development and significant variations in governance and legal systems, the historical roots in culture and religion stem from a European imperial past. It is argued that the unique diversity of this region can be fused into an "Asian way" and that the most powerful agent of fusion is the remarkable growth performance of the past few decades. Even if that were the case, of course, the disparity in views among APEC members would challenge the concept of "shared norms" that are supposed to represent a necessary condition for the construction of regimes and institutions.

The weakness of shared norms need not be a determining factor impeding institutionalization, because even in the case of the OECD, the concept of embedded liberalism was not quite as robust as first appeared. Further, in the context of an OECD model for APEC, there exist other starkly contrasting conditions between the postwar period and the present post–Cold War period: the nature of U.S. hegemony; the absence of congruence between economic and security arrangements; and the move from shallow to deeper integration of the global economy.

This section will first review the background to the creation of APEC and then consider the implications for a Pacific OECD of the region's diversity as well as the three conditions cited above.

Origins of APEC

In the Asia-Pacific region, economic integration led by foreign direct investment (FDI) was the main catalyst generating an evolutionary search process for institution-building. For the Europeans, economic integration was a means to achieve binding political linkages in order to avoid a repetition of the disastrous wars of the preceding century. The creation of the Common Market and later the European Union proceeded in fits and starts, but at each stage the depth of economic integration was more intensive, extending from border barriers to coordination or even harmonization of a growing range of domestic policies. So the pattern in Europe was politics—economics—institutions—deeper integration.

In the Asia-Pacific, a key agent of integration was and is the multinational enterprise (MNE), especially the Japanese MNE, but also U.S. and more recently Overseas Chinese corporations. Locational competition for FDI and export-led industrial strategies stimulated unilateral liberalization in many countries, and adherence to the GATT amplified this through multilateral liberalization, producing remarkable growth rates. East Asia is often presented as a model: a virtuous circle of liberalization to attract investment that generates trade and attracts more investment, thus sustaining the momentum of liberalization with no need for burdensome institutional mechanisms to thrive. Economic integration in the region is still shallow. There is no institutional mechanism, limited cooperation, or coordination or harmonization of domestic policies. Indeed, as noted, there is remarkable diversity of both polities and policies, or system diversity. Will natural economic integration foster integrating modalities?

This section will present some of the background information on this "natural integration" and the growth of intraregional trade. The debate about the nature of the East Asian Miracle will also be touched on in order to emphasize the increasing importance of technology transfer to improve productivity growth. And it will also discuss the other unique characteristic of the region, the role of international nongovernmental organizations or INGOs, which in effect laid the groundwork for APEC.

Natural Integration: The Initiation

The term East Asian Miracle,[15] was coined by the World Bank to capture the extraordinarily rapid growth rates of the East Asian members of APEC (excluding Japan). Since the mid-1960s, their GNP growth rates have been more than twice the OECD average and real income per capita quadrupled in the Four Tigers (Hong Kong, Singapore, Taiwan, and Korea—now termed the Newly Industrializing Economies or NIEs) and nearly doubled in ASEAN. More recently, mainland China has been added to the miracle group, with growth rates outstripping even the NIEs.

While there is no single East Asian model, there are some common characteristics of the growth pattern, such as unusually high domestic savings and investment rates, priority to improving the basic educational and skill levels, and rapid increases in exports. This improved efficiency provided for technology access from the advanced markets of the OECD. Their share of world manufacturing exports ballooned from less than 2 percent in 1965 to nearly 20 percent in 1994.

This export growth pattern differs in a number of fundamental respects from the postwar catch-up of Japan and other members of the convergence club. Thus, for example, the role of improvements in overall technology capability, as captured by total factor productivity, was far less important in fostering rising living standards in East Asia than it was for the OECD countries. The growth of inputs rather than overall productivity accounted for most of the rise in living standards.

Another significant difference from the postwar catch-up model is that rapid structural change was a major force in increasing productivity in East Asia. Resources shifted to higher productivity manufacturing industries, which raised their efficiency through competition in export markets. Apart from the shrinkage of the agricultural sector after the war, which provided a supply of low-wage labor, structural change played a relatively minor role in the creation of the convergence club. But in East Asia as a region, the supply of lower-wage workers is more elastic both because of rapid structural change within as well as among countries. The lesser role of unions and government regulation than that in Europe's labor markets facilitates rapid structural change in most of these countries. Further, within the region as a whole, foreign investors can if necessary shift parts of their production process to offset rising wages in the more advanced countries. This makes the region a very attractive location for foreign investors, not only to serve rapidly growing regional markets but as a global export platform.

And thus perhaps the most significant difference between the East Asian miracle and the building of the OECD convergence club is the role of FDI and its impact on trade and technology transfer. Although the degree of openness to FDI varies within the region, all countries have sought technology transfer either by welcoming the establishment of foreign subsidiaries or by contracts for manufacturing equipment as well as by so-called new forms of investment such as strategic alliances of various types. But unlike the period after the war—when there was only one significant technology provider, the United States—there are now in East Asia three major foreign investors: the United States, Japan, and the Overseas Chinese (O/C) in Malaysia, Singapore, Taiwan, and Indonesia. European companies have fallen behind in the investment race, although more recently there are signs of changing priorities. Hence, in sharp contrast with the postwar situation, the existence of multiple players in East Asia makes the game much more complex than one dominated and governed by a single hegemon. Moreover, since there is no "nesting" of security and economic institutions in East Asia but rather a hub-and-spoke arrangement with the United States, and since the Cold War is now over, there is no political "glue" to foster integration but instead—especially vis-à-vis China—a "reverse spillover" from economic to political friction. This, of course, adds to the difficulty of fusion or shared norms, whether Asian or otherwise.

There are other problems with the pattern of natural integration as a source of fusion. The East Asian countries seem en route to creating a new convergence club and are mobilizing their efforts to do so. But to sustain further growth over the long run will require higher levels of technology since the returns to increasing inputs and to major structural transformation as well as the advantage of less expensive labor will inevitably diminish.

As was the case for the OECD countries, upgrading the knowledge base through improvement and expansion of higher education and investment in R&D is a necessary but not sufficient condition for catch-up. But the key funnel for technology acquisition in this region overall has been foreign investment, which has transferred not only technological know-how but management expertise and access to export markets. Competition for "good" investment has become a prominent feature of industrial policy in many of these countries and especially in China. And these industrial policies will be the source of increasing friction as investment issues assume a higher profile in the global trade agenda.

Another concern is whether East Asian, but more particularly Chinese, growing bilateral trade deficits with the United States will echo the "asymmetry problem," which has created a good deal of heat in U.S.-Japanese relations. Thus, as may be seen in Table 13.1,

TABLE 13.1

MEASURES OF REGIONAL INTERDEPENDENCE, 1979-1993

REGION	1979	1985	1990	1992	1994
Intraregional Trade as a Share of Regional Trade					
North America	0.287	0.330	0.313	0.314	0.365
European Union	0.535	0.542	0.607	0.611	0.565
East Asia *	0.332	0.363	0.407	0.453	0.525
Gravity Coefficients[a] of Intraregional Trade					
North America	1.95	1.71	1.84	1.86	1.87
European Union	1.53	1.70	1.53	1.55	1.68
East Asia	2.64	2.05	2.09	2.13	2.24

* Hong Kong, Singapore, Taiwan, Korea, Malaysia, Indonesia, Philippines, Thailand

[a] ([Intraregional Trade]x[World Trade])/([Total Exports of Region]x[Total Imports of Region])

Sources: Peter Petri, "Corporate Links and Direct Foreign Investment in Asia and the Pacific" (PAFTAD, Hong Kong, June 1-3, 1994, mimeographed), 7; figures for 1994 and European Union calculated using data from International Monetary Fund, *Direction of Trade Statistics*, various issues.

intraregional trade has increased significantly since the late 1980s, after a marked decline over the previous decade. This increase reflects the impact of trade liberalization in East Asia and growing penetration of world markets as mentioned earlier. More important, it reflects the differing strategies of the MNEs from different countries. While it would take us too far afield to describe these developments in detail, a brief description is necessary to highlight the basic issue, i.e., whether natural integration is a catalyst for institutional change.

As may be seen in Tables 13.2 and 13.3, the East Asian trade surplus with the United States grew very rapidly, but its deficit with Japan grew even more, especially after the mid-1980s because of rising imports of capital goods and technology intensive components from Japan. This dependence on Japan is evident in the pattern of trade for both the more advanced NIEs and ASEAN. Thus a pattern of triangular trade has emerged,

TABLE 13.2

TRADE BALANCE AND SHARES OF VARIOUS COUNTRIES AND REGIONS IN TOTAL IMPORTS AND EXPORTS OF EAST ASIA

	1980			1985			1994		
	EXPORTS TO	IMPORTS FROM	BALANCE[a]	EXPORTS TO	IMPORTS FROM	BALANCE[a]	EXPORTS TO	IMPORTS FROM	BALANCE[a]
UNITED STATES	22%	17%	6,467	29%	16%	28,084	22%	14%	53,783
WESTERN EUROPE[b]	14%	9%	6,936	10%	11%	-909	13%	13%	-798
JAPAN	21%	24%	-4,646	17%	26%	-12,622	13%	23%	-80,384
EAST ASIA[c]	21%	22%	0	25%	27%	0	38%	37%	0
REST OF WORLD	22%	27%	-6,488	19%	20%	1,535	14%	13%	2,925
WORLD	100%	100%	2,269	100%	100%	16,089	100%	100%	-24,474

Source: Calculations based on data from U.N., *International Trade Statistics Yearbook*, various issues; OECD, *Foreign Trade by Commodities*, various issues

a. U.S.$ millions
b. East Asia = China, Hong Kong, Indonesia, South Korea, Malaysia, Philippines, Singapore, Taiwan, and Thailand
c. Western Europe = Austria, Belgium, Luxembourg, Denmark, Finland, France, West Germany, Greece, Iceland, Ireland, Italy, Netherlands, Norway, Portugal, Spain, Sweden, Switzerland, and the United Kingdom

manifested by growing surpluses with the United States and growing deficits with Japan.

The Japanese intrafirm investment networks in East Asia, in which higher value-added production is kept in Japan, the production process is allocated within the region, and finished goods are exported abroad and back to Japan ("reverse imports"), is now undergoing change. This is due to both domestic factors (the prolonged recession and the yen shocks of the 1990s) as well as growing criticism from many host governments about the allegedly parsimonious technology- transfer policy of the Japanese MNEs. When and to what extent these changes will significantly alter the behavior of the corporations or of governments is not at all clear. However, because the dominant strategy of U.S. manufacturing firms has been to use the region as an inexpensive industrial base for processing products to sell to the U.S. market—outsourcing, in

TABLE 13.3

TRADE BALANCE AND SHARES OF VARIOUS COUNTRIES AND REGIONS IN MANUFACTURED IMPORTS AND EXPORTS OF EAST ASIA

	1980			1985			1993		
	EXPORTS TO	IMPORTS FROM	BALANCE[A]	EXPORTS TO	IMPORTS FROM	BALANCE[A]	EXPORTS TO	IMPORTS FROM	BALANCE[A]
UNITED STATES	27%	17%	6,860	40%	14%	3,161	25%	13%	62,983
WESTERN EUROPE	19%	15%	1,212	12%	14%	-2,239	17%	17%	2,191
JAPAN	8%	35%	-25,316	7%	32%	-32,158	9%	25%	-82,700
EAST ASIA	22%	19%	0	23%	23%	0	36%	38%	0
REST OF WORLD	26%	13%	9,049	18%	18%	-209	14%	7%	35,135
WORLD	100%	100%	-8,194	100%	100%	-2,995	100%	100%	17,609

Source: Calculations based on data from U.N., *International Trade Statistics Yearbook,* various issues; OECD, *Foreign Trade by Commodities,* various issues
Note: SITC: 6,7,8
a. U.S.$ millions
b. East Asia = China, Hong Kong, Indonesia, South Korea, Malaysia, Philippines, Singapore, Taiwan, and Thailand
c. Western Europe = Austria, Belgium, Luxembourg, Denmark, Finland, France, West Germany, Greece, Iceland, Ireland, Italy, Netherlands, Norway, Portugal, Spain, Sweden, Switzerland, and the United Kingdom.

effect—these "reverse imports" have far outweighed the export of components and equipment from U.S. headquarters and thus added to the triangular trade pattern. But here also there are signs of change as the corporations are vying for regional market share. Rivalry among MNEs, wherever their home base, is bound to intensify in this rapidly growing region. And U.S. investment, which has lagged behind that of Japan, is scrambling to catch up.

Finally, the U.S. and Japanese firms are not the only big players in this high-stakes game. Some Korean and Taiwanese firms have already established market presence both in the East Asian region and world markets and compete with OECD firms in certain products in both consumer and industrial electronics. U.S. and Japanese firms have formed alliances of various kinds with these firms for both defensive reasons as well as to gain share in host country markets. However, the most important new actors by far are the Overseas Chinese firms, or rather networks. The networks are "international clan associations based on dialect."[16] The potent combination of wealth, power, and influence is a valuable asset everywhere.

The ethnic Chinese states are major players in a number of East Asian countries as well as, of course, China. With the opening up of mainland China, the asset value of the O/C family corporations was greatly amplified. Language, culture, and history are "capabilities" essential to navigate the labyrinth of the mainland. The Chinese term for this asset is *guanxi,* personal connections. The O/C use *guanxi* in China "to make up for the lack of the rule of law and transparency in rules and regulations."[17]

Many observers have commented on the remarkable entrepreneurial savvy of the Overseas Chinese and the rapid adaptive capacity of the networks. But of course, the chief assets of the Japanese and U.S. corporations in East Asian—capital, technology, and global distribution capabilities—are far greater than those of the O/C. Since the O/C networks are private and closed, equity purchase is impossible. That leaves only one possibility: mutually advantageous strategic alliances based on an exchange of complementary assets—that is, capital, technology, and third-country market access for O/C *guanxi.* And, while data are scarce, press reports and other sources suggest that joint ventures with Japanese, U.S., and European MNEs are proliferating.

By far the most elaborate and sophisticated example of *guanxi* is Singapore's undertaking to build industrial parks for foreign multinationals. The biggest undertaking in Suzhou will export a Singaporean "soft infrastructure" to China (legal, financial, and administrative arrangements) and serve as a base for attracting foreign multinationals.

China's open-door policy started by using tax and other incentives to bring investment to the special economic zones (SEZs). This investment was primarily low-cost assembly operations for export. But by the end of the 1980s a new industrial policy was developing, geared to technology transfer. Thus the government recently announced that its top priority is "a rapid upgrade of technology to the most advanced available in such fields as machinery, electronics, and telecommunications."[18] In the contest to gain a foothold in the Chinese market, the Chinese authorities can play one MNE against another to secure the best deal. Since the Chinese foreign investment policies are rather opaque (to say the least), such deal-making is normal practice. But China is not alone in this shift to high-tech industrial policy. Indeed, fear of investment diversion to China has added a new concern to the need for a policy geared to "catch up." Malaysia, Korea, and Indonesia have all announced new high-tech industrial policies.[19] And a number of other countries in the region are gearing both domestic and foreign investment policies to upgrade their industrial structure. These policies often conflict with any investment agreement in APEC.

In summary, the process of natural integration and export-education-led growth has indeed been remarkably successful and has also increased regional economic integration. But the pattern of trade and investment linkages both within the region and with respect to the global economy have also created a number of structural imbalances that are potentially divisive. Thus far, then, natural integration is not a strong candidate as catalyst for a metaregime.

Yet it is possible to define principles and norms at such a high level of generality that even dissenting actors can agree. But to move from a metaregime to an institution requires agreement on more tricky issues—reducing transaction costs and reducing opportunistic behavior by various means of control. Yet some of the actors in East Asia want to increase transactions costs (less transparency, fewer enforceable rules) in order to minimize constraints on highly rewarded opportunistic behavior. Thus the barest possible institution would be much more desirable—the less the better.

The rapid growth of East Asia did generate one binding norm or objective for the East Asian miracle countries—to build a new Asian convergence club. This commitment to rapid economic growth, in turn, generated another catalytic force unique to this region—the INGOs.

Asia-Pacific International Non-Governmental Organizations (INGOs)

If natural economic integration alone is unlikely to generate a metaregime in East Asia, what about the other actors unique to this region, the INGOs? Prior to World War II, the role of the INGOs was to promote "cooperative relationships based on a mutual understanding of religion, society, and culture."[20] Economics was not mentioned.

Thus the most active and most influential organizations were launched after the onset of rapid economic growth in the 1960s. The major actors in the formation of the INGOs have been Australian and Japanese academics and officials and a number of MNEs. The newer INGOs, also instrumental in the creation of APEC, include the Pacific Trade and Development Conference, or PAFTAD (1968); the Pacific Basin Economic Council, or PBEC (1967-1968); the Pacific Economic Cooperation Conference (now Council), or PECC (1980). The main product of the INGOs is the diffusion of ideas through books, articles, papers, and conferences. The term "epistemic communities" has been used to capture their role in influencing the evolution of a new international regime in the Asia-Pacific.[21] Their credo is, indeed, economism. But the terminology of liberalization is couched in the postwar language of shallow integration: liberalization will promote economic growth by eradicating trade reducing or trade distorting impediments. Does this mean border barriers? Obviously, yes. Does it mean domestic regulatory differences which impede access? Probably, but maybe not. Does it mean transparency, due process, direct access to domestic courts for dispute settlement? No answer. And so on.

Nonetheless, the INGOs have played an important role in the creation of APEC. It has been argued that because of the diversity of the region that precluded the formation of intergovernmental institutions, an innovative communication medium had to spring from private actors. The message that flowed within this medium was economic growth. The medium was built in stages: first academics, then businessmen, and then government officials. This patient construction strengthened and broadened the communication links and thus established the foundation for constructing APEC. Just before the first APEC Ministerial Meeting held in Canberra in 1989, Saburo Okita, a former Japanese Minister of Foreign Affairs who was prominent in both PBEC and PECC, published a comment in the *Nihon Keizai Shinbun:*

> It was about 20 years ago that people started to propose various ideas on Asia-Pacific cooperation, which finally led to the creation of PBEC, a non-governmental body. There was then already a feeling that eventually this region would need an international governmental organization. In this sense, I feel a certain profound emotion vis-à-vis the coming Ministerial Meeting. The Asia-Pacific region embraces countries in both the South and the North. In addition, these countries are considerably heterogeneous. When we start promoting cooperation in this area, we should keep this situation fully in mind.[22]

Dr. Okita was a visionary noted for his long-range viewpoint, patience, and careful planning.

APEC

APEC may arguably be termed a triumph of Australian foreign policy. It is the only example of an institution created by a middle power, albeit with a good deal of help from a dominant regional power, Japan. Thus, far from being the creation of a global hegemon, as was the OECD, APEC was not a high U.S. priority at its inauguration. Indeed, the negative spillover from U.S. policies—unilateralism and regionalism in the form of NAFTA—was an important factor in the launch of APEC. The changes in U.S. trade policy during the 1980s (i.e., the move away from the overriding commitment to multilateralism that reflected the postwar hegemony, to a multitrack policy that included regionalism—first in the United States–Canada Free Trade Agreement and then the NAFTA—and 301–based unilateralism) created widespread concern in Japan, Australia, and other countries in the region about the future of the Uruguay Round negotiations, largely because of the transatlantic battle over agriculture and the fear of exclusion from two protectionist regional blocs—a Fortress Europe and a Fortress North America.

When APEC was established in 1989, it was accorded a low-key U.S. endorsement. Active American participation dates from the 1993 Seattle Summit, the first meeting of heads of government. What caused this change?

Several reasons for this turnaround in American policy have been proffered. It provided a means of allaying Asian concerns about NAFTA as well as a threat to the EU over the prolongation of the Uruguay Round agriculture dispute. Most of all it was seen as good for the president's image. In an era of "photo-op diplomacy," since the president's domestic advisers "without knowing the substance of the issue, thought it would be really positive to have 15 leaders of the free world from Asia meeting in Seattle on the West Coast since it would show the change from the past: new generation, new leaders, looking to Asia, not absorbed with a European focus (and) Clinton himself liked the idea from the start. It was an easy sell to the President, it took two sentences and he was positive."[23] It's important to underline the contrast by recalling Okita's remarks. The first APEC Ministerial Meeting involved twenty years of planning, but the Seattle Summit was launched in hours by two sentences. It was difficult to convince the governments in the region that meetings of ministers would serve any purpose. But if one leader, especially from a powerful country, decides on a summit, then it's done.

It's also important, however, to spell out the implications of APEC as a policymaking modality. Due to rotating leadership, summit agendas will strongly reflect domestic priorities as well as unpredictable current events (in the Economic Summit of the G7, some examples are Chernobyl and the terrorist attack in Saudi Arabia). The outcomes in policy terms reflect this ad hoc, episodic nature of the forum and the now-pervasive photo-op context. But because the Economic Summit is underpinned by a comprehensive policymaking infrastructure, which links all the postwar institutions, there is an entirely separate summit agenda of international policy cooperation and coordination and the Summit per se is (or can be) a focal point and catalyst for policy momentum.

This brings us to the most pertinent question with respect to institution-building—what is the APEC infrastructure at present? The INGOs play a role in generating policy-analytic knowledge. Another INGO was created by APEC itself at the Bangkok Ministerial Meeting in 1991, namely the Eminent Persons Group or EPG. The EPG, through a series of reports, has acted partly as a quasi-secretariat (agenda setting, documentation) but more significantly as a forum to spell out a workable metaregime by setting overall target objectives with dates and means of implementation. Thus the Bogor Declaration, announced at the 1994 APEC Summit in Indonesia, established a consensus on a goal of "free trade" by 2010 for "advanced" countries and 2020 for "developing" countries. Unresolved debate continues on, however, defining APEC-speak "open regionalism" or "concerted unilateral action."

The precise meaning of these new APEC-speak terms is not a debate about words but about profound policy differences. "Open regionalism" is not about WTO-conformity since the WTO rules provide for preferential arrangements that discriminate in favor of members. So the explanation sometimes proffered to clarify the terms adds to the confusion—why not just regionalism, i.e., a free trade agreement or a customs union? Or why not just MFN, perhaps within some given time frame? Some members of APEC might accept such a proposal. But certainly it would be difficult to sell to the Americans.

The conflict about open regionalism concerns U.S. insistence on reciprocity—broad reciprocity for all liberalization measures to prevent "free-riding" by the EU and even more important, as WTO negotiations have recently demonstrated, sector-specific reciprocity in sectors such as financial and telecommunications services where the barriers are not transparent border measures but the extent and nature of domestic regulation. The services negotiations thus involved an exchange of access to the American market for regulatory reform in other countries. Indeed, the precise type of reform was spelled out as part of the negotiating modality in the case of the telecommunications negotiations. A definition of "open regionalism" as "conditional MFN" perhaps might allay U.S. concerns regarding EU free-riding. But "conditional MFN" might not be acceptable to the proponents of "concerted unilateralism"—no reciprocity, indeed no negotiations.

"Concerted unilateralism" is described as an Asian way—voluntary liberalization encouraged by peer group pressure. It would not necessarily cover all sectors—for example, agriculture might be too sensitive for some or intellectual property enforcement for others. It would not necessarily involve reciprocity, even in the broadest sense of an overall balance of benefits. Indeed, it would be difficult to estimate who did what because no monitoring arrangements exist. It would not necessarily include investment, or at least not necessarily for all countries. And so on.

And it certainly would not be popular in Congress. If the Asian way can be described as "Trust," the American way is "Trust, but Verify." As the trading system has become more legalized and moved inside the border, the "verification" of commitments has become more important and more difficult. The diversity of systems in East Asia and most particularly the diversity of legal cultures and legal institutions make monitoring anything but tariffs and other border barriers virtually impossible. And if there is no monitoring system or secretariat infrastructure, how would peer group pressure work? In the OECD, by way of contrast, the nonbinding investment codes adopted in the 1960s and 1970s were regularly reviewed in committees established for that purpose. A process of continuing review and discussion led to successive improvements in the codes and increasing liberalization of member countries' policies. But the peer group pressure and the resulting liberalization depended on the secretariat and committee infrastructure.

This comparison with the OECD brings us back to our original question: Is the OECD an appropriate model for a future APEC institution?

V. CONCLUSION

The origins of the OECD rested on several key features of the postwar period. As this chapter has argued, these systemic factors were: the Cold War; the unique nature of the U.S. hegemony; and the shared norms of the founders engendered by vivid memories of a bitter past. The founding momentum stemmed from politics, and economic issues were "nested" in broader global security objectives. The United States was able to mobilize support for the Marshall Plan by forging domestic coalitions of the main nongovernment actors, business, and labor. While there were system differences among member countries, these did not come into focus until the 1970s and 1980s.

In APEC, the United States is still by far the dominant player. But the twenty-first century will be bipolar, with China becoming the other pole. The other regional power—Japan—is undergoing a major structural transformation domestically and groping for a new Asian foreign policy that offends neither the United States nor China. The system differences within the region and most significantly between the United States and China are far greater than within the OECD in the postwar decades or today.

Further, the political glue of the Cold War has dissolved. There is no "nesting" of economic and security regimes and no agreed definition of the public good of comprehensive security. The new domestic coalitions—the greens and human rights organizations—are not supportive of trade liberalization per se and are increasingly willing and able to become global players in the international policy domain.

Finally, by way of contrast, the OECD strategic assets were described as a knowledge infrastructure in the form of a secretariat; a meeting infrastructure for knowledge diffusion, monitoring, and the exercise of peer group pressure; and a hard-power network for policymaking momentum and coordination. The argument is made by some that a knowledge infrastructure can be mobilized more easily today by using think tanks, INGOs, member government research, etc. to form a "virtual secretariat." Moreover, APEC has an *embarras de richesse* of meetings of different groups of ministers, subject-specific working groups, senior officials and so on (at last count there were 31 expert working groups). Perhaps, as the Canadians have argued (and this was a major theme of the 1997 meeting in Vancouver),[24] better management of all this activity could provide some form of "virtual meeting infrastructure." Most of the working groups deal with trade facilitation, however, so new groups would have to be established for monitoring trade policy. Could these rotating and migrating intergovernmental groups be substitutes for the OECD location-based continuity-based meeting infrastructure? Perhaps.

That would leave one other asset to cover—the hard power network. Some members of APEC are also members of the OECD, the Summit, the Bretton Woods institutions, and the WTO. So in theory these members could link into the network and coordinate

APEC, with other regional initiatives (NAFTA-extended or NAFTA-Mercosur or EU-ASEAN, etc.) and the overall international policy process—unless the other members objected, as has Malaysia, for example, in the case of investment negotiations or Indonesia and the national car policy, and so on. But even if it were possible to forge a consensus on most policy issues, there's one gaping hole in this potential hard power network. China is not a member of the WTO. And the terms of China's accession to the WTO are highly contentious and unlikely to be easily resolved, either by APEC—which excludes the EU—or by the WTO itself. It's thus difficult to predict the outcome of the Chinese endorsement of the APEC targets. If the Chinese commitment is uncertain, where does that leave APEC? Or Asian security concerns?

In sum, the case for an APEC-OECD merits the Scottish verdict: Not proven.

NOTES

1. Yoichi Funabashi (1995, pp. 55-58). The Japanese regarded the OECD model as too "rigid" for the Asia Pacific (p. 60).
2. Lawrence T. Woods (1993, p. 43).
3. Richard N. Cooper (1987, p. 301).
4. William Diebold, Jr. (1987, p. 286).
5. For a discussion of "nesting" see Chapter 2 (Aggarwal 1998a) in this volume.
6. J. J. Servan-Schreiber (1968, p. 8).
7. For a full exposition of this unique program, see Sylvia Ostry (1997, forthcoming).
8. John A. C. Conybeare (1987, p. 251).
9. Jacob Viner (1947, pp. 621-22).
10. William Diebold, Jr. (1952, p. 14).
11. OECD (1973, pp. 5-12). All references to the OECD Convention are taken from this document.
12. Don Cook (1989, p. 187).
13. See OECD (1970). These studies were launched at the second meeting of ministers responsible for science and technology in January 1966.
14. Raymond Aron (1974, p. 191).
15. *The East Asian Miracle* (1993).
16. For a fuller exposition of the FDI patterns, see Ostry (1997).

17. Louis Kraar, "The Overseas Chinese: Lessons from the World's Most Dynamic Capitalists," *Fortune,* October 31, 1994, p. 104.
18. Ryuji Sato, "China High-Tech Spree Pays Dividends," *The Nikkei Weekly,* November 7, 1994, p. 24.
19. For Malaysia, see *International Trade Reporter,* January 31, 1996, Washington, D.C., pp. 170-71. For Korea and Taiwan, see Richard G. Lipsey and Russell M. Wills, December 1995 (mimeo.).
20. Ernst B. Haas (1990, p. 41), cited in Mack and Ravenhill, eds., (1994, p. 9).
21. Michio Yamaoka (1996, p. 4).
22. Yamaoka (1996, p. 18).
23. Funabashi (1995, p. 79).
24. John Klassan (1996).

CHAPTER 14

EUROPEAN INTEGRATION AND APEC: THE SEARCH FOR INSTITUTIONAL BLUEPRINTS

Cédric Dupont

I. INTRODUCTION[1]

Created in 1989 by Japan and Australia as a regional discussion forum for economic growth, the Asia-Pacific Economic Cooperation (APEC) forum has gradually grown in scope to encompass more ambitious goals, in particular the objective of free and open trade and investment to be achieved no later than 2020. In addition to trade liberalization, member countries have committed themselves to several measures of trade facilitation and economic cooperation to promote growth and reduce disparities and asymmetries in the region. This expanding agenda has prompted the question of institutionalization—that is, the strength, nature, and scope of regulatory arrangements that would be both feasible and needed to implement the enlarged agenda. Institutional mechanisms that would serve as either commitment or coordination devices between member countries can take many forms, and it is still unclear which one would be best adapted to the regional agenda in the Asia-Pacific.

Whereas most analysts tend to acknowledge that there are few if any theoretical answers to this question,[2] there has been little effort to look for empirical answers. In particular, scholars have refrained from putting current challenges in the Asia-Pacific in comparative perspective with the evolution of integration in Western Europe. This chapter aims at filling this gap and makes two distinct uses of institutional build-ups that have gone hand in hand with efforts toward regional integration in Western Europe since the mid-fifties. First, it analyzes the dual experiences of the European Community (EC) and of the European Free Trade Association (EFTA) as two exemplars of different institutional mechanisms linked to different economic agendas.[3] Focusing on the first decade of existence of the two organizations—to control for path-dependent arguments—the chapter shows the successes and failures of the two exemplars. Second, the chapter explores the efforts to enhance regional economic cohesion in Western Europe in a search for lessons for coping with subregional trends inside APEC. The economic division of Western Europe between EFTA and EC has fostered a permanent concern for erasing differences, preserving mutual compatibility, and enhancing European unity— a quest for harmony in diversity. This chapter analyzes the two attempts to design a large encompassing structure that supposedly had to serve as a "nest" for subregional structures, the wide free-trade zone inside the Organization of European Economic Cooperation (OEEC) and the European Economic Area (EEA).

The first section discusses the current situation in the Asia-Pacific in terms of institutional setting and bargaining processes. It provides a benchmark for assessing the feasibility and optimality of alternative institutional paths for the future achievement of the goals of the organization. The second section examines the individual experiences of the EC and EFTA in their early years. For the sake of comparison with APEC, the discussion centers on the link between institutional procedures and measures of trade liberalization, trade facilitation and economic cooperation, with a specific focus on nonborder-related measures that are included in the Osaka Action Program adopted by APEC in December 1995. In the third section, I discuss the issue of harmony in diversity and the difficulty of creating nested institutions. I first show how APEC can be considered as a case study of institutional nesting of various subregional trading arrangements (SRTAs) into a larger regional structure. I then look at two European experiences, the OEEC wide free-trade zone story and the more recent EEA story, examining the institutional path that the various actors followed in the two experiences. I conclude with lessons that European integration processes can bring to our understanding of the institutional future of APEC.

II. APEC AND ECONOMIC INTEGRATION IN THE ASIA-PACIFIC: INSTITUTIONAL FEATURES AND PLANNED DEVELOPMENTS

APEC was created in November 1989 by Australia, Brunei, Canada, Indonesia, Japan, South Korea, Malaysia, New Zealand, Philippines, Singapore, Thailand, and the United States. It was initially not much more than a loose forum for discussion of economic cooperation in the region. Political and security issues were explicitly left aside. Members agreed on the broad objectives to sustain growth and development in the region to contribute to improving living standards and, more generally, to enhance the growth of the world economy. Since then the forum has evolved both in terms of membership and in terms of institutional structures and objectives. With respect to membership, APEC widened to China, Taiwan, and Hong Kong in 1991, to Mexico and Papua New Guinea in 1993, and to Chile in 1994. Regarding institutional scope and structures, the first significant step was made at the Bangkok Summit in September 1992. Members agreed to create a secretariat and a fund to support APEC activities. The secretariat was established in February 1993 in Singapore as a "support mechanism" for the coordination and facilitation of the organization's activities. Members also created an Eminent Persons Group (EPG), which is an advisory body charged with formulating visions for the future of APEC.

The institution went one step further during the Bogor (Indonesia) summit in November 1994. The Bogor Declaration, which concluded the meeting, set the firm objective of achieving free trade and investment in the Asia-Pacific no later than 2010 for industrialized economies and no later than 2020 for developing economies. While members set the vision in Bogor, they agreed on a more specific program one year later in Osaka. They adopted the Action Agenda that states the principles, scope, procedures, and structures of APEC. The agenda's principles pertain to how free trade should be achieved, and include comprehensiveness, WTO consistency, and nondiscrimination. With respect to the scope of activity, the focus is on the promotion of convergence and harmonization of laws and regulations affecting trade and investment flows. More specifically, members should engage in: (1) trade liberalization (gradual liberalization through "concerted unilateral actions," that is unilateral nonbinding commitments to undertake actions toward free trade and investment); (2) trade facilitation (cooperation on standards, customs procedures, competition policies, dispute mediation); and (3) economic cooperation (regional development and assistance on projects in human resources, energy, transportation, telecommunications, and the environment).

In terms of procedures, the agenda confirms the so-called principle of mutual benefit, and there is a commitment to open dialogue and consensus-building. Annual ministerial meetings shape the direction and nature of APEC activities. Decisions are then developed by senior officials' meetings supported by the secretariat and by working groups. Composed of representatives of the member economies, these working groups each pursue one aspect of the work program. Finally, with respect to external relations, participation is open to economies that have strong economic linkages in the Asia-Pacific. The agenda restates the key principle of open regionalism vis-à-vis nonmembers. As defined in the second EPG Report, this consists of the following elements: (1) commitment to further reduce trade and investment barriers toward non-APEC countries; (2) offer to extend the benefits of APEC liberalization to nonmembers on a reciprocal basis; and (3) recognition that any individual APEC member can extend its APEC liberalization toward free trade to nonmembers on a conditional basis (via free trade arrangements) or on an unconditional basis (all nonmembers in conformity with GATT rules). After this major push to the process, the results of the Manila Summit in November 1996 appear very limited but seem to reflect the concern of member countries to keep the bicycle moving. They agreed on an agreement to eliminate tariffs "substantially" by 2000 in the trade of information technology but recognized "the need for flexibility." Contrary to the previous moves toward more comprehensiveness, the recent strategy has thus been to focus on some selected products in which APEC economies have a large interest in moving fast. It is not clear, however, whether this piecemeal approach will extend to the remaining items of the agenda.

To sum up and help put the institution in the context of bargaining processes in the Asia-Pacific, APEC is currently a broad but weakly constraining regime, highly liberal based on the founding principle of open regionalism. Can it promote free trade and investment by 2020 in a context of rising interactions? The answer largely depends on whether the institution will be able to reduce the scope and strength of national controls in the region in domains such as rules of origins, intellectual property rights, and competition policy, among others. "Casual empirism" (Hufbauer and Schott 1995, p. 40) tells us that at least a modest institutionalization of APEC is necessary for addressing these controls.[4] The EPG acknowledged the idea in its first report but warned against "over-institutionalization and over-bureaucratization" in its second report. In particular, the EPG stated that "the approach followed by the European Community is one that is neither possible nor productive for the Asia-Pacific." The aim of this chapter is to go beyond such caricatures of the European Community and of European integration in general. A more careful reading of regional integration in Europe brings useful lessons for the future institutionalization of APEC. In particular, this chapter makes explicit use of the dichotomy between EC and EFTA as two different experiences toward regional integration.

III. WHICH INSTITUTIONS FOR IMPLEMENTING THE OSAKA ACTION PROGRAM? SOME LESSONS FROM THE EC AND THE EFTA IN THE 1960s

The roots of regional economic cooperation in Western Europe are both internal and external to the region. Internally, the success of European economic recovery after the end of the Second World War exacerbated the need for liberalizing trade and payments. This could only be done while preserving the security of those who would embark on extensive cooperation. Externally, the manifest emergence of the Soviet threat and its challenge to the U.S. interests around the world provided European countries with both the willingness and the financial means to build new institutional arrangements. These strong roots did not, however, prevent major conflicts among Western European countries on how to proceed to enhance growth and peace in the region. Despite their massive financial aid through the Marshall Plan and the OEEC, the United States was not able to prevent these conflicts and lacked the leverage to impose its preferences.[5] The consequence was a power game between France and the United Kingdom, and the end result was a division of Western Europe in two economic blocks—the EC and EFTA.

Whereas EFTA was originally designed as a potential bridge-builder with the EC, failure to immediately come up with concepts encompassing the two organizations de facto transformed EFTA as a true alternative to EC for addressing economic integration in Europe. For almost a decade, from 1962-1963 to the first significant EC/EFTA rapprochement in the early 1970s, the two institutions appeared as rival solutions to the economic development of Western Europe. EFTA aimed mostly at achieving free trade on industrial products and was designed as a strictly intergovernmental structure. With the objective of bringing peace and unity in Europe, the EC launched the idea of a common market with common external barriers and common policies. It gave supranational powers to institutional organs. This section analyzes how the two parallel organizations performed during their first decade of existence. In particular, it tries to assess how the different institutional set-ups accounted for the successes and failures of the two groupings.

The EFTA Experiment: How Far Can One Go with Minimal Institutions?

Following the failure of OEEC members to come up with a wide free-trade zone,[6] seven countries—Austria, Denmark, Norway, Portugal, Sweden, Switzerland, and the United Kingdom—decided to create their own free trade area and established EFTA in 1960. In doing so, the seven countries restated their interest in a wider European market, ultimately embracing all the OEEC countries, and agreed on the following objectives: (1) to promote in the area of the association and in each member state a sustained expansion of economic activity, full employment, increased productivity, and the rational use of resources, financial stability, and continuous improvement in living standards; (2) to secure that trade between member states take place in conditions of fair competition; (3) to avoid significant disparity between member states in the conditions of supply of raw materials produced within the area of the association; and 4) to contribute to the harmonious development and expansion of world trade and to the progressive removal of barriers to it.[7]

In line with these objectives, member countries agreed on a ten-year timetable to create a free trade area for industrial goods protected by complex rules of origins. They also adopted measures of trade facilitation, in particular rules of competition designed to avoid the offsetting effects of government aids, restrictive business practices, dumping, or restrictive rights of establishment. The institutional structure was kept very simple. The cornerstone was the EFTA Council, which could make binding decisions for member states and had a broad mandate regarding internal developments and external relations. Given that decision making inside the council mostly followed unanimity rule, members engaged in consensus-building through permanent consultation processes— an approach that strikingly resembles APEC's current functioning mode. To help administer the convention, the council established a secretariat and several standing committees.[8]

How did EFTA perform? On the trade liberalization side, prima facie evidence based on net trade creation and economic/political cooperation speaks in favor of great success.[9] EFTA members completed the elimination of tariffs and quotas on industrial products three years earlier than the initial projections.

The picture is different with respect to trade facilitation. EFTA did very little with respect to nonborder restrictive practices. First, on public procurement, there was no significant development until 1966, when the council modified the official interpretation of Article 14 of the Stockholm Convention, which rules out discrimination on grounds of nationality,[10] and adopted some measures that significantly improved its implementation. In particular, the council prepared guidelines for public tenders and for greater exchange of information on major national projects. These changes aimed at multilateralizing public procurement by informing the parties, and avoided harmonization of tender procedures. As a consequence, several trans-EFTA contracts on public procurement emerged in the late sixties, and they did not originate only from public entities of small countries.

There was also little progress with respect to restrictive business practices. According to the Stockholm Convention (Article 15), harmed economic actors had to lodge complaints with their respective national governments, which would then take up the matter to the EFTA council. The council would then exert pressure on the member where the practice took place. This procedure made life quite hard for plaintiffs and a natural consequence was that no complaint of any kind was notified to the council until the mid-sixties. In 1965, the members publicly admitted that the absence of any complaints could not constitute indirect proof of the absence of restrictive business practices. They agreed that an investigation could be launched on prima facie evidence without a formal complaint or a fully documented case. Governments could take up the matter bilaterally to determine the facts on the basis of a formal constraint. If bilateral measures failed, members could use the multilateral consultation and complaints procedure. But administrative measures were always given priority over legal ones. Overall performance improved after 1965, but coverage was not comprehensive. For instance, EFTA did nothing to curb exclusive dealership arrangements.

Work on the matter of technical standards began in early 1962 when a working party put up a list of administrative measures that could potentially distort trade flows. To curb the negative externalities of these measures, member states committed to a series of coordination and consultation procedures between national administrations. A bolder move took place in 1968 when the council agreed to proceed along the lines of the mutual recognition of technical tests. These agreements committed national testing stations to recognize the test reports of other members' stations that are properly permitted to perform tests in their respective countries. They opened the way toward significant progress against trade inhibiting standards. Mutual recognition did not require elaborate institutional structures but rather a high level of trust among members. The social fabric of institutionalized cooperation had boosted this trust, and reduced the need for enforcing powers at the supranational level.

The EC Way: An Overinstitutionalized Solution?

The Treaty of Rome in 1957 laid down a large agenda of trade liberalization, trade facilitation, and economic cooperation. From the ultimate perspective of preserving and strengthening peace and liberty, member countries stated their willingness to promote economic development and growth and reduce disparities between them. In line with these broad objectives, they agreed on a timetable for the implementation of a common market for industrial and agricultural products with a common external tariff and harmonization of fiscal and economic policies. This included harmonization of policies in agriculture, energy, transport, and competition as well as the development of fiscal transfers to promote regional developments.

The Treaty of Rome created an elaborate institutional structure to help achieve the broad agenda of the organization. In contrast to the intergovernmental structure of EFTA, the EC structure tilted the balance of power in favor of supranationalism. In addition to the creation of three main supranational organs, the commission, the European Court of Justice (ECJ) and the European parliament, selected majority decision making inside the Council of Ministers was supposed to boost institutional momentum and power.[11] In the early years of the community, however, unanimity decision making was the rule, in particular after the so-called Luxembourg Compromise of 1966 gave veto power to every individual member. This transformed the EC into a de facto intergovernmental body with very few supranational powers.

How did the EC perform? Starting with the abolition of border measures, most customs duties on intra-EEC trade were achieved by July 1968 as well as the implementation of the common external tariff. A favorable macroeconomic environment—characterized by rapid growth and low unemployment—helped to absorb the costs of increased trade exposure and thus facilitated consensus in the Council of Ministers.[12]

The EC was less efficient with respect to nonborder measures. At first, efforts to curb preferential treatment for national firms in government procurement remained limited.[13] The commission tried to fill the gap left open by the Treaty of Rome, but governments resisted any major implementation.[14] Insufficient supranational power blocked progress on this issue.

In contrast, there was some progress, although limited, on the issue of cartels and competition policy. Under Articles 85 and 86 of the Treaty of Rome and EC Regulation 17,[15] the commission had both investigation and sanctioning powers, whereas the court acted as an organ of control. Aggrieved actors had to notify the commission, which would then deal with the case and come up with negative clearance or with a statement of violation with fines. But most of the results fell in between these two extreme cases. Firms wanted to avoid sanctions, and they "voluntarily" modified their behavior under the guidance of the commission. In some cases, however, compliance with the pressure of the commission proved more problematic. In a famous case of exclusive dealership over the French territory given to the German electronic firm Grunding, the ECJ had to intervene in confirming the decision made by the commission.

Finally, there was little achievement on trade related transportation issues. The Treaty of Rome (Articles 75, 79, 80, and 81) called for an harmonization of costs and technical standards.[16] But these articles did not include precise rules due to strong divergence among member states on how to proceed. No specific and detailed program filled this gap until 1962-1963. The first measures were rather timid, mostly limited to the removal of special railway rates and some restrictions on the carriage of specific items. Governments disagreed on the extent of government intervention leading to high variation in licensing regulations, rules on road freight charges and technical specifications.[17] Change came in 1968-1969 with the reduction of the number of licenses for road haulage operations, the regulation of charges for haulages, and increased convergence between national taxations of fuel.

Which Bottom-Line for APEC?

The analysis of the performance of EFTA and EC as two stark institutional alternatives to regional integration helps go beyond the traditional discussion on the choice between a free trade area and customs union. It highlights the powers and limits of various institutional mechanisms for implementing various agendas. First of all, liberalization can be achieved within institutions that function on an intergovernmental mode. Both EC—forced to work in an intergovernmental mode with package deals given the individual veto power—and EFTA achieved free trade on industrial goods after less than a decade of existence. Such an achievement greatly bene-fited from good macroeconomic performance in the region much more than from a preexisting social fabric. This seems to be good news for APEC's trade liberalization agenda, but there are two important caveats. On the one hand, trade liberalization in Western Europe was of a concerted multilateral type and collectively binding, whereas APEC currently opts for a concerted unilateral approach. It is unclear whether a favorable macroeconomic context will be sufficient to promote liberalization with that kind of commitment. On the other hand, success might be harder to achieve inside APEC due to the larger number of members. Package deals and other strategies to reach consensus are more difficult to implement in a larger setting than they are in a smaller one.

The EC and EFTA experiences also show that the intergovern-mental mode of functioning is ill-adapted to an agenda of trade facilitation. In the EC, progress came only when supranational organs joined forces to attack national interests. This was the case in competition policy in which the EC Commission and the EC

Court of Justice combined to bind the actions of nation states. In contrast, EFTA members built on a high level of mutual trust to achieve some progress. In particular, they applied the principle of mutual recognition to curb trade-inhibiting effects of different technical standards. These lessons are bad news for APEC. First, there is no short-term perspective for the creation of supranational organs with enforcement power. Second, there is little likelihood that members will get such a high level of mutual trust as to commit to the principle of mutual recognition. Even if we assume they will, the use of mutual recognition would have to be closer to the one that the EC has adopted since the Cassis de Dijon ruling in 1979 than to EFTA's limited use of the principle. But then it is hard to imagine that such an extensive use of mutual recognition could take place without third-party enforcement.

IV. REGIONAL HARMONY AND SUBREGIONAL DIVERSITY: THE CHALLENGE OF INSTITUTIONAL NESTING IN COMPARATIVE PERSPECTIVE

Since the beginning of the 1990s, the Asia-Pacific region has contemplated a trend toward subregional trading arrangements (SRTAs) with the creation of regional fora in North America (NAFTA), Southeast Asia (AFTA and EAEC), as well as the emergence of special multinational economic zones. Analysts have different views on the effects of these developments for the future of the region. Some view them as the quickest way to eliminate obstacles to trade and investment and thus as the foundations for pan-regional prosperity. From this perspective, decision makers should let a hundred flowers bloom and not worry about regulating them. Other analysts are less optimistic and argue that the uncoordinated build-up of subregions will create net negative externalities. Entrenched interests may develop behind new subregional barriers and block progress at the wider regional level. At a minimum, this will create significant delays and inefficiencies on the road toward liberalization. But a bigger concern is that trade conflicts might emerge and induce larger conflicts given the fragile and noninstitutionalized security context in the region. From this perspective, there is an urgent need to find institutional means to prevent subregional diversity from eroding the potential for pan-regional harmony.

Decision makers have tended to subscribe to the second view and have put the issue of pan-regional harmony high on the agenda. Yet they have not come up with convincing solutions to the problem. Should subregional organizations such as NAFTA, AFTA, EAEC, or the Australia New Zealand Closer Economic Relations and Trade Agreement (ANZCERTA) be hierarchically encompassed inside APEC in a nested design? If so, how should one proceed? This section goes beyond abstract discussions and puts the APEC dilemma in comparative perspective with two specific episodes in European integration, the OEEC wide free-trade zone attempt and the EEA agreement between EFTA and the EC. These cases share interesting similarities with the current situation of APEC. First, the underlying objective was to promote regional harmony and keep regional diversity. Second, the institutional context consisted of different arrangements, which varied both with regards to the metaregime and the regime. Third, externalities in the initial bargaining context had an asymmetric impact on the various actors. Lastly, the favored solution to address the problem was multilateral. This section draws on these similarities and tries to derive some lessons for the future of APEC. The discussion follows the theoretical lines presented by Vinod Aggarwal in chapter 2 of this volume.[18]

APEC as an Institutional Nest for Subregional Trading Arrangements in the Asia-Pacific: Challenges and Options

Whereas trade expansion in East Asia and the Asia-Pacific up to the beginning of the nineties was virtually free of collective discriminatory trade schemes—ANZCERTA being the only major exception—there have recently been some significant new developments along these lines.

The first significant one, and according to many analysts the trigger for the whole process, was the move toward a perceived "North American Fortress." This culminated in the conclusion of the North American Free Trade Agreement in 1993. NAFTA is a comprehensive and preferential trade agreement that removes all barriers to trade (after 15 years) and discriminates against outsiders. It has a wider scope than GATT/WTO, encompassing liberalization of trade/exchange in agriculture, investment, and key services such as telecommunication, financial services, and transportation. It includes a substantial package on government procurement that covers both services and construction, and very strict rules of origins on sensitive products such as textiles, several electronic products, and automobiles.[19] The institutional structures are moderately elaborated, the center piece being the Dispute Settlement Mechanism (DSM) with special provisions regarding investment, labor, and environmental issues.

A second major development has been the emergence of the idea of an exclusively Asian economic grouping. Malaysia first proposed the formation of an East Asian Economic Group (EAEG) consisting of a preferential trade arrangement for intra-Asian trade, investment, and collaboration on economic policy.[20] Most ASEAN countries opposed this initial idea and amended the proposal to an East Asian Economic Caucus (EAEC). This is a softer version of subregional defensive behavior. It is limited to an informal consultative mechanism embracing ASEAN, China, Hong Kong, Japan, South Korea, and Taiwan.

A third expression of subregional reaction was the conclusion of an ASEAN Free Trade Area (AFTA) at the fourth ASEAN Summit in Singapore in January 1992. AFTA calls for a progressive reduction of tariffs on manufactured goods and processed agricultural products to 0 to 5 percent within 15 years beginning January 1,

1993.[21] To supervise the process, members created a ministerial-level council, the AFTA council, which receives support from the secretariat and the Senior Economic Officials' Meeting. Regarding relationships with other regional groupings, ASEAN members explicitly attach importance to cooperation and participation in APEC and the EAEG and consider the implementation of AFTA as fitting into the growth and dynamism of the region. Given that some rules of origin require a 40 percent content from member states, the real effects on trade and investment patterns in the Asia-Pacific are still unknown.

Fourth, there has been a growing interest in the formation of subregional special economic zones. Generally speaking, these zones aim at promoting exports, attracting foreign investment, developing natural and human resources, and infrastructure, and they consist of loose intergovernmental structures with a prominent role left to the private sector. The most active one is the Singapore-Riau-Johor Growth Triangle, and other examples include the Great Mekong Zone (Cambodia, Laos, Myanmar, Thailand, Vietnam, and the Yunan Province in China), the South China Growth Triangle (South China, Hong Kong, and Taiwan), the Northern Growth Triangle (southern Thailand, northwestern Malaysia, and western Sumatra), and the Tumen River Delta Area (eastern Russia, China, Mongolia, and South and North Korea).[22] In terms of externalities to the larger region, it is unclear what the effects of these developments could be. One view is to consider them as positive for the promotion of economic interdependence in the region. From this perspective, APEC members should increasingly engage in such efforts. A different view emphasizes the possibility of a race to the bottom between the different zones, each trying to attract investment and production facilities. Such a prospect is enhanced by the fact that there is very little overlapping in terms of national membership between the existing or projected zones.

In addition to these new developments, ANZCERTA—often simply called CER (Closer Economic Relations)—has proven to be a successful and far-reaching free trade area that may be heading toward a single market.[23] There is now complete free trade in all goods and most services, and free movement of residents. Restrictions remain on capital flows.

In terms of Aggarwal's framework, the recent subregional developments within the Asia-Pacific region constitute a shock that creates negative externalities, in particular trade deflection through the imposition of complex rules of origins. Trade distortions are currently difficult to assess but the mere potential for their emergence already constitutes a stimulus for institutional change. Figure 14.1 depicts the initial bargaining game in the wake of the new challenges. The fear of political and economic fragmentation coming from managed trade negatively affects all actors, but it does so in an asymmetric manner. The small and export-oriented ASEAN countries and the geographically isolated Australia and New Zealand are much more sensitive to the new challenges than are Japan, China, and the United States. No wonder there is no consensus among members on how to address the problem but rather a continuation of the developments at the subregional level.

How to Cope with the Problem?

Asia-Pacific countries have considered several options toward regional harmony. In particular, they have engaged in bargaining at both the bilateral and multilateral levels, and also pursued unilateral courses of action (see Figure 14.2). At a bilateral level, between two SRTAs, there has been some discussion of a possible direct link between AFTA and NAFTA since the formation of the two arrangements. Most recently, United States Trade Representative Mickey Kantor mentioned such a possibility at the Osaka Summit in November 1995. Still at the bilateral level but between a country and one SRTA, Singapore expressed an interest in joining NAFTA. Bargaining has also taken place directly between countries. Besides the U.S. strategy toward Japan and China, Japan recently courted

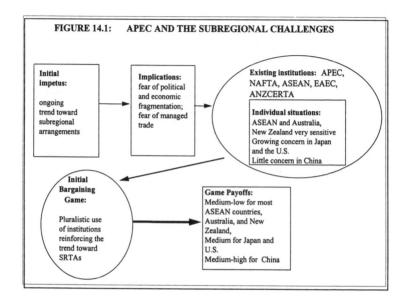

FIGURE 14.1: APEC AND THE SUBREGIONAL CHALLENGES

economic ties with Mexico and Chile.[24] Finally, the unilateral option to liberalize unconditionally has been popular in some Asian countries.

But the stronger calls have been for a multilateral approach within APEC and the use of a nested linkage. In Seoul in November 1991, members stated that "APEC should play a central role in promoting harmonious and balanced development of the trans-Pacific relations by embracing subregional economic groups within the Asia-Pacific region."[25] At the Bangkok meeting one year later, the joint statement mentioned that "APEC's prospects as a possible bridge between the major subregional free trade areas in the Asia-Pacific region should be carefully explored."[26] The first report of the EPG pursued the idea and mentioned the possibility of the SRTAs being "harmonized within the arrangements of APEC itself."[27] It called for an annual review of the progress of each of the subregional arrangements within APEC. The EPG again raised the issue of compatibility between SRTAs in its second report. To

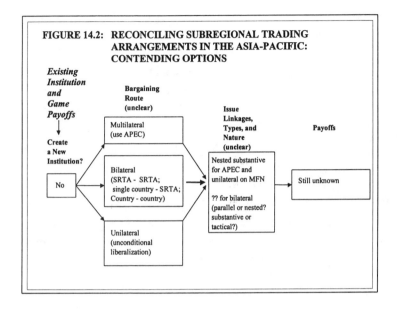

FIGURE 14.2: RECONCILING SUBREGIONAL TRADING ARRANGEMENTS IN THE ASIA-PACIFIC: CONTENDING OPTIONS

accommodate the SRTAs into the broader APEC arrangement, the Report recommended that the members equalize their margin of preferences, and adopt simple, transparent and across-the-board applicable rules of origins.[28]

In addition to linkages between SRTAs and APEC, linkages between SRTAs were a key concern in the third report of the EPG. The reason was that these linkages could either facilitate the achievement of the long term goal of free trade and investment in the region by 2010 and 2020 or hinder it by creating "new entrenched interests." In terms of proposals, however, the EPG remained vague and simply expanded on the basic APEC principles of "open subregionalism" and "WTO-consistency." Regarding the latter, the report proposed that "any new initiatives within APEC be promptly submitted to the WTO for confirmation that they meet these tests and for surveillance of their performance in practice."[29] Strict consistency with the WTO is believed to ensure "automatically" harmonious relationships between SRTAs. But the problem with this view is that most existing SRTAs are already GATT/WTO consistent, and therefore hardly any change could come from this approach. The EPG's vision of open subregionalism is to promote an extended use of unilateral linkages based on the Most Favored Nation (MFN) rule. There is little reason to expect this policy recommendation to solve the potential conflicts between the SRTAs, mostly because there are no enforcement mechanisms that could compel the countries to stick to the principle of open regionalism.[30]

In addition to the reluctance of ASEAN countries to agree on any proposal that would grant APEC stronger prerogatives, the EPG stumbled on the lack of any blueprint and could not go beyond vague policy recommendations on how to reach regional harmony through institutional means. I now discuss how European integration can provide some useful lessons.

Nesting in European Integration: The Failed Search for Harmony and Diversity

The idea of reconciling different SRTAs with a common regional envelope has been a major concern in the history of European economic integration. It began in the late fifties with the attempt to reconcile the creation of the European communities with the wider OEEC. Failure to come up with a solution led to the demise of the regional envelope and the parallel development of two SRTAs, the EC and the EFTA. Whereas the two organizations maintained ties, mostly through a transfer of members, and through the building of a complex web of bilateral agreements, no new attempt to come up with a common regional envelope was tried until the late 1980s EEA-process. The basic idea behind this effort was to reduce the externalities related to the dual structure of trade arrangements in Western Europe.

The OEEC and the Wide Free-Trade Zone

Created in April 1948 to administer the Marshall Plan, the OEEC aimed at fostering trade liberalization and promoting economic cooperation. Notably, it pushed through the adoption of the Liberalization Code for the elimination of quantitative restriction to trade and for the restoration of multilateral payments among its members with the creation of the European Payments Union (EPU).[31] As a consequence, in the mid-1950s, trade had doubled in volume and only 10 percent of the 1948 volume of imports still encountered quantitative restrictions.[32] However, some members still found this progress too slow. Dissatisfaction stemmed from two main weaknesses. First, the organization was too weak to compel states that were falling short of their commitments. Second, the removal of quantitative restrictions led to sharp asymmetry regarding protection levels based on existing tariffs. The so-called low-tariff club including the Benelux and Scandinavian countries, Switzerland, and Austria felt particularly aggrieved by the situation and pushed for progress on tariff reduction. But action at the OEEC level stumbled on a basic divergence on how to address the issue of tariffs with third countries. The Six of the European Coal and Steel Community (ECSC) argued in favor of exploiting Article 24 of the GATT to build a European market on the basis of regional discrimination. The others generally preferred to stick to nondiscrimination vis-à-vis external actors, although there was the possibility for selected exceptions to the principle. As a consequence, the Six of the ECSC took the lead and decided in Messina in June 1955 to build a common market free of any restrictions to trade.

This was the starting point of the nesting episode inside the OEEC. The Outer Six perceived the project of the Six as potentially discriminatory and thus a danger to the OEEC's objective to build peace and unity in Europe. The concern became significant with the conclusion of the Treaty of Rome in March 1957. Outer Six members wanted to avoid what they perceived to be the clearest indication of future trade discrimination. Countries such as Switzerland, Sweden, and Austria were particularly sensitive to possible trade distortions stemming from the imposition of a common external tariff. The United Kingdom was more concerned with the political aspects of the division of Europe and of the formation of a core block of countries around France. This would leave the British out of the highest European economic dynamics and would precipitate their economic and political decline. Although less concerned by the de facto division of Europe, the Six wanted to preserve cooperation with the other OEEC members and agreed on the necessity of finding a new way to institutionalize it.

If all the OEEC members agreed on the search for a new solution, they had different institutional conceptions. Two broad alternatives were on the agenda. Both were multilateral solutions, but one favored a hard core with a softer belt, whereas the second opposed the idea of a two-tiered solution. Differences between the two alternatives largely went beyond the technical debate of free trade vs. customs union. They touched upon different economic and political conceptions of European integration and resulted in a power game between the United Kingdom and France. Each considered the other's nesting solution as a tactical means of weakening the position of the other one. The prize of the battle was the EC itself. The United Kingdom consistently pushed for solutions that would dilute the newly created organization, whereas France fiercely resisted any movement down this road. The British argued that a free-trade area with rules of origins would work with minimal trade deflection. The Six followed the positions of France and Italy and opposed the idea. A free-trade formula would endanger the objectives of the community, especially because rules of origin would not prevent trade diversion through some of the low-tariff Outer Six. To address this externality, the Six first came up with a de facto common external tariff through the harmonization of tariffs across all OEEC members. A better solution appeared in March 1958 with the so-called Carli Plan after the name of the Italian minister of trade. The idea was to establish margins of tolerance for differences in tariffs vis-à-vis third countries backed by compensatory taxes each time the difference falls outside the margin of tolerance.[33] But the idea lost momentum when France came up with a different proposal in favor of a "European Economic Association" giving priority to the development of the hard core. According to this proposal, progress toward a wide common market would proceed on a sector basis, be conditional on prior harmonization of competition policies, and would follow the integration of the EC (with a time lag). There was little ground left for a common agreement, and the ultimate sign of failure came in November 1958 when France used its individual veto power to push the EC out of the negotiation process.

The failure of the wide free-trade zone was the starting point of the economic division of Western Europe, leading to the creation of EFTA in January 1960 and the demise of the wider envelope, the OEEC, in December 1990. Delouvrier, then Finance Director of the ECSC, was right when he warned in the wake of the creation of the EC, that the OEEC could persist only through major institutional reforms and a modified agenda. But he was wrong in considering that the test case would be the arrival of an economic depression.[34] The challenge of nesting was the fatal shock.

The EEA Experience

Thirty years after the failure of the wide free-trade zone, Western Europe was still characterized by a clear separation between EC and EFTA, although the two had developed ties between them.[35] This enduring separation in two regulatory environments generated transaction costs and lessened the economic potential of regional trade, despite growing interpenetration between societies. In the second half of the eighties, two shocks aggravated these externalities (see Figure 14.3). The first one was the adoption of the Single European Act by the EC in December 1985. It primarily affected EFTA countries, which feared being left out of economic integration in Western Europe. The second shock, the end of the Cold War and the new situation in Central and Eastern Europe, was of greater concern to the EC. For political reasons, the

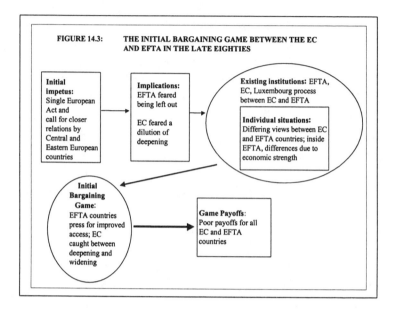

FIGURE 14.3: **THE INITIAL BARGAINING GAME BETWEEN THE EC AND EFTA IN THE LATE EIGHTIES**

community could not turn down emerging demands for new trade arrangements from newly democratic governments.[36] These agreements themselves did not endanger the pace of the community's deepening process, but there was clearly a fear that new demands would come from other countries and more worryingly that more far-reaching demands would emerge.

To address these new challenges, EC and EFTA countries decided to engage in institution-building, and they considered a nested design. In a path-breaking speech on January 17, 1989, the president of the EC Commission, Jacques Delors, envisioned EFTA as members of a second circle, a village called EEA, that would be more flexible and less demanding than the EC. EFTA countries responded positively, and exploratory talks began in Spring 1989.

Institutional choices and linkages were key considerations and a bone of contention in the exploratory phases. Figure 14.4 identifies the alternative choices that were evaluated and the path

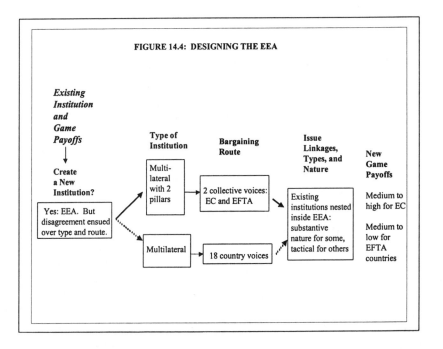

FIGURE 14.4: DESIGNING THE EEA

actually favored by the parties (in plain arrows in Figure 14.4). Both parties decided to engage in the creation of a *new institution* rather than simply using existing arrangements. Systemic imperatives and domestic considerations in EFTA countries ruled out an extended use of the community to address the externalities. Neutrality was still seen as the main obstacle for Switzerland, Sweden, and Finland. The same applied to Austria, despite the latter's official request for membership in July 1989. Domestic constituencies still valued this foreign policy stance. But adhesion was also economically suboptimal, despite the mounting pressure of increasing flows of foreign direct investments by both multinational and smaller firms in countries like Sweden and Switzerland. For these countries, rushing to the EC was not the "first best" option, because preserving the competitiveness of EFTA economies would require compatibility between European integration and world competitiveness. On the EC side, priority had clearly been given to the completion of the internal market before any widening to new members.

Turning to the more intriguing aspect of *institutional type,* the EC had given top priority to deepening, and any new development with EFTA had to respect this commitment. Whereas a truly multilateral framework would fall out of bounds, a two-pillar (EC and EFTA) structure with some common decision shaping offered a credible and feasible option. This implied a strengthening of EFTA as a collective organization. The EC considered that such a development would provide a more efficient bargaining platform than a truly multilateral system with 18 voices. The dominant view inside EFTA was against the two-pillar structure, but power asymmetries enabled the EC to successfully push this mixed institutional form onto the agenda.

A direct consequence of the two-pillar structure was the choice of a bilateral *bargaining route.* From the EC's perspective, negotiations were to serve as a test case for a strengthened EFTA. The EC was particularly keen to have the EFTA countries speak with one voice, both for efficiency concerns and to help overcome the resistance of laggard countries. Indeed, the commission wanted to avoid having to consider individual demands from each EFTA country based on domestic specificities and constraints. Forcing them to speak together shifted the onus of reconciling divergent domestic demands to EFTA, where opposition from individual countries could be overcome.

In terms of *linkages,* there were both substantive and tactical reasons to proceed with a nested design. Substantively, nesting was believed to be the only feasible route to cope with both deepening and widening issues in European integration. It allowed for a variable geometric approach that would be compatible with the different economic and political conditions of Western European states. From an economic point of view, there was a clear interest in coming up with concentric circles. Enhanced performance required a careful hierarchical ordering with different integration speeds embedded in a common framework.[37] Politically, the strengthening of EC-EFTA cooperation could also be the basis for discussions with the countries of Eastern Europe.

But these sound motivations could not hide more tactical purposes. From the EC's perspective, the EEA offered a tactical response to systemic developments in Europe and at a global level. Additionally, the new relationship with the EFTA combined the wish to open the internal market gradually to outsiders—under the pressure of trade liberalization at the global level—and the desire to prevent a disorganized flow of new applications for EC membership. The new structure could be used to welcome Eastern and Central European countries through association treaties.[38] In addition, at the global level, the EC could use the EEA to increase its influence in international regimes and world commercial negotiations. Tactical reasons also guided the behavior of several EFTA countries, especially Norway, Sweden, and Austria. The EEA was the best way to please both those domestic constituents concerned with economic necessity and those concerned with political security. These countries used substantive reasons to cover up long term goals, initially seeing only the tactical dimension of the new structure.

Formal negotiations on the creation of an EEA began in June 1990 and were officially concluded in February 1992.[39] The agreement was a significant economic achievement. It created a kind of single market in which goods, capital, services and persons were to move almost freely.[40] It also provided member countries with a set of facilitating measures and economic cooperation in domains such as research and development, education, consumer policy, social policy, and the environment. The agreement, however, fell short of EC membership in several areas. It did not create a customs union but established a free trade area. Thus it did not include a common external tariff and did not require the removal of border controls or the harmonization of indirect taxes. Moreover, it did not include participation in the EC common policies (agriculture, fisheries, transport, trade) or in the European

Monetary System. As a consequence, it was not perceived as a sufficiently strong signal to EFTA distressed markets.

Moreover, the agreement was politically asymmetric. Since, the EC had the key decision-making role, EFTA countries were left with few prerogatives. They may be informally consulted in the legislative preparation phase and later have an individual right to raise any matter of concern (*droit d'évocation*) and may collectively ask for the suspension of new rules (collective opting-out). They do not have any right of co-decision, although they might unilaterally call for a general safeguard clause for some areas of vital interest. This made it hard to sell to domestic constituents in EFTA countries, and of little interest for the concerns of Central and Eastern European countries.

The lack of psychological appeal of the economic dimension of the treaty and the asymmetry of the political dimension left most parties unsatisfied with the new institutional setting. These failed expectations cleared the way toward EU adhesion for the EFTA countries that had officially applied for it—Austria in July 1989 (prior to the conclusion of the EEA), Sweden in July 1991 (during the negotiation process), Finland in March 1992, Switzerland in May 1992, and Norway in November 1992. Enlargement negotiations with these countries, minus Switzerland, started in February 1993 (April for Norway) and were successfully concluded in March 1994.[41] Failure to ratify the EEA forced the Swiss government to freeze its application. Domestic opposition also affected Norway in November 1994 when the "no" vote won the referendum on EC adhesion. As for the other applicants, voters agreed to get into the EC nest, leaving only four birdies in the EFTA nest.

V. LESSONS FROM NESTING IN WESTERN EUROPE: PROSPECTS FOR THE ASIA-PACIFIC

The two attempts to nest Western European subregional economic institutions into a larger regional structure brings us three main lessons. The first is one of overall danger for existing institutions. The attempt to come up with a wide free-trade zone led to the demise of the OEEC, the organization that was supposed to act as the common envelope. The creation of the EEA precipitated the quasi-destruction of EFTA, one of the two inner organizations. Nesting was finally resolved in Europe through a bilateral way of individual countries gradually rearranging around a core.

Second, the scope and depth of the common institutional envelope is the thorny issue. Opting for a minimal common denominator (the OEEC way) lessens the worthiness of a common denominator at the regional level, especially when there are global institutions that are of similar scope and depth. Choosing a strong envelope (the EEA way) tends to give priority to one model and thus forces some reshuffling among the inner organizations, which either kills the diversity or creates destabilizing tensions. The choice depends primarily upon the stage of development and the relative strength and stability of inner organizations. Nesting in the OEEC failed because the EC feared having its characteristics diluted; on the other hand, nesting in the EEA failed because the EC believed it could fully impose its characteristics and way of life.

Finally, nesting significantly depends on the cognitive underpinnings of existing institutions. European problems stem from the stark dichotomy between two visions of regional integration. One has far-reaching economic and political goals and relies on strong institutions. The other one has pragmatic, purely economic goals without political implications. This dichotomy has precluded stable nesting of existing institutions inside a pan-regional framework.

What can we extrapolate from the European cases for the future of APEC? Regarding the first two general lessons—danger for existing institutions and scope and depth of the common envelope—they help highlight the stakes of the current discussion on APEC and WTO. If APEC becomes a WTO front-runner, i.e., if the common envelope is relatively strong (with large scope and elements of deep integration), it is hard to see how AFTA will not be threatened. As one observer puts it, "ASEAN would find it uncomfortable if the APEC outfit is not loose enough."[42] If APEC simply remains a kind of WTO outpost in Asia and the Pacific, there is little reason to care for the regional institution once the global agenda gets going. It would soon prove to be ill-adapted for lobbying purposes. More generally, integration in the Asia-Pacific might well follow a kind of hub-and-spoke pattern, ultimately leading to some type of merging into one or two powerful groups. But this institutional reshuffling seems to be out of the question for the moment; it would prove too costly at home for most governments. The EEA case should, however, warn us that this does not allow for safe bets on institutional evolution in the regional integration processes.

Turning to the cognitive underpinnings, it has been argued often that there are two approaches to economic integration inside APEC—a North American institutional approach based on conditional reciprocity and clear endorsement of free trade, and an Asian evolutionary view driven by consensus and cautionary liberalizing steps. This division is not a very encouraging sign. But some authors have argued that there has recently been convergence between the two positions, which stems from the fact that both views focus on economic integration without a willingness to develop political integration. From this perspective, the cognitive gap is smaller than it was in Western Europe despite much lower "social capital."

VI. CONCLUSION

Which institutional path should APEC follow if it wants to implement the Osaka Action Program? Lessons from regional integration in Western Europe from the mid-fifties to the mid-nineties do not offer easy recipes, but they warn against false hope and preconceived ideas. First, the ambitious agenda of trade liberalization, trade facilitation, and economic cooperation cannot be implemented simply by concerted unilateral actions and open regionalism. Whereas the individual experiences of EFTA and EC in the sixties leave alive the likelihood to achieve trade liberalization within strict intergovernmental bodies, they clearly rule out major achievement on trade facilitation and economic cooperation measures within such institutional structures. From this perspective, the story of the EC in the sixties is not one of administrative inefficiency—a kind of overbureaucratization—but rather one of deep intergovernmental differences and national pressures against the integration momentum. Stronger institutionalization is also needed for keeping the compatibility between various subregional trading arrangements.

Second, the chapter highlights that the dual search for regional harmony and subregional diversity is for the time being an illusion in the Asia-Pacific. The lowest level of institutionalization at the regional level that could preserve harmony seems to be a kind of "WTO plus" arrangement. Below this level, the episode of the OEEC-wide free trade area shows that there is little role left for the regional institutional envelope. The problem for APEC is that anything at or above this threshold would endanger subregional diversity. In particular, the ASEAN Free Trade Area would need to undergo a kind of upgrading to be able to fit inside a "WTO plus" arrangement. As shown by the EFTA experience during the EEA process, strengthening an inner organization while building the envelope may lead to failure on both accounts and to even less optimal situations.

What then is left for the members of APEC? The safest, most feasible road seems to try to gain time and carefully select some "easy" items on the broad Osaka action agenda. Trade liberalization of products that can benefit the largest number of countries at a minimal cost appears feasible without further institutionalization. By the time the process gets going, the feasibility of stronger institutions might increase, thus preserving the chances of implementing the full agenda. APEC currently appears to be proceeding down this road. Members recently agreed on selected liberalization on products in information technology, and this agreement was then broadened through the WTO. This type of issue focus, rather than organizational focus, is a more promising path. The price of this choice is that there will not be much control over subregional developments, leaving open the possibility of both institutional decay and rising conflicts. But if member states succeed in building momentum toward liberalization, harmony in diversity might well become more than an illusion.

NOTES

1. Earlier versions were presented at a workshop on "APEC and Regime Creation" at the APEC Study Center, University of Washington, Seattle, August 13-15, 1996; at the APSA meetings in San Francisco, August 29-September 1, 1996; and at the International Relations Theory Colloquium at the University of California at Berkeley. I am grateful to the East-West Center and the Center for Global Partnership for financial assistance. I am particularly indebted to Vinod Aggarwal for extensive comments on earlier versions. I would also like to thank Joe Grieco, Andrew Moravcik, Charles Morrison, Sylvia Ostry, Eoghan Peavoy, Mike Plummer, and Ole Waever.

2. Existing hypotheses on the design of international institutions are either too general or lack empirical evidence. Inductively derived propositions suffer from small-N problems, whereas deductive attempts generally lack substantive content or remain too vague in their prescriptions. For inductively derived hypotheses, see Kahler (1995). For research avenues in the formal analysis of institutions, see Calvert (1995). For trade liberalization and institutional forms, see Yarbrough and Yarbrough (1992).

3. For the sake of convenience, I use the European Community as a generic title for the integration process from the Treaty of Rome to the current situation.

4. The historical case that comes closest to an institution-free integration process is the period from 1880 to 1914. In the words of John Maynard Keynes, this was "an extraordinary episode in the economic progress of man" (Keynes 1920, p. 10). There was a high mobility of goods, persons and capital among a core group of countries. This happened without the presence of formal institutions. On the trade side, countries used the bilateral most-favored-nation clause to exchange concessions on tariffs. On the monetary side, currency convertibility through the gold standard helped secure trust and stability. The gold standard was the cement of a functionally

self-organized system, a cement that qualifies as a regime or as an institution in the sense of North's (1990) "rules of the game." But as Gallarotti (1995) points out, the key to the success of this largely diffuse institutional setting was a deep cognitive consensus on economic liberalism that pervaded in the core countries—the United States, Great Britain, France, and Germany. There was no need for commitment at the international level given the harmony of domestic economic policies. This is clearly different from the current situation inside APEC. In depth discussion of the lessons from the pre–World War I period is beyond the scope of this paper (see Dupont and Hefeker 1997).

5. For a detailed discussion of this view, see Milward (1984).

6. See the next section for a detailed account of this episode.

7. Article 2 of the EFTA Convention.

8. For details, see, for instance, EFTA (1980).

9. For evidence along these lines, see Fukuda (1970, p. 46).

10. Article 14 of the Stockholm Convention rules out discrimination on grounds of nationality "in so far that it frustrates the benefits expected." In 1966, the council agreed that public undertakings should "give equivalent treatment" to domestic goods and goods of EFTA origin. On public procurement inside EFTA during the sixties, see Liesner (1969) and Curzon (1974).

11. The commission is the watchdog of the implementation of community law and policies. It is mandated to develop new initiatives in the areas of the treaty. The council was and still is, albeit in a less significant manner, the main legislative body of the EEC. It meets in different composition according to the issue considered but always represents the different national interests. According to the Treaty of Rome, decision making follows either qualified majority voting or unanimity.

12. For data on macroeconomic performances, see Tsoukalis (1993).

13. See Liesner (1969).

14. Treaty of Rome did not address the problem of government procurement explicitly. Article 7 rules out discrimination on the basis of nationality.

15. See Young and Metcalfe (1995), Swann (1969), and Hallstein (1970).

16. See Lee (1995).

17. See Hallstein (1970).

18. Aggarwal (1998a). For more details, see Aggarwal (1998b).

19. In these products, domestic value added requirements go as high as 62.5 percent.

20. For more on the EAEG, see, for instance, Yan, Heng, and Low (1992).

21. In September 1994, AFTA members shortened the implementation period to 10 years, and included unprocessed agricultural goods. AFTA was established on the exception given to developing countries to enter into preferential trading arrangements.

22. Others are on the drawing board, such as the Yellow Sea Economic Zone (Japan, South Korea, northern China), and the Japan Sea Economic Zone

(Japan, eastern Russia, northeastern China, and South and North Korea). For more details on these zones, see Tang (1995, pp. 224-30) and Yue and Lee (1994).

23. Lloyd (1994) makes the argument that the CER is a project parallel to the Single European Act that might well lead the Australia and New Zealand toward a single market.

24. Cameron, chapter 11 in this volume.

25. Joint Statement, Asia-Pacific Economic Cooperation Ministerial Meeting Seoul, November 12-14, 1991.

26. APEC Ministerial Meeting, Bangkok, September 10-11, 1992, Joint Statement.

27. APEC (1993, p. 32).

28. APEC (1994, p. 48).

29. APEC (1995, p. 34).

30. This argument is made by Cameron, chapter 11 in this volume.

31. The liberalization code established a multilateral system of barriers reduction. Each OEEC member committed to a 50 percent reduction of restrictions on imports from all other members without specific reciprocity. The percentage was gradually increased to 90 percent in the mid-fifties (Snoy et d'Oppuers 1959, pp. 575-76). See also Heilperin (1957) and Kitzinger (1960).

32. According to one source, trade increased by 97 percent between 1949 and 1955 (Snoy et d'Oppuers 1959, p. 579).

33. See Hurni (1987, p. 29).

34. Delouvrier (1957, p. 120).

35. In particular, the transfer of United Kingdom and Denmark from EFTA to EC in the early 1970s facilitated the conclusion of bilateral free trade agreements between each EFTA member and the EC.

36. In November 1988, Hungary was the first member of the Council of Mutual Economic Assistance (CMEA) to get such an agreement. It included a schedule for the abolition of specific quantitative restrictions on Hungarian exports to the EC. Czechoslovakia signed a less wide-ranging agreement on industrial goods in March 1989. In September 1989, Poland signed an agreement similar to the Hungarian one. See Nicolaïdis (1993) for more details on these accords.

37. See Baldwin (1994) for an economic argument about concentric circles.

38. See the interview of Horst Krenzler, EC chief negotiator, in *EFTA-Bulletin*, April 1990, p. 20.

39. For a detailed account of the negotiations, see Dupont (1994, chapter 5).

40. See Dupont (1998) for a summary of the agreement. For the full text of the agreement, see *Official Journal of the European Communities*, L1, 1994.

41. On enlargement negotiations, see, for instance, Granell (1995) and Dupont (1998).

42. Ariff (1994, p. 172).

CHAPTER 15

THE FUTURE OF APEC

Vinod K. Aggarwal and Charles E. Morrison

I. INTRODUCTION

Regionalism has become a prominent feature of international relations in the second half of the twentieth century, but it is one whose significance for the international order is not yet fully understood. This volume has examined one crucial area of the world, the Asia-Pacific, where a distinctive but late form of regionalism is developing in the shape of the Asia-Pacific Economic Cooperation (APEC) forum. Evolving in an environment of rapid economic growth, growing interdependence, possible underlying political-military tension, and very limited historical experience with institutionalization, APEC seeks to establish free trade and investment and economic cooperation through a new mechanism of "open regionalism" based on concerted but voluntary actions. How successfully will this organization evolve? What impact will it have on the relations among states and firms in its region? How will APEC regionalism influence and be influenced by globalism and by subregional arrangements? Will APEC and its form of open regionalism be influential in the establishment of international values, norms, or rules at either the global or regional level?

Based on the theoretical framework developed by Vinod Aggarwal in chapter 2, the papers in this volume examine a number of distinctive aspects of APEC's development. The objective of this approach has been to clarify the causal factors and empirical developments relevant to APEC's institutional trajectory. The task of this chapter is to review the findings of this volume and to present some likely scenarios for APEC's evolution. In doing so, our discussion is structured around the five parts of the book: Section II begins by providing a summary of the theoretical structure, followed by Section III, which identifies the key economic trends that we have seen in the Asia-Pacific. Sections IV and V discuss national policies toward APEC and the reconciliation of APEC with both broader and narrower arrangements respectively. In conclusion, Section VI speculates on the future of APEC in light of other institutional exemplars.

II. THE THEORETICAL FRAMEWORK SUMMARIZED

Existing approaches to examining the development of international institutions have contributed much to our understanding of institutional change. Each of the three main schools—neorealist institutionalism, neoliberal institutionalism, and the cognitive approach—provide us with a different analytical lens to examine institutional changes. While the neorealist institutional approach emphasizes the role of power and control, the neoliberal institutionalist school focuses on transaction costs and the importance of existing institutions in constraining and motivating the development of new institutions. Finally, the cognitive approach emphasizes the role of scientific consensus and interaction of "epistemic communities" with interest groups in affecting the course of institutional development. But as suggested in chapter 2, the leading contenders miss capturing important aspects of the phenomenon of institutional evolution. In particular, standard analytic approaches cannot single-handedly explain how actors develop new institutions and reconcile them with old ones or adequately help us to understand the problem of institutional modification.

To better understand APEC's development and likely future, chapter 2 provided a comprehensive framework to capture the institutional bargaining process. Specifically, the chapter identified two distinct phases in the institutional bargaining process—an initial bargaining game and a game change phase. In brief, it was suggested that actors respond to an initial impetus, conditioned by the "goods" involved in the resulting negotiations, the actors' individual situations, and the institutional context. In turn, the payoffs of this bargaining game provide a stimulus to the institutional game change phase (see Figure 2.2 and Figure 2.4 in chapter 2).

Faced with favorable or unfavorable payoffs, actors may promote changes in the game. Of the three strategies available—the direct manipulation of goods, changing individual situations, or institutional innovation—this book has concentrated on the latter. As depicted in Figure 2.4 in chapter 2, if actors choose to go down the institutional change road, they must agree on the type of institution (multilateral or bilateral) and pursue either a multilateral, bilateral, or unilateral bargaining path. During the bargaining process, actors can engage in linkage bargaining. In so doing, they can use either (1) nested or parallel linkages; or (2) substantive or tactical connections among issues or institutions. This effort may lead to a new game structure with a different set of payoffs for actors.

To better understand the dynamics of this process, chapter 2 presented a number of hypotheses about the stages of institutional bargaining. In particular, our objective has been to understand two key choices: the decision to create APEC and reconcile it with the GATT and WTO; and the process by which greater institutionalization of APEC might take place. The sets of hypotheses focused on several questions relevant to APEC's development and future. These include: (1) how to handle possible free-riders, both inside an institution and outside it, given the porous nature of open regionalism; (2) the benefits of using existing institutions vs. creating new ones; (3) the decision to focus on multilateral versus bilateral institutions and unilateral, bilateral, or multilateral bargaining strategies in institutional creation; and (4) linkages among issues and institutions, both with respect to tactical and substantive connections and in terms of parallel or substantive ties.

III. ECONOMIC TRENDS AND IMPLICATIONS

The Asia-Pacific's increasing economic interdependence has coincided with rapid domestic economic growth. As recounted by Paolo Guerrieri in chapter 3, corporate activity in the region has driven economic integration. From 1980 to the mid-1990s, the level of trade among the APEC economies increased from 57 to almost 75 percent. According to Shujiro Urata, there has been a similar increase in intra-APEC flows of direct foreign investment (DFI), rising from 41 percent of the future members' outflow in 1980 to 51 percent in 1992. The DFI inflow to developing Asian APEC members rose remarkably, with China becoming a major destination of foreign investment despite relatively low rates of return. Although the growth of trade and investment has been associated with the strong growth performance of the region, it has also generated political tensions. In terms of the theoretical framework, economic interactions have been the driving force in international institutional developments, whereas international governance mechanisms have been relatively insignificant.

There is no reason to believe that the forces of East Asian economic integration have been played out. The rapid growth of the developing East Asian economies means that even if there is no special regional trade or investment bias, intraregional trade and investment will continue to grow. This, over time, is eroding East Asia's dependence on the North American market. But the United States remains the single most important export market for many

East Asian countries and is also very significant as a source of technology and capital. This partly accounts for the cognitive consensus in much of Asia for the need to preserve strong connections to the United States and resistance to exclusive East Asian economic groupings. North America's dependence on East Asia is gradually rising, the region absorbing about 30 percent of U.S. exports in 1994 compared with 24 percent in 1980.

Economic interdependence creates many winners from trade and investment flows on both sides of the Pacific. In China, for example, the demonstrable benefits of openness have made the policies of openness irreversible, although, as Zhang Yunling argues, the Chinese believe they need time to tackle the remaining sectors (especially state industries) and develop adjustment strategies to deal with globalization. Similarly, the United States seems unlikely to significantly increase protectionism. In the case of its bilateral trade with China, American calculations are that the ratio of exports to imports is more than 3 to 1 in China's favor. Although import-substituting groups have been abetted by a powerful U.S. human rights lobby, diplomatic and export interests have repeatedly defeated efforts to withdraw Most-Favored-Nation (MFN) treatment. Admittedly, the withdrawal of MFN is a very drastic and therefore a politically unattractive form of protectionism. More palatable for American administrations is continued pressure "to open markets." Indeed, so long as there are large U.S. deficits in the region, the U.S. government will be under constant pressure to improve export performance by "leveling the playing field."

Thus trade and investment trends suggest both continued integration and continued imbalances. These forces have pushed the region's governments toward negotiations and efforts to build regimes to reduce transaction costs and to attempt to manage their relationships with their counterparts to cope with conflicts that might otherwise threaten their economic and political relationships as a whole. In the context of the vast and heterogeneous Pacific Basin, major differences in actors' individual situations, created by quite different national regimes, business, and cultural practices, potentially can accentuate tensions. East Asia's rise to importance in the global economy is outpacing institutional convergence, so that international businessmen are frequently faced with national regimes (or their absence), social values, or traditions that seem unfair to them. The APEC forum is thus one effort to deal with distinctive Asia-Pacific problems rather than relying solely on the WTO.

Intellectual property provides a good example of potential tensions. As Asian societies grew richer, American companies became less tolerant of intellectual property piracy. As Sumner La Croix describes, since the existing international intellectual property regime was weak, especially as applied in Asia, the United States resorted to bilateral pressures backed up by threats of retaliation. This has resulted in severe disputes, especially with Thailand and China. These disputes reflected differing economic interests, differing views about the property rights for intellectual activities, an Asian reluctance to yield to coercive diplomacy, and weak capabilities or will for enforcement in many Asian countries even where legal regimes existed. Yet each crisis was resolved just as it reached a crescendo, partly due to accommodations by Asian countries as well as recognition by the U.S. government and/or the industries in question that they had pushed as far as they could for the moment.

This is a gradual and often conflict-ridden process of regime-building. In the case of intellectual property regimes, as La Croix points out, APEC has contributed through exchanges of information on the implications and respective actions to enforce the global Trade-Related Aspects of Intellectual Property Rights (TRIPS) Agreement, workshops, and training projects. It may also consider establishing an APEC-wide trademark system. While the United States is the only APEC economy pushing actively for higher standards, many others want to achieve the level of compliance necessary at a minimal cost. This is enough to put an international property regime (IPR) on the agenda. Some concrete measures such as patent cooperation may occur, but divergent interests and domestic laws make unlikely a true APEC regime in this area as opposed to strengthening each APEC economy's compliance with the global regime.

Paolo Guerrieri and Shujiro Urata reach similar conclusions about trade and investment. Guerrieri sets out a trade bloc scenario but believes that it is much more likely that APEC will work with and support existing global regimes. In his view, unresolved trade asymmetries, economic tensions, differences in the levels of liberalization, and disparate views in many trade areas make likely a less ambitious effort that avoids formal institutions and legally binding obligations. In the case of investment, Urata points to potential advantages for negotiating investment agreements in an APEC forum as opposed to a global or OECD context: agreement should be more easily achieved among the smaller number of partners. China and Taiwan are members of the regional group but not the WTO or OECD, and APEC is becoming more congruent with the principal FDI suppliers. But he also notes how APEC's diversity inhibits agreement. In fact, APEC's only significant venture so far into rules-making, the 1994 agreement on Non-Binding Investment Principles (NBIP), falls short of the WTO Trade-Related Investment Measures (TRIMS) agreement in some respects. Urata suggests, however, that with growing awareness of the economic benefits of FDI in East Asia, opposition to a stronger, regional regime may weaken in the future.

IV. NATIONAL POLICIES

National governments provide a crucial lens through which to view the prospects for regime formation. Our country case studies, as well as Michael Plummer's discussion of ASEAN in chapter 12, reinforce the conclusion that substantial rules-building at the regional level, separate from and in advance of the global level, is unlikely. As noted, economic forces of interdependence suggest the need for substantial effort to develop rules of the game to reduce costly conflicts. Governments respond to these pressures. But the rules that might appeal to the dominant interests in one economy may be anathema in another.

Interestingly, the country studies in this volume suggest substantial similarity at the metaregime level in the most engaged bureaucracies (basically foreign and trade ministries) of the key APEC member economies. Countries that once pursued strong import-substitution policies in the manufacturing sector, including China, most of the ASEAN group, and Australia, have discarded these. Moreover, the APEC economies, from different starting points and at different speeds, have all been moving toward increased deregulation and privatization. Ironically, Japan, in the 1980s a strong model of government-promoting industrialization, has become in the 1990s the region's leading example of what can happen when the economy is overregulated.

In fact, these bureaucracies often look to APEC and each other for reinforcement of a liberal economic policy line against domestic interests who do not share the free market ideology. Zhang Yunling reports that it would have been impossible for China to make the across-the-board tariff cuts it offered at the 1995 Osaka APEC meeting without the justification of needing an impressive down payment for APEC. Richard Baker notes that some in the U.S. government (and many in other governments) hope that APEC will help moderate U.S. trade unilateralism, and Yoshinobu Yamamoto and Tsutomo Kikuchi argue that APEC can help Japan to carry out needed deregulation.

The similarity at the metaregime level was sufficient in the initial bargaining stage to get APEC launched and encourage efforts to reconcile APEC with the GATT. From the perspective of the member economies at that stage, APEC was largely an empty vessel yet to be filled. Ideas about the purposes of APEC, however, did impact on the issues relevant at the time. For example, from a Japanese perspective, if the organization were to play a role in moderating U.S. trade pressures, it needed to include the United States. As described in chapter 1, the APEC process gradually developed institutional definitions and objectives. This ongoing process increasingly engages national economic interests and sharpens at the bargaining and issue linkages. As discussed in several chapters, a key question is whether the diffuse reciprocity offered through APEC's voluntary and concerted liberalization approach will be as effective as the explicit reciprocity offered through traditional trade negotiations in the GATT/WTO. On the one hand, some of the chapters on national policies offer encouragement. ASEAN, after many years of limited liberalization efforts, has moved forward rapidly in developing a free trade area on the basis of setting out the principle first and negotiating the details afterwards. But as Michael Plummer notes, trade within ASEAN is limited, and thus the internal adjustments costs of freer trade are reduced while the agreement is seen to have major benefits in inducing investment. Other supporting evidence is the trend through the past decade of the APEC economies engaging in deregulation and liberalization—even in the absence of reciprocity because they recognized this was in their own economic interests.

Our examination of the domestic political dynamics of trade liberalization in some of the most important APEC economies, however, yields a less sanguine assessment. The United States has demanded explicit reciprocity since the Reciprocal Trade Act was first adopted in the 1930s as a means of mutually reducing trade barriers. The U.S. situation is complicated by the Congress's authority to regulate foreign commerce. Congress requires reciprocity in its advance grant of authority to the president to engage in trade negotiations, and on nontariff issues it has a second shot to ensure its standards of reciprocity after the negotiations through the need for its approval of the necessary implementing legislation.[1]

Japan's situation is both very different and somewhat similar. The legislative process does not require a prior grant of authority, but political interests groups in Japan, including elements in the bureaucracy itself, have been quite effective in slowing or blocking liberalization in many sectors. The tried and true formula for moving ahead is usually heavy handed *gaiatsu*, or foreign pressure. Yamamoto and Kikuchi point out, however, that in the eyes of Japan's Ministry of International Trade and Industry (MITI), APEC may help to alleviate foreign pressures. But if it is successful, will the positive examples of other economies liberalizing be enough to force Japan into the same pattern in the more sensitive sectors, such as agriculture? Or must APEC try to exert a strong form of *gaiatsu* to substitute for the American unilateral *gaiatsu*?

Another dimension to this problem arises from the preference of Asian countries for a strong commitment to "open regionalism." In some economies, notably the United States, Canada, and Australia, there is concern about potential free-riders. These would undercut political support for APEC trade liberalization and compel APEC governments to seek equivalent concessions from all major trading partners, thus forcing the negotiations from the regional to the global level. As described below, APEC, in fact, successfully did this in the Information Technology Agreement. However, it is difficult to see how this effort could have succeeded had APEC sought a regional agreement and then multilateralized its benefits to non-APEC markets. This experience suggests that a rigid adherence to open regionalism will make it very difficult for APEC to move toward deeper institutionalization at the regional level as compared to the global level. This, in fact, may be exactly what some adherents of open regionalism hope to achieve.

The country perspectives point to another potential problem involving the linkage between trade and investment liberalization and facilitation on one hand and economic and technical (or development) cooperation on the other. The APEC economies have privileged the former, but some are willing to see APEC in almost exclusive liberalization/facilitation terms. For example, John Ravenhill notes that the Australian fathers of APEC were so steeped in the presumed self-benefits of unilateral liberalization that they gave scant intellectual or policy attention to either adjustment assistance or technical cooperation. The United States, according to Richard Baker, often appears to see APEC's value almost exclusively in terms of liberalization. But China and the ASEAN group have argued for a clear substantive link among these issues: liberalization should be counterbalanced, or even compensated for, by cooperation. Japan has been sympathetic to this argument. Its major financial contribution to APEC was to be in the area of economic cooperation until American pressures caused a reformulation summed up by the title of Japan's $100 million contribution to APEC: "The Trade and Investment Liberalization and Facilitation Special Fund."

So far APEC has moved ahead at an unequal pace on both fronts, with some mostly informal linkage recognized between them. Thus the APEC group during the 1996 Philippine year wrestled simultaneously with establishing individual action plans for trade and investment while developing a declaration on economic and technical cooperation. However, there is a potential for tension as the going gets tougher and developing APEC economies feel pressured to reduce trade and investment barriers. They may demand a stronger linkage or argue that the failure of the developed economies to support development adequately is ample cause to slow down liberalization and deregulation tactically.

V. RECONCILING APEC WITH OTHER INSTITUTIONS

In considering APEC's relationship to other institutions, the question of nesting has been a central concern. At one level, APEC members have attempted to reconcile the institution with the WTO and broader political-security arrangements. At another level, they have worked to bring arrangements involving some APEC members, which include such institutions as NAFTA, ASEAN, and the CER, among others into conformity with APEC. It might also be noted that nesting is not the only mode in which reconciliation might take place: although not the case at present, some type of division of labor or parallel institutional linkages could also be possible.

Turning first to broader arrangements, Joseph Grieco finds that the originators of APEC chose to nest it within the GATT (now the WTO). But he observes that although "vertical nesting" within the same broad issue area has been quite successful, the absence of cooperative security and political arrangements has prevented APEC from being well entrenched in a broader "horizontal nest." Drawing primarily on realist arguments, Grieco is pessimistic about APEC's prospects for future institutionalization because of the negative pressures arising from the broader political-military system in the Asia-Pacific. As a result, he suggests that APEC could become a drag on—rather than a stimulus to—economic liberalization at the global level through the WTO.

Grieco's skepticism about APEC's role in economic liberalization as a result of political-military problems that the Asia-Pacific region is a useful corrective to the overly optimistic view of pure economic liberals who see harmony in the security system as a natural outcome of economic cooperation or ignore it altogether. By pointing to the important connections that exist in nested systems, Grieco draws out attention to the two-way interplay among economic and security systems.

On the other hand, Grieco's pessimism, deriving from realist hypotheses, may not be fully warranted. Recent events give us cause for greater optimism about APEC's role in trade liberalization. As noted, at the APEC Manila/Subic meetings, the participants agreed to commit to zero tariffs in information technology. This APEC-based agreement was then broadened at the December 1996 Singapore WTO ministerial meeting, providing for WTO-based liberalization in this sector. This development is more consistent with neoliberal and cognitive notions that agreements in smaller fora may be easier to come by and may be a basis for broader consensus-building. In this case we see the possibility of upward pressure from consensus developed in narrower, substantively connected arrangements. While one case hardly gives us cause to reject the pessimism of realist conceptions, it does point to the need to follow a more integrated analysis as advocated in chapter 2.

The difficulties of creating highly institutionalized and nested institutions become readily evident from Maxwell Cameron's analysis of the notion of nesting NAFTA in APEC in chapter 11. Cameron points to the quite different underlying factors in the creation of APEC and NAFTA. The United States used NAFTA to increase its bargaining power. As an FTA, the NAFTA agreement deals with potential free-riders simply by excluding them and pressuring members of the group through the use of political and economic pressure. The weakness of the Canadians and Mexicans as compared with the Americans becomes clear from Cameron's analysis. Thus, the problem of substantive nesting is a difficult one, given the differing nature of the two arrangements and the quite different packages of issues that underlie these institutions.

The implication of Cameron's study is that at present, NAFTA and APEC fit together uneasily. Indeed, existing connections, while nested, appear to be more tactically related in view of U.S. policy objectives to avoid choosing between the pursuit of connections to Asia and Latin America while maintaining the United States as a hub. Although some suggest that the open regionalism formula can overcome the tensions between the drive to create subregional accords while pursuing liberalization at the APEC level, Cameron is skeptical. He argues that open regionalism runs counter to the U.S. effort to force liberalization and pursue other political goals by excluding nonparticipants—an approach that cannot be followed in the APEC context in view of its emphasis on open regionalism and lack of exclusionary mechanisms.

In theory, substantive nesting could be achieved by changing the nature of APEC to bring it more in line with NAFTA—that is, creating an APEC free trade agreement rather than simply pursuing the notion of open regionalism. But as noted above, our country studies showed that an Article 24 free trade agreement with formal negotiations on trade liberalization and exclusion of free-riders is anathema to most Asian participants. Thus, this avenue does not appear to be a promising road to institutional reconciliation. In short, for the time being, the tactical substantive route, in view of the differing nature of the metaregimes and regimes of NAFTA and APEC, would appear to be the only available one. However, consistent with the theoretical arguments of chapter 2, Cameron views such an effort as an unstable one over the long run in view of shifting power capabilities in the region.

Plummer provides a more sanguine view of the substantive nesting of institutions in his chapter on ASEAN. He argues that ASEAN has a strong commitment to open regionalism. Thus, in terms of the overall principles and norms of the organization (the metaregime), there appears to be built-in compatibility between the two institutions. An important underlying factor in the sharply divergent views presented by the Cameron and Plummer papers is the contrast between Asian perspectives on development and enduring focus on export promotion in East Asia, and the long-term policy of import substitution that has only recently, if in some cases dramatically, changed in Latin America. An additional reason may be Plummer's focus on economic factors to the relative exclusion of political variables that might complicate the harmonious reconciliation of APEC and ASEAN. To summarize, at least in the short run, there would appear to be little doubt of the "better fit" of ASEAN and APEC, particularly in view of the leading role played by Asian states in the APEC process itself.

What does the future of nesting in the Asia-Pacific look like in view of the three papers by Grieco, Cameron, and Plummer? The short answer is that APEC's commitment to open regionalism and compatibility with the WTO, as well as the notion of the smooth nesting of subregional accords, is by no means a forgone conclusion. A focus on economic factors that is only concerned with how liberalization will proceed at different levels without attention to the broader security and political system gives us only a portion of the picture of the future. Substantive nesting may not be out of the question. But the notion that open regionalism by itself will solve the potential conflict among institutions at different levels would appear to be naive.

The future of nesting in the Asia-Pacific is likely to be characterized by bureaucratic conflicts among institutions, possible spillovers from the political security system into economic liberalization discussions, and tension over the use of bilateral and unilateral instruments by the United States and others in pursuit of their perceived self-interest. Without a careful understanding of the political and economic dynamics in each institution, we must be circumspect in yielding to excessive optimism about successful substantive nesting. In short, there is much work to be done by policymakers and their advisers in attempting to reconcile institutions at different levels in the Asia-Pacific.

VI. WHITHER APEC?

We now turn to speculation about the future of APEC. How will this forum evolve? Will it fit well as an intermediate-level institution between subregions and the WTO, or will it be squeezed institutionally from "above" and "below"? And will APEC move beyond its metaregime and very weak regime to a significantly more institutionalized arrangement? To address these questions, our discussion can be divided into two parts. The first considers exemplars for APEC, namely the EU and the OECD, as possible paths that APEC might follow. By looking at how these institutions have evolved, we hope to gain insight into APEC's future. The second section takes these institutional examples and uses them to speculate about APEC's future in light of the economics trends, national policies, and nesting issues discussed in the book and summarized in this chapter.

Exemplars for APEC: The EU and OECD

In thinking about APEC's future, it is useful to learn from other institutional experiences. We have chosen two extreme cases to set the parameters for this book. The first is the OECD as the exemplar of a loose consultative organization and the other is the EU, a highly institutionalized bureaucratic organization that has increasingly taken on state functions. In looking at these examples, we are not suggesting that the conditions in the Asia-Pacific are necessarily conducive to the formation of either of these two types of organization. Indeed, the task of our authors entrusted to write about the OECD and EU, Sylvia Ostry and Cédric Dupont respectively, was to not only evaluate these organizations as agents of international cooperation but to assess the implications of their experience for APEC.

In chapter 13, Ostry reviews the role of the OECD as an actor in fostering international economic cooperation and conducts a political-economic analysis of its origins and evolution. She then considers the question of whether an OECD-type organization would be useful in the Asia-Pacific and examines the likelihood of such an arrangement coming into being in view of the differing conditions in the region.

Ostry is circumspect in her appraisal of the OECD's success. In analyzing the tasks that this institution has undertaken in the postwar era, however, it seems quite evident that OECD helped promote multilateral trade liberalization and an open economic system. In particular, Ostry suggests that OECD helped to diffuse knowledge to actors (soft power) and also was able to draw on a hard power network of key officials from major states that pushed forward on various agendas and served as a forum for peer group pressure, usually outside the framework of the OECD itself. In addition, its parallel substantive connection to the GATT/WTO has prevented conflict by ensuring a division of labor. As for OECD's evolution, Ostry finds the Cold War critical to the creation and evolution of the OECD. She also notes that domestic pressures from business supported the notion of the OECD and multilateral liberalization and that cognitive factors also favored cooperation among the developed capitalist states.

In thinking about an OECD model for the Asia-Pacific, Ostry focuses mainly on the difference in the origin of the OECD and APEC. On the whole, an OECD-type model would seem to benefit the region and could facilitate the economic liberalization process in a manner similar to the OECD. But Ostry is skeptical of whether as a practical matter APEC could be modeled on the OECD. She systematically considers security-political factors, domestic political economic strategies, and cognitive agreement on shared goals. But in each case, Ostry finds the factors that were crucial to OECD's success wanting in the APEC case. Although some of the economic drivers in the APEC case may substitute for the lack of some of the factors that facilitated OECD's creation and evolution, she argues that while it lasts, the absence of China in the WTO will prove to be a major impediment to developing an APEC organization with broader clout in the international economic system. In short, while an APEC-OECD might be desirable, the many potential obstacles identified in the theoretical discussion in chapter 2 and Ostry's empirical analysis of the OECD cast doubt on a straightforward evolution of APEC in this direction.

If not the OECD, what about the EU? At first blush, this would appear absurd in view of the difficulty in developing a much looser initial institution such as the OECD. But it is worth examining the EU not only in its current incarnation but in the evolutionary process that began in the 1950s. Cédric Dupont's careful analysis in chapter 14 of both the question of institutional strength and competence as well as the problem of nesting in the European context provides an insightful analysis that may hold important lessons for APEC.

Dupont argues that liberalizing without deeper institutionalization is a chimera. He suggests that both the paths of the free trade agreement taken by EFTA and the customs union approach of the EC both showed that there are important limits to unilateral liberalization. Instead, governments followed an intergovernmental path that often ran into conflict over the types of policies that would be changed. Multilateral negotiations and binding agreements moved the process forward. And when the process of liberalization stalled as national differences came to the fore, he suggests that supranational arrangements helped to sustain the momentum of liberalization. We think the fears of a Brussels bureaucracy are not overdrawn. Supranational arrangements are necessarily the same as bureaucracy. The problem here is the absurdity of the comparison. Liberalization will require reciprocity, but not necessarily agreements. To see the EU Commission as the impediment to liberalization is to misunderstand the liberalization process in Europe and to put excessive faith in the good intentions of member states—at least in Dupont's view.

On the question of nested institutions, Dupont points to the danger that existing institutions might be undermined as new ones such as APEC are created. This in fact has been an oft-voiced fear of ASEAN members, and it delayed the creation of an Asia-Pacific intergovernmental organization for most of the 1980s. In addition, the question of the scope and depth of the institutional envelope within which subregional organization might fit also poses a potential problem in view of the examples from Europe. In that case, the thin envelope along OEEC lines did little to bind European integration while a strong institutional focus like the EEA undermined EFTA. APEC is in a difficult position if caught between attempting to supplant the WTO while avoiding strong opposition for fear of diluting subregional organizations. Still, if movement takes place on some issues in APEC that are not addressed in either broader or narrower fora, then APEC may come to be seen as a useful organization that merits bolstering and fitting into a nest of organizations. As noted earlier, the information technology agreement provides an example of the path that APEC might fruitfully follow. It remains to be seen whether the organization can find other issues in which it might provide leadership without threatening narrower or broader arrangements.

Regime Formation

What then might APEC become? As this review shows, APEC does not seem likely to become a rule-making institution. International rules-making in the Asia-Pacific region occurs at other levels: bilaterally, subregionally in specific geographical areas such as North America, and globally. Unlike the OECD, APEC's societies are at diverse levels of economic development, and although the building of a "community" is an APEC objective, there is not now a strong sense of shared values, interests, and vulnerabilities. But like the OECD, APEC has a socializing function—helping to develop a consensus on the basic norms and values that should govern international behavior and underlie rules and to defend the metaregime from threats within the APEC societies. The growing breadth of APEC activities (which includes trade, investment, the environment, labor, finance, transport, tourism, fisheries, and the promotion of small and medium-sized business), has involved the creation of consultative mechanisms at both the technical and ministerial levels that did not previously exist. At a minimum, this facilitates the development of a common vocabulary and, more ambitiously, common understandings of the basic challenges and objectives in the issue areas.

Open regionalism may retard the development of rule formation, implementation, and enforcement at the regional level and support it at other levels. To a large extent in the APEC context, open regionalism has been a code phrase against what many Asian regard as "Western-style institution-building," serving as a defense against formal regional rules-making. However, open regionalism does direct the attention of the APEC countries to the GATT/WTO regime in trade, and similar global conventions covering such areas as intellectual property protection, customs classification, value-added network services, and transportation. In these areas, there are considerable deficiencies in some APEC member economies' compliance with the global regimes, sometimes because of political or technical problems in implementation. Through information exchange and training, APEC may apply pressure for improved enforcement or help overcome technical deficiencies or simply ignorance. Moreover, the normative APEC vocabulary is full of other more operationally meaningful principles—transparency, nondiscrimination, comprehensiveness, WTO-consistency, mutual benefit. These serve both as guiding principles influencing national, bilateral, and subregional rules-making and as a basis for other governments to challenge actions inconsistent with them.

Thus in the operational rules-making, implementation, enforcement, and adjudication arenas, APEC also facilitates the development of regimes but more by acting to strengthen the operation of global regimes at the regional level than by either creating new regional regimes or by pushing for major extensions of global regimes. Rather than breaking new ground, the early efforts of APEC's working groups have been focused on understanding existing national regimes and global obligations.

The jury remains out on the extent to which APEC may result in significant trade liberalization among its members that would not have already occurred anyway. The success of the 2010/2020 targets in this respect may depend less on what is done within the APEC institutional context itself and more on the broad fortunes of traditional trade barriers in a world that is liberalizing anyway. APEC's targets, however, may help maintain the momentum in this direction and serve the interests of its member governments in moving ahead in a direction that its technocratic and big business elites favor. But when it comes to rule formation, APEC will likely lead to greater national efforts to conform to existing but often weak regional regimes, and, to a lesser extent, collective efforts to move forward global regime formation. The emphasis on the former process may be somewhat disappointing to those who would like to see APEC first and foremost as a strong institution to ratchet up global freer trade and investment regimes. Yet leveling up for the economically important APEC developing economies is also central to the effective operation of regional and global regimes. Moreover, it probably provides a needed basis for any APEC role at the cutting edge in the future.

Finally, the political-security aspects of APEC should not be ignored. As APEC has turned from vision and action agenda toward the humdrum of year-to-year efforts to bring about its vision, there has been increasing concern among some APEC supporters that heads of government and state will lose their interest. In this, the Group of Seven may prove instructive. Like the G7, APEC may incorporate a number of functional activities that have little obvious relationship to each other. In the APEC case as well, the leaders' meetings may be sustained more for their convenience in international relations and domestic political terms than for trade, investment, and development cooperation. Much of the emphasis in the preparation and use of leaders' time for APEC affairs is focused on bilateral side meetings. Thus, APEC summits are an effective and regularized way for consultation at the highest levels on a variety of political and security issues that are unconnected with the formal APEC work program.

Ultimately, APEC will sink or swim with the general importance of its region. In this respect, we are APEC-optimists. As long as basic economic growth trends continue, the APEC economies are becoming more important to each other. This in itself provides a political and economic imperative for broad-gauged consultations among the leading economies of the region. Although the political-security tensions may retard or disrupt economic cooperation and institution-building, such effects are likely to be temporary. Even the serious financial crisis that began in mid-1997 will be overcome in time. The forces that helped bring APEC into being at the beginning are likely only to grow stronger.

NOTES

1. It is for this implementing process that the president has found he needs "fast track" authority as a practical matter. The Congress's reluctance to provide new fast-track legislation at the end of the Uruguay Round crippled the U.S. ability to make credible individual action plans in the APEC process.

REFERENCES

ABAC [APEC Business Advisory Council] (1996) *APEC Means Business: Building Prosperity for Our Community.* Asia-Pacific Economic Cooperation Secretariat, Singapore.

Abbott, Kenneth, and Duncan Snidal. (1995) "Mesoinstitutions in International Politics." Paper presented at the ISA meetings, February.

Abe, Shigeyuki, and Michael G. Plummer. (1996) "Implications of the Asia-Europe Meeting for the World Trading System." *Kobe Economic and Business Review* 41, Annual Volume.

Aggarwal, Vinod K. (1985) *Liberal Protectionism: The International Politics of Organized Textile Trade.* Berkeley: University of California Press.

————. (1989) "Interpreting the History of Mexico's External Debt Crises." In Barry Eichengreen and Peter Lindert, eds., *The International Debt Crisis in Historical Perspective.* Cambridge: MIT Press, pp. 140-88.

————. (1994) "Comparing Regional Cooperation Efforts in Asia-Pacific and North America." In Andrew Mack and John Ravenhill, eds., *Pacific Cooperation: Building Economic and Security Regimes in the Asia Pacific Region.* Sydney: Allen and Unwin, pp. 40-65.

————. (1996) *Debt Games: Strategic Interaction in International Debt Rescheduling.* New York: Cambridge University Press.

————. (1998a) "Analyzing Institutional Transformation in the Asia-Pacific." In Vinod Aggarwal and Charles Morrison, eds., *Asia-Pacific Crossroads: Regime Creation and the Future of APEC.* New York: St. Martin's Press.

————., ed. (1998b) *Institutional Designs for a Complex World: Bargaining, Linkages, and Nesting.* Ithaca: Cornell University Press.

Aggarwal, Vinod K., and Pierre Allan. (1983) "Evolution in Bargaining Theories: Toward an Integrated Approach to Explain Strategies of the Weak." Paper presented at the American Political Science Association, Chicago, September.

Aggarwal, Vinod K., and Cédric Dupont. (forthcoming) "Good Games." UC Berkeley, ms.

Ajia-Taiheiyo Kyouryoku Suisin Konndannkai. (1989) Hirakereta Kyouryoku Ni Yoru Jidaihe (Asia-Pacific Cooperation Promotion Committee, Towards an Era of Open Economic Cooperation). Tokyo, Japan: MITI.

Akrasanee, Narongchai, and David Stifel. (1994) "The Political Economy of the ASEAN Free Trade Area." In Ross Garnaut and Peter Drysdale, eds., *Asia Pacific Regionalism.* Sydney: Harper Educational.

Alatas, Ali. (1992) "Basic Principles, Objectives and Modalities of APEC." In Hadi Soesastro, ed., *Indonesian Perspectives on APEC and Regional Cooperation in Asia Pacific.* Jakarta: Centre for Strategic and International Studies.

Allan, Pierre. (1984) "Comment Négocier en Situation de Faiblesse? Une Typologie des Stratégies à Disposition." *Annuaire Suisse de Science Politique* 24.

Amsden, Alice. (1989) *Asia's Next Giant.* Oxford: Oxford University Press.

Anderson, Kym, et al. (1985) "Pacific Economic Growth and the Prospects for Australian Trade." Canberra: Australia-Japan Research Centre, Australian National University, Pacific Economic Papers 122 (May).

APEC Economic Committee. (1995) *Foreign Direct Investment and APEC Economic Integration.* Singapore: Asia Pacific Economic Cooperation Secretariat.

APEC Economic Leaders. (1994) "APEC Economic Leaders' Declaration of Common Resolve," Bogor, Indonesia. Distributed by United States Embassy in Indonesia, November 15, l994, pp. 4, 7.

APEC Secretariat. (1993) *A Vision for APEC: Towards An Asia Pacific Economic Community.* Report of the Eminent Persons Group. Singapore: Asia Pacific Economic Cooperation Secretariat.

————. (1994) *Achieving the APEC Vision: Free and Open Trade in the Asia Pacific.* Second Report of the Eminent Persons Group. Singapore: Asia Pacific Economic Cooperation Secretariat.

————. (1995a) *The Osaka Action Plan: Roadmap to Realising the APEC Vision.* Singapore: Asia Pacific Economic Cooperation Secretariat.

————. (1995b) *1995 Report on the APEC Regional Economy.* Singapore: Asia Pacific Economic Cooperation Secretariat.

————. (1995c) *Implementing the APEC Vision: Free and Open Trade in the Asia Pacific.* Third Report of the Eminent Persons Group. Singapore: Asia Pacific Economic Cooperation Secretariat.

————. (1995) Selected APEC Documents, 1989-1994.

————. (1995) *Selected APEC Documents: 1995* (APEC #95-SE-05.3), December.

————. (1995) "APEC Economic Leaders' Declaration for Action." November 19, Osaka, Japan.

————. (1996) *Update on Activities Within APEC.* (APEC #96-SE-05.3), March.

APEC Study Center of Nankai University. A report prepared by the center.

Appleton, Barry. (1994) *Navigating NAFTA: A Concise User's Guide to the North American Free Trade Agreement.* Toronto and Rochester: Carswell and Lawyers Cooperative Publishing.

Ariff, Mohamed. (1994) "APEC and ASEAN: Complementing or Competing?" In Siow Yue Chia, ed:, *APEC: Challenges and Opportunities.* Singapore: Institute of Southeast Asian Studies. pp. 151-174.

————. (1996) "Outlooks for ASEAN and NAFTA Externalities." Chapter 12 in Shoji Nishijima and Peter H. Smith, eds. *Cooperation or Rivalry?: Regional Integration in the Americas and the Pacific Rim.* Boulder: Westview.

Aron, Raymond. (1974) *The Imperial Republic. The United States and the World, 1945-1973.* New Jersey: Prentice-Hall.

Asahi Shimbun. (various issues). *ASEAN-Japan Statistical Pocketbook.* (1987, 1991, 1992) Tokyo: ASEAN Promotion Centre on Trade, Investment, and Tourism.

Asia-Pacific Economic Cooperation (1996), *Joint Statement of the Eighth APEC Ministerial Meeting,* November 22-23, 1996.

Australia-Japan Research Centre. (1995) *Implementing the APEC Bogor Declaration.* Canberra: Australia-Japan Research Centre, Australian National University.

Australian Chamber of Commerce and Industry. (1995) "Business and the APEC Process." Brisbane, Melbourne, Sydney: Department of Foreign Affairs and Trade, Series on "Business and APEC."

Baker, Richard W., ed. (1994) *The ANZUS States and their Region: Regional Policies of Australia, New Zealand, and the United States.* Westport: Praeger.

Baldwin, Richard E. (1994). *Toward an Integrated Europe.* London: Center for Economic Policy Research.

Barber, Lionel. (1995) "Bonn Sets Agenda for Monetary Union," *Financial Times,* October 2.

Barkun, Michael. (1968) *Law without Sanctions: Order in Primitive Societies and the World Community.* New Haven: Yale University Press.

Beijing Review (various issues).

Bergsten, C. Fred. (1994a) "APEC and World Trade: A Force for Worldwide Liberalization." *Foreign Affairs* 73, 3 (May-June).

———. (1994b) "APEC: The Bogor Declaration and the Path Ahead." Remarks at the Institute for International Economics, Washington: mimeo, December 7.

———. (1996) "An Asian Push for World-Wide Free Trade," *Economist,* January 6-12, pp. 62-63.

Betts, Richard K. (1993/1994) "Wealth, Power, and Instability: East Asia and the United States After the Cold War." *International Security* 18, pp. 34-77.

Bhagwati, Jagdish, and Anne O. Krueger. (1995) *The Dangerous Drift to Preferential Trade Agreements.* Washington, D.C.: AEI Press.

Bora, Bijit. (1993) "Investment Cooperation in the Asia-Pacific Region: The PECC Asia-Pacific Investment Code." In Gili Yen, ed., *New Directions in Regional Trade Liberalization and Investment Cooperation: A Tripartite Approach.* Pacific Economic Cooperation Council.

Bora, Bijit and Monte Graham. (1996) "Non-Binding Investment Principles in APEC." In Bijit Bora and Mari Pangestu, eds., *Priority Issues in Trade and Investment Liberalization: Implications for the Asia Pacific Region,* Pacific Economic Cooperation Council.

Borden, William S. (1984). *The Pacific Alliance: United States Foreign Economic Policy and Japanese Trade Recovery, 1947-1955.* Madison: University of Wisconsin Press.

Borrus, Michael. (1993) "The Regional Architecture of Global Electronics: Trajectories, Linkages and Access to Technology." In Peter Gourevitch and Paolo Guerrieri, eds., *New Challenges to International Cooperation: Adjustment of Firms, Policies, and Organizations to Global Competition.* La Jolla: University of California, San Diego.

Braendli, Paul. (1995) "Utilization of Patent Protection in Europe—The EPO Comments." *Patent World* (March), pp. 16-22.

Brunelle, Dorval, and Christian Deblock. (1995) "New Issues on the NAFTA Front." *International Journal* 50, pp. 619-29.

Burley, Ann-Marie, and Walter Mattli. (1993) "Europe Before the Court." *International Organization* 47, pp. 46-71.

Buzan, Barry. (1995a) "Japan's Defense Problematique," *The Pacific Review* 8, 1.

———. (1995b) "The Post - Cold War Asia-Pacific Security Order: Conflict or Cooperation?" In Andrew Mack and John Ravenhill, eds., *Pacific*

Cooperation: Building Economic and Security Regimes in the Asia-Pacific Region. Boulder: Westview Press.

Buzan, Barry, and Gerald Segal. (1994) "Rethinking East Asian Security." *Survival* 36, 2.

Calvert, Randall L. (1995) "The Rational Choice Theory of Social Institutions: Cooperation, Coordination, and Communication." In Jeffrey S. Banks and Eric A. Hanushek, eds., *Modern Political Economy.* New York: Cambridge University Press. pp. 216-267.

Cameron, Maxwell A. (1991) "North American Free Trade, Public Goods, and Asymmetrical Bargaining: The Strategic Choices for Canada." *Frontera Norte* 3, 6, pp. 47-64.

———. (1992) "The l992 Initiative: Causes and Consequences." In Alberta M. Sbragia, ed., *Euro Politics: Institutions and Policymaking in the "New" Euro Community.* Washington, D.C.: Brookings Institution, pp. 23-74.

———. (1995) "Conflict and Cooperation in NAFTA and APEC: Nested or Parallel Institutions." Norman Paterson School of International Affairs, Carleton University, mimeo.

———. (1996) "From Free Rider to Free Trader: Modelling Trade Negotiations with Mexico." In Louis Perret, ed., *Vers une Amérique sans frontière/Toward a Borderless America.* Montreal: Collection Bleue/Wilson & Lafleur, pp. 425-40.

———. (1997) "North American Trade Negotiations: Liberalization Games Between Asymmetric Players." *European Journal of International Relations* 3, 1.

Cameron, Maxwell A., and Vinod K. Aggarwal. (1996) "Mexican Meltdown: States and Markets in Post-NAFTA Financial Turmoil." *Third World Quarterly* 17, 5, pp. 1015-27.

Cameron, Maxwell A., and Lisa North. (1996) "Las sendas del desarrollo en una encrucijada: La agricultura del Perú a la luz de la experiencia del este asiático." *Socialismo y Participación* 73 (March, pp. 127-40).

Cameron, Maxwell A., and Brian W. Tomlin. (1995) "Canada and Latin America in the Shadow of U.S. Power: Toward an Expanding Hemispheric Agreement?" In Donald Barry, ed., *Toward a North American Community.* Boulder: Westview Press.

Cartiglia, James R. (1994) "The Patent Cooperation Treaty: A Rational Approach to International Patent Filing." *Journal of the Patent and Trademark Office Society,* 76 (April), pp. 261-74.

Castles, Francis G. (1988) *Australian Public Policy and Economic Vulnerability.* Sydney: Allen and Unwin.

Cecchini, Paolo. (1988) *The Costs of Non-Europe.* Bruxelles: Commission of the European Communities.

Centeno, Miguel Ángel. (1994) *Democracy Within Reason: Technocratic Revolution in Mexico.* University Park: The Pennsylvania State University Press.

China Statistical Yearbook, 1996.

Ching, Frank. (1995) "APEC moving along 'Asian Way.'" *Far Eastern Economic Review,* December 7.

Choi, B. S. (1993) "Financial Policy and Big Business in Korea: The Perils of Financial Regulation." In S. Haggard, C. Lee, and S. Maxfield, eds., *The*

Politics of Finance in Developing Countries. Ithaca: Cornell University Press.

Clarke, Jonathan, and James Clad. (1995) *After the Crusade: American Foreign Policy for the Post-Superpower Age.* Lanham, Md.: Madison Books.

Cohen, Benjamin J. (1974) "The Revolution in Atlantic Relations: A Bargain Comes Unstuck." In Wolfram F. Hanrieder, ed., *The United States and Western Europe: Political, Economic, and Strategic Perspectives.* Cambridge: Winthrop Publishers.

Cohen, Stephen, and Guerrieri, Paolo. (1995) "The Variable Geometry of Asian Trade." In Eileen Doherty, ed., *Japanese Investment in Asia. International Production Strategies in a Rapidly Changing World.* San Francisco: The Asia Foundation and the Berkeley Roundtable on the International Economy.

Commonwealth Bureau of Census and Statistics. (Various) *Trade and Customs and Excise Revenue of the Commonwealth of Australia.* Canberra: Australian Government Printing Service.

Conybeare, John A. C. (1987) *Trade Wars: The Theory and Practice of International Commercial Rivalry.* New York: Columbia University Press.

Cook, Don. (1989) *Forging the Alliance NATO, 1945-1950.* New York: Arbor House/ W. Morrow.

Cooper, Richard N. (1987) "Trade Policy as Foreign Policy." In Robert M. Stein et al., eds., *U.S. Trade Policies in a Changing World Economy.* Cambridge, Mass.: Harvard University Press.

Cornes, Richard, and Todd Sandler. (1986) *The Theory of Externalities, Public Goods, and Club Goods.* New York: Cambridge University Press.

Crone, Donald. (1993) "Does Hegemony Matter? The Reorganization of the Pacific Political Economy." *World Politics* 45 (July), pp. 501-25.

Curzon, Victoria (1974) *The Essentials of Economic Integration: Lessons of EFTA Experience.* London: Macmillan.

Cushing, Higley, et al. (1993) *The Challenge of NAFTA: North America, Australia, New Zealand and the World Trade Regime.* Austin: University of Texas Press.

Dae Jung, Kim. (1994) "Is Culture Destiny? The Myth of Asia's Anti-Democratic Values." *Foreign Affairs* 73, 6, pp. 189-94.

Delouvrier, Paul. (1957) "Economic Integration: Problems and Possibilities." In C. Grove Haines, ed., *European Integration.* Baltimore: John Hopkins University Press. pp. 114-24.

Destler, I. M. (1986) *American Trade Politics: System Under Stress.* Washington: D.C.: Institute of International Economics.

Diebold, William, Jr. (1952) "The End of the I.T.O." *Princeton Essays in International Finance* 16, October.

———. (1987) "Political Implications of the U.S.-E.C. Economic Conflicts: American Trade Policy and Western Europe." *Government and Opposition: A Journal of Comparative Politics* (Summer).

Dixit, Avinah, and Robert Pindyck. (1994) *Investment Under Uncertainty.* Princeton: Princeton University Press.

Dobson, Wendy. (1995) "Pacific Triangles: U.S. Economic Relationships with Japan and China." Paper presented at the Industry Canada Conference on "The Growing Importance of the Asia-Pacific Region to the World Economy: Implications for Canada." (December 1-2) Vancouver, B.C.

Dobson, Wendy, and Frank Flatters, eds. (1994) *Pacific Trade and Investment: Options for the 90s*. Kingstone: John Deutsch Institute for the Study of Economic Policy.

Dornbusch, R. W. (1990) "Policy Options for Freer Trade: The Case for Bilateralism." In R. Z. Lawrence and C. L. Schultze, eds., *American Trade Strategy: Options for the 1990s*. Washington, D.C.: The Brookings Institution.

Dratler, Jay, Jr. (1996) *Intellectual Property Law: Commercial, Creative, and Industrial Property*. New York: Law Journal Seminars Press.

Drysdale, Peter. (1988) *International Economic Pluralism: Economic Policy in East Asia and the Pacific*. Sydney: Allen and Unwin.

———. (1991) "Open Regionalism: A Key to East Asia's Economic Future." Canberra: Australia-Japan Research Centre, Australian National University, Pacific Economic Papers 197 (July).

Drysdale, Peter, and Ross Garnaut. (1989) "A Pacific Free Trade Area?" In Jeffrey J. Schott, ed., *Free Trade Areas and U.S. Trade Policy*. Washington, D.C.: Institute for International Economics, 217-54.

———. (1992) "NAFTA and the Asia Pacific Region: Strategic Responses." Paper presented at the Institute for International Economics, September 10-12, Washington, D.C.

———. (1993) "The Pacific: An Application of a General Theory of Economic Integration." In C. Fred Bergsten and Marcus Noland, eds., *Pacific Dynamism and the International Economic System*. Washington, D.C.: Institute for International Economics, 183-223.

Drysdale, Peter, and Hugh Patrick. (1981) "An Asia-Pacific Regional Economic Organization: An Exploratory Concept Paper." In Sir John Crawford and Greg Seow, eds., *Pacific Economic Co-operation: Suggestions for Action*. Petaling Jaya: Heinemann Educational Books Ltd., pp. 63-82.

Dupont, Cédric. (1994) *Domestic Politics, Information and International Bargaining. Comparative Models of Strategic Behavior in Non-Crisis Negotiations*. Geneva: Graduate Institute of International Studies.

———. (1998b) "The Failure of the Nest-Best Solution: EC-EFTA Institutional Relationships and the European Economic Area." In Vinod K. Aggarwal, ed., *Institutional Designs for a Complex World: Bargaining, Linkages, and Nesting*. Ithaca: Cornell University Press.

Dupont, Cédric, and Carsten Hefeker. (1997) *Does Economic Integration Need International Institutional Foundation? The Political Economy of Institutions, Money and Trade*. Geneva and University of Basel: Graduate Institute of International Studies, mimeo.

Dyster, Barrie, and David Meredith. (1990) *Australia in the International Economy in the Twentieth Century*. Cambridge: Cambridge University Press.

Eby-Konan, Denise, Sumner J. La Croix, James Roumasset, and Jeff Heinrich. (1995) "Intellectual Property Rights in the Asia-Pacific Region: Problems, Patterns, and Policy." *Asia-Pacific Economic Literature* 9 (November), pp. 13-35.

Economic Commission for Latin America and the Caribbean (ECLAC). (1994) *Open Regionalism in Latin America and the Caribbean: Economic Integration as a Contribution to Changing Production Patterns with Social Equity*. Santiago de Chile: United Nations Economic Commission for Latin America and the Caribbean.

Economist. (various issues).

Eden, Lorraine, and Maureen Appel Molot. (1993) "Fortress or Free Market? NAFTA and its Implications for the Pacific Rim." In Richard Higgott, Richard Leaver, and John Ravenhill, eds., *Pacific Economic Relations in the 1990s: Cooperation or Conflict?* Boulder: Lynne Rienner, pp. 201-22.

EFTA. (1980) *EFTA Builds Free Trade.* Geneva: EFTA.

Elek, Andrew. (1992a) "Pacific Economic Co-operation Policy Choices for the 1990s." *Asia-Pacific Economic Literature* 6, 1, pp. 1-15.

———. (1992b) "Trade Policy Options for the Asia-Pacific Region in the 1990s: The Potential of Open Regionalism." *American Economic Review* 82, 2 (May).

———. (1995) "APEC Beyond Bogor: An Open Economic Association in the Asian-Pacific Region." *Asia-Pacific Economic Literature* 9, 1 (May), pp. 1-16.

Ernst, Dieter. (1995) *Carriers of Regionalization: The East Asian Production Networks of Japanese Electronics Firms.* BRIE Working Paper 73. Berkeley: University of California Press.

Ernst, Dieter, and Guerrieri, Paolo. (1995) "International Production Networks and Changing Trade Patterns in East Asia: The Case of the Electronics Industry." BRIE Working Paper. Berkeley: University of California Press.

Evans, Gareth, and Bruce Grant. (1991) *Australia's Foreign Relations.* Melbourne: Melbourne University Press.

Evans, Peter. (1992) "The State as Problem and Solution." In Stephan Haggard and Robert Kaufman, eds., *The Politics of Economic Adjustment: International Constraints, Distributive Conflicts, and the State.* Princeton: Princeton University Press.

Fajnzylber, Fernando. (1990a) *Unavoidable Industrial Restructuring in Latin America.* Durham: Duke University Press.

———. (1990b) "The United States and Japan as Models of Industrialization." In Gary Gereffi and Donald L. Wyman, eds., *Manufacturing Miracles: Paths of Industrialization in Latin America and East Asia.* Princeton: Princeton University Press.

Fane, George. (1995) "APEC: Regionalism, Globalism, or Obfuscation?" *Agenda* 2, 4, pp. 399-409.

Finn, Richard B. (1992) *Winners in Peace: MacArthur, Yoshida, and Postwar Japan.* Berkeley: University of California Press.

Fishlow, Albert. (1989) "Latin American Failure against the Backdrop of Asian Success." *Annals, AAPSS* 505, pp. 117-28.

Foreign Investment in China 8, 1995.

Foster, R. A., and S. E. Stewart. (1991) *Australian Economic Statistics 1949-50 to 1989-90.* Occasional Paper No. 8. Sydney: Reserve Bank of Australia.

Frankel, Jeffrey A. (1991) 'Is a Yen Bloc Forming in Pacific Asia?" In R. O'Brien, ed., *Finance and the International Economy* 5. The AMEX Bank Review Prize Essays. New York: Oxford University Press.

———. (1993) "Is Japan Creating a Yen Bloc?" In Jeffrey Frankel and Miles Kahler, eds., *Regionalism and Rivalry: Japan and the U.S. in Pacific Asia.* Chicago: University of Chicago Press.

Frankel, Jeffrey A., and Miles Kahler. (1993) "Pricing Strategies and Trading Blocks in East Asia." In Jeffrey Frankel and Miles Kahler, eds., *Regionalism and*

Rivalry: Japan and the United States in Pacific Asia. Chicago: University of Chicago Press.

Frankel, Jeffrey, Ernesto Stein, and Jan Wei. (1995) "Trading Blocs and the Americas: The Natural and the Supernatural." *Journal of Development Economics* 47, 1 (June), p. 43.

Frankel, Jeffrey A., Shang-Jin Wei, and Ernesto Stein. (1994) "APEC and Regional Trading Arrangements in the Pacific." In Wendy Dobson and Frank Flatters, eds., *Pacific Trade and Investment: Options for the 90s.* Kingstone: John Deutsch Institute for the Study of Economic Policy, pp. 289-312.

Friedberg, Aaron L. (1993-1994) "Ripe for Rivalry: Prospects for Peace in a Multipolar Asia." *International Security* 18, Winter, pp. 5-33.

Fukami, Hiroaki. (1993) "An Evolution of the Movement Toward Regional Integration." In *The Global Trend Toward Regional Integration.* Tokyo: Foreign Press Center.

Fukuda, Haruko. (1970) "First Decade of EFTA's Realization." In Hugh Corbet and David Robertson, eds., *Europe's Free Trade Area Experiment. EFTA and Economic Integration.* Oxford: Pergamon Press. pp. 43-77.

Funabashi, Yoichi. (1995) *Asia Pacific Fusion: Japan's Role in APEC.* Washington: D.C.: Institute of International Economics.

Gaikou-Seisyo 1 (Diplomatic Blue Book) (1996) Tokyo: Ministry of Foreign Affairs.

Gallarotti, Guilio M. (1995) *The Anatomy of an International Monetary Regime: The Classical Gold Standard, 1880-1914.* New York: Oxford University Press.

Garnaut, Ross. (1989) *Australia and the Northeast Asian Ascendancy.* Canberra: Australian Government Publishing Service.

———. (1994) "Open Regionalism: Its Analytic Bases and Relevance to the International System." *Journal of Asian Economics* 5, 2 (Summer).

———. (1995) "The Bogor Declaration on Asia-Pacific Trade Liberalisation." *Australian Quarterly* 67, 2 (Winter), pp. 28-42.

George, Aurelia. (1983) "The Changing Patterns of Japan's Agricultural Import Trade: Implications for Australia." Canberra: Australia-Japan Research Centre, Australian National University, Research Paper 100 (January).

Gereffi, Gary. (1989) "Development Strategies and the Global Factory," *Annals, AAPS* 505, pp. 92-104.

Gillingham, John. (1991) *Coal, Steel, and the Rebirth of Europe, 1945-1955: The Germans and French from Ruhr Conflict to Economic Community.* Cambridge: Cambridge University Press.

Gilpin, Robert. (1975) *U.S. Power and the Multinational Corporation: The Political Economy of Foreign Direct Investment.* New York: Basic Books.

———. (1987) *The Political Economy of International Relations.* Princeton: Princeton University Press.

Gowa, Joanne. (1989) "Rational Hegemons, Excludable Goods, and Small Groups: An Epitaph for Hegemonic Stability Theory?" *World Politics* 41, 3 (April).

———. (1994) *Allies, Adversaries, and International Trade.* Princeton: Princeton University Press.

Grieco, Joseph M. (1996) "Realism and Regionalism: American Power and German and Japanese Institutional Strategies During and After the Cold War." Prepared for delivery at the annual meeting of the American Political Science Association, San Francisco, CA, August 29-September 1.

———. (forthcoming) "Realism and Regionalism: American Power and German and Japanese Institutional Strategies During and After the Cold War." In Ethan Kapstein and Michael Mastanduno, eds., *Unipolar Politics: Realism and State Strategies After the Cold War*. New York: Columbia University Press.

Grimm, Margo. (1991) "Japan and the North American Free Trade Agreement." *JEI Report* 39A. Washington, D.C.: Japan Economic Institute.

Grinspun, Ricardo, and Maxwell A. Cameron, eds. (1993) *The Political Economy of North American Free Trade*. New York: St. Martin's Press.

Grinspun, Ricardo, and Maxwell A. Cameron. (1994) "Restructuring North America: The Impact of Unequal Integration." In Theodore Georgakopoulos, Christo C. Paraskevopoulos, and John Smithin, eds., *Economic Integration between Unequal Partners*. Aldershot, England: Edward Elgar.

———. (1996) "NAFTA and the Political Economy of Mexico's External Relations." *Latin American Research Review* 31, 3, pp. 161-88.

Gruen, Nicholas, Ian Bruce, and Gerard Prior. (1996) *Extending Patent Life: Is It in Australia's Economic Interests?* Staff Information Paper, Australia Industry Commission (June).

Guerrieri, Paolo. (1993) "Patterns of Technological Capability and International Trade Performance: An Empirical Analysis." In M. Kreinin, ed., *The Political Economy of International Commercial Policy: Issues for the 1990s*. London: Taylor & Francis.

———. (1995) *Trade Integration and Changing Specialization Patterns in the East Asia Electronics Industry*. BRIE. Berkeley: University of California Press.

Guerrieri, Paolo, and Tylecote, Andrew. (1996) "Interindustry differences in technical change and national patterns of technological accumulation." In Charles Edquist and Francis Pinter, eds., *Systems of Innovation: Technologies, Institutions and Organizations* (forthcoming).

Guisinger, Stephen, and Diane McNulty. (1996) "Private Sector Responses to Investment Rules: Evidence on U.S. Investors in the APEC Region." In Bijit Bora and Mari Pangestu, eds., *Priority Issues in Trade and Investment Liberalization: Implications for the Asia Pacific Region*. Pacific Economic Cooperation Council.

Haas, Ernst. (1980) "Why Collaborate? Issue-linkage and international regimes." *World Politics* 32, 3, pp. 357-405.

———. (1990) *When Knowledge is Power: Three Models of Change in International Organizations*. Berkeley: University of California Press.

Haas, Peter. (1989) "Do Regimes Matter? Epistemic Communities and Mediterranean Pollution Control. *International Organization* 43 (Summer).

———. (1992) "Knowledge, Power, and International Policy Coordination." Special Issue of *International Organization* 46, 1.

Haggard, Stephan. (1995) *Developing Nations and the Politics of Global Integration*. Washington, D.C.: The Brookings Institution.

Hallstein, Walter. (1970) *L'Europe inachevée*. Paris: Robert Laffont.

Hanrieder, Wolfram F. (1989) *Germany, America, Europe: Forty Years of German Foreign Policy*. New Haven: Yale University Press.

Harris, Stuart. (1989) "Economic Cooperation and Trading Blocs." *Australian Foreign Affairs and Trade: The Monthly Record* 60, 3 (March) pp. 63-66.

———. (1991) "Varieties of Pacific Economic Cooperation." *The Pacific Review* 4, 4 (December) pp. 301-11.

———. (1992) "Concepts and Objectives of Pacific Economic Cooperation." Canberra: Australia-Japan Research Centre, Australian National University, Pacific Economic Papers 213 (November).

Hawes, Michael. (1994) "NAFTA, Regional Integration and Japan: A Canadian Perspective." In Charles F. Doran, et al., eds. *Pacific Partners: Canada and the United States*. Washington: Brassey's, pp. 58-89.

Hawke, Bob. (1989) "Challenges for Korea and Australia: Speech by the Prime Minister, Mr. Bob Hawke, at a lunch of Korean Business Associations in Korea, on January 31." *Australian Foreign Affairs and Trade: The Monthly Record* 60, 1 (January) pp. 5-7.

———. (1994) *The Hawke Memoirs*. Port Melbourne: William Heinemann.

Heilperin, Michael A. (1957) "European Integration: Commercial and Financial Postulates." In C. Grove Haines, ed., *European Integration*. Baltimore: John Hopkins University Press. pp. 125-36.

Helliwell, John F. (1995) "Growth and Social Capital in Asia." Paper presented at the Industry Canada Conference on "The Growing Importance of the Asia-Pacific Region to the World Economy: Implications for Canada." Vancouver, B.C. (December 1-2).

Helpman, Elhanan. (1993) "Innovation, Imitation, and Intellectual Property Rights." *Econometrica* 61 (November), pp. 1247-80.

Higgott, Richard, and Andrew Fenton Cooper. (1990) "Middle Power Leadership and Coalition Building: Australia, the Cairns Group and the Uruguay Round of Trade Negotiations." *International Organization* 44, 4 (Fall) pp. 589-632.

Higgott, Richard, Andrew Fenton Cooper, and Jenelle Bonnor. (1990) "Asia-Pacific Economic Cooperation: an evolving case-study in leadership and cooperation building," *International Journal* 45, 4, pp. 823-66.

Hill, Hal. (1996) "Towards a Political Economy Explanation of Rapid Growth in Southeast Asia." *The Australian National University Working Papers in Trade and Development* 96, 2, (July).

Hirata, A. (1995) "The coherence or lack of coherence in Japan's economic policies towards developing countries." In K. Fukasaku, M. Plummer, and J. Tan, eds., *OECD and Asean Economies*. Paris: OECD.

Hogan, Michael. (1987) *The Marshall Plan: America, Britain, and the Reconstruction of Western Europe, l947-l952*. Cambridge: Cambridge University Press.

Hufbauer, Gary, and Jeffrey Schott. (1995) "Toward Free Trade and Investment in the Asia-Pacific." *Washington Quarterly* 18, 3, (Summer) pp. 37-45.

Hughes, Helen. (1991) "Does APEC Make Sense?" *ASEAN Economic Bulletin* 8, 2 (November), pp. 125-36.

Hurni, Bettina. (1987) "The Failure to Establish the Large Free Trade Area." In Pierre Du Bois and Bettina Hurni, eds., *EFTA From Yesterday to Tomorrow*. Geneva: EFTA. pp. 27-35.

Ikenberry, G. John. (1989) "Rethinking the Origins of American Hegemony." *Journal of Politics* 104, pp. 375-400.

Imada, P. and S. Naya. (1992) *AFTA: The Way Ahead*. Singapore: Institute of Southeast Asian Studies.

International Trade Reporter. (1996) Washington, D.C.: Bureau of National Affairs (January).

Jackson, John H. (1994) "Managing the Trading System: The World Trade Organization and the Post-Uruguay Round GATT Agenda." In Peter B. Kenen, ed., *Managing the World Economy: Fifty Years After Bretton Woods.* Washington: Institute for International Economics.

Japanese Ministry of Foreign Affairs. "The Osaka Action Agenda: Implementation of the Bogor Declaration." Provided by the APEC 1995 Osaka Official Information website (http://apec.tokio.co.jp/agenda/agenda/html).

————. "The Osaka Initial Actions," provided by the APEC 1995 Osaka Official Information website, (http: //apec.tokio.co.jp/agenda/initial/html).

Japanese National Committee for Pacific Economic Cooperation. (1988) *Review on Pacific Economic Cooperation Activities.* Tokyo: Japan Institute of International Affairs.

JETRO. (1994) JETRO White Paper on Foreign Direct Investment. Tokyo: Japan External Trade Organization.

Johnson, Chalmers. (1993) "History Restarted: Japanese-American Relations at the End of the Century." In Richard Higgott, Richard Leaver, and John Ravenhill, eds., *Pacific Economic Relations in the 1990s: Cooperation or Conflict?* Boulder: Lynne Rienner, pp. 39-61.

Johnstone, Christopher B. (1996) "APEC in 1996: Mixed Results, Uncertain Future," JEI Report. Washington: Japan Economic Institute of America, December.

Kahler, Miles. (1994) "Institution Building in the Pacific." In Mack and Ravenhill, eds., *Pacific Cooperation: Building Economic and Security Regimes in the Asia-Pacific Region.* St. Leonards, NSW: Allen & Unwin.

————. (1995) *International Institutions and the Political Economy of Integration.* Washington, D.C.: The Brookings Institution.

Kaufman, Burton I. (1990) "Eisenhower's Foreign Economic Policy with Respect to East Asia." In Warren I. Cohen and Akira Iriye, eds., *The Great Powers in East Asia 1953-1960.* New York: Columbia University Press.

Keohane, Robert. (1984) *After Hegemony: Cooperation and Discord in the World Economy.* Princeton: Princeton University Press.

Keohane, Robert, and Elinor Ostrom. (1994) "Local Commons and Global Interdependence: Heterogeneity and Cooperation in Two Domains." *Journal of Theoretical Politics.* Special Issue 6, 4 (October).

Keynes, John Maynard. (1920) *The Economic Consequences of the Peace.* New York: Harcourt, Brace and Howe.

Kikakucho, Keizai. (1988) *Sekai to tomoni ikiru Nihon: Keizai un'ei 5 ka nen keikaku* (Japan Living with the World: The Five-Year Economic Plan). Tokyo.

Kim, Kihwan, and Danny M. Leipziger. (1993) *Korea: A Case of Government-Led Development.* Washington, D.C.: World Bank Country Study.

Kindleberger, Charles P. (1973) *The World in Depression, 1929-1939.* Berkeley: University of California Press.

Kitzinger, U. W. (1960) "Europe: The Six and the Seven." *International Organization* 14, 1, pp. 20-36.

Klassan, John. (1996) "Prospects for Changing APEC in 1997." CIS Conference on the Future of APEC. Toronto, Canada (May 15 mimeo.).

Knight, Jack. (1992). *Institutions and Social Conflict*. Cambridge: Cambridge University Press.

Kraar, Louis. (1994) "The Overseas Chinese: Lessons from the World's Most Dynamic Capitalists." *Fortune* (October 31).

Krasner, Stephen D. (1983) *International Regimes*. Ithaca: Cornell University Press.

————. (1991) "Global Communications and National Power: Life on the Pareto Frontier." *World Politics* 43, 3 (April).

Kratochwil, Friedrich, and John Gerard Ruggie. (1986) "International Organization: A State of the Art on an Art of the State." *International Organization* 40.

Kreinin, M. E., and M. G. Plummer. (1994) "Structural Adjustment and Regional Economic Integration in East Asia." *International Economic Journal*, Summer.

Krugman, Paul. (1991) "Regional Trade Blocs: the Good, the Bad and the Ugly." *The International Economy*, November/December, pp. 54-56.

Kurth, James R. (1989) "The Pacific Basin Versus the Atlantic Alliance: Two Paradigms of International Relations." *Annals of the American Academy of Political and Social Science* 505, September, pp. 34-45.

La Croix, Sumner J. (1992) "The Political Economy of Intellectual Property Rights in Developing Countries." In James Roumasset and Susan Barr, eds., *The Economics of Cooperation: East Asian Development and the Case for Pro-Market Intervention*. Boulder, Co.: Westview Press.

————. (1994) *Intellectual Property Rights in ASEAN and the United States: Harmonization and Controversy*. Business Environment in ASEAN No. 14. Private Investment and Trade Opportunities (PITO). Honolulu: East-West Center.

————. (1995) *The Rise of Global Intellectual Property Rights and Their Impact on Asia*. Asia Pacific Issues Paper No. 23. East-West Center, August.

Lardy, Nicholas R. (1994) *China in the World Economy*. Washington: Institute for International Economics.

Lavin, Franklin L. (1962) "After NAFTA: Free Trade and Asia." The Heritage Lectures, No. 418. Washington, D.C.: The Heritage Foundation.

Lawrence, Robert Z. (1991) "Emerging Regional Arrangements: Building Blocs or Stumbling Blocs?" In R. O'Brien, ed., *Finance and the International Economy 5*. The AMEX Bank Review Prize Essays. New York: Oxford University Press.

————. (1994) "U.S. Trade and Investment Priorities: Asia's Place." In Wendy Dobson and Frank Flatters, eds., *Pacific Trade and Investment: Options for the 90s*. Kingstone: John Deutsch Institute for the Study of Economic Policy.

Lee, Norman. (1995) "Transport Policy." In Mike Artis and Norman Lee, eds., *The Economics of the European Union*. Oxford: Oxford University Press.

Lee, Tsao Yuan. (1994) "The ASEAN Free Trade Area: the Search for a Common Prosperity." In Ross Garnaut and Peter Drysdale, eds., *Asia Pacific Regionalism*. Sydney: Harper Educational.

Lees, Clifford. (1995-1996) "Strategic Reflections on the European Patent Office." *Patent World* (December 1995/January 1996), pp. 24-29.

Li Jingwen. (1995) *Chinese Economy toward the 21 Century*. Economic Management Publisher.

Liberal and National Parties. (1996) *Meeting the Challenges: The New Global Economy: Liberal and National Party Trade Strategies for the Future.* Canberra: Liberal and National Parties.

Liesner, H. H. (1969) "Policy Harmonization in the EEC and EFTA." In Geoffrey R. Denton, ed., *Economic Integration in Europe.* London: Weidenfeld and Nicolson.

Lincoln, Edward J. (1992) *Japan's rapidly emerging strategy toward Asia.* Working Paper 38. Paris: OECD Development Centre.

Lipsey, Richard G., and Russell M. Wills. (1995) *Science and Technology Policies in Asia Pacific Countries: Challenges and Opportunities for Canada.* (December) Vancouver, B.C. (mimeo).

Lloyd, P. J. (1994) "The Future of the CER Agreement: A Single Market for Australia and New Zealand." In Ross Garnaut and Peter Drysdale, eds., *Asia Pacific Regionalism.* Sydney: Harper Educational.

Luce, Edward, and Guy de Jonquières. (1996) "Clinton in Drive for IT Trade Pact." *Financial Times,* London Edition, Nexus, November 25.

———. (1996) "Confusion Greets Clinton's Big Deal." *Financial Times,* London Edition, Nexus, November 26.

Mack, Andrew, and Ravenhill, John, eds. (1994) *Pacific Cooperation: Building Economic and Security Regimes in the Asia-Pacific Region.* St. Leonards, NSW: Allen & Unwin.

Mahathir, Mohamad. (1981) "Tak Kenal Maka Tak Cinta." In Sir John Crawford and Greg Seow, eds., *Pacific Economic Co-operation: Suggestions for Action.* Petaling Jaya: Heinemann Educational Books Ltd.

Mahbubani, Kishore. (1995) "The Pacific Way." *Foreign Affairs* 74, 1, pp. 100-11.

Manning, Robert A., and Paula Stern. (1994) "The Myth of the Pacific Community." *Foreign Affairs* 73, 6, pp. 79-93.

Markusen, James R., James R. Melvin, William H. Kaempfer, and Keith E. Maskus. (1995) *International Trade: Theory and Evidence.* New York: McGraw-Hill.

Martin, Lisa. (1992) "Interest, Power, and Multilateralism." *International Organization* 46, 4 (Autumn).

Maskus, Keith, and Denise Eby-Konan. (1994) "Trade-Related Intellectual Property Rights: Issues and Exploratory Results." In A. V. Deardorff and R. M. Stern, eds., *Analytical and Negotiating Issues in the Global Trading System.* Ann Arbor: University of Michigan Press.

Maskus, Keith E., and Mohan Penubarti. (1995) "How Trade-Related Are Intellectual Property Rights?" *Journal of International Economics* 39, p. 227-48.

Mehmet, Ozay. (1994-1995) "AFTA-NAFTA Links: Canada as a Catalyst?" *Canadian Foreign Policy* 2, 3, pp. 61-75.

Messing, Joel. (1995) "Toward a Modern APEC Investment Policy." In *APEC at the Crossroads.* Seattle: National Bureau of Asian Research.

MFA. (1988) "The Fourth Medium-Term Target of the Japanese Government on Official Development Assistance (ODA)." (June)

Milward, Alan S. (1984) *The Reconstruction of Western Europe. 1945-51.* London: Routledge.

Minister's Office, MITI, ed. (1988) *Nihon No Sentaku* (Japan's Options). Tokyo: Tsuyo Sangyo Kyosakai (June).

Ministry of Foreign Affairs, Japan. (1995a) *APEC Economic Leaders' Declaration for Action.* Osaka, November 19.

————. (1995b) *The Economic Leaders Meeting: The Osaka Initial Actions*. Osaka, November 19.

————. (1995c) *The Osaka Action Agenda: Implementation of the Bogor Declaration*. Osaka, November 19.

Mitchell, Ronald. (1994) "Regime Design Matters: International Oil Pollution and Treaty Compliance." *International Organization* 48, 3 (Summer).

Morgenthau, Hans. (1958, 1966) *Politics Among Nations*. New York: Knopf, pp. 497-98, and (1966), pp. 531-34.

Morrison, Charles. (1994) "The United States and Cooperation in the Asia-Pacific." *The Australian Journal of International Affairs* 48, 1 (May), pp. 63-73.

————. (1995) "NAFTA and Northeast Asia: Accommodation or Conflict." In Kee, Woo Sik, In-Taek Hyun, and Kisoo Kim, eds., *APEC and a New Pacific Community*. Seoul: Sejong Institute.

————. (1997) "APEC: The Road to Subic." *The Review of Asian Pacific Studies* 14.

————. (1998) "APEC: The Evolution of an Institution." In Vinod Aggarwal and Charles Morrison, eds., *Asia-Pacific Crossroads: Regime Creation and the Future of APEC*. New York: St. Martin's Press.

Morrison, Charles, and Suhrke Astri. (1978) *Strategies of Survival: The foreign policy dilemmas of smaller Asian states*. Queensland: University of Queensland Press.

Nell, Philippe G. (1990) "EFTA in the 1990s: The Search for a New Identity." *Journal of Common Market Studies* 28, 4, pp. 327-358.

Nicolaïdis, Kalypso. (1993) "East European Trade in the Aftermath of 1989: Did International Institutions Matter?" In Robert O. Keohane, Joseph S. Nye, and Stanley Hoffmann, eds., *After the Cold War: International Institutions and State Strategies in Europe, 1989-1991*. Cambridge: Harvard University Press.

Noland, Marcus. (1995) "Implications of Asian Economic Growth," Asia project working paper. New York: Council on Foreign Relations.

North, Douglass C. (1990) *Institutions, Institutional Change and Economic Performance*. Cambridge: Cambridge University Press.

OECD. (1973) *History, Aims, Structure*. Paris: OECD Information Service (June).

————. (1970) *Gaps in Technology: Comparison between Member Countries in Education, R&D, Technological Innovation, International Economic Exchange*. Paris: OECD Directorate for Scientific Affairs.

Olson, Mancur. (1965) *The Logic of Collective Action*. Cambridge: Harvard University Press.

Orr, Robert M. (1990) *The Emergence of Japan's Foreign Aid Power*. New York: Columbia University Press.

Ostrom, Elinor (1990) *Governing the Commons: The Evolution of Institutions for Collective Action*. New York: Cambridge University Press.

Ostry, Sylvia. (forthcoming) *The Post Coldwar Trading System: Who's On First?* Chicago: University of Chicago Press.

Oxford Analytica. (1995) "Japanese relations part of grand strategy in Asia-Pacific region." Reprinted in *The Globe and Mail* (November 29, p. A9).

Oye, Kenneth. (1979) "The Domain of Choice," Oye et al., 1979, pp. 3-33.

————. (1992) *Economic Discrimination and Political Exchange*. Princeton: Princeton University Press.

———. (1992) Robert Lieber, and Donald Rothschild, eds., 1983. *Eagle Entangled: U.S. Foreign Policy in a Complex World.* New York: Longman.

Paarlberg, Robert L. (1995) *Leadership Abroad Begins at Home: U.S. Foreign Economic Policy after the Cold War.* Washington, D.C.: The Brookings Institution.

Pacific Economic Cooperation Council (PECC). (1995) *Pacific Economic Development Report.*

———. (1995) *Pacific Economic Outlook, 1995-1996.* Report prepared by the U.S. National Committee for Pacific Economic Cooperation. San Francisco: The Asia Foundation.

Pacific Research. (1992) Peace Research Center Periodical, Australian National University, Vol. 5, no. 3 (August).

Panestu, Mari. (1992) "APEC and Investment Facilitation." In Hadi Soesastro, ed., *Indonesian Perspectives on APEC and Regional Cooperation in Asia-Pacific.* Jakarta: Centre for Strategic and International Studies.

Park Y. C., and Won-Am Park. (1991) "Changing Japanese Trade Patterns and the East Asian NICs." In Paul Krugman, ed., *Trade with Japan: Has the Door Open Wider?* National Bureau of Economic Research. London and Chicago: University of Chicago Press.

Pastor, Manuel, Jr. (1994) "Mexican Trade Liberalization and NAFTA." *Latin American Research Review* 19, 3, pp. 170-71.

Pelkmans, Jacques, and Balaoing, Annette. (1996) "Europe Looking Further East Twinning European and Multilateral Interests." Paper presented at the Transatlantic Workshop entitled "Toward Rival Regionalism," July.

People's Daily (various).

Petri, P. (1993) "The East Asian Trading Bloc: An Analytical History." In J. Frankel and M. Kahler, eds., *Regionalism and Rivalry: Japan and the United States in Pacific Asia.* Chicago: University of Chicago Press.

Petri, Peter A. (1997) "Foreign Direct Investment in a Computational General Equilibrium Framework." A paper presented at the conference, "Making APEC Work: Economic Challenges and Policy Alternatives," March 13-14, Keio University, Tokyo, Japan.

Petri, Peter A., and Michael G. Plummer. (1996) "The Multilateralization of Regional Preferences: The Case of Asia." GSIEF Working Paper, Brandeis University, March.

Preeg, Ernest H. (1990) "Rationale, Objectives and Modalities of APEC." In Richard Grant et al., eds., *Asia Pacific Economic Cooperation: The Challenge Ahead.* Washington, D.C.: The Center for Strategic and International Studies.

Primo Braga, C. A. (1995) "Trade-Related Intellectual Property Issues: The Uruguay Round and its Intellectual Property Implications." Unpublished paper, World Bank Conference on The Uruguay Round and the Developing Economies, January 26-27.

Purdum, Todd S. (1996a) "APEC's Lost Opportunity." *Financial Times,* London Edition, Nexus, November 27.

———. (1996b) "At Asian Meeting, Support for Free Trade." *New York Times,* Nexus, November 26.

Pusey, Michael. (1991) *Economic Rationalism in Canberra.* Cambridge: Cambridge University Press.

Putnam, Robert D., Robert Leonardi, and Raffaella Y. Nanetti. (1993) *Making Democracy Work: Civic Traditions in Modern Italy.* Princeton: Princeton University Press.

Ravenhill, John. (1995a) "Bringing Politics Back In: The Political Economy of APEC." Seoul: Institute of East and West Studies, Yonsei University, Conference on the Future of APEC, November.

———. (1995b) "Competing Logics of Regionalism in the Asia-Pacific." *Journal of European Integration* 18, 2-3, Winter/Spring, pp. 179-99.

———. (1995c) "Economic Cooperation in Southeast Asia: Changing Incentives." *Asian Survey* 35, 9 (September), pp. 850-66.

———. (1998) "Australia and APEC." In Vinod Aggarwal and Charles Morrison, eds., *Asia-Pacific Crossroads: Regime Creation and the Future of APEC.* New York: St. Martin's Press.

Ravenhill, John, and Trevor Matthews. (1991) "Australia's Economic Malaise: A Northeast Asian Solution?" *Pacific Review* 4, 1, pp. 45-55.

Reichman, J. H. (1994) "Further Reflections on the TRIPS Components of the GATT's Uruguay Round." Unpublished paper. Washington University Conference on East Asian Intellectual Property Law, St. Louis, Missouri, February 24-27.

Riedel, J. (1991) "Intra-Asian Trade and Foreign Direct Investment." *Asian Development Review* 9, 1.

Roy, Dennis. (1994) "Hegemon on the Horizon? China's Threat to East Asian Security." *International Security* 19 (Summer), pp. 149-68.

Rudner, Martin. (1992) "ASEAN, Asia Pacific Economic Co-Operation, and Hemispheric Free Trade For the Americas." *World Competition* 16, 2, pp. 131-46.

———. (1995) "APEC: The Challenges of Asia Pacific Economic Cooperation." *Modern Asian Studies* 29, 2, pp. 403-37.

Ruggie, John. (1992) "Multilateralism: The Anatomy of an Institution." *International Organization* 46, 3 (Summer).

Ruggiero, Renato. (1996) "The Road Ahead: International Trade Policy in the Era of the WTO." The Fourth Annual Sylvia Ostry Lecture, Ottawa, May 28, published in *World Trade Organization Press Release,* May 29.

Samuels, Jeffrey B., and Linda B. Samuels. (1993-94) "The Changing Landscape of International Trademark Law." *George Washington Journal of International Law and Economics,* 27, pp. 433-55.

Sato, Ryuji. (1994) "China High-Tech Spree Pays Dividends." *The Nikkei Weekly.* Tokyo: Nikkei (November 7).

Saxonhouse, Gary R. (1993) "Pricing Strategies and Trading Blocks in East Asia." In J. Frankel and M. Kahler, eds., *Regionalism and Rivalry: Japan and the United States in Pacific Asia.* Chicago: University of Chicago Press.

Sazanami, Yoko. (1993) "GATT and Regional Arrangements can Live Together." In *The Global Trend Toward Regional Integration.* Tokyo: Foreign Press Center.

Schmidt, Gustav. (1995) "Tying (West) Germany into the West—But to What? NATO? WEU? The European Community?" In Clemens Wurm, ed., *Western Europe and Germany: The Beginnings of European Integration, 1945-1960.* Oxford and Washington: Berg Publishers.

Schoenberger, Karl. (1991) "Asia Seeks Leading Role in Pacific's Destiny." *Los Angeles Times*. Nexus, October 21.

Schott, Jeffrey. (1995) "Paths to Hemispheric Integration." *Policy Options*, November, pp. 22-24.

Schwabe, Klaus. (1995) "The United States and European Integration, 1947-1957." In Clemens Wurm, *Western Europe and Germany: The Beginnings of European Integration, 1945-1960*. Oxford and Washington: Berg Publishers.

Segal, Gerald. (1995) "Tying China into the International System." *Survival* 37, pp. 60-73.

———. (1996) "East Asia and the 'Constrainment' of China." *International Security* 20, (Spring), pp.107-35.

Servan-Schreiber, Jean-Jacques. (1968) *The American Challenge*. New York: Atheneum.

Shigeie, Toshimori. (1996). A Speech by Deputy Secretary-General Shigeie. Economic Affairs Bureau, MFA. Tokyo: Sekai Keizai Hyoron.

Snape, Richard H. (1986) "Should Australia Seek a Trade Agreement with the United States?" Canberra: Economic Planning Advisory Council, EPAC Discussion Paper 86/01.

Snidal, Duncan. (1979) "Public Goods, Property Rights, and Political Organization." *International Studies Quarterly* 23, 4 (December).

———. (1985a) "Coordination Versus Prisoners' Dilemma: Implications for International Cooperation and Regimes." *American Political Science Review* 79, (December).

———. (1985b) "The Limits of Hegemonic Stability Theory." *International Organization*, 39.

Snoy et d'Oppuers, Baron. (1959) "La Zone de Libre Echange." *Chronique de politique etrangere* 12, 5-6, pp. 569-623.

Soesastro, Hadi. (1994a) *Economic outlook for Asia region towards the 21st century*. Jakarta: Centre for Strategic and International studies.

———. (1994b) "The Institutional Framework for APEC: An ASEAN Perspective." In Siow Yue Chia, ed., *APEC: Challenges and Opportunities*. Singapore: Institute of Southeast Asian Studies. pp. 36-53.

———. (1996) "Keeping Regionalism Open in the Asia Pacific." A paper presented at the Conference on "Europe in Asia Pacific," May 28-31, Bali.

Stein, Art. (1980). "The Politics of Linkage." *World Politics* 33, 1 (October).

———. (1983) "Coordination and Collaboration: Regimes in an Anarchic World." In Stephen Krasner, ed., *International Regimes*. Ithaca: Cornell University Press.

Summers, Lawrence. (1991) "Regionalism and the World Trading System." In *Policy Implications of Trade and Currency Zones*. Federal Reserve Bank of Kansas City.

Swann, Dennis. (1969) "Cartels and Concentrations—Issues and Progress." In Geoffrey R. Denton, ed., *Economic Integration in Europe*. London: Weidenfeld and Nicolson. pp. 171-93.

Tang, Min. (1995) "La cooperation economique en Asie: opportunites et defis." In Kiichiro Fukasaku, ed., *Cooperation et Integration Regionales en Asie*. Paris: OCDE. pp. 221-52.

The Policy Recommendations on "The Future of Regionalism and Japan." The Japan Forum on International Relations (June). Tokyo, Japan.

The Round Table on Japan and the Asia-Pacific Region in the 21st Century. (1992) "Japan and the Asia-Pacific Region in the 21st Century—Promotion of Openness and Respect for Plurality." Tokyo, Japan.

Thompson, Jeffrey L. (1993-1994) "The North American Patent Office? A Comparative Look at the NAFTA, the European Community, and the Community Patent Convention." *George Washington Journal of International Law and Economics* 27, pp. 501-29.

Tsoukalis, Loukas. (1993) *The New European Economy.* Oxford: Oxford University Press.

Tsuusho Hakusyo (Annual Report of MITI). (1996) Tokyo: Ministry of International Trade and Industry.

United Nations Development Programme. (1994) *Human Development Report, 1994.* New York: Oxford University Press.

United Nations. (1995) World Investment Report 1995: Transnational Corporations and Competitiveness. New York: United Nations.

———. Commodity Trade Statistics. New York: United Nations (various issues).

Urata, Shujiro. (1993) "Changing Patterns of Direct Investment and the Implications for Trade and Development." In C. F. Bergsten and M. Noland, eds., Pacific Dynamism and the International Economic System. Washington, D.C.: Institute for International Economics.

Viner, Jacob. (1947) "Conflicts of Principle in Drafting a Trade Charter." *Foreign Affairs* 4 (July).

Wade, Robert. (1990) *Governing the Market.* Princeton: Princeton University Press.

———. (1992). "East Asia's Economic Success: Conflicting Perspectives, Partial Insights, Shaky Evidence." *World Politics* 44, pp. 270-320.

Wanandi, Jusuf. (1990) "APEC and Other Regional Organizations." Reprinted in Hadi Soesastro, ed. (1992) *Indonesian Perspectives on APEC and Regional Cooperation in Asia-Pacific.* Jakarta: Centre for Strategic and International Studies.

Warner, Geoffrey. (1993) "Eisenhower, Dulles, and the Unity of Western Europe, 1955-1957." *International Affairs* 69, (April), pp. 319-29.

Watanabe, Toshio. (1994) "Ajia-Taiheiyou ni okeru Boueki-Tousi no Sin-Choryu" (New Trends of Trade and Investment in Asia and the Pacific). A paper delivered at the symposium organized by the Japan Forum on International Affairs. Japan.

Weber, Steve and J. Zysman. (1992) "The Risk that Mercantilism Will Define the New Security System." In W. Sandholtz et al., eds., *The Highest Stakes: The Economic Foundations of the New Security.* Oxford University Press.

Wendt, Alexander. (1995) "Constructing International Politics." *International Security* 20, 1 (Summer).

Whitwell, Greg. (1986) *The Treasury Line.* Sydney: Allen and Unwin.

———. (1993) "Economic Ideas and Economic Policy: The Rise of Economic Rationalism in Australia." *Australian Economic History Review* 33, 2 (September) pp. 8-28.

Willis, F. Roy. (1968) *France, Germany, and the New Europe.* Stanford: Stanford University Press.

Woods, Lawrence T. (1993) *Asia-Pacific Diplomacy: Nongovernmental Organizations and International Relations.* Vancouver: University of British Columbia Press.

Woolcott, Richard. (1989) "Regional Economic Cooperation." *Australian Foreign Affairs and Trade: The Monthly Record* 60, 4 (April).

World Bank. (1993a) *The East Asian Miracle.* World Bank Policy Research Report. Washington, D.C.: The World Bank.

———. (1993b) *The East Asian Miracle.* London: Oxford University Press.

———. (1993c) *The East Asian Miracle: Economic Growth and Public Policy.* Oxford: Oxford University Press.

———. (1995) *The World Development Report: Workers in an Integrating World.* New York: Oxford University Press.

WTO [World Trade Organization]. (1996) *Trade and Foreign Direct Investment.* World Trade Organization Press Release, October 9.

Yamaoka, Michio. (1996) *PBEC, PECC and APEC.* Tokyo: APEC Study Center, Waseda University and Institute of Developing Economies (March).

Yamazawa, Ippei. (1992) "On Pacific Economic Integration." *The Economic Journal* 102, November.

———. (1997) *Eipekku Manira Koudou-keikaku to Ajia Taiheiyou no Keizai Titujyo* (The APEC Manila Action Program and a New Economic Order in the Asia-Pacific). Tokyo: Sekai Keizai Hyoron (February).

Yan, Tan Kong, Toh Mun Heng, and Linda Low. (1992) "ASEAN and Pacific Economic Cooperation." *ASEAN Economic Bulletin* 8, 3, pp. 325-28.

Yang Guanqun. (1994) "The Effects of APEC." *Journal of Asia-Pacific Studies* 2: 3.

Young, David, and Stan Metcalfe. (1995) "Competition Policy." In Mike Artis and Norman Lee, eds., *The Economics of the European Union.* Oxford: Oxford University Press. pp. 119-38.

Young, Oran. (1979) *Compliance and Public Authority: A Theory with International Applications* Baltimore: Johns Hopkins University Press.

———. (1991) "Political Leadership and Regime Formation: On the Development of Institutions in International Society." *International Organization* 45, 3 (Summer), pp. 281-308.

Yue, C. S., and L. T. Yuan. (1993) "Subregional Economic Zones: a New Motive Force in Asia-Pacific Development." In C. F. Bergsten and M. Noland, eds., *Pacific Dynamism and the International Economic System.* Washington, D.C.: Institute for International Economics.

Zhu Shoushen. (1995) "Suggestions for Policy Reflections to Osaka Meeting." *International Business*, October 28.

INDEX

* numbers in bold are for tables and figures